Child Poverty and Public Policy

Judith A. Chafel, Editor

Child Poverty and Public Policy

THE URBAN INSTITUTE PRESS
Washington, D.C.

Library of Congress Cataloging in Publication Data

Child Poverty and Public Policy/Judith A. Chafel, editor.   1. Poor children—United States.   2. Child Welfare—United States.   3. United States—Social policy—1980–I. Chafel, Judith A.

HV741.C487   1993   93-27329
362.7'08'6942--dc20   CIP

ISBN 0-87766-610-5 (alk. paper)
ISBN 0-87766-609-1 (alk. paper; casebound)

Urban Institute books are printed on acid-free paper whenever possible.
Printed in the United States of America.

Distributed by University Press of America
4720 Boston Way   3 Henrietta Street
Lanham, MD 20706   London WC2E 8LU ENGLAND

THE URBAN INSTITUTE is a nonprofit policy research and educational organization established in Washington, D.C., in 1968. Its staff investigates the social and economic problems confronting the nation and public and private means to alleviate them. The Institute disseminates significant findings of its research through the publications program of its Press. The goals of the Institute are to sharpen thinking about societal problems and efforts to solve them, improve government decisions and performance, and increase citizen awareness of important policy choices.

Through work that ranges from broad conceptual studies to administrative and technical assistance, Institute researchers contribute to the stock of knowledge available to guide decision making in the public interest.

Conclusions or opinions expressed in Institute publications are those of the authors and do not necessarily reflect the views of staff members, officers or trustees of the Institute, advisory groups, or any organizations that provide financial support to the Institute.

For all children who live in poverty.

ACKNOWLEDGMENTS

This book has been brought to press with the help of many people. The chapter authors researched their topics well, graciously responded to requests for revision, and dutifully met their deadlines. Marion McNairy, Bruce Tone, Bud Spodek, and James A. Chafel provided valuable comments at various stages of the book's completion. Molly Ruzicka did a skillful job of editing.

A Congressional Science Fellowship from the Society for Research in Child Development enabled me to spend a year in Washington, D.C., learning about child poverty and the policymaking process. Without that support, this book would not have been possible.

I am gráteful to them all.

CONTENTS

Tables

Figures

FOREWORD

As the population ages, and globalization increasingly affects our economy, getting the most out of our human resources—our children—becomes an economic as well as a moral imperative. Yet 30 years after the War on Poverty began, growing up poor still prevents millions of American children from realizing their full potential.

Ever since the Urban Institute Press published Thomas J. Espenshade's *Investing in Children* a decade ago, child well-being and policies to improve it have been central to the Institute's mission. The first rigorous comparison of parental expenditures on children across the economic and demographic spectrum, this work documented the extreme disparities among income groups in the amounts parents spend on their children. Subsequent work at the Institute and elsewhere has documented the link between poverty and developmental risk, and designed numerous policy alternatives to alleviate child poverty and its attendant hazards.

Child Poverty and Public Policy documents how far we still are from putting our knowledge into effective practice. It provides an overview of the changing nature of child poverty in the United States today, and the challenges we face as a society if we are to reach the goal of giving all our children a fair chance. The contributing authors use a number of quantitative and qualitative approaches to look at the many faces of poor children and their parents; the complex interplay of factors giving rise to poverty; how poverty interacts with other stressors to sabotage parental care; changing public perceptions of the poor; the successes and failures of the 101st ("children's") Congress as an example of the dynamics involved in public policy formation; a proposal to use the Social Security surplus to set up a Human Capital Account to fund public investment in children; and ways to advocate effectively on behalf of poor children.

The Urban Institute welcomes the opportunity to publish this collection of essays. The evidence presented here drives home an obvious but frequently neglected point: If poor children are to make it in today's world, they and their parents must try harder than better off Americans simply because poverty magnifies the effects of any other barriers to full achievement of human potential.

The Clinton Administration has raised expectations about a new commitment to children in this country. Let us hope that this commitment can be translated into effective action, and that the considerable body of knowledge now available about child poverty will be used effectively to help equalize opportunity for all our children.

William Gorham
President

Chapter One

CHILD POVERTY: OVERVIEW AND OUTLOOK

Judith A. Chafel

They lived in a trailer that had no screens. The first home visit was in August . . . I estimated 500 to 600 flies in the trailer. The mother had just bathed the 5-month-old and the amount of water that she was using was in a 10-inch skillet. She had running water. She didn't know she needed more water than that to clean the infant. . . . She had a gallon of milk sitting on the counter. When I asked if she wasn't afraid it would sour, she said, "Yes, but it's just too hard to get it in the refrigerator." So, I said, "Why?" The refrigerator in the trailer did not work . . . the refrigerator that was working was outside, down an embankment with the door tied shut and a heavy box pushed against it. I took the milk to the refrigerator and it took me 12 minutes from the time I left the trailer with the milk 'til I got back.
—As told by a Head Start teacher[1]

The difficult life circumstances depicted above are not uncommon. Today, millions of American children and their families live in poverty. "Poverty" is defined by the federal government as a pretax cash income below $13,860 for a family of four, or less than $10,973 for a family of three (1991 figures from Scarbrough, chapter 3, this volume). The "poverty line" changes by family size and composition and is intended to signify the yearly annual income required by a family to realize a "minimally adequate" standard of living (Scarbrough, chapter 3, this volume).

Although the threshold defines a category of persons and suggests an absolute standard, poverty is not a static construct. The condition of being "poor" differs according to the extent to which family income falls below the poverty line and the number of years lived in poverty. These dynamics profoundly affect life circumstances and are not reflected in the official federal definition of poverty. A child residing in a family whose income is 100 percent *below* the poverty line for 10 years of his or her life is far more disadvantaged and substantially at greater risk developmentally than one living in a family at the poverty margin for a single year. Unquestionably, poverty acts as a stressor for both children, but one child's experience with impoverishment is far more chronic and acute.

The figures verifying the existence of child poverty, as defined by the federal government, and the growing proportion of the population affected by it are startling. Today, 14.3 million children in our society, about 1 out of every 5, are poor. This figure comprises 46 percent of African-Americans; 40 percent of Latinos; 32 percent of Native American, Asian-American, and other cultural groups; and 12 percent of whites (1991 figures; Scarbrough, chapter 3, this volume). Over the past two decades, child poverty rates (the proportion of those poor), while fluctuating somewhat, have been rising: from 15.1 percent in 1971 to 21. 8 percent in 1991 (Scarbrough, chapter 3, this volume). In the foreseeable future, these estimates are expected to remain high.

The economic stress that defines poverty harms children and places them at risk of long-term disadvantage. Children of the poor endure myriad deficits in their life circumstances—deficient nutrition, substandard housing, restricted access to quality health care, unsafe environments, and less-than-effective schooling, to cite but a few (National Center for Children in Poverty 1990). Exposed to conditions such as these, they are likely to suffer from a number of serious risk factors: premature birth and low birthweight, malnutrition, physical and psychological stress and abuse, chronic and untreated health problems, and learning disabilities (Committee for Economic Development 1987).

Any society impervious to the plight of its poor will inevitably suffer the material consequences resulting from its neglect, thereby endangering its economic well-being. More importantly, left unresolved, the problem of child poverty has profound ethical implications for our society. What can be said of a nation that does not assume responsibility for nurturing the most vulnerable among its young? Only that its moral integrity has been compromised.

During the decade of the eighties, the United States witnessed a predilection on the part of government to scale back services for the poor. An unprecedented number of domestic programs were cut or eliminated, as a political philosophy of retrenchment took hold (Danziger, Haveman, and Plotnick 1986). The Reagan and Bush administrations succeeded in mobilizing a broad coalition of Americans against the impoverished and in focusing public sentiment on the "stigma of poverty" (Waxman 1983). As a result, many groups in our society became indifferent, if not overtly hostile, to the plight of the poor population.

A more promising outlook has emerged under the administration of Bill Clinton. Clinton's commitment to "an expanding, entrepreneurial economy of high-skill, high-wage jobs" assumes a domestic policy of greater equity for the impoverished (Merry 1992: 2138). His human capital investment proposals advocate an expansion of the Earned Income Tax Credit (EITC) for poor working families, increased provision for childhood immunization, an enlargement of WIC (Special Supplemental Food Program for Women, Infants, and Children), an enhancement of Head Start funding, and welfare reform, to mention but a few components of his economic agenda ("Clinton Outlines His Plan" 1993). Elected on a mandate for "change," he envisions the concept to mean activism by government in the pursuit of brighter economic prospects for all (Germond and Whitcover 1993).

Although the outlook for the poor has changed considerably in recent months and has become far more sanguine, it is tempered by profound antigovernment sentiment that persists among a large cross-section of the American people skeptical of any "tax and spend" policy (Barnes 1993). Similarly, a skyrocketing federal deficit restricts the amount of money available for social programs. These political realities operate as constraints on the construction of a domestic agenda designed to alleviate the hardships of those living in poverty.

Nationally, a concern for children's issues is escalating. Increasingly, public attention is being directed to the plight of poverty-stricken children by the media, with the appearance of articles vividly describing their life circumstances (e.g., Wilkerson 1993), detailing data on the incidence of child poverty (e.g., "Report Says Poor Children Grew Poorer in 1980's" 1992), and telling of its effects (e.g., "Commission Warns Child Poverty Poses Threat" 1990). In addition, a variety of organizations have begun to collaborate in constructing nonpartisan advocacy networks to win legislative support for children in need. "Intergenerational action," for example, has been cited as a priority of the American Association of Retired Persons (AARP), which has united with the Coalition for America's Children, a national group, to promote a children's agenda ("Seniors and Juniors" 1992). Moving from an orientation of insensibility, to one of concern, to one of political commitment in support of action on behalf of children in poverty necessitates several large leaps, but noticeable steps are being taken in this direction.

The purpose of this volume is to provide the reader with a broad overview of child poverty, as it exists in the United States today. Its aims are to delineate important parameters of the topic, to focus attention on key issues, and to stimulate research, public policy initiatives, and advocacy efforts on behalf of children in poverty. An edited collection of original essays, the volume discusses case examples, demographics, the causes and effects of poverty, changing conceptions of those who are impoverished, recent legislation, social policy, and child advocacy. Through the selection of the topics addressed and the authors chosen to reflect upon them, it is designed to provide a comprehensive, multidisciplinary perspective on the problem of child poverty.

As the incidence of child poverty rises, the number of professionals concerned with the phenomenon is multiplying. This book's intended audience includes all those individuals whose areas of expertise focus on children (such as educators, health care workers, pediatricians, psychologists, public policy analysts, social workers, and sociologists, to name but a few). Whether researchers or practitioners, these professionals will benefit from this volume's substantive discussion of the issues. To assist readers in surveying the book's contents, a brief synopsis of each of the succeeding chapters follows.

OVERVIEW OF CHAPTERS 2 THROUGH 10

In chapter 2, Judith S. Musick presents a psychological ethnography of child poverty. Two case examples are highlighted, each illuminating a specific developmental dimension: first, the gender and sexual socialization of disadvantaged females and, second, disadvantaged parents as mediators of their children's environment. Readers are immersed in a "stream of experience" that vicariously places them in "the shoes of those who walk in poverty." A broad sample of subjects is portrayed, representing diverse geographic locales, racial and ethnic groups, and family structures. The case examples shed light on what it means to contend with the multifaceted dilemmas associated with living in poverty and its influence on human development.

Using key demographic variables, William H. Scarbrough, in chapter 3, describes and analyzes the composition of the child poverty population in the United States today: by age, race and ethnicity, family structure, family size, and geographic locale. The data underscore the "heterogeneity" that characterizes the poor as well as the numerous dimensions of child poverty. A number of concepts critical to understanding poverty are clarified in the chapter: the "official" (federal) definition; conceptual, methodological, and computational problems pertaining to the definition's reliability and validity; proposed alterations to the measure; and the distinction between "transitory" versus "persistent" poverty. By analyzing past trends and projecting future ones, the chapter provides the reader with a historical perspective on the problem of child poverty.

Chapter 4, by Suzanne M. Bianchi, emphasizes the complex interplay of factors giving rise to poverty. Among the many variables examined are: macroeconomic elements, the growing inequality of earnings, government income transfers and taxation, and changing family structure. Bianchi ponders whether female-headed families are a cause or effect of impoverishment. Critical to the debate is a consideration of the politically conservative view of welfare as rewarding dependency, fostering a lack of paternal responsibility for children, and promoting marital dissolution and out-of-wedlock childbearing. These are among several themes weighed as the author reflects upon the problem: "Is welfare antiwork and antifamily?" The chapter helps readers appreciate the convolution of issues surrounding a consideration of causes, as well as the fact that any discussion of them is unavoidably "politicized."

Reviewing research on ways in which poverty interacts with other stressors to sabotage parental care, Joan I. Vondra, in chapter 5, emphasizes poverty as a "predictable risk factor" for children. As she points out, a complex constellation of variables is involved in child maltreatment, including poverty, parental psychology, community resources, as well as societal values. Any discussion of child maltreatment must take into consideration sociocultural influences. Attitudes, values, and family practices vary according to social class and ethnicity. Such factors render more enigmatic not only the processes and dynamics of child maltreatment but also its very definition. By clarifying the link between child maltreatment and poverty, the chapter explains why there is a disproportionate occurrence of abuse and neglect among economically disadvantaged families.

Elsie G. J. Moore analyzes evolving conceptions of the impoverished in chapter 6. Basic as well as applied research has sought to explain why children in poverty fail to develop knowledge and skills at the same rate as children from more economically advantaged circumstances. Emanating from this research are a number of explanatory paradigms: the deficient child (genetic source) perspective, the deficient child (environmental source) perspective, and the cultural difference perspective. The chapter offers a critical historical examination of these conceptions, demonstrating how prevailing assumptions about the nature and meaning of developmental outcomes relate to how intervention for children in poverty is conceived. The discussion highlights the complexity of the issues involved, as well as the danger of oversimplifying problems and their accompanying solutions.

In chapter 7, Sandra L. Hofferth examines the 101st Congress (the "Children's Congress"). As a result of growing recognition in the 1980s that public intervention on their behalf was necessary, the executive and legislative branches of the federal government directed an unprecedented degree of attention toward children. Significant legislation was passed pertaining to child care, Head Start, extended Medicaid coverage, and family and medical leave. Hofferth analyzes the contributions of the 101st Congress and, to a lesser extent, later ones, including issues surrounding passage of legislation, the dynamics involved in public policy formation, and an appraisal of the achievements. By examining the multiple forces (demographic, social, economic, and technological) that prompted legislative enactment, the author places congressional action in context. The detailed legislative history contained in the chapter enables the reader to appreciate how the formation of a broadly based national coalition, application of political pressure, and the negotiation of key concessions served as "dynamics" responsible for successful passage of legislation on behalf of children and families in poverty.

Drawing upon the concept of "human capital," Harold Watts, in chapter 8, interprets the developmental deficits emanating from child poverty in terms of the nation's economic well-being. Seeing human capital as "the biggest deficit" of child poverty, Watts spells out the consequences of failing to recognize this tenet. As he defines it, human capital refers to an individual's ability to contribute positively to self and society, whether as a wage earner, family member, or a participant in the broader community. Watts outlines specific elements of a social policy focusing on human capital investment and suggests that a portion of the Social Security Trust Fund be set aside for this purpose. By establishing the link between child development and the nation's economic well-being, the chapter presents a cogent argument for intervention on behalf of the poor. It details, as well, a concrete plan of action.

In chapter 9, Kevin Condit and I present a rationale for societal intervention on behalf of poverty-stricken children, whom we characterize as representing a "powerless constituency." Believing that society has a responsibility to alleviate these children's plight as an essential exercise of social justice, we describe and analyze facets of the advocacy process. Focusing on both government and philanthropy, we review literature on specific ways of influencing the legislative process, and analyze the dynamics and dimensions of nonprofit activity. The chapter further discusses how issues arise on the national domestic policy agenda (i.e., how a "policy window" opens) and how to take advantage of politically favorable occasions to press for change. To assist potential advocates, the chapter provides an appendix that lists both private- and public-sector organizations committed to serving impoverished children and their families.

Chapter 10, the concluding essay of the volume, highlights and synthesizes the themes that echo through the book. In the chapter, I seek to emphasize the many wide-ranging and interconnected aspects of the dilemma of child poverty. In the end, it is only by comprehending the multidisciplinary nature of the challenges of child poverty that we will properly address the problem.

Note

1. I would like to express my appreciation to Mary Lou Paurazas for providing this example.

References

Barnes, J. 1993. "To Clinton's Public, Less May Be More." *National Journal* 25 (Mar. 6): 582.

"Clinton Outlines His Plan to Spur the Economy." 1993. *Congressional Quarterly* 51 (Feb. 20): 399–404.

"Commission Warns Child Poverty Poses Threat of National Tragedy." 1990. *New York Times*, Apr. 27: A9.

Committee for Economic Development. 1987. *Children in Need: Investment Strategies for the Educationally Disadvantaged*. New York: Author.

Danziger, S., R. Haveman, and R. Plotnick. 1986. "Antipoverty Policy: Effects on the Poor and the Nonpoor." In *Fighting Poverty: What Works and What Doesn't*, edited by S. Danziger and D. Weinberg. Cambridge, Mass.: Harvard University Press.

Germond, J., and J. Witcover. 1993. "The Next Move Is the Electorate's." *National Journal* 25 (Feb. 20): 477.

Merry, R. 1992. "Clinton's First Test: Defining His Party." *Congressional Quarterly* 50 (July 18): 2138.

National Center for Children in Poverty. 1990. *Five Million Children*. New York: Author.

"Report Says Poor Children Grew Poorer in 1980's." 1992. *New York Times*, Mar. 24: A22.

"Seniors and Juniors." 1992. *New York Times*, Sept. 30: A14.

Waxman, C. 1983. *The Stigma of Poverty: A Critique of Poverty Theories and Policies*. New York: Pergamon Press.

Wilkerson, I. 1993. "First Born, Fast Grown: The Manful Life of Nicholas, 10." *New York Times*, Apr. 4: A1.

Chapter Two

PROFILES OF CHILDREN AND FAMILIES IN POVERTY

Judith S. Musick

This chapter offers a portrait of the psychological consequences of growing up poor in the United States, and of the connections between social-economic, and developmental factors. The ideas put forward are based on lessons I have learned in over 10 years of research and psychological practice in intervention programs for disadvantaged families—programs designed to help families build a better future for themselves and their children. The chapter immerses the reader in the stream of experience to which children raised in poverty are exposed, and sheds light on the developmental and psychological costs of that experience—costs so high they significantly deplete our country's human resources. Although the chapter suggests how public policy might play a role in preventing or reducing the problems associated with childhood poverty, no simple solutions are proposed.

The life circumstances of poor children and their parents may vary from community to community, and among separate subgroups and cultures within communities.[1] In spite of this diversity, certain invariant childrearing themes can be found across diverse groups. These are the universal building blocks of human experience that *all* families and communities must provide for their children. Poverty rearranges or removes these building blocks.

The chapter is composed of two case studies focusing on the developmental roots of two interlocking problems associated with childhood poverty: teenage motherhood and school failure. These problems were chosen because they repeatedly surface in the debate about the intergenerational transmission of poverty, a debate that has largely overlooked the developmental and psychological dimensions of this phenomenon. Each of the case studies reflects a central theme or concept. The theme of the first case study is that the sexual and gender socialization experiences of many poor girls make early childbearing almost inevitable for them, not simply by shaping their sexual behavior and relationships to men but also their motivation, efficacy, and sense of personal control. The developmental consequences of victimization and exploitation diminish their capacity to seek routes—other than motherhood—to achieve key developmental tasks.

The second concept, reflected in the second case study, concerns the extraordinary parenting challenges facing poor families today. Paradoxically, they are called on to do and be far more than their middle-class counterparts, with fewer resources to support them in this role and many more burdens to contend with. The second case study describes how the present circumstances of poverty force disadvantaged parents to take on almost superhuman roles as mediators of their children's environment, especially if they wish them to succeed in school.

BACKGROUND, METHOD, SAMPLE, AND SOURCES

Background

In developing these concepts, I have drawn on and integrated data from a variety of disadvantaged communities, including information on participants and staff in programs I developed for the Ounce of Prevention Fund, a statewide system of family support programs for disadvantaged families in Illinois. A unique public-private partnership established in Illinois in 1982, the Fund's principles and practices serve as models for programs throughout the United States. Its mission is to promote the well-being of disadvantaged children and adolescents by working with families, communities, and policymakers. Efforts focus on communities with very limited resources. Recognizing the family's critical role in determining children's futures, the Fund strives to strengthen family relationships and the family's ability to care for its members. Programs are based on the conviction that it is more caring and effective to promote healthy child and adolescent development than to treat problems later in life. The services range from parent education and support groups for teenagers who are already pregnant or parenting, to school-, social-service-agency-, or clinic-based prevention programs for those who are not. The fund has not only developed nearly 40 community-based family resource and support programs for teen parents and their children but has established—and now administers—three adolescent health clinics in large urban high schools, as well as the Center for Successful Child Development (the "Beethoven Project")—a comprehensive program for parents and young children in Chicago living in and around one of the nation's largest public housing projects. The Fund's network of services includes numerous home-visiting programs in large urban areas, small towns, and isolated, underserved rural communities; teen and family drop-in centers; Head Start and infant day-care programs; and middle-school and junior high school projects aimed at building literacy and other skills in youth at risk for a variety of problems including early parenthood.

Method

The rules of traditional social science are very limiting in terms of understanding the developmental and psychological dimensions of phenomena such as school failure and teenage childbearing. Although large-scale research studies are important for getting a sense of the breadth of such phenomena, they provide only one relatively narrow perspective on them, omitting some of the most potent, personally significant forces in people's lives—forces that interact to organize their attitudes and behavior and to furnish the affective fuel for their openness or resistance to change. They tell us what people do, but not why they do so. Thus, to properly evaluate what I have encountered in programs and in the lives of the participants for whom they are designed, I draw on clinical as well as research-based knowledge from diverse fields and populations. The deliberate use of multiple sources is a safeguard against the biases and limitations of only one or two perspectives. Those concerned with creating climates for change can ill afford narrow-sightedness.

The vantage point of this chapter is that of a practitioner-scholar, the approach a form of psychological ethnography. Miller and Sperry (1987) described such an approach as seeking and validating patterns through the use of various sources of evidence. They point out that each type of data raises questions about the interpretation of the others. Although utilizing findings from the larger, quantitative studies of others, as well as some of my own, the main ideas in this chapter are based on smaller, and for me, more fruitful, qualitative studies, and from my direct clinical work and field observations. That is, I have synthesized and interpreted data gathered on hundreds of children, adolescents, parents, and teachers, but the most revealing and enlightening material has often come through closer, deeper examination of individual lives. In the "study of lives" tradition, much of the evidence presented is in the words of adolescents and adults—many of whom I know personally—as they reflect on their lives. Like Bumiller (1990) in her study of the women of India, I believe that larger truths may come from the exploration of individual lives. Of course, there are limitations to this perspective: "what emerges is always a highly subjective, partial and fragmentary—but also deeply felt and personal—record of human lives based on eyewitness and testimony" (Scheper-Hughes 1992: xii). The insights and ideas contained here are only that. The objective is to direct the attention of policymakers, researchers, and practitioners to key processes and mechanisms underlying the problems of childhood poverty and adolescent childbearing, to look deeply rather than broadly, and to raise issues for others to consider. The sample and sources used for this purpose are described next and in appendix 2.A.

Sample Characteristics

Whereas most research on poverty has focused on black, urban, single-parent families—making it difficult to generalize to other groups—the data on which this chapter is based were collected from a broader representation of poor families living in small towns and isolated rural communities as well as large cities in the midwestern and southeastern United States. The parents and children are African-American, white, and Hispanic (Puerto Rican and Mexican). They reside in single-parent, two-parent, and extended family households. Most of the parents are young, or were young when they first gave birth. All are poor, but some are poorer than others. By the same token, some have greater social resources and family support than others. Poverty takes many forms, affecting different groups in different ways.

The subjects (or respondents) consist of infants and young children in early intervention programs, child care and Head Start centers, family support programs, and homes; preteen and teenage girls participating in school- and agency-based prevention programs; adolescent and adult mothers in health, social service, educational, and comprehensive family support programs; and preschool, primary, and secondary school teachers, as well as direct service providers and supervisors in community-based intervention and family support programs. Although the numbers of children and parents within each study tend to be relatively small, over the years, several thousand adolescent mothers and their children have participated in the programs described here.

Sources

My data sources consist of surveys; individual and focus group interviews; observations done in homes, schools, and programs; videotapes; and clinical case material collected over a 10-year period from 1981 to 1991. The data were gathered by other researchers and clinicians, as well as by me; these sources are described in appendix 2.A.

One additional source of data was especially rich: the diaries of adolescent mothers in the Ounce of Prevention Fund's Heart-to-Heart sexual abuse prevention program and the Dear Diary journal writing project. These diaries are mixtures of private writing and "journal dialogues"; that is, the journal is not only a place for private thoughts but also for ongoing written interaction between the writer and someone who writes back every few months. Letters are sometimes included in these journals when girls address their children, boyfriends, parents, and other significant people. In the pages of their journals teens express thoughts and emotions they are unable to tell others directly—laying out their personal histories as they interpret them. More than an exercise in self-expression, this also promotes a sense of mastery over life experiences that were often painful and puzzling.

At the same time that personal writing serves the teen, it serves the researcher or practitioner as well. In examining the journals of young people, one gains access to their inner world and a unique perspective on the social forces and psychological themes that motivate their behavior. As adolescent writers create their own distinctive narratives, their unique perspectives rise to the surface, revealing how they perceive and comprehend themselves and their world.[2] They tell us what they must cope with and how they cope. And although some adolescent mothers may initially tell only their "good stories," gradually, as they continue to write, their "real stories" are unveiled. These stories enable us to see sexual and other significant relationships through the eyes of the adolescent and the little girl she was in the recent past. With adolescent mothers the picture, whether past or present, is seldom pretty. For them, the "lessons" of self and others have been hard and harmful, teaching ways of thinking and relating that will be very difficult to change—even with opportunity and encouragement. Through internalization these lessons have become the psychological themes that structure and guide their lives (Musick 1993).

CASE STUDY 1. LESSONS OF SEX ARE LESSONS OF SELF: GROWING UP FEMALE IN POVERTY

I knew that it was going to be a pattern [because] I lived it with my parents. Like they say, if they do it once they will do it again. My father used to hit my mom all the time . . . it happened every day. It haunted me all the time, I thought it would happen to me. When my second boyfriend did it to me, I found myself in my mother's shoes and I had always said I wasn't going to let it happen to me. [But] I got involved in the relationship in the first place. I had already felt it when we were going out. During the first year, everything was getting stricter and stricter—no tight clothing, no makeup; my hair was supposed to be the way he wanted it. I couldn't go out with my friends. It started with pushes and yelling and then a little pinch to let me know he was angry. Then he would do this [thump her on the forehead with two fingers]. His family is like mine. His father drinks and hits his mother. It goes from generation to generation. . . . my mother said I should stay with him since he was the father of my daughter. I finally realized I didn't need him. I was going to school, I have a job. Yet I was scared to come home, fearing that as soon as I turned the lights on he was going to jump me 'cause I'm an hour late. He didn't even have a high school education. He would tell me, "You go to [the young parent support group] meetings, they are changing you and brainwashing you." The night before I told him to leave, he beat me up and I went to school all marked up.

Marla was a mother in her teens. Now, age 20, she is in college and doing well. She lives alone with her two children.

Description

This case study provides a profile of family and environmental influences on the socialization of disadvantaged females. Specific emphasis is given to the sexual exploitation of preadolescent girls by older males who should be in protective and nurturing roles—fathers, father-figures, and others such as uncles, brothers, cousins, and grandfathers. It considers how development-thwarting experiences such as sexual victimization and psychological maltreatment affect adolescent girls' relationships with males, fertility, and risk-taking behaviors, as well as their capacity for achievement in the domains of school and work.

The primary data on which these ideas are based come from three basic sources: (1) over 300 journal entries from participants in the Heart-to-Heart and Dear Diary programs, (2) interviews with several hundred "graduates" of Heart-to-Heart and other programs, and (3) results of the sexual abuse prevalence survey of 445 pregnant and parenting young women described previously (Gershenson et al. 1989). Although the girls are highly diverse, their words have a striking similarity.[3] They speak of childhoods marked by repeated exploitation, terror, and betrayal of trust, and by the loneliness that comes from shame. As one adolescent mother described her sexual abuse while growing up, "After it happened I was in a world by myself."

Analysis of the Problem

Approximately 1 million adolescent pregnancies occur each year, with 50 percent resulting in live births (Forrest and Singh 1990). For a decade, the birthrate among U.S. teens has remained nearly constant, at a level much higher than in comparable Western countries. Of equal concern is the significant increase in births to girls under age 15 (Hayes and Panel on Adolescent Pregnancy and Childbearing 1987; Moore 1991), and the small but significant rise in births to teens aged 15 to 17 (Moore 1991). Today, once a birth has occurred, very few adolescent mothers elect to relinquish their child for adoption (Kalmuss, Namerow, and Cushman 1991). This is just one difference between teenage motherhood in the present and that in the past.

Today, when an adolescent becomes a mother, it generally means that she is not engaged in the process of becoming something else— not on her way to becoming a college student, a career woman, a wife. When she becomes a mother in her teens, it all too often means that she and the children she bears are more likely to remain very poor, and to do very poorly. Whereas in past generations, the burdens of adolescent childbearing were at least partially alleviated by marriage—if not before the birth of the child, then fairly soon afterward— this is far less often the case today (Guttmacher Institute 1992). In addition, the young mother of yesterday was more likely to receive substantial help from her family in raising her child and getting her life back on track. Today there are far fewer grandmothers (or grandfathers) able or willing to take over and provide good-quality care for an adolescent's child. At best, a 33-year-old grandmother may be too busy getting her own life in order, or starting a new family of her own, to devote herself to grandmotherhood. At worst, she may be even more troubled and unstable than her daughter. Indeed, the childbearing climate she created in her home—she and the men in her life—may well have led to her daughter's premature parenthood.

Recent research has found sexual abuse to be a common background factor for poor young women, especially those who engage in early, unprotected sex and who become teenage mothers (Boyer and Fine 1992; Butler and Burton 1990; Gershenson et al. 1989; Moore, Nord, and Peterson 1989). Even before these empirical studies were undertaken, there was increasing clinical evidence of high sexual abuse prevalence rates among this population (Musick 1993). In this regard, the Ounce of Prevention Fund conducted a study of the nature and extent of sexual abuse among our participants. A survey specifically designed for adolescents was administered to a mixed sample of 445 white, African-American, and Hispanic pregnant and parenting teens (Gershenson et al. 1989) in the Fund's programs across Illinois. The results of this survey were striking even to those who had suspected the extent of the problem. Sixty-one percent of the adolescents had been sexually abused, the majority by more than one perpetrator. For many of the girls, abuse was an ongoing situation. Although some girls were victimized as young children, abuse was most common during puberty and early adolescence, with first occurrence at 11½ years of age on average.[4]

In addition to answering the questions on the survey, 333 respondents wrote comments on the test protocols, in which they revealed their rage and resentment at being forced to engage in acts they found debasing and repugnant. They described trickery and betrayal, sexual assaults at knife point, men inviting their friends to "share" the victim, and other experiences similar to those described in the clinical sexual abuse literature.

If a preadolescent girl's psychological energies are focused predominantly on defensive and security measures, her attention is diverted from key developmental tasks that pave the way for adolescent, and later, adult competence. This is precisely the case for many poor girls. Instead of being free—let alone encouraged—to concentrate on developing critical educational and social skills, they are being coerced or forced into premature sexual relations, and into coping with the burden of keeping shameful secrets.

A mixed sample of Hispanic, African-American, and white teenage mothers described the sexual experiences of their pre- and early adolescent years.

It was like a family thing . . . repeatedly. . . . It was a relative . . . and he scared me and told me he was going to kill me and my mom. . . . When he done it he told his brothers and they wanted to do it, and they was forcing me into, "well if you don't let us do it then we'll tell that so and so did it." So I didn't say anything, no I was just keeping it inside . . . and I didn't know any better [that he wouldn't make good on his threats] and I know that was wrong and bad, but I didn't want him to kill anybody. . . . Somebody should have seen that in me . . . because when it happened to me I wasn't a kid anymore, I was just different. . . . I've had so many problems with disease infection . . . and some of it I believe is from that childhood experience. . . . My body, I'm not lying. . . . It's gone! Messed up already. . . . My mind, it's blocked.

* * *

. . . such bad memories I've had to keep from my mother and sister.

* * *

When this experience happened to me I did not know that it was wrong. If only I had known it was wrong.

* * *

My grandfather . . . put his hand up my pajamas while I was sleeping. He made me feel his body in the dark. He made me hold my vagina open so he could look inside. He made me put my fingers in my vagina and then put my fingers in my mouth. I have many painful memories from many different times.

* * *

My stepfather beat my mother hoping to make me have sex with him. He also hit me.

* * *

My mom she married J. when I was about 4 years old and I just assumed his last name. He never adopted me. And it was in [junior high school] . . . my mom wanted to finally get straight which last name I would have before I started high school, and she couldn't understand why I didn't want his last name. . . . and she just kept asking different questions and then she just finally asked me if he hurt me or touched me and I started crying and she figured it out.

* * *

My daughter's father is in jail. He abused me physically, sexually, and mentally [for many years]. He is a total mistake to have come to this earth. . . . I could never forget what he did to me but I want to prevent that from happening to any of my children. So help me God I will kill anyone who hurts my kids the way I was hurt.

* * *

I have been through hell. My Dad did everything to me. . . . took me out in the country and raped me. . . .

Taken together, the findings of the survey, interviews, and diary data reveal a pattern whereby preadolescent and early adolescent girls are sexually socialized into passive victim roles by a variety of older male kin and "near kin" such as stepfathers and mothers' boyfriends. Only 18 percent of the abusers were 2 or fewer years older than their victims, another 18 percent were 3 to 5 years older, and 17 percent were 6 to 10 years older. The remaining 46 percent were more than 10 years older than their victims. Very large age differences were especially common among girls abused before age 14. Thus, before and during pubertal development, these girls were left unprotected. In many instances the girls' own young mothers were in victimizing relationships themselves, and may have been afraid to acknowledge, let alone interfere, with what was happening to their daughters. A 16-year-old white mother reflected on her mother's refusal to believe her, or intervene to stop her abuse:

> One of the hardest things I've had to deal with is trying to get someone to believe me. These people are not thought to ever do anything like this. My 2nd and 3rd times were the most traumatic. I had nightmares.

In light of the findings in regard to the age differences between victims and perpetrators, it is interesting to note that data on a larger sample of 1,500 program participants indicated that only half the fathers of the teen mothers' children were teenagers themselves; half were older men. Although I have not studied the phenomenon closely, there is strong anecdotal evidence that girls who consistently "choose" older partners are more likely to come from troubled, multi-problem homes where there was more abuse of all types—sexual, physical, and emotional—while they were growing up. Further, the relationships they form with these older males often turn out to be violent and destructive, both for the young mothers and their children. It appears that girls who were sexually exploited at home are more likely to be drawn into exploitive relationships outside the home when they reach adolescence. Nearly one-quarter of the victims in our study reported that they became pregnant by an abuser, with 91 percent of these pregnancies resulting in live births. Although the fathers were seldom immediate family members such as fathers and grandfathers, many were considerably older than the girls. A black teenage mother recalled her first sexual experience:

> He was [older]. . . . I was only a freshman in high school. He took my virginity away . . . I got pregnant. . . . I finally told him after I was 3 months pregnant. He laughed and said, "Little girl you can't be

pregnant from me, I'm sterile." I said, "It was you." He said he wasn't my first.

Although there may not always be direct links between sexual victimization and adolescent childbearing, it does appear that there are strong indirect associations between these two phenomena. In her psychological struggle to defend herself against, or to adapt to an environment that provides too little care and protection; in searching for the acceptance and love she craves—and which she believes is based solely on her sexuality—a girl who has been sexually exploited will take many risks and few precautions. The capacity to care for oneself and one's body is, after all, predicated on being protected by caring others while still too young to do this for oneself. An Hispanic adolescent mother described the effects of sexual abuse on sexual behavior:

> For girls, I think they don't give a care if they are alive because they got sexually abused and they will go around just jumping into any other guy's bed. After it happens they feel so cheap and fleezy [sic] and they don't care about life anymore. "They are hurting me, so why shouldn't I hurt myself."

Today, with the risk of AIDS and other sexually transmitted diseases so great, pregnancy is not the only outcome of risk-taking sexual behavior. For the preadolescent girl who is unable to resolve the developmental tasks of the school years—tasks that confer a sense of industry, of personal efficacy, and pride in self (Erikson 1963)—the price will be high, and she may eventually pay for it with her life, and perhaps with the life of her child, if not in adolescence, then in early adulthood.

Enmeshing a girl in sexually precocious behavior confuses her about what is and is not appropriate behavior, and repeated violation of her body makes her feel powerless. It is a kind of brainwashing that robs the girl of will and self-efficacy, and inculcates a sense of helplessness in relation to men, a fatalism that may some day hurt her children as well. When I asked one 17-year-old mother, "What do you think you could do to protect your children from suffering the kind of abuse and problems you have suffered?" she responded, "I personally don't know what can be done, simply because when you feel you know someone, suddenly that person changes, then you don't know who to trust or not trust." Another young mother said, "There's nothing you can protect them from . . . as far as drugs, sex, or anything."

The emotional energy required to cope with (or suppress the effects of) severe emotional trauma depletes the girl's psychological resources, interfering with her ability to concentrate on academic tasks (Conte and Schuerman 1987).[5] In this way, the consequences of deviant sexual socialization reach beyond the realms of sexual and social behavior to disrupt cognition and learning. By distorting the girl's images of herself and others, sexual exploitation pushes her toward self-defeat and away from self-enhancement, not only in regard to her relationships but also in regard to school, and later perhaps, in regard to work. The expressions of futility, and difficulties with school and work so often noted with poor young women, are clearly not exclusively the results of sexual abuse, but are at least partly a consequence of having been used by others without regard for their needs as developing children. That so many developing young people are harmed by those charged with nurturing and protecting them is evidence of a major social— and societal—failure.

Supports and Resources Available to Families

Although the phenomenon of sexual exploitation is by no means exclusive to poor communities, it is more pervasive there for a variety of reasons to be discussed here. Further, its effects are likely to be more toxic where there are fewer family and structural supports. The middle-class victim of sexual abuse is no less likely to be hurt by this experience than her disadvantaged counterpart; she is, however, much more likely to have a range of other compensating factors in her life, including access to private counseling or therapy. For those, relatively few, poor girls who report or try to stop their own abuse, the only sources of support are often understaffed and substandard services offered by public child welfare, medical, and mental health institutions, or overburdened private social service agencies. Immediate, and often ongoing, treatment, by professionals who know what they are doing is of critical importance for victims of sexual abuse and their families (Haugaard and Reppucci 1988). Yet, very few poor families have access to any but the most fragmented of services. Treatment is the first step in preventing further cycles of abuse. An untreated female victim is much more likely to continue to embroil herself (and later her children) in abusive situations; an untreated male victim is much more likely to become an abuser himself, often by early adolescence.

In addition to a lack of ameliorative/therapeutic or preventive services in poor communities, more families in poverty are headed by single women, often single young women. Thus, there is a greater likelihood of a pre- and early adolescent girl being exposed to her mother's boyfriend(s) or stepfather(s)—men who may have only a transient interest (if that) in her care and well-being. This also means that there is no stable male figure in the home to protect her, and, in the risk-saturated context of poverty, girls need all the protection they can get—both in the home and in the wider world. As Elijah Anderson (1989) observed:

> . . . in those domestic situations in which there is but one adult—say, a woman with two or three teenage daughters and with no male presence—the dwelling may be viewed [by local males] as essentially an unprotected nest. . . . In such settings, a man, the figure the boys are prepared to respect, is not there to keep them in line (68).

Anderson noted that "when it does survive," the conventional inner-city family unit of two parents with the extended network of kin forms a "viable supportive unit engaged to fight in a most committed manner the various problems confronting so many inner-city teenagers" (68). We have found this to be the case in impoverished rural areas and small towns, as well as in inner-city urban communities. Decreased employment opportunities for skilled, as well as unskilled, workers have significantly reduced the pool of men able to fulfill the role of family breadwinner, or at least to contribute significantly to the family's economic and social welfare.

Fathers and other older family or extended family members who abuse young girls are clearly deviant, but what about the men who seek out much younger females as "dates"? Is a less-severe form of pathology at work when 25-year-old men seduce or coerce 14-year-old girls? Are these men merely immature, or are they in fact deviant as well? A 16-year-old Hispanic mother wrote: "My boyfriend is much older than I and I sometimes feel like . . . he really abused me. I knew what was happening between us, but I was always afraid to say no to him." Probably many such men are marginal individuals who compensate for feeling powerless by asserting power over whomever they can. Preadolescent girls are more naive and more easily intimidated than adolescents, especially older adolescents; they are also less likely to tell. Where there is widespread male joblessness and hopelessness, it should not be surprising that sexuality becomes an arena in which men seek to gain and maintain a sense of power.[6]

Unresolved Issues

The factors that promote the widespread sexual victimization of young women are highly complex. They are rooted not only in familial and economic problems but in societal attitudes about females, about sexuality, and especially about female sexuality, as highlighted recently by the controversy surrounding the Anita Hill–Clarence Thomas hearings. Can social policies influence something as deeply personal and private as sexual behavior? Can they heal the pain of the past that leads to repeated cycles of psychological damage? Most significantly, can social policies alter the underlying attitudes that permit or promote the mistreatment and exploitation of developing young people, and modify socialization patterns based on the need to control and dominate females? Behavior develops in context; and although it is clear that the impoverished circumstances of the men in poor communities contribute to their tendency to "use" young girls to make themselves feel better, it is important to remember that only certain men are likely to act in this way. We do not know who is most likely to become a sexual abuser, nor what means of early identification and intervention might result in the prevention of abusive situations. Obviously, improved economic opportunities will help to some degree, but middle-class and wealthy men also seek to control and exploit females.

Other unresolved issues concern the interlocking mechanisms connecting girls' preadolescent socialization experiences to their later sexual attitudes, and, further, to both their sexual and fertility-related behaviors. A girl who unconsciously perceives childbearing as a way out of an abusive situation at home is not only unlikely to use contraceptives herself, but she is equally as unlikely to insist that her partner use a condom. Thus, as noted earlier, she is putting herself at risk for AIDS and other sexually transmitted diseases, as well as early pregnancy.

Next Steps in Policymaking

Perhaps policy can *directly* affect changes only by making the consequences of sexual exploitation (including sexual harassment) much more serious for the offender; by consistently and relentlessly enforcing the laws against such behavior. It can, however, have a significant *indirect* impact, both through the creation of greater social and economic opportunities for poor families, and through support for interventions that enable disadvantaged young people (male and female) to engage in productive and life-affirming activities for themselves. Policy can promote and sustain programs that equip youth to seek, recognize, and take advantage of whatever opportunities are available. Then, when these young men and women become parents themselves (as adults, it is hoped, not adolescents), they will be able to provide more nurturing, protective, and healthier caregiving environments for their children.

Recent years have seen a proliferation of such programs, especially programs for adolescent mothers (or those at risk of becoming adolescent mothers) and their children. As the needs have become more widely recognized, these programs have gained greater acceptance by policymakers, community leaders, and especially the young women for whom they have been created. In developing the programs in its network, the Ounce of Prevention Fund has brought state-of-the-art knowledge to everyday practice, testing the validity of that knowledge against practice under difficult conditions. By examining and refining intervention strategies in action, we seek to understand why particular strategies are or are not working, and for whom. This recurring cycle of program development, field-testing, refinement, and assessment yields important lessons for policymakers and has led to the creation of new programs directed to special populations and special needs. These "programs-within-programs" target issues such as substance abuse, job training, and preventing/solving parent-child relationship problems, and, in the case of Heart-to-Heart, preventing sexual victimization.

Lessons from Heart-to-Heart

The goal of the Heart-to-Heart prevention program is to prevent sexual abuse by strengthening the abilities of adolescent mothers—especially current or former victims of abuse—to protect their children and themselves from sexual and other forms of victimization. In a specially designed 12-week curriculum embedded in an ongoing young mothers' support group, participants learn about and discuss children's social-emotional and sexual development, sexual victimization and its prevention, and indicators and treatment of sexual abuse. Discussions of the young mothers' own childhoods and their past and current relations with family members and partners are core features of this program. Heart-to-Heart groups are led by facilitators from the community who have undergone an extensive 20-hour training program. Most of these women are former adolescent mothers themselves, and many are adult survivors of childhood sexual abuse.

Group leaders are supervised by professional clinicians connected to area child welfare and social-service agencies.

One of the most important lessons learned through practice concerns the positive changes that occur in conceptually sound interventions, in spite of considerable variation from program to program. Although, for example, the Heart-to-Heart program requires each service site to provide the same core prevention curriculum, there is still substantial variation among them. Yet, most Heart-to-Heart programs have had a strong, positive impact on participants' self-image, self-confidence, parenting behavior, and attitudes in relation to men. Similar outcomes have been found in regard to school enrollment, employment, and delay of subsequent pregnancies among a larger sample of 1,004 participants in our teen parent programs (Ruch-Ross, Jones, and Musick 1992). How could there be equal success across programs given such diversity? An examination of the data suggests that underneath the apparent diversity, similar processes are at work across program sites. These processes originate in the relationships girls form with staff members who serve as nurturers and mentors; as teachers, role models, and as rescuers in times of crisis. A conceptually sound intervention for adolescent girls is therefore one that is grounded in the belief that change is an outgrowth of healing and enabling relationships. The Ounce of Prevention Fund's experience in this regard is not unique: the significance of such relationships is mentioned in virtually every study of programs for adolescent girls and young mothers in the United States (see, for example, the research on Project Redirection discussed by Dryfoos 1990; and Polit, Quint, and Riccio 1988).

If an intervention is conceptually valid, it may work even when not fully executed. If the program has the potential to genuinely fill a void or solve a problem, the adolescent will sense and respond to its "promise." Participants benefited from Heart-to-Heart, even in those groups that were somewhat disorganized. Girls in such groups asked for extra time (often private time with staff members), used their journals to ask questions or to seek help, and pressed group leaders to cover topics in the curriculum that had been passed over that week. Appreciating and making the most of whatever they received—even when it was not enough—their experience of support went beyond what was actually given (Musick 1993).

Evidence of the power of relationships forged in this program to effect positive personal change has been demonstrated repeatedly. Whenever young women speak of the role of programs in such transformations, they identify people as the predominant influence, individuals who have guided, enabled, and enhanced their positive growth as parents and as people. In study after study, these kinds of relationships have been found to be the essential building blocks of effective intervention strategies; they are the "universals" that hold true across communities and cultures, and apply to a wide range of settings.

In their relationships with participants, staff members have clear expectations that girls will be better at certain things when they leave the program than when they entered. They envision their role as directly imparting new knowledge and teaching new skills, or connecting girls with others who can do this for them. Thus they promote and reinforce positive change, both in their formal functions as guides, role models, and teachers, and through the personal, nurturing relationships they build with the girls. This blend of curative new relationships and valuable new competencies helps to break dysfunctional patterns of childrearing. Two young women described their experiences—and gains—in a community-based program for teenage mothers: "The program was different from the way I grew up. And probably if I didn't have [the program], then I would probably have raised him the way I was raised, which I really wouldn't have wanted." And on relating to men: "They taught me don't let a man run over you, don't be used by men, don't be used by the words, 'I love you,' cause 'I love you' don't always mean I love you. They might just love you as a body, but not as a person."

Many positive effects of teen parent programs are indirect results of the combination of rehabilitative relationships and new knowledge and skills. For example, when teens know that a program is empathic to them, this helps them, in turn, identify with and be empathic to their children. As they become more aware of how they feel (and how they felt when they were children), they become aware that their children have similar feelings. They thus begin to monitor their behavior and its affects on their children.

I never knew how babies feel. You know you're upset, and I never knew that they feel that way too.

Boy them sisters [program staff] talked to you. . . . they made me think about a lot of the things that I do now. . . . I learned to sit back and watch my kids. . . . I don't want them to say when they get bigger, "Man, my mamma be beating me up." My mamma . . . threw anything she seen or anything she put her hand on. Or . . . she hit you with one of these [fist]. I try not to be like that with my kids.

If I hadn't been in [the parent support group] . . . I would be like those other girls, beating that child and in jail. I was on the edge of hitting him. And I had to find somebody to talk, to hold myself to keep from abusing him. I was on the edge of wanting to hurt him.

When an adolescent feels comfortable telling her story—when the forbidden is no longer forbidden—a spell is broken. As secrets (from herself, as well as others) surface, unspoken words lose their power, and her history loosens its grip on her life. As three Heart-to-Heart participants described it:

> Today I shared my most innermost secret . . . and for once in my life I feel normal . . . a new way has open(ed). I feel better. This knowledge also makes me feel that I know how to define my problems.

> When I can talk about this (sexual abuse), I can talk about anything.

> My heart feels so clean.

Speaking the unspeakable shifts the adolescent's sense of control from others to the self, as the past becomes more than what happened *to* her, but a series of events that she can objectify. When, in a healing relationships, she tells her story, she *acts*, and in acting, stops protecting (and psychologically collaborating with) those who have done her harm. For many, this process is a first step away from victimhood.

The process of putting words to things—of making the amorphous, concrete and "conscious"—is applicable to a wide range of intervention issues. When the young woman speaks or writes about things that have hurt her, she puts a cognitive framework on an emotional experience. This helps her to master it and put it in a manageable place. Language, whether spoken or written, also puts psychological "space" or a "wedge" between feeling and action. It encourages reflection and self-awareness; thinking before automatically doing. Such mechanisms promote personal and parental responsibility. Things do not just happen; we can make them happen, or not. In an open letter to girls just beginning the program, a former Heart-to-Heart participant counseled:

> There is help out there, you just have to look for it. If you just sit home and don't do nothing about it you'll keep running and continue, but if you look out and seek help, you find it, believe it or not. But you just got to look for it.

Putting words to things is not, by itself, sufficient to encourage change. If allowed to go on too long, complaining can become yet another way to avoid doing what needs to be done. Unlike adults, adolescents need large doses of "guided" talking: candid, direct, and sometimes confrontive conversations. A skilled, sensitive listener leads the teenager to connect her past to her present, and to see the psychic purposes behind what she does. For example, one adolescent was helped to conclude: "You mean I keep involving myself with destructive men because that's the only way I managed to get along with all the different men in my mother's life when I was growing up?"

Preadolescents and younger adolescents have questions they need to ask and to have answered directly by adults they trust. As two seventh-grade girls asked the counselor guiding their prevention group discussion, "Mrs. Patten, if your uncle is not really a relative is it O.K. for him to kiss you on the mouth?" And "If a person you know says they'll pay you to have sex, is that prostitution?" Girls are empowered by accurate knowledge about what is and is not appropriate sexual behavior:

If I hadn't been in [Heart-to-Heart] . . . I would be ignorant. If something happens and you don't know, it's just like 'O.K. I'm not going to say nothing.' It's gonna stay like that . . . and now you know you have to do something about it. You know what to do, what to say.

* * *

Heart-to-Heart has helped me in many ways. Well just one week ago I was over at my boyfriend grandparents' house and his uncle was kissing my son in the mouth but I stop that but if it was not for Heart-to-Heart I may not known what to do. . . . So be very careful about who you leave your kids with.

Accurate knowledge also disconfirms negative evidence in regard to themselves:

I know now that it's my body and no one can tell me what to do with it.

* * *

I realized that I was abused by an uncle and cousins too.

* * *

As I grew up at times I felt guilty like maybe I did something to have this guy approach me. But I understand a lot more now since I've went through Heart to Heart. I now know its not my fault and never was.

* * *

As a child I was physically and emotionally abused by my father. And had a hard time with guilt. I learned not long ago that he also sexually abused my [younger] sister and niece. I only wish I knew then what I know now. I can see signs now that would have helped me to stop his abuse long ago. . . . All the time my sister was being abused I had this

sick feeling that something was wrong. . . . I just didn't believe in
myself enough and she suffered for it. . . . I still have problems
sometimes, but being in Heart-to-Heart has relieved the guilt and made
me feel as if I can finally get past the pain.

* * *

I am glad that I have finally reached out and faced facts about my past.
Now with the information I found out I can make sure that what
happened to me will not happen to my kids and no one else that is
close to my heart.

To be listened to and genuinely heard is very self-affirming, especially for young females (Fine 1990; Gilligan, Lyons, and Hanmer
1990). Girls tend to be "pleasers" who fear they might offend others—
especially males—by saying the wrong thing. A process of transfor-
mation is set in motion when they have a chance to be who they are,
and say what they have to say—without fear of criticism, retaliation,
or estrangement from those to whom they are attached. One teenager
commented: "It makes me understand that you can have someone
to trust and take your hardest and most painful things in mind and
heart."

If relationships are the foundation of many of the problems encountered, they are also the foundation of their solution. In the words of
another program participant, "Everybody cares [at the program]. . . .
Its not like if you didn't want to do anything they would just leave
you alone. They would get on you and hound you and make sure
you do it."

Especially for adolescent females, relationships are the stepping
stones to growth and change. Recognizing this, effective policies
must make relationships their most critical concern—whether the
principal goals of the program are preventive health care, preparation
for work, completion of school, improvement of mental health, parenting, child development, or family planning. Like good families,
good interventions provide both emotional support and consistent
guidance firmly anchored in strong, positive values. Finally, to be
effective, programs must do for low-income youth what more advantaged families are able to do "naturally" for their children—link high
expectations with the *means* to fulfill them.

CASE STUDY 2. BEING BETTER THAN GOOD: THE ROLE OF PARENTS IN AN ENVIRONMENT OF RISK

Description

The second case study describes the experiences of a group of young
children living in an extremely deprived, socially isolated inner-city

community, one characterized by row after row of barely maintained high-rise public housing projects, vacant lots littered with broken glass and garbage, and boarded-up buildings peopled by drug users, dealers, and others involved in crime. Danger and disorder are omnipresent, in the homes as well as in the streets.

The qualitative material used to support this case study comes from transcripts of conversations with parents raising children under these conditions, and with the teachers in the school serving these children. These transcripts are part of a larger study of family and educational factors contributing to successful school experiences for low-income young children (Hans, Musick, and Jagers 1992) described in appendix 2.A. The larger dataset includes observations of young children at their schools, in their homes, and at the previously mentioned Center for Successful Child Development, an early intervention demonstration project developed jointly by the Ounce of Prevention Fund and the Chicago Urban League. The data were collected from parents living in the community where the center is housed, and from teachers in the nearby elementary school. To understand the roots of early school success for poor children, we examined the perceptions and attitudes of these important adults with regard to their children and their school expectations for them. As in the first case study, the purpose of using qualitative data was to bring to the surface underlying processes that mediate—and help to explain—child outcomes that I and others have observed in disadvantaged young children.

A relatively small percentage, approximately 10 percent, of the children in this study were doing very well—cognitively, academically, socially, and emotionally—but most were not.[7] The comments and personal narratives of their parents and teachers help to explain these differences and illustrate a central finding of the research— that parents in such high-risk environments must be better than good to save their children from failure or worse. Their children's future depends on more than the relationships they have established with them; it depends on what they have learned through these relationships about what to expect and how to relate in the world beyond the home.

Analysis of the Problem

During the earliest years—and far longer in the highest-risk communities—parents are the most significant aspects of their child's environment. All parents act as mediators between the world and their young children, but within the context of severe poverty, where there are many dangers and few safeguards, their role is literally as well as symbolically a life-saving one. Read the words of two mothers, whose children were identified by kindergarten teachers as entering school well-adjusted and socially competent, intellectually ready, and eager to learn. It is worth noting that these mothers are adults, not adolescents.

> No way would I send my child through these buildings at five years old. . . . So many kids get snatched off. . . . Not only will somebody snatch them, the older kids, they take their money. They beat them up. All kinds of things. That's too small. Maybe I'm over-protective. . . . That's just my opinion. Mine wouldn't be doing it.
>
> * * *
>
> She wants to come back home by herself. Like maybe I let her get a little head start . . . and I stand on the porch, and I watch her. When I see her get about right there I hit the steps. So when she gets about right there, I say, "You walked all the way home by yourself, didn't you?" . . . I always tell her, Robin, if I should be late don't just stand in a lonely spot. A pervert looks for alone kids. Don't just stand in one spot. Start walking towards home cause I'll meet you before you get home. Sometimes I let her make those steps. Because sometimes she thinks that she is doing something so grown. Believe me, I'm on her. Four or five [pairs of] eyes are on her.

These parents strongly recognize—and consistently act on the recognition—that the world is a very threatening place for their children. At the same time, they are aware of the developmental importance of promoting a child's autonomy and self-confidence. They take pains to protect children when they are little, and act proactively to prepare them to protect themselves when they are older. What is more, they promote their children's sense of pride at being able to do so. Such parents do more than merely caution their children; they clearly and repeatedly demonstrate what to do in dangerous situations, rehearsing and replaying these situations with them, and praising them for their efforts, no matter how small. Aware that danger lurks within homes as well as streets, these parents realize that what they teach may be at the cost of the child's innocence and capacity to trust other adults and children. Still, they believe that certain lessons must be taught.

> And as far as aunts and uncles, I taught her that they aren't supposed to touch you in certain places. Don't sit on no man's lap because men do get stimulated. They might not do it intentionally. And women too. I taught her don't sit on people's laps. You sit on mine or her father's or grandma. You know, people like that.

In a context where no one else looks out for their children's psychological well-being, the parent's role as champion of his or her children is especially critical. As one mother responded to the dentist who told her to spank her child for squirming while he was treating her:

> "You don't know why she's like this, and you don't tell me how to raise my kids." I didn't like the way he said what he said. As if kids don't have any rights. . . . I mean this child was so scared. . . . She is terrified of needles because when she was younger she had to have surgery.

Parents such as this serve as strong advocates on behalf of their children, forging links with outside institutions and refusing to be intimidated, even if it means going up against authority figures such as teachers or health care providers.

Far more than their middle-class counterparts, poor parents are called on to mediate the effects of an unforgiving environment, to counteract the effects of harmful or antisocial values, and to shield their children from the consequences of social pathology. Risk factors such as these impinge directly on parents, who then must meet these risks head on while sheltering the child through their caregiving and at the same time empowering him or her to act confidently in his or her world. In this way, the disadvantaged child's parents *are* his or her environment to a much greater degree than that of a more advantaged child. Bruno Bettelheim has written:

> It is quite possible to be a good enough parent—that is, a parent who raises his child well. To achieve this, the mistakes we make in rearing our child—errors often made just because of the intensity of our emotional involvement in and with our child—must be more than compensated for by the many instances in which we do right by our child (1987: ix).

But, for poor parents today, being "good enough" is far from sufficient. When a child's parents are virtually all he or she has, they must be more than merely good enough, they must be extraordinary. Where there is environmental risk, a family's childrearing burdens are compounded. They must *proactively* buffer, mediate, and protect their children from the dangerous elements in the world; they must guide, enable, and validate, fostering the growth of sturdy and resilient egos; and they must provide an enriching interpersonal matrix for the development of psychosocial and cognitive skills (Clark 1983; Comer 1985; Musick 1987, 1993; Musick and Stott 1990). All this low-income parents must do, absent most of the material and social supports of their middle-class counterparts. That a good many of them do just that is powerful testimony to their love and their strength. How many parents fall into this category? One can only speculate, but considering the present conditions and those of the recent past, one could fairly say that any parent who has raised a son or daughter who finishes high school, stays out of trouble, relates well to others, and moves ahead to become a productive adult has done a great many things right.

Supports and Resources for Poor Parents and Children: The Case of the School

As just mentioned, a major reason why the low-income parent's role as mediator is so critical concerns the paucity of childrearing resources for poor families, and the absence or inferior quality of virtually all of the material and social supports that middle-income families take for granted in raising and educating their children. From the start, poor children are disadvantaged by a host of serious family and community problems; by a lack of decent, accessible, perinatal and pediatric care; by substandard housing; by highly dangerous surroundings; by parental social isolation; by few positive role models and mentors in the community (i.e., mature, concerned adults to step in and weave a web of care and protection for children whose parents do not or cannot do so; by the obvious absence of adequate—let alone developmentally appropriate and affordable—child care for infants, preschoolers (Schorr, with Schorr 1988) and school-aged children during summer and after school; and, of equal importance, by the distressingly low quality of their schools.

Nowhere is the disparity between the haves and have-nots more glaringly apparent than in the educational institutions that serve the poor. In a mainstream community parents and teachers alike become concerned, if not alarmed, if a formerly motivated child suddenly begins to experience problems in school—whether in relation to behavior or learning. The more-privileged child's parents may provide him or her with therapy or tutoring—or even send the child to private school. In cases where middle-class parents are not willing or able to help, if their child is attending a high-quality school in the community—with smaller classes, more teachers, guidance counselors, and learning disability and other specialists—the school itself often serves as a psychic safety net, preventing temporary difficulties from becoming permanent ones. For the middle-class child, a problem in school may be simply a detour; for the child of poverty it is all too often a dead end.

In poor communities the schools are generally as impoverished as the children. Thus, with so much missing at school, it is up to parents to fill in the educational gaps. The following comments are from inner-city parents:

[Before Donnie was old enough for school] we played school practically every day—what he called school. And when he went to school he could read simple words, he could write his name, ABCs. He could count to a hundred. He could write his address. He knew his phone number, his grandmother's phone number and his grandmother's address. Oh, we did lots!

* * *

He is in first grade and he's reading at third grade now. . . . You should start teaching him right off. [say] This is an "A," and show him the letter "A." And they know that's an "A". And you just keep teaching them. A child will learn as far as you teach them. It's not a certain point where they will stop, because he comes home every day with another mystery word. And Camille is the same way. She wants to know more and more. But if you take their attention off of learning they will forget about it.

* * *

It starts at home. I don't care what anybody says, learning starts at home.

* * *

My kids, I buy them educational toys, flash cards. When I wasn't able to buy them, sometimes I would just make them up myself. Like right now, they got stacks of cards like "Sesame Street."

* * *

[I am] involved in her work with her. . . . You know that the teacher can only tell you so much and the rest you have to take it upon yourself.

* * *

You can teach them with anything. . . . catalogue book, newspapers . . . I always tell my kids that anything that they can find, get anything and read! . . . Get a piece of paper and write your name. Go write Cs all over it. My baby wrote all over there on everything. But she's writing. She's trying to learn.

Further, if these parents want their children to get the best of what is available in school, to be the beneficiaries of the most their often overwhelmed teachers have to give, they must be ever-vigilant and vocal on their behalf. The same inner-city mothers stated:

[I'm] participating in the PTA, or the fundraising. Or just popping up at school and asking the teacher what's going on.

* * *

Every time I pick him up [from school] I always ask his teachers how he's doing—what he's doing.

* * *

Well maybe he didn't quite catch on to that [at school]. He can figure it out at home. I can help him with it. Then I can know what's going on with him and what he is learning and what he's doing, when he brings home homework. When he doesn't, I don't know what's going on. I go to the school and ask. I go to his class.

* * *

I always tell them, if you go and tell your teacher that you don't understand, and she doesn't explain it to you, you come tell me. I will go up the next day and say, "He's having this problem." And I've done it on occasion, and the teacher has acknowledged that [and said] "Yes I did [know], but I'll be with him today."

To succeed in life, to become competent and contributing members of society, poor children must first succeed in school. To do that, they need not just good, but excellent, schools—qualitatively different schools than currently exist in all but a few places. As James Comer recently observed, "American education is structured to serve children who have had the average family experience or better" (Comer 1989: 215). Such family experience is clearly not the case for growing numbers of poor children. While increasing social, occupational, and economic pressures are having a profound influence on all families' capacities to provide nurturing, growth-fostering environments for their children, these pressures are played out much more strongly in the families of poor children, and are ultimately expressed in patterns of poor performance or failure in school. With few exceptions, schools are simply not prepared to deal with students whose experience, styles of learning, and educational motivation differ from those of mainstream children—let alone those whose outlook and behavior have been shaped through adaptation to family and community conditions that are in so many ways toxic to developing children.

In the course of my research, the questions my colleagues and I asked of teachers were designed to tap into their feelings and ideas about the students and their parents, and about the teaching styles they saw as being most effective with low-income, inner-city children. Examples of some of the questions include: How adequately prepared for school were these children? What were their clearest strengths and weaknesses? What roles did parents appear to play in their children's school readiness and general educability? What did they view as the best type of education for disadvantaged children? Just as importantly, in raising such questions we hoped to learn how teachers perceived themselves and their roles in helping to create a new and more successful generation of young people. For instance: Did they believe that teachers could really make a difference in the lives of these children? Did they believe that *they* had made a difference? Although, as could be expected, there was some variation, the answer to these last two questions was a basic, although not unequivocal no.

Examining the content, tone, and language of the teachers' responses, one sees that they know a good deal about young children, and although they would like for children to have a basic working knowledge of letters, numbers, colors, and so forth, they place a higher value on readiness skills such as eagerness to learn, curiosity, persistence, ability to focus attention, ability to relate well to others, and desire to please the teacher. These educators clearly know what it takes for children to be socially and educationally competent; to successfully make the transition to kindergarten; to do well in school and in life. They just do not believe that most of the children they teach have what it takes to accomplish this. And, as just indicated, they do not feel that teachers can really make a difference with these children or that *they themselves* have made a difference with them. Or, perhaps, it might be more accurate to say that they do believe that they could make a difference, but only with certain kinds of children—children raised by certain kinds of parents. The quotations from inner-city teachers in the following pages make this point glaringly apparent.

Teacher A: "Like when they come to the kindergarten room just knowing nothing at all. . . . teachers go through the motions. Many teachers teach, many teachers don't teach. They're doing the best they can. But those kids sit there in that room all year, and they just don't know anything. . . . You invent all kinds of ways and everything, and they still don't know. You know? They do a little bit better. A teeny weeny bit better. A spark of improvement. But there is something wrong."

Teacher B: "I believe that it's all in the supported home."

Teacher A: "Yes, that's it."

Teacher C: "I think that the main thing that's missing from our children . . . is experience. You know?"

Teacher B: "Yeah, the basic problem is listening skills. They don't have

listening skills, and until they have that, we can't do anything. As long as they come with basically good listening skills we can teach the rest."
Teacher A: "And you only get that from home."

The comments of these teachers tell us that they believe most of the children they teach possess neither the cognitive and social abilities nor the personal attributes and attitudes to do well in school. The teachers feel strongly about this, sometimes blaming the school system, sometimes even themselves. Mostly, however, they blame the families. These well-meaning, committed teachers care about the small children in their charge, often deeply, but they are frequently very angry at their parents. As one teacher stated, "Got so many people who are asleep. They're not able to do anything. Most of our children are taking care of themselves. . . . *Our little children!*"

If one attends closely to the words of these teachers, one senses that eventually, inevitably, these teachers could become angry at the children as well as their parents: angry at them for thwarting their earnest desires and efforts to be good teachers; for destroying their sense of competency and of hope; for robbing their work of its mission and meaning, and for making a mockery of their caring. They are not yet angry at the children, or at least not openly so. Rather, they focus on and fault those who they view as having failed in their childrearing roles. Strongly expressed, and heartfelt, their testimony is sometimes very harsh.

They turn the children off. They never turn their children on before they come to school. So here we are "Good morning, so and so." And they're looking at us like we just stepped off Mars. We are totally foreign to these children. . . . Yes, these children have lived for five years, but it's like they've just been brought out of a cage. It's sad to say but true.

* * *

In working with these children for the first time in kindergarten they really need quite a bit. . . . They are so badly . . . maybe I shouldn't use the word "damaged." They are so far behind . . . they don't have any of the things that they should have. . . . I guess what I'm trying to say is that what you're starting with is children who don't know anything at all. It's like if I would go to Siberia today, and you would just take me from the airport and leave me on my own. And I don't know the language or anything at all. Look how lost I would be! What could I do? . . . When they come to us they are totally lost. . . . And you know we blame the parents. . . . Nobody takes them anywhere. Nobody talks to them. There are no newspapers in the home. No magazines. Nothing. Very little language is spoken. And when the check comes, the young

mothers . . . they go out and do what's important to them. And the
children just don't get any . . . get any nourishment or anything at all.
All the things that they need to know in kindergarten, they just come
here and they just don't know it. . . . When they come here everything
is so foreign to them . . . . All they hear in the home is "Sit down and
shut up. . . . Go out and play!" This kind of thing. How can you expect
something? What should we [expect] with the homes they're coming
from. When you talk of expectations, I know what I would expect from
a normal situation, but with the children we teach, I don't expect
anything, and you don't get anything.
* * *

Those lazy girls [teenage mothers] will sit there knowing that school
opens the first day of September, they won't walk across that field and
bring that kid. . . . They're right at home not doing anything.
* * *

And not only are these mothers asleep, but they're high. You know,
let's be real.

The teachers earnestly try not to act on their anger, realizing as
they do that many of these parents, especially the adolescent mothers,
lack experience and models of good parenting from their own childhoods. They know that these mothers need support themselves to
be able to prepare their children for school.

But we have to go further. Blame the parents' parents . . . parents'
parents . . . so back on down the line.
* * *

The parents need parenting. You know what I mean?
* * *

I think that a lot of these mothers don't know. It's not that they don't
do it, I don't think they know *how* to do it. And what they should
do. . . . Like after the child is born, either the Board [of education] or
something like the Urban League, or the University [of Chicago] should
provide inservices. Tell the parents how to work with their kids.
Telling them how to teach them.
* * *

I know the girls are young, and they don't know how to do and what to
do. Then why would they want their children to succeed? . . . If you
didn't do anything for five years, and when your kid gets his report
card in kindergarten and he didn't get such a good grade, . . . maybe D
or something . . . you know you're broken-hearted. But how can we
have them understand that they're supposed to be doing things with
these children from birth until they're five years old? . . . I guess they
have their own problems where they just can't do it. Right?
* * *

Nobody comes knowing how to parent. I think what you do more than anything else, you adopt the style you saw in your home. But how do you really know? Especially these young people having babies. They really don't know.

* * *

I think a lot of the teenage mothers *would* do better if they *could* do better. If they were taught to do better. A lot of them don't know they're not doing the right thing for these children. . . . They want their children to do well, but they don't know how to go about it.

Ambivalence about the parents of the students who are not doing well—the majority of the children—is a pervasive theme, one that surfaces repeatedly, regardless of the topic discussed. Teachers seem to struggle against the temptation to blame, because they are aware of the importance of being able to work with parents in a partnership for the good of the child, and because they feel that although few parents actually know what to do about it, most truly do place a high premium on education.

They don't know how. If your mother didn't know, and your grandmother didn't know; you don't know. You need help.

* * *

What I try to do with my parents. I know that the children are going to watch television, so I would say to them . . . "Does [your child] watch TV a lot?" "Yes." "Then I say, "Select the programs and sit down with your child when he watches "Sesame Street". . . . Talk to him . . . explain to your child what is going on."

Acknowledging the central role that families play in school readiness, the teachers laud some parents, such as those described earlier, for the fine job they have done.

I think that's probably the most important thing that parents can do. Now I can tell being with a child whether a parent reads to them or not. You can just tell! I don't know they're somehow more *humanized*. I don't know how to describe it, but you can tell."

* * *

. . . but sometimes you get . . . one or two that I just wish the whole class could be this way. Where they come from families that have taught them good manners. Even in communities like where Beethoven [elementary school] is you've got a few people. . . .

* * *

What I could never understand is that these same parents all live with these other parents. They all went to the same school together. They all live in the same building. Same neighborhood. So why is there such a vast difference even among the parents just as there is with the children?

Time after time variability in school readiness is attributed to variability among parents. The teachers find that parents who actively foster readiness have children who are eager to learn, who are intellectually and socially competent. Conversely, those who fail to do so have children who are "programmed," and thus destined to fail in school.

Now there's a vast, vast difference between the top group children academically. . . . This past school year, I had a lovely classroom. Parents naturally very cooperative. Very intelligent. Very everything that parents are supposed to be. And naturally, these are the children they produce.

versus:

. . . [these] children are terribly hostile. Some of them are. They come from hostile environments. So that's learned. That's all they know . . . somebody accidently steps on your foot, you haul off and knock the hell out of them. . . . The children are taught hostility, anger, shut-up, sit down, everything is negative. They never get any good positives . . . [such as] "I love you Bobby."

Students with behavioral problems can easily absorb the majority of a teacher's effort, robbing her and thus her other students of sufficient time for academics. In suburban schools there may be only one or two such students, and chances are they spend at least part of the day outside of the classroom receiving individualized help from special education teachers, speech therapists, counselors, and other resource professionals. In inner-city schools the percentage of problem to nonproblem children tends to be higher, and the alternate sources of support (and respite for the classroom teacher) minimal or absent. Much as teachers would prefer it otherwise, it is the bottom of the class that requires the greatest investment of their mental and physical energy. One teacher stated, "some days it's 80 percent nonacademic, 20 percent academic. It just depends, but . . . on the whole, I'll say 55 percent/45 percent, nonacademic being the highest percentage. . . . That's on a good day."

Given such circumstances, it is understandable that trying to educate, and in many cases to remediate, can be discouraging and exhausting. It is all too easy for educational theorists, child psychologists, and other educational reformers to judge teachers harshly for deriding disadvantaged parents and expecting too little from their children. Still, those who judge have rarely walked in the shoes of an inner-city teacher, experiencing how it feels to work, day after day, year after year, in a milieu that offers so few psychological or material supports, so little thanks for one's caring and effort.[8] Nor have the critics felt the frustration and sense of impotence that come from repeated rejection by the parents of children who need all the help they can get. Such experiences are devaluing and are devastating to a teacher's self-esteem and sense of hope.

Many would object to putting the blame and burden on parents who are already sorely tried. Yet, as these teachers observe, there are unmistakable differences in childrearing abilities among the parents of the pupils they teach. In the context and constraints of social disadvantage, these differences have heightened salience. Poor parenting magnifies and exacerbates environmental risk; good parenting ameliorates it. The teachers know this hard truth, but perhaps are not aware of the monumental—indeed the heroic effort—it takes to be "better than good," day after day, year after year, in circumstances that provide so few incentives for doing so. Teachers could learn a great deal from these parents, but to do so they need time and support to step back and reflect on what they do, and adequate educational and personal resources (e.g., better in-service training) to do more than simply survive.

The parents of the most competent children were a diverse group: some were married, others were single; some were quite young, others were in their thirties and forties; some had more education and sophistication than others; some worked, others stayed at home. Still, they were very much alike in one respect—in their ability to provide their children with the essential building blocks of early competence. Building blocks such as: focusing and maintaining attention, persistence, intrinsic motivation and challenge, and encouragement. In the words of several parents:

> As far as learning ability, [you] just teach them to take notice of things. To understand what you are saying, and really just put their mind to what they are doing. That's the most important thing. . . . They get the ability to really comprehend.
>
> * * *
>
> He'll get frustrated, but once you give him a pep talk, he'll get back on it . . . that's the challenge.
>
> * * *
>
> She always says, "I need help Mama. Come over here and help me with

this Mama." "Mama, what spells this?" She always says it backwards. And she's always conscientious about spelling. She knows all about sounds, and her vowels, and whenever she does something and learns something new, she seems to like it. She's really happy about it.

* * *

When she brings her papers home, I say, "Oh, that's pretty." I just persuade her to keep on—to keep up the good work. She said, "Mama, this [picture] is you." I said, "Okay, it's me. Hang it up in the room." . . . I put it in frames. . . . [She will] get somebody by the hand—"Come see this. I did this!" . . . It may not be nothing to nobody else, but to them it's everything.

These parents share a keen understanding of the importance of parents as educators, placing high values on education and setting high standards for their children. From an early age, they work with, monitor, and actively teach their children. Using whatever resources they possess, they provide their children with educational materials and quiet settings conducive to learning. They have an excellent grasp of key principles of motivation—principles such as the need to make learning fun and exciting for small children. They recognize the role of praise in the learning process. They have definite ideas about the differences between children and adults, and between individual children, and have adjusted their expectations accordingly. They are proud of their children's achievements, and deeply empathic to their feelings. Finally, they help their children to manage the world's difficulties—by protecting them, advocating for them, and teaching them a wide variety of positive coping skills (Hans, Musick, and Jagers 1992). These parents are alive to the suffering of their own past and are deeply committed to making it different for their children. As one parent painfully recalled:

And we were poor. We never had anything. My father never did anything for us, and my mother died so young. My auntie and my father never showed love. I can't remember when they ever hugged me or kissed me, or told me that he loved me. I said that if I had any kids, and I had one at fourteen, I'm going to love it. I'm going to let him know that I care about him, tell him that I love him and do everything that I can for him. I'm not going to be distant with my kids. Like I said, my kids they'll come tell me everything.

The teachers' disappointment and anger stems partially from their experiences and interactions with parents such as these. If some families can do it, they reason, why can't others? It is hard to answer that question, but important to remember that these parents represent a relatively small group of extraordinary individuals who manage to do what they do while carrying burdens few of us are expected (or expect ourselves) to carry. Middle-class parents can get away with being "good enough"—poor parents cannot. Even outstanding poor parents are not always able to prevent their children from succumbing to the many temptations a life in poverty offers to the young and impressionable, especially when they reach adolescence.

To explain the teachers' attitudes does not excuse them. No matter what the source, there is ample reason to be concerned about the damage such anger and negative attribution can cause. There is abundant evidence of the pernicious effects of low teacher expectations on student self-concepts and performance in school.[9] As powerful and significant others see us, so do we come to see ourselves. If teachers believe children (and their parents) are hopeless, why should either bother to try? Yet when innovative educational programs include teachers as part of the process of change, the teachers both contribute substantially and they receive substantial recognition and support. They feel validated—an important part of something special. They have hope and higher expectations, and their pupils frequently do as well as their more advantaged counterparts (Comer 1985, 1988).

Unresolved Issues

These teachers are tired, and they are discouraged. It is human nature to direct our anger at those whose failures make us feel that we have failed. But the anger here is tragically misdirected. Although one might understand their need to blame, we should be alarmed when teachers "take it out" on poor children and their families. This must be recognized for what it is: victims blaming victims—one more example of the ways in which poverty creates a house divided. The schools in socially isolated, impoverished communities are divided houses in which teachers blame parents and—albeit more subtly—the children as well. Without power or prestige, teachers dare not blame those above them in the system. Like the children they teach, these educators are victims themselves, of a school system with far too many problems and far too few rewards. They suffer from the death of their own dreams, as well the broken hearts and broken dreams of families whose children they teach. Yet, their superiors in the educational system have not dared to say, "If we are charged with curing diseases our society has created, doing for children what their families have not been able to do, and enabling their parents to do their best, we must create radically different institutions. We must become radically different educators ourselves." It is not simply a matter of more money, either, although that would certainly help. Rather it is also a matter of commitment and inspiration—a change of heart as well as curriculum.

Although there are always new incarnations, dissatisfaction with the way our educational system works for disadvantaged children is an old story. Good schools, or at least good teachers, are capable of redirecting children's lives. However, we know that while hundreds may be helped, thousands are lost. We also have a fairly good idea of what kind of structures and processes are required to create growth-enhancing school experiences. As Edmonds (1986) has pointed out, "we know more than enough to effectively educate poor children." We simply don't know how to make it happen—consistently and continuously for most, instead of merely sometimes, for some children. Or, put another way, we know how to do it in theory, but in practice the changes required of educational institutions—and, of educators—are just too formidable. Even when funds have been obtained for educational reform, there is a multitude of barriers to their actual provision. Some barriers may be found within families themselves, but the majority are institutionally based. Our schools are a reflection of our society and its values, and of government that values its children too little in spite of its self-righteous rhetoric.

Policy Implications

Education must be restructured to engage and support families in their children's education—especially those parents who are harder to reach. This can be accomplished by providing greater financial support to schools, and greater incentives to teach in the inner city. We would do well to also incorporate family resource and support programming into the school setting, providing its considerable benefits to parents of school-age, as well as preschool-age, children. Currently such programs begin before birth, providing health care and preparation for parenthood, and then comprehensive child development services from birth to kindergarten entry. Family resource programs enable parents to become active participants in their children's lives—both within the home when they are infants, and beyond the home when they venture into preschool. As one teenage mother said about the results of her participation in a family support program when her child was an infant, "B.J. is in day care and I don't worry about her any more. And (at her day care center) they know I am the type of Mom that comes on lunch hour and wants to see exactly what they are doing."

The Ounce of Prevention Fund's Center for Successful Child Development is open to families living in an impoverished inner-city community. Because the center's goal is to help parents prepare their children for success from the beginning of their school careers, it works with parents from the time of pregnancy until their child enters kindergarten at age five or six. The center provides on-site health care, social services, and job training for parents, developmental day care, Head Start, drug and alcohol counseling, teen parent programming, and a range of other preventive services. Comprehensive child development programs similar to those at the Center for Successful Child Development are being replicated as demonstrations in a number of sites across the country, but they currently reach only a small number of the families who could benefit from their services, and are directed mainly to families with infants and preschool-aged children.

CHALLENGES FOR PUBLIC POLICY

A necessary first step for policymakers must be a clear commitment to longer-term solutions to social problems, rather than ever-shifting approaches whereby one year the fashion is teenage pregnancy and the next it is drug abuse, or child abuse, or infant mortality, or welfare abuse, or school failure, or youth crime, and so on. A deeper, more comprehensive approach to multifaceted and interlocking psychosocial issues is critical to creating a climate for social change. All the problems discussed in this chapter are basically the same problem viewed from different perspectives. If the complex human dilemmas of children and families in poverty remain as rigidly compartmentalized—and politicized—as they have become in recent years, they are—and will remain—unsolvable. Surely we know enough about what works to develop an immediate agenda for action.[10] Family support approaches are well-suited to this challenge.

The family support movement (Halpern and Larner, 1988; Kagan et al. 1987; Unger and Powell 1991; Weiss and Halpern 1990) has roots in community-development approaches found both in the United States and in many developing countries. It is grounded in the idea that all families must have the power to determine their own needs and how these can best be met, and that families therefore should be encouraged to actively participate in any efforts aimed at providing them support. Rather than creating dependency, such an approach leads to strategies that empower families to advocate on their own behalf—to become authentically self-sufficient, active, and invested in their own and their children's lives. It is not hard to see how well suited such principles and practices are for the long-overdue reform of our schools.

Acknowledging the difference between the family's informal system of support and that provided by formal social programs, family resource programs also insist that any community-based intervention be grounded in norms and values that are compatible with how support is provided *naturally* within the family and community being served. Thus, for example, on home visits to African-American teens, the adolescent's mother is usually included; with Hispanic girls, the father as well as the mother may wish to be present. On the other hand, when visiting white adolescent mothers, privacy is the expected—and accepted—mode of service.

The family support model has become an increasingly popular approach to a wide range of human services in the United States. In fact, one might say that it is as much a social movement as a method of service provision. In general the services associated with this approach fit within a continuum of community-based, preventively oriented helping services, but they also fill gaps within that continuum, so that they are acceptable to a wide range of families. If a young mother needs help in returning to school, the program enables her to do that without sacrificing her child in the process. If a family needs medical and educational resources for a special-needs child, the program links them to the appropriate agencies, and, when necessary, advocates on their behalf with local, state, or federal agencies to obtain these resources. When a young person is in trouble, a family support program engages him or her in acquiring new skills, and with that, a new sense of self, all through the growth-enhancing new relationships and opportunities it offers. To do such work on a larger scale—which is what is required—is not simple, nor cheap, but it can be done.

There needs to be a national commitment to support and enable all parents to do the best they can for their children—a national network of community-based resources to support parents in their critical, irreplaceable role, and to help them help themselves. We are currently able to help some parents (although not all who could use it) of preschool-age children. But what about the parents of school-age children and adolescents? What exists for them? Do parents stop needing help when their children enter school? Hardly; a new sequence of tasks and challenges begins. And what are we doing to direct the lives of all our nation's children and youth? What do we hold up as values and goals? What models do we present for them to emulate? What safety nets are there to catch them and help them rebound from youth's inevitable missteps? Here too, we need a national agenda for youth and adolescents, a plan to help provide meaning and focus for their natural idealism and need to be something, to do something, to *mean* something.

This chapter has employed an ethnographic paradigm to illustrate the importance of engaging families and youth in enabling and empowering relationships. Years of demographic and statistical studies documenting social problems such as teenage childbearing and school failure have failed to spur us to action, largely because such studies offer so few strategies for reaching and changing the mindsets and motivations underlying behavior. It is time to pay as much attention to rewriting the inner stories of people's lives as to eradicating the problems that are their outward manifestations. If we accomplish the first, the second will follow. There is no other way.

APPENDIX 2.A
DATA SOURCES

Data sources for this study include the following:

1. Follow-up interviews with 25 adolescent mothers 18 months after their participation in programs at four urban sites. This was a qualitative component of a larger, quantitative study of former participants' status in four areas: education, employment, contraception/fertility, and parenting. The research was concerned with how aspects of program participation were (or were not) related to changes in teen mothers' relationships with their parents, their children, and with males—especially as these affect forward movement in terms of school, work, and personal goals.

2. Group interviews with 46 pregnant and parenting teens, and providers at six program sites, from a study on the attitudes of adolescents and service providers regarding adoption (Musick, Handler, and Wadill 1984). These interviews cover issues of sexuality; attitudes and feelings about motherhood; and influences of family, friends, boyfriends, and providers.[11]

3. Qualitative data, clinical case material, videotapes, and observations of adolescent mothers, children, and staff in the Developmental Program, an innovative training and intervention module incorporated into some Ounce of Prevention Fund teen parent programs (Musick and Stott 1990). This program-within-a-program focuses on the adolescent in her parenting role. Material covers parent-child relationships and childrearing practices; attitudes and behaviors of lay and professional service providers; and changes in teens, staff, and children in these domains.

4. Data from the Peer Power Project, a junior-high-school-based prevention project (Handler 1987). This survey and interview material with several hundred pre- and early adolescent girls portrays the developmental and psychological effects of growing up and living in high-risk environments.

5. Findings from a survey of 445 pregnant and parenting teens concerning the prevalence of coercive sexual experience in childhood and adolescence (Gershenson et al. 1989). This was the first study of its kind to examine possible connections between a history of sexual victimization and adolescent childbearing. It is currently being replicated by other researchers in different regions of the country.

6. Interview and observational data on the causes and correlates of rapid, repeated childbearing among teens in Ounce of Prevention Fund programs (Ruch-Ross and Mosena 1991). This material provides insights about the effects of environmental, developmental, and psychological factors, and about the interactions between and among them.

7. Interviews with community-based service providers, most of whom are former teenage mothers. The focus is on adolescent mothers in their roles as parents and partners. The issue here is not only the young women themselves but also the attitudes and actions of the mentors, models, and help-givers who are supposed to function as agents of change.

8. Research on the home and school experiences of children living in circumstances of extreme urban poverty. The qualitative data presented here are only part of a larger study of family functioning as it relates to early cognitive and social competence in disadvantaged preschool and kindergarten children (Hans et al. 1992). The 60 children in this study live in the same community as the Ounce of Prevention Fund's Center for Successful Child Development. Many of the parents are young, but few are still in their teens, since their children are now of preschool or kindergarten age; many have older children as well. Some fathers are also included in this study. The transcripts presented here come from a small subgroup of parents (10 out of the larger sample of 60) who are raising very competent children—that is, children identified and rated by their teachers as entering public kindergarten emotionally and academically well-prepared. Transcripts of conversations with the children's teachers are included as well.

9. Material from Project Match, an award-winning welfare-to-work demonstration program developed by Toby Herr at Northwestern University's Center for Urban Affairs and Policy Research (Herr and Halpern 1991). Although not technically part of the basic dataset, this program's unique tracking system and clinical observations provide information about the motivations, abilities, and conditions neces-

sary for disadvantaged young people to use opportunities beyond their family and peer networks. Housed in the same community-based health service agency as an Ounce of Prevention Fund teen parent program, Project Match serves some of the same participants.

10. Selected material from 35 group interviews with economically disadvantaged women in six southeastern states that are part of a study of Best Start: Breastfeeding for Healthy Mothers and Healthy Babies Campaign (Bryant et al., 1989). Bryant and colleagues documented a variety of factors influencing a mother's choice of feeding method. These data are equally pertinent to a range of other issues, including motivation for childbearing, pregnancy resolution choices, and feelings about motherhood; family planning and preventive health care; childrearing practices; attitudes toward marriage; relations with family, partners, and peers; and responses to preventive programs such as Best Start and Special Supplemental Food Program for Women, Infants, and Children (WIC). Bryant's subjects are identified by age (including a division between younger and older adolescent mothers), ethnicity (mostly black or white with only a few Hispanic), residence (rural or urban), method of feeding (breast or bottle), and parity (pregnant, primiparous, or multiparous). Only the responses of the adolescent subjects have been used in my analysis.

Notes

The ideas in this chapter are based on work supported by grants from the Rockefeller Foundation and the Harris Foundation. I thank James Gibson, now at the Urban Institute; Phoebe Cottingham, of the Rockefeller Foundation; and Irving Harris, for their support and belief in this work. Thanks also to the Spencer Foundation and the Woods Charitable Fund for supporting the research on which much of this chapter is based. Portions of this chapter are based on data and ideas in my book, *Young, Poor, and Pregnant: The Psychology of Teenage Motherhood* (Yale University Press 1993). I also thank my collaborators on the study of inner-city parents, teachers, and children described in this chapter: Sydney Hans of the University of Chicago and Robert Jagers of the University of Illinois at Chicago.

1. The research of Clark (1983); DeCubas and Field (1984); Heath (1983, 1987); Burton (1990); Codega, Pasley, and Kreutzer (1990), Norton (1990), Werner (1990) and Werner and Smith (1982) indicates that, in spite of many commonalities, there is also marked variation in the childrearing environments of different ethnic and cultural groups living in poor communities in the continental United States and Hawaii (Werner).

2. No matter who the adolescent is, personal writing can provide an authentic means of self-expression, a new route to self-awareness. Especially for an adolescent at risk, it can also provide a certain distance between feeling and doing—a way to help him or her think before acting. Personal writing may not be right for every adolescent,

and it is clearly only one part of a total intervention package; still, because it is so psychologically authentic, it should be attempted wherever possible. See, for example, "Middle Adolescence: The Diary of Anne Frank," in Dalsimer (1986).

3. Approximately 40 percent of participants are white, coming mostly from small cities and rural areas in the "downstate" region of Illinois, and about 45 percent are African-American, living in the Chicago area, although some are from southern Illinois as well. The remaining teens are Hispanic, being either Mexican or Puerto Rican. Almost all of these young women live in the Chicago area.

4. It is important to bear in mind that this was a nonclinical sample; that is, it was not a sample of girls in treatment because of sexual abuse. The evidence indicates that among clinical samples, the age of onset of abuse is often considerably younger (Jones and McCurdy 1992).

5. See the special issue of the *Journal of Interpersonal Violence* devoted to "The Lasting Effects of Child Sexual Abuse," edited by Wyatt and Powell (1987).

6. When some of these data were presented at The Ms. Foundation and Valentine Foundation conference on Programs that Work for Girls, June 8, 1992, at Bryn Mawr College, in Bryn Mawr, Pa., psychologist Carol Gilligan remarked that the pugnacious, feisty behavior typical of preadolescent girls is especially threatening to some males. She suggested that such men may use sexual victimization as a way of "teaching them who's boss" and "putting them in their place." This interpretation would seem to make particular sense for economically and vocationally marginal individuals.

7. The designation "doing well" is based on a range of criteria including standardized tests, teacher and parent ratings, and evaluations by an outside, trained observer.

8. Indeed, many inner-city teachers buy school supplies and books out of their own money because the schools in which they teach are so resource poor. In a recent radio broadcast, I heard a Chicago educator who has studied this issue comment that teachers in inner-city school spend an average of $500 per year of their own money on supplies, books, and even food and clothing for the children.

9. See, for example, "The Education of African-American Youth" by Boykin and Jagers (1991). This review examines factors found to be especially pertinent to the education of children such as those in our study. It considers issues such as academic self-esteem, cultural factors in the content and context of education, teacher motivation and influence, administrative leadership, and family factors affecting school achievement.

10. See the discussion of this issue in Schorr with Schorr (1988).

11. This is an understudied topic because of the current rarity of adoption among adolescent mothers. Currently only about 5 percent of infants born to unwed adolescent mothers are placed for adoption; adoption was far more prevalent in the not-so-distant past. As Kalmuss, Namerow, and Cushman noted, "While we know that very few young women choose adoption, we do not know why so few do" (1991: 17).

References

Anderson, Elijah. 1989. "Sex Codes and Family Life among Poor Inner-city Youths." *ANNALS, AAPSS* 501: 59–78.

Bettelheim, Bruno. 1987. *A Good Enough Parent: A Book on Child-Rearing.* New York: Alfred A. Knopf.

Boyer, Debra, and D. Fine. 1992. "Sexual Abuse as a Factor in Adolescent Pregnancy and Child Maltreatment." *Family Planning Perspectives* 24, 1: 4–11, 19.

Boykin, Wade, and R. Jagers. 1991. "The Education of African-American Children: A Selective Interpretive Review of Recent Research." Photocopy.

Bryant, Carol, D. Bailey, J. Coreil, S. D'Angelo, and M. Lazarov. 1989. "Determinants of Breastfeeding in the Southeast Region: Research Findings from the Best Start: Breastfeeding for Healthy Mothers and Healthy Babies Campaign." Photocopy.

Bumiller, Elisabeth. 1990. *May You Be the Mother of a Hundred Sons: A Journey among the Women of India.* New York: Random House.

Burton, Linda. 1990. "Teenage Childbearing as an Alternative Life-Course Strategy in Multigeneration Black Families." *Human Nature* 1, 2: 123–43.

Butler, Janice, and L. Burton. 1990. "Rethinking Teenage Childbearing: Is Sexual Abuse a Missing Link?" *Family Relations* 39, 1: 73–80.

Clark, Reginald. 1983. *Family Life and School Achievement: Why Poor Black Children Succeed or Fail.* Chicago: University of Chicago Press.

Codega, Susan, B. K. Pasley, and J. Kreutzer. 1990. "Coping Behaviors of Adolescent Mothers: An Exploratory Study and Comparison of Mexican-Americans and Anglos." *Journal of Adolescent Research* 5, 1: 34–53.

Comer, James. 1985. "Empowering Black Children's Educational Environments." In *Black Children: Social, Educational, and Parental Environments,* edited by H. McAdoo and J. McAdoo. Beverly Hills, Calif.: Sage Publications.

—————. 1988. *Maggie's American Dream: The Life and Times of a Black Family.* New York: New American Library.

Conte, John, and J. Schuerman. 1987. "The Effects of Sexual Abuse on Children: A Multidimensional View." *Journal of Interpersonal Violence* 2, 4: 380–90.

Dalsimer, Katherine. 1986. *Female Adolescence: Psychoanalytic Reflections on Literature.* New Haven: Yale University Press.

DeCubas, Mercedes, and T. Field. 1984. "Teaching Interactions of Black and Cuban Teenage Mothers and Their Infants." *Early Child Development and Care* 16: 41–56.

Dryfoos, Joy. 1990. *Adolescents at Risk: Prevalence and Prevention.* New York: Oxford University Press.

Edmonds, R. 1986. "Characteristics of Effective Schools." In *The School Achievement of Minority Children,* edited by U. Neisser. Hillsdale, N.J.: Lawrence Erlbaum Press.

Erikson, Erik. 1963. *Childhood and Society,* 2nd ed. New York: W. W. Norton.

Fine, Michelle. 1990. "Creating Space." *Women and Foundations Newsletter* (Fall/Winter).

Forrest, Jacqueline, and S. Singh. 1990. "The Sexual and Reproductive Behavior of American Women, 1982–1988." *Family Planning Perspectives* 22, 5: 206–14.

Gershenson, Harold, J. Musick, H. Ruch-Ross, V. Magee, K. Rubino, and D. Rosenberg. 1989. "The Prevalence of Coercive Sexual Experience among Teenage Mothers." *Journal of Interpersonal Violence* 4, 2: 204–19.

Gilligan, Carol, N. Lyons, and T. Hanmer, eds. 1990. *Making Connections: The Relational Worlds of Adolescent Girls at Emma Willard School.* Cambridge, Mass.: Harvard University Press.

Guttmacher Institute. 1992. "Teenage Sexual and Reproductive Behavior in the U.S." *Facts in Brief.*

Halpern, Robert, and M. Larner. 1988. "The Design of Family Support Programs in High-Risk Communities: Lessons from the Child Survival/ Fair Start Initiative." In *Parent Education as Early Childhood Intervention: Consequences for Children and Families,* edited by D. Powell (181–207). Norwood, N.J.: Ablex.

Handler, Arden. 1987. "An Evaluation of a School-Based Adolescent Pregnancy Prevention Program." Ph.D. dissertation, University of Illinois, School of Public Health, Chicago.

Hans, Sydney, J. Musick, and R. Jagers. 1992. "Giving Children What They Need: Parents Raising Competent Children in High-Risk Environments." Photocopy.

Haugaard, Jeffrey, and N. Reppucci. 1988. *The Sexual Abuse of Children.* San Francisco: Jossey-Bass, Publishers.

Hayes, Cheryl, ed., and The Panel on Adolescent Pregnancy and Childbearing. 1987. *Risking the Future: Adolescent Sexuality, Pregnancy, and Childbearing.* Washington, D.C.: National Academy Press.

Heath, Shirley Brice. 1983. *Ways with Words: Language, Life, and Work in Communities and Classrooms.* Cambridge, Mass.: Cambridge University Press.

————. 1987. "The Children of Trackton's Children: Spoken and Written Language in Social Change." Paper presented at 1987 Chicago Symposium on Culture and Human Development, Nov. 5–7.

Herr, Toby, and R. Halpern. 1991. *Changing What Counts: Rethinking the Journey out of Welfare.* Evanston, Ill.: Northwestern University, Center for Urban Affairs and Policy Research.

Jones, Elizabeth, and K. McCurdy. 1992. "The Links between Types of Maltreatment and Demographic Characteristics of Children." *Child Abuse and Neglect* 16: 201–15.

Kagan, Sharon, D. Powell, B. Weissbourd, and E. Zigler. 1987. *America's Family Support Programs: Perspectives and Prospects.* New Haven: Yale University Press.

Kalmuss, Debra, P. Namerow, and L. Cushman. 1991. "Adoption versus Parenting among Young Pregnant Women." *Family Planning Perspectives* 23, 1: 17–23.

Miller, Peggy, and L. Sperry. 1987. "The Socialization of Anger and Aggression." *Merrill-Palmer Quarterly* 33, 1: 1–31.
Moore, Kristin. 1991. *Facts at a Glance*. Washington, D.C.: Child Trends.
Moore, Kristin, C. Nord, and J. Peterson. 1989. "Nonvoluntary Sexual Activity among Adolescents." *Family Planning Perspectives* 21, 3: 110–14.
Mosena, Pat. 1987. "Repeated Pregnancy and Childbearing among Adolescent Mothers." Report prepared for Parents Too Soon and the Illinois Department of Public Health, Chicago. Photocopy.
Musick, Judith. 1987. "The Psychological and Developmental Dimensions of Adolescent Pregnancy and Parenting: An Interventionist's Perspective." Paper prepared for the Rockefeller Foundation. Photocopy.
————. 1993. *Young, Poor, and Pregnant: The Psychology of Teenage Motherhood*. New Haven: Yale University Press.
Musick, Judith, and F. Stott. 1990. "Paraprofessionals, Parenting and Child Development: Understanding the Problems and Seeking Solutions." In *Handbook of Early Intervention*, edited by Samuel Meisels and Jack Shonkoff (651–67). Cambridge, Mass.: Cambridge University Press.
Musick, Judith, A. Handler, and K. Wadill. 1984. "Teens and Adoption: A Pregnancy Resolution Alternative?" *Children Today* 13, 6: 24–29.
Musick, Judith, S. Hans, and R. Jagers. 1992. "A Change of Heart: Conversations with Teachers of Inner-city Children." Photocopy.
Norton, Dolores. 1990. "Understanding the Early Experience of Black Children in High-Risk Environments: Culturally and Ecologically Relevant Research as a Guide to Support for Families." *Zero-to-Three* 10, 4: 1–7.
Polit, Denise, J. Quint, and J. Riccio. 1988. *The Challenge of Serving Teenage Mothers: Lessons from Project Redirection*. New York: Manpower Demonstration Research Corporation.
Ruch-Ross, Holly, and P. Mosena. 1991. "Inner-City Perspectives on Rapid Repeat Childbearing." Paper presented at the annual meeting of the American Public Health Association, Atlanta, November.
Ruch-Ross, Holly, E. Jones, and J. Musick. 1992. "Comparing Outcomes in a Statewide Program for Adolescent Mothers with Outcomes in a National Sample." *Family Planning Perspectives* 24, 2: 66–71, p. 96.
Scheper-Hughes, Nancy. 1992. *Death without Weeping: The Violence of Everyday Life in Brazil*. Berkeley, Calif.: University of California Press.
Schorr, Lisbeth, with D. Schorr. 1988. *Within our Reach: Breaking the Cycle of Disadvantage*. New York: Anchor Press.
Unger, Donald, and D. Powell. 1991. *Families as Nurturing Systems: Support across the Life Span*. New York: Haworth Press.
Weiss, Heather, and R. Halpern. 1990. *Community-Based Family Support*

and Educational Programs: Something Old or Something New? New York: National Center for Children in Poverty, Columbia University.

Werner, Emmy. 1990. "Protective Factors and Individual Resilience." In Handbook of Early Intervention, edited by Samuel Meisels and Jack Shonkoff (97–116). Cambridge, Mass.: Cambridge University Press.

Werner, Emmy, and R. Smith. 1982. Vulnerable but Invincible: A Longitudinal Study of Resilient Children and Youth. New York: McGraw-Hill Book Co.

Wyatt, Gail, and G. Powell, eds. 1987. "The Lasting Effects of Child Sexual Abuse." Special Issue of Journal of Interpersonal Violence 2: 4.

Chapter Three

WHO ARE THE POOR? A DEMOGRAPHIC PERSPECTIVE

William H. Scarbrough

According to recent figures from the U.S. Bureau of the Census, nearly 36 million people living in the United States in 1991 were poor, the largest number of poor people since the beginning of President Lyndon Johnson's War on Poverty. That number translates to a poverty rate—the proportion of all people who are poor—of 14.2 percent, or one out of every seven people living in the U.S. Being poor in 1991 meant that, for example, a four-person family's pretax cash income (including cash public assistance such as Aid to Families with Dependent Children [AFDC]) fell below the federal government's poverty threshold of $13,860, while a three-person family's income would have had to fall below $10,973 (U.S. Bureau of the Census [henceforth, Census Bureau] 1992c). The recently released (preliminary) poverty thresholds for 1992 are $11,187 for a three-person family and $14,343 for a four-person family (poverty statistics for 1992 will not be available until late summer 1993).

Although the recent statistics regarding the large number of poor people living in one of the richest nations in the world is a reason for great concern, the dramatic increase and stability in the number of poor children in the United States over the past 20 years is also cause for alarm. Between 1971 and 1991, for example, the number of the nation's poor children increased from 10.3 million to 14.3 million (and the poverty rate increased from 15.1 percent to 21.8 percent of all children under age 18).[1] The rise in poverty among U.S. children puts a large proportion of tomorrow's work force at increased risk of serious health problems, school dropout, and social isolation. Today, with business competition and national economies becoming more globalized (in the words of the Children's Defense Fund) we can afford to "leave no child behind" (1991).

This chapter details the extent and character of childhood poverty in the United States, using key demographic variables. The data presented are derived from government reports and special analyses, studies by economists and poverty researchers, and original analyses conducted by me.

The chapter begins by discussing the official (federal) definition of poverty, including proposed changes to the poverty measure and the implications of those changes for program operation and policy-making. The second major section of the chapter describes childhood poverty on the basis of key demographic variables, and reviews important historical trends. The third section addresses the distinction between transitory and persistent poverty and describes the populations affected. The chapter concludes with a discussion of public policy issues.

HOW IS POVERTY DEFINED AND WHAT DOES IT MEAN?

Poverty in the United States is officially measured by comparing an individual's or family's pretax cash income to a set of federally established dollar amounts known as the poverty thresholds. If the individual/family's income falls below the income thresholds, the individual/family is defined as "poor." As shown in table 3.1, the poverty thresholds change according to family size and composition. In 1991, as stated, the average poverty threshold for a four-person family was $13,860; for a family of three it was $10,973.

It is important to understand that the official poverty measure consists of two major components: individual/family income and income thresholds. Individual/family income consists of before-tax cash income (i.e., salaries, wages, tips, etc.), including cash public assistance such as AFDC. Individual/family income does not include the value of noncash benefits (such as Food Stamps or Medicaid), nor does it account for payroll, Social Security, sales taxes, rental property income, or assets.

The income thresholds are officially defined as the annualized proportion of income the average family spends on a low-cost government food plan adjusted for families of various sizes and compositions. When the income thresholds were developed in the early 1960s at the Social Security Administration (SSA), data from the 1955 National Food Consumption Survey suggested that U.S. families spent, on average, one-third of their cash income on food (Orshansky 1965). Using the same survey, analysts at the SSA estimated in 1964 that the annual cost of the federal government's Economy Food Plan (a plan designed by the U.S. Department of Agriculture for "tempo-

Table 3.1 AVERAGE U.S. POVERTY THRESHOLDS BY FAMILY SIZE AND NUMBER OF CHILDREN UNDER AGE 18: 1991

Family Size	Poverty Thresholds ($) by Number of Children								
	None	One	Two	Three	Four	Five	Six	Seven	Eight +
One person									
—Under 65	7,086								
—65 or over	6,532								
Two persons									
—HH[a] under 65	9,120	9,388							
—HH[a] 65 or over	8,233	9,352							
Three persons	10,654	10,963	10,973						
Four persons	14,048	14,278	13,812	13,860					
Five persons	16,941	17,188	16,662	16,254	16,006				
Six persons	19,480	19,563	19,160	18,773	18,199	17,859			
Seven persons	22,241	22,561	22,078	21,742	21,115	20,384	19,582		
Eight persons	25,076	25,297	24,842	24,443	23,877	23,158	22,410	22,220	
Nine + persons	30,165	30,311	29,908	29,569	29,014	28,249	27,558	27,386	25,331

Source: U.S. Bureau of the Census (1992c).

a. HH, head of household

rary or emergency use when funds are low") was roughly $824 for a family of three. Using the cost of the food plan and the proportion of income spent on food, analysts calculated the average poverty threshold for a family of three to be $2,472—or $824 multiplied by three. In 1969 a revised version of the SSA poverty threshold methodology was installed as the standard poverty measure for governmental statistical purposes.

It is important to note that poverty thresholds used for counting the number of poor persons living in the United States—also known as the "statistical poverty thresholds"—are distinct (and yield different poverty statistics) from the U.S. Department of Health and Human Service's poverty guidelines, which are used primarily for administrative purposes such as determining individual or family financial eligibility for assistance or services under a particular federal program. The statistical poverty threshold is today much as it was in the early 1960s; and it is updated annually for changes in prices using the consumer price index (CPI).

Problems in Measuring Poverty

Although it is important to have an indicator such as poverty status to track individual and family welfare and to allocate scarce governmental resources to assist those in need, certain conceptual, methodological, and computational problems associated with the poverty measure cast doubt on how reliably and accurately it identifies "poor" people. Further, the official poverty measure does not distinguish degrees of poverty (how poor one is), nor does it measure the duration of one's impoverishment.

The most frequently cited problems with the official poverty measure include: (1) how well the official poverty measure reflects current conditions, (2) the exclusion of the value of noncash benefits such as Food Stamps, Medicaid, and public housing in the calculation of income, (3) the lack of an adjustment for regional differences, and (4) inconsistencies between how the poverty measure components themselves are defined, measured, and used.

ACCURACY OF OFFICIAL POVERTY MEASURE

The official poverty measure, affectionately referred to as a "relatively absolute" standard by its developer Molly Orshansky (1965), was originally developed on a normative, not an empirical, basis. Orshansky based her poverty measure methodology on the assumption that consumption patterns of all persons in 1955 were roughly the same. The major problem with this "relatively absolute" measure is that the measure cannot change as consumption patterns change. Analysts have pointed out that some of the goods and services consumed today did not even exist in 1955 and others were relatively rare— such as telephones and child care (Ruggles 1990). As goods and services available for consumption continue to change, our perception of need may change; and the current practice of annually adjusting the poverty measure for changes in prices (via the CPI) means the measure will fall further and further behind the average standard of living (Danziger 1988; Ruggles 1992).

An alternative to the official poverty measure that is designed to change as the average standard of living changes is one tied to some proportion of aggregate family income, such as one-half the median family income. For example, in 1990, one-half the median income for a family of four was $17,853. This figure was $3,993 higher (or 29 percent higher) than the 1990 official poverty threshold for a family of four ($13,860). The merit of a relative measure such as this is that it automatically adjusts for changes in prices as well as in need. The problem with a relative measure of poverty, however, is that it presents a "moving target" for policy purposes (because income fluctuates so dramatically and because it is more difficult to carry out income redistribution policies than it is to improve consumption opportunities for the poor) (Ruggles 1992).

The inadequacy of both the official poverty measure and the median income measure methodologies has led experts to agree, in principle, that a measure that periodically assesses and adjusts a minimally adequate market basket of goods and services would be superior to the current poverty measure (Danziger, 1988; Ruggles 1992; U.S. General Accounting Office [henceforth, GAO] 1987). The updated food multiplier measure depicted in table 3.2 is a crude illustration of this. The measure assumes that the market basket is complete, that its components are cost quantifiable, and that the proportion that poor families spend on the various components can be accurately measured. Using the same market basket as the official measure, the adjusted food multiplier poverty threshold is $1,990 larger (or 14 percent larger) than the official poverty threshold.

NONCASH BENEFITS

The second issue related to the reliability and validity of the current poverty methodology involves the completeness of the income com-

Table 3.2 AVERAGE U.S.POVERTY THRESHOLDS FOR FOUR-PERSON
FAMILIES, NUMBERS OF POOR CHILDREN, AND POVERTY RATES
UNDER ALTERNATIVE POVERTY MEASURES: 1991

		Poverty Measures	
	Official	50% Median Family Income	Updated Food Multiplier[a]
Income threshold ($)	13,860	17,853	15,850
Number of poor children (millions)	14.3	18.0	16.3
Poverty rate (%)	21.8	27.2	25.1

Sources: U.S. Bureau of the Census (1992c: table b) and author's calculations based
on published and unpublished data from 1992 Current Population Survey.

a. This income threshold was calculated using an adjusted food multiplier (.29) and
the official method (see Ruggles 1990).

ponent. Many analysts and policymakers argue that the income component excludes important additional forms of "income" such as
government noncash benefits (e.g., Food Stamps, public housing, and
Medicare and Medicaid). In 1979, the U.S. Bureau of the Census
developed three methods for valuing these noncash benefits for the
purpose of assessing the effect of a more complete definition of
income on the national poverty statistics (Census Bureau 1980). This
work clearly showed that to varying degrees, each of the valuation
methods had the same overall effect, that of significantly decreasing
the number of poor individuals and families.

Shortly after the publication of the Census Bureau's work, the U.S.
General Accounting Office conducted a series of studies to evaluate
the effect of various adjustments to the official poverty measure,
including the Census Bureau's noncash benefit valuation methods
(see table 3.3) (GAO 1986, 1987). The findings revealed that many
of the adjustments examined had sizable effects on the number of
poor people, sometimes reclassifying or misclassifying poor persons
as nonpoor. The findings also showed that certain population subgroups were much more adversely affected by the adjustments; key
among them were African-Americans, persons living in families
headed by women, and the elderly.

REGIONAL DIFFERENCES

Another poverty measurement issue that has gained much attention
in recent years is the fact that the national poverty threshold ignores
regional differences in earnings, available goods and services, and

Table 3.3 CONSEQUENCES OF ADJUSTING THE OFFICIAL U.S. POVERTY
MEASURE FOR NONCASH BENEFITS AND TAXES ON THE CHILD
POVERTY RATE: 1981, 1986, 1991

	Year		
Income Source	1981 (%)	1986 (%)	1991 (%)
Cash only	20.0	20.5	21.8
Cash and means-tested food and housing benefits	17.4	17.6	19.0
Cash, means-tested food and housing benefits, and fungible value of Medicaid	16.1	16.8	17.7
Cash, means-tested food and housing benefits, and fungible value of Medicaid and taxes[a]	17.4	18.4	18.1

Source: U.S. Bureau of the Census,1992b "Measuring the Effect of Benefits and Taxes
on Income and Poverty: 1979 to 1991" *Current Population Reports*, ser. P-60, no. 182-
RD, table 2:98 (Washington, D.C.: U.S. Government Printing Office).

a. Social Security payroll, federal and state income, and Earned Income Tax Credit
taxes.

prices. For example, a family of four living in New York City earning
less than $14,000 has a much more difficult time making ends meet
(i.e., feeding, housing, clothing, and taking care of themselves) than
a family of four with the same income living in rural Mississippi.
The reason for this is that, according to a study by Nelson (1991),
the cost of living in New York (Index = 113.2) is considerably higher
than in Mississippi (90.3) (see table 3.4). What this means to the
average consumer is that a family with a minimum-wage job paying
$7,438 per year in New York has an actual earning power of $6,456
compared to a family in Mississippi with the same minimum-wage
job whose earning power is $8,159. When cost of living is combined
with the fact that some states in the nation have significantly higher
AFDC benefit levels (particularly in the higher cost-of-living states),
this could help explain why individuals and families cross state lines
or move monthly: to take advantage of living in a lower cost-of-living
state while receiving benefits from a higher cost-level state.

POVERTY MEASURE INCONSISTENCIES

The final issue deals with the inconsistencies that exist between
the income and the income threshold components of the poverty

Table 3.4 COST-OF-LIVING INDEXES AND MAXIMUM MONTHLY AFDC BENEFITS FOR FAMILY OF THREE IN THE UNITED STATES: 1991

State	COL[a] Index	Maximum AFDC ($)[b]	State	COL[a] Index	Maximum AFDC ($)[b]
Alabama	91.9	124	Nebraska	92.9	364
Alaska	N.A.	891	Nevada	98.1	330
Arizona	100.8	293	New Hampshire	107.9	526
Arkansas	90.9	204	New Jersey	125.8	424
California	105.9	694	New Mexico	92.9	310
Colorado	99.8	356	New York	113.2	703
Connecticut	125.8	680	North Carolina	93.6	272
Delaware	103.2	338	North Dakota	92.2	401
Washington, D.C.	121.0	428	Ohio	95.8	334
Florida	97.3	294	Oklahoma	92.5	341
Georgia	94.1	280	Oregon	94.2	444
Hawaii	N.A.	632	Pennsylvania	101.3	421
Idaho	91.3	317	Rhode Island	106.8	554
Illinois	97.4	367	South Carolina	92.6	210
Indiana	92.9	288	South Dakota	91.6	385
Iowa	93.6	426	Tennessee	93.1	195
Kansas	91.7	409	Texas	94.1	184
Kentucky	92.1	228	Utah	92.9	402
Louisiana	93.4	190	Vermont	93.9	679
Maine	92.0	453	Virginia	97.1	354
Maryland	110.8	406	Washington	97.0	531
Massachusetts	121.8	539	West Virginia	91.9	249
Michigan	95.4	555	Wisconsin	94.4	517
Minnesota	95.6	532	Wyoming	93.4	360
Mississippi	90.3	120			
Missouri	92.9	292			
Montana	91.1	370	U.S. average	100.0	367

Sources: Nelson (1991) and U.S. Congress (1992: table 12, 547–48).

Note: Alaska and Hawaii are excluded from the COL index because of unique factors involving climate and transportation.

a. COL, cost of living.   b. AFDC, Aid to Families with Dependent Children.

measure. The official poverty measure compares pretax family income (i.e., gross income) with a posttax income threshold (i.e., net income). Adjusting family income for this inconsistency by removing payroll and Social Security taxes, for example, makes the comparison of the two components of the poverty measure more consistent. The net effect of this adjustment is to lower family incomes, thus increasing the number of poor people.

To illustrate this point, when Census Bureau analysts adjusted 1991 income for Social Security payroll taxes, federal, state and local income taxes, and the Earned Income Tax Credit, the poverty rate increased from 14.2 percent to 14.9 percent (this translates to an increase of roughly 2 million persons reclassified as poor) (Census Bureau 1992b). Analysts have also found that failure to adjust this discrepancy in the tax bases of the income and income threshold components of the poverty measure differentially affected families with children (GAO 1987).

In summary, although the federal poverty measure is flawed, it is the only measure the United States has ever recognized as an indicator of the nation's social welfare. Given the Clinton administration's focus on improving the lives of low-income Americans, particularly children living in low-income families, the official poverty measure may be reevaluated as a means to more accurately identify those in need and thus more effectively target and deliver assistance. For purposes of consistency and comparison, only the official poverty definition is utilized in subsequent sections of this chapter.

COMPOSITION OF POVERTY POPULATION AND HISTORICAL TRENDS

There are many commonly held stereotypes about poor families with children in the United States. For example, many believe that all poor families are alike—that they are lazy (in that their parents do not work), that they are persons of color, that they are uneducated, that they have many unrelated members, and that they have been poor all of their lives. The facts are that many of these families are white, are composed of a relatively small number of related individuals, and the adults in the families generally work and have high school educations (Census Bureau 1992a; National Center for Children in Poverty 1990, 1992a; 1992b; U.S. Congress 1990). The problem is that these and other important facts rarely receive adequate media or public attention, thus perpetuating the stereotypes.

To dismantle these and other stereotypes regarding poor people, and to better understand the heterogeneity of the poor population and the dynamics of poverty, it is important to examine, in detail, who is considered poor in the United States and how the poverty population has changed over time. This section describes poor children and their families using the most recent data available and compares those statistics with data from past decades across five key demographic variables: age, race/ethnicity, family structure, family size, and geographic locale.

Age

CURRENT SITUATION

According to a recent Census Bureau report (1992c) in 1991 there were approximately 251 million people living in the United States; over one-fourth (26 percent) of these were children under age 18; 62 percent were between ages 18 and 64; and 1 in 8 (12 percent) were aged 65 or over. The age composition of the poor population is considerably younger; 40 percent of all poor people in 1990 were children; 49 percent were aged 18 to 64; and 11 percent were aged 65 or over. Therefore, it should not be surprising that children were the poorest of all the age groups (22 percent, over 1 in 5), followed by adults aged 18–64 (13 percent, nearly 1 in 8), and then the elderly (12 percent, or nearly 1 in 10). However, even among children, poverty was not evenly distributed. In 1991, preschool-age children—those aged 5 and under—registered the highest poverty rate at more than 24 percent, compared to 20 percent for children aged 6–17.

TRENDS

Over the past three decades, the total number of children under age 18 living in the United States has fluctuated around 65 million. During the 1960s, the number of children rose from 64 million to 70 million, and then declined to 63 million at the end of the 1970s. The number of children declined further into the mid-1980s (62 million), only to return to roughly 65 million by the close of the decade.

The dramatic rise and stabilization of poverty rates among children in the late 1970s through the 1980s occurred at a time when the poverty rate among adults aged 18–64 was inching up slowly, and when poverty among the elderly was decreasing consistently. The

Figure 3.1 POVERTY RATES BY AGE GROUPS IN THE UNITED STATES:
1959–91

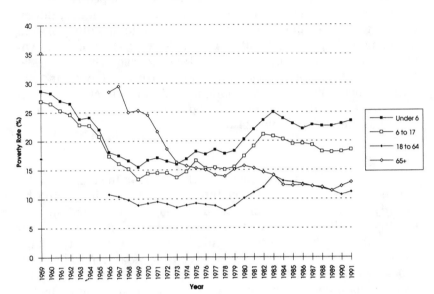

Sources: Author's calculations based on published and unpublished data 1959–1965;
and U.S. Bureau of the Census, various years, 1966–91, *Current Population Reports,*
Ser. P-60 *(Washington, D.C.: U.S. Government Printing Office).*

change in child poverty was preceded by a number of factors, some
of which were economic and others demographic and social. For
example, although family incomes increased substantially and steadily in the two decades following World War II, they stopped growing
around 1973 (U.S. Congressional Budget Office 1988). In addition,
inequality of incomes increased for families with children. In 1970,
families with children and household incomes in the lowest quintile
accounted for 7 percent of the total aggregate income, yet only 4
percent in 1990 (CBO 1988).

Figure 3.1 depicts the poverty rates for children aged 0–5 and
6–17, elderly adults aged 65 and over, and adults aged 18–64 from
1959 to 1991. Generally, poverty rates for each of these groups
declined dramatically over the period 1959 to 1973. From 1974 to
1979 the poverty rates for each of these groups remained relatively
steady (with the exception of a short-term increase due to the economic recession between 1973 and 1975); roughly 17 percent for
children under age 6 and 15 percent for older children; about 9

percent for adults; and 14 percent for the elderly. Starting in 1979, the poverty rates for children rose dramatically to a peak in 1983—25 percent for children under age 6 and 21 percent for older children; the rate was 14 percent for adults. In spite of the double-dip recession in this period, the poverty rate for the elderly began another downward trend that would continue until 1984. Between 1984 and 1989, the poverty rates for all age groups hovered just below their 1983 levels. Since 1989, poverty among all children under age 18 has increased to nearly 22 percent, while poverty among children under age 6 has increased to over 24 percent.

PROJECTIONS

According to the Census Bureau (1989), the size of the child population is expected to rise slowly through the 1990s (increasing by roughly 3 million) and then decline through 2010 (decreasing by roughly 2 million). The growth rate will stabilize between the years 2010 and 2030. Given the economic recession of the early 1990s, child poverty rates can be expected to continue to rise until the mid-1990s. If changes in the labor market and in the health care and social welfare systems that are currently under consideration by the Clinton administration are implemented and modestly effective, child poverty rates can be expected to stabilize and even fall slowly in the mid-1990s (even with continually changing family demographics and increasing numbers of poor children who are poor for longer time periods). For children of color, the fastest growing segment of our population, the nation's economic and family demographic trends will provide the clearest picture of their prospects for the 1990s: children of color can expect to experience poverty more frequently and for longer time periods. Changes in social welfare and labor policy will serve to mitigate some of the trend toward more widespread and deeper poverty.

Race/Ethnicity

CURRENT SITUATION

In 1991, roughly one-third of all children living in the United States were African-American, Latino, Native American, Asian-American, or from other racial and ethnic backgrounds (see figure 3.2). Yet these children represented more than half of all poor children. When each of these groups is examined independently, one finds that the poverty rates among minority children are three to four times that of white children. Specifically, in 1991 there were 65.9 million children under age 18 living in the U.S., of which 44.3 million were white (67 percent) and 21.6 million (33 percent) were children of color. The distribution of poverty among these children, however, was very different. Of the 14.3 million poor children under age 18 living in U.S. families, 5.6 million were white, representing 39 percent of the poor child population. The remaining 8.7 million children (61 percent) were children of color (figure 3.2).

What these numbers mean is that African-American children, Latino children and children from other racial and ethnic backgrounds are more likely to be poor than are white children. The following poverty rates illustrate this point. (Poverty rates are calculated by taking the number for the appropriate year and race in figure 3.2, Part B, and dividing it by the corresponding number in figure 3.2, Part A). The poverty rate for African-American children in 1991 was 46 percent (or nearly 1 of every 2 African-American children). Among Latino children, the poverty rate was 40 percent (or 2 of every 5 Latino children). The poverty rate for children from Native-American, Asian-American, and other cultural backgrounds was 22 percent. By way of comparison, the poverty rate for white children was 12 percent (just over 1 of every 10 white children).

TRENDS

Over the past three decades, the child population has become considerably more diverse, as has the poor child population. In 1960 roughly 14 percent of the entire child population comprised children of color; 26 percent of the poor child population comprised children of color. In 1991, 32 percent of the entire child population were children of color; yet, they represented over half (61 percent) of the poor child population (see table 3.5).

Clearly, the poverty status of African-American children relative to white children has worsened over the past three decades; African-American children are approximately four times more likely than white children to be poor (the poverty rate for white children was 12 percent compared to 46 percent for African-American children in 1991). In 1960, African-American children were three times more likely to be poor than white children (55 percent versus 18 percent) (O'Hare 1987).

Owing in large part to higher-than-average fertility, a low death rate, and high levels of immigration, the largest growth in the child population between 1960 and 1991 has occurred among Latinos—

Figure 3.2 PERCENTAGE DISTRIBUTIONS OF ALL CHILDREN AND POOR
CHILDREN IN THE UNITED STATES BY RACE/ETHNICITY: 1991

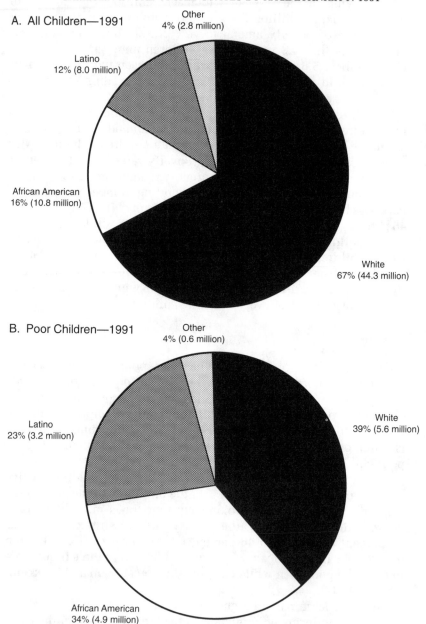

A. All Children—1991

Other
4% (2.8 million)

Latino
12% (8.0 million)

African American
16% (10.8 million)

White
67% (44.3 million)

B. Poor Children—1991

Other
4% (0.6 million)

Latino
23% (3.2 million)

White
39% (5.6 million)

African American
34% (4.9 million)

C. All Children—1960

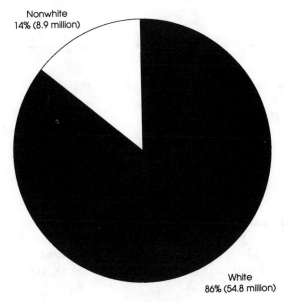

Nonwhite
14% (8.9 million)

White
86% (54.8 million)

D. Poor Children—1960

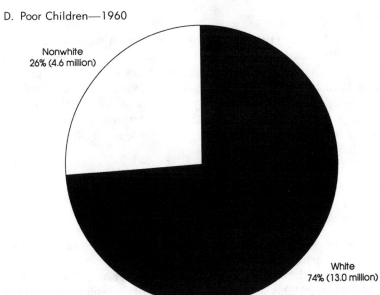

Nonwhite
26% (4.6 million)

White
74% (13.0 million)

Sources: Author's calculations using data from March 1992 Supplement to the Current Population Survey; and Bianchi (1990).

Table 3.5 PERCENTAGES AND POVERTY RATES FOR ALL NONWHITE
CHILDREN AND POOR NONWHITE CHILDREN, IN THE UNITED STATES: 1960
AND 1991

	1960 (%)	1991 (%)
Percentage of all children who are nonwhite	14	32
Percentage of all poor children who are nonwhite	26	61
Poverty rate for nonwhite children	45	43
Poverty rate for white children	18	11

Sources: U.S. Bureau of the Census (1992c); also author's calculations based on published and unpublished data.

an increase of 2.6 million children (U.S. Department of Commerce 1992; Census Bureau 1991b). In 1960, it is estimated that Latino children were roughly two and one-half times as likely to be poor as white children (47 percent versus 18 percent, respectively). In 1991, Latino children were over three times as likely to be poor as were white children.

PROJECTIONS

The Census Bureau (1989) estimated that growth rates for African-American and white populations will continue to decline through the early 21st century. However, growth rates for minority groups such as Latinos and Asian-Americans are expected to continue to grow through this period. Child poverty rates follow the general direction and magnitude of the change for the entire population subgroup (e.g., African-Americans), but are always 50–60 percent higher than the rates for adults.

Family Structure

CURRENT SITUATION

Proportionately fewer children today than 30 years ago can count on growing up in a household that includes both their mother and father (Bianchi 1990). Moreover, it is estimated that over half of all children born in the early 1990s will spend some part of their childhood living in a single-parent family (Duncan and Rodgers 1991); and children of color will be more likely than white children to live with a single mother or other family member (Ellwood 1989).

In 1991, 26 percent of all children under age 18 (i.e., 16.9 million children) lived in single-parent families (see table 3.6). A vast majority of these children—14.6 million—lived with single mothers; one-third (4.8 million) lived with mothers who never married; 37 percent (5.4 million) lived with divorced mothers; 24 percent (3.5 million) lived with mothers who were separated or whose spouse was absent; and 6 percent (875,000) lived with mothers who were widowed (author's calculations based on data from the 1992 Current Population Survey, March Supplement).

Children living with single mothers are more likely to be poor than children living with two parents because (1) one earner rarely earns as much as two earners, (2) women earn less than men, (3) full-time minimum-wage employment pays less than the poverty line for every family size except one or two persons, and (4) less than half of all single mothers ever receive child support, including a very small percentage of low-income single mothers (Census Bureau 1987). In 1991, the poverty rate among children living in single-mother families was 56 percent—more than five times that of two-parent families (11 percent) (table 3.6). However, it should be noted that the number of children living in poor two-parent families has recently been on the rise (U.S. Department of Commerce 1992).

TRENDS

According to government reports (U.S. Department of Commerce 1992; U.S. Congress, Committee on Ways and Means 1992), between 1960 and 1991, the proportion of children living in families headed by two parents decreased 16 percent (from 88 percent to 74 percent). Among white and Latino children, the proportion dropped 13 percent and 18 percent, respectively, while among African-American children the proportion dropped 41 percent. At the same time that the proportion of children living with two parents was decreasing, the number and proportion of children living with single parents was increasing dramatically. Between 1960 and 1991, the proportion of children living in single-parent families rose 189 percent (from 9 percent to 26 percent).

The increase in female-headed families over the past three decades has been linked to the increase in out-of-wedlock births and to the increasing divorce rate (O'Hare 1987). Births to unmarried women rose from 5 percent of all births to 25 percent of all births between 1960 and 1989; and in 1989, African-American women (64 percent of all births to unmarried women) were three times more likely to

Table 3.6 DISTRIBUTION OF ALL CHILDREN AND OF POOR CHILDREN IN THE UNITED STATES BY FAMILY TYPE AND AGE: 1991

Age, Family Type	All Children		Children above Poverty Line		Children below Poverty Line		Poverty Rate (%)
	Number (millions)	%	Number (millions)	%	Number (millions)	%	
Children under 18							
All families	64.8	100.0	51.2	100.0	13.7	100.0	21.1
Two-parent families	48.0	74.1	42.9	83.8	5.1	37.3	10.6
One-parent families:	16.9	25.9	8.3	16.2	8.6	62.7	50.9
Mother-only	14.6	21.1	6.5	10.9	8.1	59.1	55.5
Other	2.3	4.8	1.8	5.3	0.5	3.6	21.7

Source: U.S. Bureau of the Census (1992c: table 5).
Notes: Data in table cover children living in families (i.e., related children only). "Other" category includes father-only, relative, and nonrelative families.

bear children out-of-wedlock than white women (19 percent of all births to unmarried women) (U.S. Department of Commerce 1992: table 89). Further, researchers assert that the growing economic independence of women and the relatively poor economic situation among African-American men have influenced African-American women to leave a marriage or even forgo marriage (Wilson 1987).

The increase in female-headed families is an important factor contributing to the increase in child poverty (see Bianchi, chapter 4, this volume). For example, Bane and Ellwood (1989) argue that one-half of the overall increase in childhood poverty in the 1980s was due to the rise in mother-only families (the other half coming from the declining value of wages among fathers living in married-couple families). However, some analysts argue that the rise in child poverty since the late 1960s has been due primarily to the poor performance of the economy. Using a demographic method to standardize children's living arrangements, researchers found that one-third of the difference in child poverty rates is due to increases in female-headed families, while two-thirds is due to the failure of the economy to restore poverty to the level of the 1960s (Danziger 1988).

PROJECTIONS

If the trend of the past 10 years is any indication of the future trend, the rate of growth of single-mother families is slowing. Between 1960 and 1980 the proportion of children living with single mothers increased, from 8 percent to 18 percent. Between 1980 and 1991, the proportion grew by only 4 percentage points (from 18 percent to 22 percent). The U.S. Census Bureau (1989) and Haveman (1988) have projected that the growth rate of families headed by single mothers will continue to slow through the 1990s.

Although the growth rate of families headed by single mothers has slowed for all racial/ethnic groups, African-American families have recently topped the 50 percent mark. Based on the author's calculations of the trend data and population projections from the Census Bureau (1989), it appears that the growth of single-mother families will slow for all population subgroups, but will reach 55 percent among African-American families, 30 percent among Latino families, and 20 percent among white families by the turn of the century.

Family Size

CURRENT SITUATION

Poor parents, on average, have more children than nonpoor parents (National Center for Children in Poverty 1990); however, poor families are not, on average, larger than the typical American family. According to government data (Census Bureau 1992c), the average family size in 1991 was 3.91 persons (including 1.86 children). Among poor families in 1991, the average family size was 3.83 persons (including 2.21 children) (see figure 3.3). Further examination of family size by race/ethnicity shows that white and African-American families averaged 3.90 and 3.84 persons, respectively (with 1.83 and 1.95 children, respectively). Latino families were larger (4.33 persons with 2.22 children). Among the poor, white families averaged 3.84 persons (2.17 children), African-American families averaged 3.76 persons (2.26 children), and Latino families averaged 4.28 persons (2.45 children).

Further examination of family size by family structure shows that among two-parent and single-mother families, the average family sizes were 4.18 persons (including an average of 1.89 children) and 3.22 persons (including 1.82 children), respectively. Among poor families, two-parent families averaged 4.73 persons (including an average of 2.41 children), while single-mother families averaged 3.43 persons (including an average of 2.14 children). In 1991, over half of all poor children under age 18 lived in families with two or fewer children (see figure 3.3) (Census Bureau 1992c).

TRENDS

According to government reports, the average number of persons living in families with children under age 18 remained relatively constant—3.88 in 1960 and 3.91 in 1991 (U.S. Department of Commerce 1992; U.S. Congress, Committee on Ways and Means 1992; Census Bureau 1992c). However, the average number of children under age 18 living in those U.S. families dropped from 2.65 to 1.86. Among poor families, these averages fell sharply. The average number of persons living in poor families with children under 18 dropped from 4.51 to 3.83, while the average number of children living in those families fell from 3.55 to 2.21. The preceding analysis shows that in 1991, the average number of persons living in poor families with children was slightly smaller than the number living in the typical American family. However, the number of *children* living in poor families is larger than the typical family. Much of the difference found between average family size and average number of children for typical and low-income families between 1960 and 1991 can be explained by the dramatic change in family structure and marriage/ divorce patterns (particularly among the poor) from two-parent to single-parent families.

Figure 3.3 AVERAGE NUMBER OF CHILDREN LIVING IN U.S. FAMILIES BY
POVERTY STATUS AND YEAR

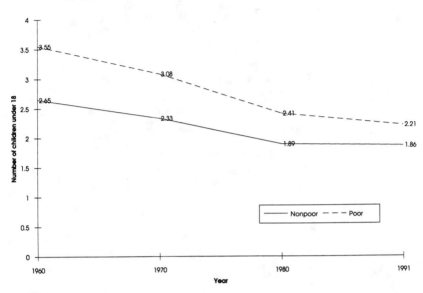

Sources: U.S. Bureau of the Census. *Current Population Reports*, P-60, nos. 43 (1960),
81 (1970), 133 (1980), and 181 (1991) (Washington, DC: U.S. Government Printing
Office).

PROJECTIONS

Given the changes in family structure, the increased divorce rate,
the increase in children born out-of-wedlock, and the changes in
the economy, family size and average number of children living in
families are expected to continue to decline, in spite of the increasing
total fertility rate.

Geographic Locale

CURRENT SITUATION

In 1991, child poverty was most concentrated in the southern region
of the country as well as the central cities (see table 3.7). Recent
government data show that the child poverty rate was 24 percent in
the South as compared to 22 percent in the West, 20 percent in the
Midwest, and 20 percent in the Northeast (Census Bureau 1992c).
As for residence areas, child poverty was most concentrated in central

Table 3.7 POVERTY RATES (AND TOTAL NUMBER) FOR ALL U.S. CHILDREN BY REGION AND RESIDENCE: 1991

| Residence | All (%) (65.9 million) | Region | | | |
		Northeast (%) (12.5 million)	South (%) (22.2 million)	Midwest (%) (16.1 million)	West (%) (14.9 million)
All (65,918)	21.8	19.7	24.1	19.8	22.2
Central cities (19,957)	31.9	34.4	32.0	37.4	27.0
Suburban areas (31,104)	14.7	10.8	17.0	10.5	19.0
Rural areas (14,857)	22.6	20.0	27.3	16.8	23.0

Source: U.S. Bureau of the Census (1992b: table 8).

cities, affecting nearly one of every three children (32 percent) living there. Impoverishment remains a significant threat to children living in rural areas (23 percent, or nearly one in four), and is a growing problem in the nation's suburbs (15 percent).

Further examination of child poverty rates in the nation's regions by residence areas shows that central cities of the Northeast and Midwest were the highest, at 34 percent and 37 percent, respectively (table 3.7). Poverty rates in the South were high in both central cities (32 percent) and rural areas (27 percent). Child poverty rates were lowest in suburban areas of the Northeast and Midwest, where one in nine (11 percent) children was poor. Child poverty rates in suburban areas of the South (17 percent) and West (19 percent) are approaching the levels experienced by rural areas one decade ago.

TRENDS

In 1959, the South contained 49 percent of the nation's poor people and its poverty rate was more than twice that of the rest of the nation (O'Hare 1987:15). In the decades following, the poverty rate in the South dropped steadily, then turned upward at the end of the 1970s. Meanwhile, the poverty rates in the Northeast, Midwest, and West also dropped steadily and then increased more quickly beginning in the late 1970s. In similar fashion, the poverty rates in the nation's rural areas in 1959 were roughly twice those of central city and suburban areas. However, poverty in rural areas dropped by nearly two-thirds through the late 1970s to a point lower than that of central cities, and since then has increased much the same as poverty rates in central cities and suburban areas. Poverty in central cities is higher today than in the late 1950s.

In 1959, the poverty rate among African-Americans living in the South was twice that of African-Americans living outside the South (69 percent versus 34 percent, respectively). Through the 1970s and 1980s, the poverty rate among African-Americans living in the South remained relatively stable around 35 percent, yet it increased dramatically outside the South (O'Hare 1987), from 19 percent in 1970 to 34 percent in 1985. Today, the poverty rates of African-Americans in the South and outside the South are nearly identical.

According to a recent study (Joint Center for Political and Economic Studies 1990), in 20 metropolitan areas around the country, poverty increased among African-American children from 30 percent in 1970 to 35 percent in 1985. During this same period, the economic situation of African-American children living in the South improved (poverty fell from 43 percent to 37 percent). The report's authors suggest that the improvement is related to expansion of employment opportunities in the South.

PROJECTIONS

Poverty in central cities of metropolitan areas in the United States has gradually increased since the early 1960s. According to poverty concentration analysts, poverty in central cities is not *spreading* as fast as it is *deepening* in areas with historically high poverty rates (Coulton and Pandey 1992; O'Hare 1987). Another disturbing recent trend is the growth in the proportion of poor persons living in areas outside the central cities (i.e., suburban areas), particularly among families with children. Poverty in suburban areas in each of the regions just described increased in a manner similar to poverty in the central cities of those same regions (Census Bureau 1992c). Until recently, changes in suburban poverty were not detectable from year to year. Without significant change in the macro economy, or greater support provided to metropolitan areas, increases in poverty among families with children living in metropolitan areas can be expected to continue.

DYNAMICS OF CHILD POVERTY: DEPTH AND DURATION

To this point in the chapter, child poverty has been illustrated using a rather static, one-dimensional definition of poverty—that is, poor versus nonpoor. Although this was necessary to clearly describe the complex and interrelated array of factors associated with child poverty, it ignores the dynamics of child poverty, its varying degrees of depth and duration. This section further analyzes child poverty by exploring those dynamics.

Depth of Child Poverty

According to a recent Census Bureau (1992c) report, of the 13.7 million poor children living in the United States in 1991, 63 percent (8.6 million) live in families whose incomes were at or above 50 percent of the poverty line. For a family of three, this translates to between $5,487 and $10,973 annually, or between roughly $457 and $915 per month (before taxes), to feed, clothe, house, and care for its members (regardless of geographic region or residence). Moreover, more than one-third (37 percent) of all poor children (many of whom are preschool age children) live in families whose annual incomes do not exceed 50 percent of the poverty line (the "deeply poor"). This data suggest that a sizable portion of the poor child population faces substantial risks—more serious than those faced by less-disadvantaged poor children—to their health and development, such as living in substandard or transient housing, inadequate nutritional and health care, abuse and neglect, accidental injury or death, and a host of other environmental risks. Although it is true that government programs such as AFDC, the Special Supplemental Food Program for Women, Infants, and Children (WIC), Food Stamps, housing, and Medicaid are available to assist these very poor families, the fact is that few deeply poor families are engaged with the social welfare system (Census Bureau 1992b).

Duration of Poverty

The preceding "snapshot" of poor families with children has applied to a single year. What this data cannot do is illustrate the duration of poverty for those families. To examine this dynamic phenomenon, research using longitudinal data (information pertaining to the same families collected over a period of time) such as from the Michigan Panel Study on Income Dynamics (PSID) and the Survey of Income and Program Participation (SIPP) has flourished in the past several years. The work of researchers such as Hill (1981), Bane and Ellwood (1989), Ellwood (1989), Duncan et al. (1984), Duncan and Rodgers (1991), Mayer and Jencks (1989), Weinberg (1988), and Williams (1986) has shown that poor families with children cycle in and out of poverty over time, and a small yet troublesome proportion of the poor cannot escape poverty entirely.

This body of research reveals a number of important issues:

☐ Approximately one-third of all children will be poor at some point in their childhood;
☐ Three percent to 5 percent of all children will experience poverty for a majority of their childhood;
☐ Twenty percent to 25 percent of all poor children are born poor;
☐ Those who experience short-term poverty (less than three years) are more demographically similar to those in the overall population than to the long-term poor (more than seven years in poverty);
☐ Changes in family events (e.g., family dissolution, job loss, and

birth of a new baby) account for more than half of all childhood spells of poverty—and about 25 percent of spells are associated with single parenthood;

□ Persistently poor children (more than seven years in poverty) are overwhelmingly children of color (most frequently African-American) and live with unmarried mothers in rural parts of the South;

□ Large, and largely offsetting, changes in key demographic variables have occurred over the past two decades—an increase in single-parent families; declines in the earnings of young workers, in the age of first-time parents, and in the average number of children living in families; and an increase in the number of years of education completed by adults.

David Ellwood's (1989) work on child poverty spells has shown that growing up in a two-parent family does not guarantee that a child will avoid poverty; in his study, roughly 20 percent of all children who grew up in a two-parent household experienced at least a short spell of poverty (see table 3.8). Still, some 2 percent of these children were poor in nearly every year of their childhood. By comparison, among children who grew up part of the time in a two-parent family and part of the time in a single-parent family, 33 percent avoided poverty entirely, while over half experienced temporary and short-term poverty (between 1 and 6 years of the child's first 10 years) and 12 percent experienced long-term poverty (7 or more years). Further, Ellwood's work showed that many children growing up exclusively in single-parent families endured long-term poverty spells. Only 7 percent of such children avoided poverty entirely, whereas 32 percent endured temporary and short-term spells of poverty and 61 percent were poor for a vast majority of their childhood.

Further examination of these poverty spells reveals that persistent poverty is much more likely among children of color and among younger children (Ellwood 1989). For example, for children born around 1970, 73 percent of all white children avoided poverty entirely as compared to 22 percent of black children; 19 percent of white children were temporarily poor (1–3 years) compared to 22 percent of black children; 5 percent of white children endured short-term poverty spells (4–6 years) compared to 22 percent of black children; and 3 percent of white children spent much of their early childhood (7–10 years) in poverty compared to 34 percent of black children (see figure 3.4).

Table 3.8 EXTENT OF POVERTY DURING FIRST 10 YEARS OF CHILDHOOD FOR U.S. CHILDREN BORN IN LATE 1970s, BY YEARS SPENT IN VARIOUS LIVING ARRANGEMENTS

Living Arrangement	Never Poor (%)	Extent of Poverty		
		Temporarily Poor (1–3 yrs.) (%)	Short-term Poor (4–6yrs.) (%)	Long-term Poor (7–10 yrs.) (%)
Always in two-parent family	80.0	13.3	4.4	2.0
Some years in single-parent family	32.8	40.7	14.7	11.7
Always in single-parent family	6.7	11.9	20.8	60.6

Source: Ellwood (1989).

Figure 3.4 EXTENT OF POVERTY DURING FIRST 10 YEARS OF CHILDHOOD
FOR U.S. CHILDREN BORN AROUND 1970, BY RACE

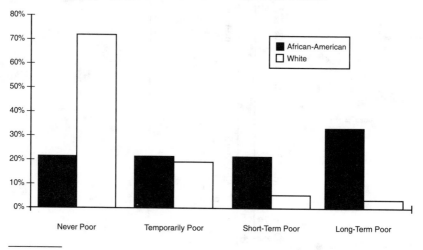

Source: Ellwood (1989).

Note: Temporary poverty (1–3 years); short-term poverty (4–6 years); and long-term poverty (7–10 years).

WHAT DOES ALL THIS MEAN?

Poverty, by definition, is simply inadequate income necessary to purchase a minimally adequate standard of living. Although conceptually this definition is appealing (because helping those who cannot help themselves is a goal of public service and public policy), operationally the poverty measure used in the United States is increasingly inaccurate and outdated. The facts that the income definition that is used is incomplete and there is a built-in inconsistency between the income measure and threshold measure, in addition to the fact that the measure does not adjust family income for regional differences in cost of living, suggest that people are sure to be misclassified as poor or nonpoor when in fact they are not. This is significant because this distorted view of impoverishment is used to distribute benefits and services to the poor and provide Americans with a barometer of social welfare.

Over the past three decades major changes have occurred within the poor population living in the United States, the most significant of which have been the increases in the numbers of poor youth, children of racial/ethnic minorities, single, never-married female-headed families, and families living outside the southern states and in rural and urban areas. Today, for the first time since the federal government began collecting poverty statistics in the late 1950s, children represent the poorest age group in America. Moreover, young children are at the greatest risk of being poor. But we must keep in mind that it is not children who are poor, but their parents (National Center for Children in Poverty 1990). Increasingly, families with children are younger (Childrens Defense Fund 1992) and therefore less able to command wages and salaries necessary to avoid poverty. As Ellwood (1989) and Duncan et al. (1984) have both pointed out, an increasing number of children in both two-parent and single-parent families will spend some of their childhood years living in poverty.

What this means for poor children is increased risk for poor health and poor nutrition, school failure and dropout, accidental injury and death, homelessness, and a host of other problems often associated with, if not directly a consequence of, impoverishment (National Center for Children in Poverty 1990). These risks increase as the persistence of poverty increases. Therefore, not surprisingly, children born into a persistently poor family are believed to be at greatest risk of poor birth outcomes (such as very low birthweight, infant mortality, and morbidity), and those who spend a majority of their childhood impoverished are expected to less often stay in school or complete their schooling, to be under- or unemployed, and to more frequently experience behavioral problems (Danziger and Stern 1990; Klerman 1991). The problem we face is collecting data rich enough to shed light on the relationship of impoverishment and child health, education, and welfare outcomes.

Historically, social, economic, and demographic forces have ebbed and flowed resulting in more or less poverty in America. The result of deteriorating economic conditions for American families and the dramatic increase in the proportion of children growing up with single mothers, particularly among African-American children, has been a persistently high poverty rate (Bane and Ellwood, 1991). This is significant because as the population becomes more diverse racially and ethnically, new ways of solving old problems (such as deep poverty, poor health, and poor housing) will be necessary. If nothing else, the riots in Los Angeles in 1992 showed us that the people of South Central are tired of being ignored and are desperately seeking a way of communicating their frustration and need for help.

Another issue illustrated by the Los Angeles tragedy is the

increased concentration of poverty in our nation's central cities and the social isolation that accompanies it. The tensions are obvious, yet the solutions are elusive. It is not simply a matter of providing jobs, although employment opportunities would go a long way toward strengthening any effort to improve resident self-sufficiency. In their review of the effects of poor neighborhoods on children and adolescents, Mayer and Jencks (1989) and Coulton and Pandey (1992) reported frequent negative outcomes such as low birthweight, infant death, teen childbearing, juvenile delinquency, dropping out of high school, and poor school performance. These effects, although more concentrated in central cities, are true also in suburban and rural areas as well. The point is poverty is a complex social, economic, and demographic phenomenon that requires a multidisciplinary approach to prevent its occurrence and reduce its effect on those impacted.

ISSUES EMANATING FROM THE ANALYSES

Three major themes emerge from this analysis of child poverty: first, poverty, as officially measured in this country, is an arbitrary and inadequate way to understand who is in need and what to do about it. Second, poverty increasingly affects people of all colors, creeds, and nationalities, particularly children. Third, policy strategies to assist poor children must focus on preventing poverty in families as well as on dealing with the impoverishment that affects so many American children.

Poverty Measurement

The poverty rate is a widely used standard whose purposes are to: determine how well we are doing as a society (a statistical function); distribute public assistance (an administrative function); and allocate increasingly scarce resources to improve the lives of those who cannot otherwise support themselves (an administrative function). However, the poverty measure is an arbitrary measure of material well-being that is conceptually, methodologically, and computationally flawed. The result of these problems is a classification system that inappropriately identifies some families and individuals deserving assistance as nonpoor (thus disqualifying them from many forms of assistance) while others who could make it on their own (with only periodic assistance) are certified as eligible for aid. The effect of correcting the various technical flaws discussed earlier can be significant—changing the poverty rate up or down by 5 percent to 25 percent and reclassifying between 1 million and 10 million persons as poor or nonpoor. This is especially important when those being affected are the same persons antipoverty policy is designed to help. Reexamination of the poverty measure and redevelopment of the poverty methodology should be priority items in any new war on poverty.

Poverty and Growing Cultural Diversity

Each year the American population becomes more culturally diverse—that is, the proportion of nonwhite persons in the population grows faster than the proportion of white persons in the population. Analysts project that between 1990 and 1995, the child and young adult populations in the United States will change so that the proportion of children and young adults of color will increase between 3 percent and 10 percent, whereas the proportion of white children and young adults will decrease by between 1 percent and 3 percent (U.S. Bureau of the Census 1991b).

The growing diversity of the American population and increased poverty rates among some racial and ethnic groups can be explained, in large part, by immigration patterns, changes in family structure, and stagnation of the total fertility rate among white women. Between 1968 and 1988, the number of immigrant children grew by nearly 50 percent (Joint Center for Political and Economic Studies 1990), whereas the proportion of children living in mother-only families increased three-fold and the total fertility rate (1.8 children) remained below replacement (2.1 children) and was lower still for white women. Increased poverty among some groups, particularly among recent immigrants, is explained, in part, by education levels being lower than those of earlier cohorts (due to many fewer recent immigrants who speak English), translating to fewer job opportunities and greater economic isolation.

The policy and program implications of a rapidly growing cultural diversity among the U.S. population, particularly for children, include finding new ways to appropriately educate, train, and employ all members of society, and to provide necessary support to those who cannot support themselves; implementing effective multicultural educational curricula in our schools; expanding English as a

Second Language (ESL); strengthening programs known to work for disadvantaged children and their families (many of whom are persons of color)—programs such as Head Start, WIC, summer youth employment, community youth centers, and employment training and job assistance; and providing poor parents with the tools to help themselves—such as affordable, high quality child care and health care.

Policies for Children *and* Families

From a policy perspective, growing impoverishment among our families with children spells disaster for the future of America. Poor children are more likely than nonpoor children to experience many health, education, and welfare problems including premature and low-weight birth; death within the first year of life; acute and chronic illnesses; injuries; maltreatment; slow or erratic intellectual, social, and emotional development; exposure to HIV/AIDS; and lack of access to quality health and childcare. Analysts argue that policies making poor children's lives worth living, not just keeping them alive, are important to the future of America (Danziger and Stern 1990; Klerman 1991). Policies most frequently discussed focused on children include (1) changing appropriations-limited programs such as WIC and Head Start to entitlement programs; (2) enforcing laws focused on eliminating lead poisoning, improving housing quality, immunization, and seat belt use; and (3) increasing the number of direct service programs in areas without an adequate number of private providers or where private providers will not go.

Policies most frequently discussed focused on low-income families with children include (1) increasing tax credits and lowering personal income taxes; (2) enacting a system of universal health care and developing strategies to offer adequate reimbursement to private practitioners serving poor families; and (3) creating or enhancing wage subsidy or other programs aimed at increasing wages, including those designed to eliminate racial and gender discrimination in the labor market. Over half of the poor families in America are headed by working adults (in some cases two working adults), and the children growing up in them are the future work force. Whereas the lack of economic resources translates directly into poorer living conditions, fewer opportunities for leisure activities, less attention paid to preventive medical and nutritional care, and a host of other difficulties, it also affects morale and motivation. For working poor families, this is not hard to understand. They are poor because they work at jobs that do not pay them a living wage. The mere opportunity to work, which two decades ago usually translated into a measure of financial security, is no longer relevant in today's world.

A productive and motivated work force requires that people who play by the rules will not have to forfeit the game. This statement, made repeatedly by David Ellwood (e.g., 1988) suggests that policies designed to (1) strengthen self-support obligations, such as child support enforcement, and (2) enhance self-sufficiency, such as welfare-to-work programs, strengthening the nation's schools, and focusing on child care will help the work force of tomorrow—that is, the children of today—grow to be productive workers and effective parents of the next generation.

Note

The views expressed in this chapter are my own, as are any errors that may be contained here. I wish to thank Suzanne Bianchi, Judith Chafel, Sandra Hofferth, and Amy Scarbrough for their valuable comments on an earlier draft.

1. In this chapter, the term "all children" refers to those persons under 18 years of age living in families (whether they are related to the householder or not) as well as those living on their own. The term "related children" refers only to those persons under 18 years of age living in families to whom the child is legally related (through birth or adoption).

References

Adams, T., G. J. Duncan, and W. L. Rodgers. 1988. "The Persistence of Urban Poverty." In Quiet Riots: Race and Poverty in the U.S., edited by F. Harris and R. Wilkins. New York: Pantheon Books.

Bane, M. J., and D. Ellwood. 1989. "One Fifth of the Nation's Children: Why Are They Poor?" Science 245: 1047–53.

————. 1991. "Is American Business Working for the Poor?" Harvard Business Review (September–October): 58–66.

Bianchi, S. 1990. "America's Children: Mixed Prospects." Population Bulletin 45, 1 (Population Reference Bureau, Washington, D.C.).

Census Bureau. See U.S. Bureau of the Census.

Children's Defense Fund. 1991. An Opinionmaker's Guide to Children in Election Year 1992. Washington, DC: Author.

————. 1992. The Children's Defense Budget: 1992. Washington, D.C.: Author.

Coulton, C., and S. Pandey. 1992. "The Geographic Concentration of Poverty." *American Behavioral Scientist* 35, 3: 238–57.

Danziger, S. 1988. "Fighting Poverty and Reducing Welfare Dependency: A Challenge for the 1990s." Paper presented at Rockefeller Foundation Conference on Welfare Reform, New York, Feb. 16–18.

Danziger, S., and J. Stern. 1990. "The Causes and Consequences of Child Poverty In the United States." Innoccenti Occasional Papers, no. 10. Florence: UNICEF International Child Development Centre.

Duncan, G. J., and W. L. Rodgers. 1991. "Has Children's Poverty Become More Persistent?" *American Sociological Review* 56, 3: 538–50.

Duncan, G. J., R. D. Coe, M. E. Corcoran, M. S. Hill, S. D. Hoffman, and J. N. Morgan. 1984. *Years of Poverty, Years of Plenty: The Changing Economic Fortunes of American Workers and Families.* Ann Arbor, Mich.: Institute for Social Research.

Eggebeen, D. J., and D. T. Lichter. 1991. "Race, Family Structure, and Changing Poverty among American Children." *American Sociological Review* 56 (December): 801–17.

Ellwood, D. 1987. *Divide and Conquer: Responsive Security for America's Poor.* New York: Ford Foundation.

————. 1988. *Poor Support: Poverty in the American Family.* New York: Basic Books.

————. 1989. "Poverty through the Eyes of Children." Harvard University, John F. Kennedy School of Government, Cambridge, Mass. Photocopy.

Fuchs, V., and D. M. Reklis. 1992. "America's Children: Economic Perspectives and Policy Options." *Science* 255: 41–46.

GAO. *See* U.S. General Accounting Office.

Garfinkel, I., and S. McLanahan. 1986. *Single Mothers and Their Children: A New American Dilemma.* Washington, D.C.: Urban Institute Press.

Haveman, R. 1988. *Starting Even.* New York: Simon and Schuster.

Haveman, R., and B. Wolfe. 1992. "On the Determinants of Children's Well-Being and Economic Success." Russell Sage Foundation Working Paper 26. New York: Russell Sage Foundation.

Hill, M. A. 1981. "Some Dynamic Aspects of Poverty." In *Five Thousand American Families: Patterns of Economic Progress,* vol. 9 (93–120). Ann Arbor, Mich.: Institute for Social Research.

Joint Center for Political and Economic Studies. 1990. *The Declining Economic Status of Black Children.* Washington, D.C.: Author.

Klerman, L. V. 1991. *Alive and Well? A Research and Policy Review of Health Programs for Poor Young Children.* New York, NY: National Center for Children in Poverty.

Korbin, J. E. 1992. "The Impact of Poverty on Children." *American Behavioral Scientist* 35 (3, special issue).

Mayer, S., and C. Jencks. 1989. "Growing Up in Poor Neighborhoods: How Much Does It Matter?" *Science* 243: 1441–45.

Murray, C. 1986. *Losing Ground.* New York: Basic Books.
National Center for Children in Poverty. 1990. *Five Million Children: A Statistical Profile of Our Poorest Young Citizens.* New York: Author.
_____. 1992a. *Five Million Children: 1991 Update.* New York: Author.
_____. 1992b. *Five Million Children: 1992 Update.* New York: Author.
Nelson, H. H. 1991. "An Interstate Cost of Living Index." *Educational Evaluation and Policy Analysis* 13, 1: 103–11.
O'Hare, W. 1987. "Poverty In America: Trends and New Patterns." *Population Bulletin* 40 (3). (Population Reference Bureau, Washington, D.C.)
Orshansky, M. 1965. "Counting the Poor: Another Look at the Poverty Profile." Social Security Bulletin 28, 1: 3–29.
Ruggles, P. 1990. *Drawing the Line.* Washington, D.C.: Urban Institute Press.
_____. 1992. "Measuring Poverty." *Focus* 14, 1: 1–9.
Sawhill, I. 1988. "Poverty in the U.S.: Why Is It So Persistent?" *Journal of Economic Literature* 26: 1073–1119.
Smith, J. 1989. "Children among the Poor." *Demography* 26, 2: 235–48.
U.S. Bureau of the Census. 1980. "Alternative Measures of Poverty: The Valuation of Noncash Benefits." *Current Population Reports, Technical Paper 50.* Washington, D.C.: U.S. Government Printing Office.
_____. 1987. "Child Support and Alimony: 1987." *Current Population Reports,* ser. P-23, no. 167, Washington, D.C.: U.S. Government Printing Office.
_____. 1989. "Population Profile of the United States: 1989." *Current Population Reports,* ser. P-23, no. 159. Washington, D.C.: U.S. Government Printing Office.
_____. 1990a. "Household and Family Characteristics: March 1990 and 1989." *Current Population Reports,* ser. P-20, no. 447. Washington, D.C.: U.S. Government Printing Office.
_____. 1990b. "Transitions in Income and Poverty Status: 1985–1986." *Current Population Reports,* ser. P-70, no. 18. Washington, D.C.: U.S. Government Printing Office.
_____. 1991a. "Poverty in the United States: 1990." *Current Population Reports,* ser. P-60, no. 175. Washington, D.C.: U.S. Government Printing Office.
_____. 1991b. "United States Population Estimates by Age, Sex, and Race: 1980 to 1990." *Current Population Reports,* ser. P-25, no. 1025. Washington, D.C.: U.S. Government Printing Office.
_____. 1992a. "How We're Changing, Demographic State of the Nation: 1992." *Current Population Reports,* Special Studies, ser. P-23, no. 177. Washington, D.C.: U.S. Government Printing Office.
_____. 1992b. "Measuring the Effect of Benefits and Taxes on Income and Poverty: 1979 to 1991." *Current Population Reports,* series P-60, no. 182-RD, table 2:98 (Washington, D.C.: U.S. Government Printing Office).

————. 1992c. "Poverty in the United States: 1991." *Current Population Reports*, ser. P-60, no. 181. Washington, D.C.: U.S. Government Printing Office.

U.S. Congress, Committee on Ways and Means. 1985. *Children in Poverty.* Washington, D.C.: U.S. Government Printing Office.

————. 1992. *Green Book.* Washington, D.C.: U.S. Government Printing Office.

U.S. Congress, Select Committee on Children, Youth and Families. 1990. "U.S. Children and their Families: Current Conditions and Recent Trends, 1989." Washington, D.C.: Author.

U.S. Congressional Budget Office. 1988. *Trends in Family Income, 1970–1986.* Washington, D.C.: U.S. Government Printing Office.

U.S. Department of Commerce. 1992. *Statistical Abstract of the United States: 1991.* Washington, D.C.: U.S. Government Printing Office.

U.S. General Accounting Office. 1986. "Noncash Benefits: Initial Results Show Valuation Methods Differentially Affect the Poor." Publ. no. PEMD-86-6BR. Washington, D.C.: U.S. Government Printing Office.

————. 1987. "Noncash Benefits: Methodological Review of Experimental Methods Indicates Many Problems Remain." Publ. no. PEMD-87-23. Washington, D.C.: U.S. Government Printing Office.

Weinberg, D. 1988. "Measuring Poverty and the Poverty Gap: 1984–1986." Paper presented at meeting of the Allied Social Science Association, New York, November.

Williams, R. 1986. "Measuring Poverty with the SIPP and the CPS." Paper presented at annual meeting of the Association for Public Policy Analysis and Management, New York, October.

Wilson, W. J. 1987. *The Truly Disadvantaged: The Inner City, The Underclass, and Public Policy.* Chicago: University of Chicago Press.

Zill, N. 1990. "Current Characteristics of Welfare Families and Their Children." Paper presented at the National Health Policy Forum, George Washington University, Washington, D.C., July 31.

————. 1992. "Children, Families, and Poverty: What We Have Learned from Recent Research." Exhibits prepared for the Columbia University School of Journalism conference on "Focus on Children: The Beat of the Future," New York, Apr. 20.

Chapter Four

CHILDREN OF POVERTY: WHY ARE THEY POOR?

Suzanne M. Bianchi

Why are children poor? The simple answer is because they live in families in which the adults are unable to provide enough income to meet their basic material needs. But this statement of the obvious is an unsatisfactory answer. Implicit in the question "Why are children poor?" is the assumption that if one could only pinpoint the root causes of poverty, one would be able to alleviate the economic deprivation that characterizes childhood for a sizable number of American children.

If one point emerges from this chapter's discussion, it is that the answer to the question "Why are children poor?" is not simple or straightforward. The causes of child poverty are multiple and interrelated. And the factors that affect the material well-being of children are becoming more numerous as the U.S. economy becomes increasingly intertwined with the economies of other nations.

This chapter begins with an overview of the long-term trend and fluctuations in the poverty of children. The interrelationships of broad, macroeconomic conditions and poverty in general (child poverty in particular) are discussed. Because earnings and family income inequality assumed greater importance in the explanation of poverty in the 1980s, the second section of the chapter focuses on the low earnings and increased earnings inequality among young men.

The increase in children living in mother-only families has been an important demographic component of the increase in child poverty. Over the long run, the growth in single-parent families may have decreased the economic security of children more than any other change. The third section of this chapter thus presents data on the increase and changing marital status distribution of mothers who are raising children alone.

The trend in child poverty cannot be discussed in isolation from changes that have occurred in public support of the poor. Consequently, the fourth section of the chapter discusses patterns in spending on public assistance and social insurance programs.

Not all trends have increased child poverty. The fifth section of the chapter highlights those factors that have lessened the incidence of poverty among today's generation of children compared with earlier generations. Changes in family size, in the educational attainment of parents, and in maternal employment have all improved the economic situation of children's families. The variation in causes of child poverty between urban and rural areas is also briefly discussed.

After reviewing macroeconomic conditions, income inequality, the growth in mother-child families, trends in public assistance, factors that have reduced poverty, and the geographic variation in poverty, the highly politicized question of whether welfare policy in the United States has been a cause, either directly or indirectly, of increased poverty among children is addressed.

The final sections of the chapter briefly examine what is known about the multiple, interrelated causes of poverty and also discuss the public policy challenges presented by the multidimensional nature of poverty. The chapter ends with a summary and conclusions.

MACROECONOMIC CONDITIONS AND THE TREND IN CHILD POVERTY

A useful introduction to causes of childhood poverty is the economist's expectation that the poverty rate in general, and among children in particular, should rise and fall with the overall performance of the economy. Children do not directly participate in the labor market, but their material well-being is tied to the well-being of the economic providers with whom they live. Since those providers tend to be relatively young, active participants in the labor force, who provide most of the support for their dependents through earnings, the ability of parents to provide for their children should be closely tied to the overall performance of the economy. During times of economic expansion and declining unemployment, poverty typically decreases. During recessions, when the demand for labor is slack, unemployment rises and poverty usually increases.

Figure 4.1 depicts the long-term trend in the poverty of children. The solid line represents the poverty rate of children in the United States using the "official" definition of poverty adopted by the Office of Management and Budget (OMB Standard Directive No. 14 as cited in U.S. Bureau of the Census 1992e: A-7). Since 1959, the U.S. Bureau of the Census (henceforth, Census Bureau), has estimated the number and proportion of the population whose pretax income in the previ-

Figure 4.1 POVERTY RATE OF U.S. CHILDREN: 1939–91

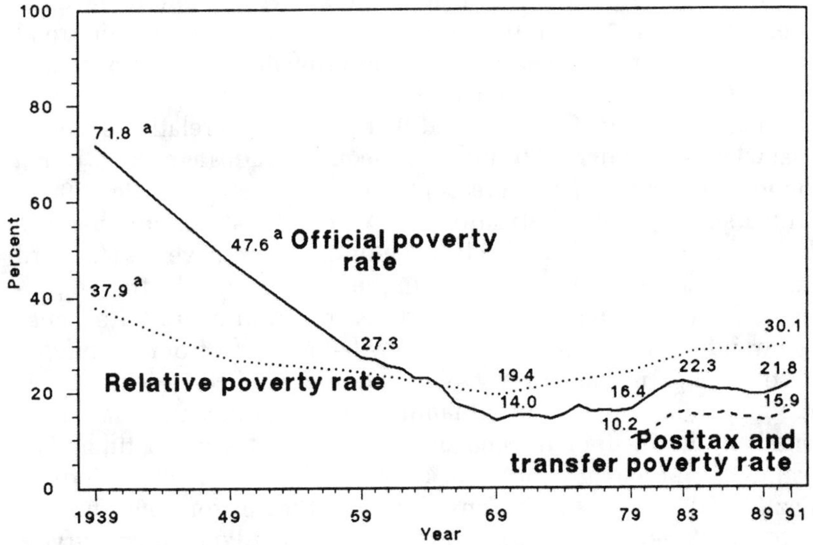

Sources: Census Bureau (1991: table B; 1992 e: table 3); and Hernandez (1993: table 9.1).
Notes: The relative poverty rate is the percentage of children in families with incomes less than one-half the median income of a two-parent, two-child family in a given year. This median income threshold is adjusted by the equivalence scale implicit in the official poverty calculations for families of sizes other than four.
a. Estimated from decennial Census data.

ous calendar year fell below a money income "poverty" threshold that varies by family size and composition.[1] The threshold is an absolute measure of poverty in that it is supposed to represent the dollar amount that a family needs to achieve a "minimally adequate" standard of living.

The annual estimate of the percentage of children under age 18 in poverty is graphed in figure 4.1 for the 1959 to 1991 period by using the Census Bureau's annual estimates of poverty, derived from the March supplement to the Current Population Survey. In addition, the line is extended back first to 1949 and then to 1939 by using poverty estimates based on income and family composition from the 1950 and 1940 Censuses of Population, respectively.[2]

The official poverty estimates have been criticized for their use of pretax rather than aftertax income and for the exclusion of in-kind sources of income, such as Food Stamps and medical coverage.[3] The

Census Bureau has developed a consistent series of poverty estimates for the 1979–91 period, which adjusts for taxes and public transfers (Census Bureau 1992c); this is also shown in figure 4.1. The trend parallels the official measure, but the estimate of the number and percentage of children in poverty is lower.

Finally, it is sometimes argued that poverty is a relative concept, that what is considered "minimally adequate" varies as average living standards increase (or decrease) (Hernandez 1993; Ruggles 1990). Under such a conceptualization, a poverty estimate should measure how far a given individual is from being able to achieve the standard of living of the "average" person in the society. For illustrative purposes, a relative measure of poverty is shown in figure 4.1 because the trend in such a measure is somewhat different from the official absolute measure of poverty. The measure graphed in figure 4.1 is the percentage of children in families in which income is less than one-half the median income of all families at a given time. The estimates in the figure for 1939, 1949, and 1959, derived by Hernandez (1993), are based on Census data. Estimates for 1964 through 1991 are based on data from the March Current Population Survey, the survey used to calculate the official poverty rate (Census Bureau 1991b: table B).

This relative poverty measure indicates much less poverty among children in the 1940s and 1950s than the absolute measure. The proportion of children in families with income less than one-half the median income of all families rose steadily for children during the 1970s and 1980s, when the absolute measure showed stability or much less increase. The relative measure also indicates a considerably higher proportion of children in poverty during the 1980s than were counted as poor using the officially accepted definition of poverty. Duncan and Rodgers (1991), who focused on the persistence of poverty over time, found similar differences between an absolute and relative measure of poverty.

According to the absolute poverty estimates (the official estimates, which remain the most widely cited and used to assess the trend in child poverty), the proportion of children in poverty was extremely high in 1939—when more than 7 in 10 children lived in poverty. Poverty declined dramatically during the 1940s and 1950s as the country emerged from the Great Depression, fought in World War II, and enjoyed a dramatic postwar economic expansion and improvement in average living standards (Hernandez 1993: table 7.1; Smolensky, Danziger, and Gottschalk 1988: table 3.1).

By 1959, when the annual series of official poverty estimates began,

27 percent of children were in poverty. The poverty rate among children continued to drop in the 1960s (to a low of 14 percent by 1969) as the economy experienced a long, uninterrupted expansion (Blank 1991: 1).[4]

During the 1970s, as economic growth slowed, the decline in poverty among children also halted. The number of children in poverty hovered around 10 million. The poverty rate of children was 15 percent during the first half of the 1970s, spiked to 17 percent during the mid-decade recession, and remained at 16 percent during the latter half of the 1970s (figure 4.1).

Poverty rose among children during the back-to-back recessions of the early 1980s, and peaked at 22.3 percent poor in 1983 (almost 14 million poor children in that year) (see figure 4.1). In 1983, the United States entered a period of sustained economic expansion. If macroeconomic performance had continued to be the major determinant of poverty, as David Ellwood and Lawrence Summers (1988) argued it was until the early 1980s, poverty should have declined substantially after 1983 as the economy grew. Poverty among children dropped from a high of 22.3 percent in 1983 to 19.5 percent in 1988, but the rate never returned to the 15–16 percent level of the 1970s. Instead, one-fifth of the nation's children were counted among those officially poor throughout the 1980s.

Poverty among children was again elevated by the recession that began in the fourth quarter of 1990. In 1991, the latest date for which figures were available at this writing, the poverty rate among children stood at 21.8 percent (see figure 4.1), a number not significantly different from the high level of 1983. In 1991, 14.3 million children were counted among the poor in the United States (Census Bureau 1992e: table 3). Hence, poor macroeconomic performance continues to move more children into poverty, but good macroeconomic performance seems less able to do the opposite. During the 1980s, macroeconomic expansion did not decrease poverty as much as expected, a failure that was particularly acute for children (Cutler and Katz 1991: table 1). We still have only a partial answer to the question of why economic growth during the 1980s failed to "trickle down" to the poor in general and children in particular.

GROWING INEQUALITY IN EARNINGS

One factor "explaining" the failure of macroeconomic growth to reach the poor in the 1980s is the decline in earnings of less-skilled,

Figure 4.2 PERCENTAGE OF MALE WORKERS, AGED 25 TO 34, WITH ANNUAL
EARNINGS BELOW POVERTY THRESHOLD FOR FAMILY OF FOUR:
1969–89

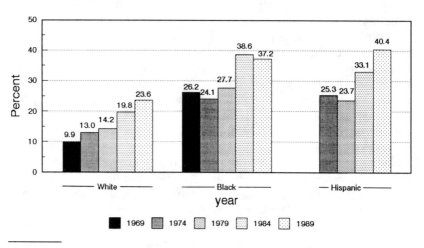

Source: Census Bureau (1992g: table 2).

less-educated workers relative to more-skilled, more highly educated
workers (Acs and Danziger 1990; Blackburn, Bloom, and Freeman
1991; Bound and Holzer 1991; Bound and Johnson 1992; Census
Bureau 1992d, f, g; Karoly 1990; Levy and Murnane 1992; Ryscavage
and Henle 1990). Average wages of younger workers decreased relative to wages for older workers among those with a high school (or
less) education. And, within educational and age groups, earnings
inequality increased (Katz and Murphy 1992). The result was that
breadwinners at the bottom of the income distribution increasingly
could not earn enough to keep a family above the poverty level.

Figure 4.2 graphs the increase from 1969 to 1989 in young white,
black, and Hispanic men who did not earn enough to keep a family
of four above the poverty level. During this period, the percentage
of young, white male workers who had low earnings more than
doubled, rising from 1 in 10 to almost 1 in 4. Among black men, the
percentage with low earnings increased from 26 percent to 37 percent,
with almost all of the increase occurring during the early 1980s. The
trend for men of Hispanic origin is similar, with 40 percent with low
earnings by 1989.

Danziger and Stern (1990: figure 2) have provided evidence that
the increase in low earnings was particularly acute among young

men with a high school education or less. During the 1950s and 1960s, the proportion of less-educated men with low earnings declined dramatically, but then rose sharply in the 1970s and 1980s. The trend over time was similar, but not nearly so accentuated, for better-educated young men (Danziger and Stern 1990: table 2).

Why did the earnings distribution become more unequal? Why did the earnings of those with a high school education or less deteriorate relative to those with a college education? This puzzle has not been completely sorted out, but the hypothesized causes include the large shifts out of low-technology industries and basic manufacturing and into professional and business services, a shift that favored college graduates. Some argue that this "industrial restructuring," and the resulting increase in demand for more highly educated workers, has been brought about by the revolution in computer and information technologies (Davis and Haltiwanger 1991; Krueger 1991; Mincer 1991).

Due to large deficits and the globalization of trade, demand for low-skill labor declined as production jobs moved overseas (Borjas, Freeman, and Katz 1992; Murphy and Welch 1992). Katz and Murphy (1992) have shown that effects of international trade were quite modest until substantial trade deficits developed in the 1980s. Adverse effects were concentrated among high school dropouts, and were larger for female dropouts (who tended to work in textiles) than for males, who were more often affected by domestic between-sector shifts (out of manufacturing and into service).

Others have investigated the decline in unions, erosion in the real value of the minimum wage, and supply factors such as the slower growth in college graduates in the 1980s than in the 1970s (Blackburn et al. 1991; Katz and Murphy 1992). A large part of the shift in earnings inequality is due to the increase in wage inequality among workers of the same age and educational attainment, an increase that is not well understood (Levy and Murnane 1992).

To summarize, the poverty of children continues to be affected by macroeconomic conditions in the United States and, increasingly, in the world economy, but the connection is mediated by an ever-more complex set of factors. Economic conditions interact directly and indirectly with decisions about family formation and dissolution, decisions that have been extremely important in moving children into and out of poverty. Economic growth remains a necessary condition for poverty reduction, but during the 1980s, it became less sufficient, in and of itself, to keep children out of poverty.

CHANGING FAMILY STRUCTURE

One of the most significant changes affecting the well-being of children over the past few decades has been the increase in single-parent families. Children are raised in families, and provision for their material needs comes via the adults who assume responsibility for them. Family structure has changed dramatically in recent years, with more children born out-of wedlock and many experiencing the dissolution of their parents' marriage. An increasing proportion of children spend all or part of childhood living with only one parent, usually their mother.

Between 1960 and 1991, the proportion of children living in mother-only families increased from 8 percent to 26 percent (Bianchi 1990: table 1; Census Bureau 1992b: table F). The rise among black children living in mother-only families was much more pronounced than for white children (Bianchi 1990 and forthcoming; Cherlin 1992; Farley and Bianchi 1991). By 1991, 54 percent of black compared with 17 percent of white children lived only with their mother (Census Bureau 1992b: table F).

Perhaps as important as the overall rise in mother-only families was the shift in marital status of single mothers. Between 1960 and 1990, the proportion of female family householders who had never married rose from 4 percent to 28 percent. In 1990, almost one-half of black single mothers had never married, a 37 percentage point increase from 1960, when 12 percent of black-mother-only families were maintained by a never-married mother (Bianchi, forthcoming: table 2).

The overall growth in single-parent families, which was extremely rapid during the 1960s and 1970s, slowed considerably during the 1980s. Prior to the early 1980s, at least among whites, the increase in divorce was the primary reason so many more children resided in mother-only families for at least part of childhood (Wojtkiewicz, McLanahan, and Garfinkel 1990: table 3). The divorce rate peaked in 1981 and had declined by 8 percent by 1991 (National Center for Health Statistics 1992: 4). As shown in table 4.1, the proportion of all children in mother-only families who live with a divorced parent declined from 41 percent to 36 percent between 1983 and 1992, although the number of such children continued to increase (by around 300,000).[5]

By 1992, there were almost as many children living with a never-married mother (5.4 million, see table 4.1) as with a divorced mother

Table 4.1 CHILDREN IN MOTHER-ONLY FAMILIES BY MARITAL STATUS OF MOTHER: UNITED STATES, 1983–92 (numbers in thousands)

	Number			Percentage Distribution		
	1983	1992	Change	1983	1992	Change
Total Children < Age 18						
Mother-only, total	12,739	15,396	2,657	100.0	100.0	100.0
Never married	3,212	5,410	2,198	25.2	35.1	82.7
Divorced	5,190	5,507	317	40.7	35.8	11.9
Separated	2,951	3,258	307	23.2	21.2	11.6
Widowed	1,004	688	− 316	7.9	4.5	− 11.9
Other spouse absent	383	533	150	3.0	3.5	5.6
White Children < Age 18						
Mother-only, total	7,616	9,250	1,634	100.0	100.0	100.0
Never married	958	2,016	1,058	12.6	21.8	64.7
Divorced	3,984	4,266	282	52.3	46.1	17.3
Separated	1,715	2,108	393	22.5	22.8	24.1
Widowed	687	503	− 184	9.0	5.4	− 11.3
Other spouse absent	271	357	86	3.6	3.9	5.3
Black Children < Age 18						
Mother-only, total	4,789	5,607	818	100.0	100.0	100.0
Never married	2,203	3,192	989	46.0	56.9	120.9
Divorced	1,062	1,040	− 22	22.2	18.5	− 2.7
Separated	1,184	1,091	− 93	24.7	19.5	− 11.4
Widowed	258	156	− 102	5.4	2.8	− 12.5
Other spouse absent	83	127	44	1.7	2.3	5.4
Hispanic Children < Age 18						
Mother-only, total	1,475	2,168	693	100.0	100.0	100.0
Never married	357	757	400	24.2	34.9	57.7
Divorced	443	633	190	30.0	29.2	27.4
Separated	460	556	96	31.2	25.6	13.9
Widowed	128	104	− 24	8.7	4.8	− 3.5
Other spouse absent	87	118	31	5.9	5.4	4.5

Source: Census Bureau (1984: table 5; 1993: table 5).

(5.5 million). Fifty-seven percent of black children in mother-only families lived with a mother who had never married, compared with 35 percent of Hispanic and 22 percent of white children. Among all race-ethnic groups, the increase in children with a never-married mother accounted for the majority of the net increase in single-parent living during the 1980s. Between 1983 and 1992, the net increase of 2.2 million children living with a never-married mother was 83 percent as large as the overall increase of 2.7 million children in mother-only families (table 4.1).

Table 4.2 affords a comparison of the economic situation of

Table 4.2 SELECTED DEMOGRAPHIC AND SOCIOECONOMIC DIFFERENCES
AMONG CHILDREN LIVING WITH A DIVORCED, SEPARATED, OR
NEVER-MARRIED MOTHER

	Divorced	Separated	Never Married
Age of Mother			
Percentage under age 25	3.6	9.3	30.1
Median age	36.0	34.0	28.5
Education of Mother			
Percentage high school graduates	81.7	66.4	59.1
Percentage college graduates	12.6	7.0	2.9
Employment/Income of Mother			
Percentage with employed mother	68.9	47.2	37.6
Median family income (1991 dollars)	17,503	10,053	8,609
Percentage below poverty in 1991	36.6	64.3	66.1
Child Support in 1989			
1. Percentage of mothers with award	76.8	47.9	23.9
2. Percentage with award who received in 1989	77.0	79.7	73.2
3. Percentage receiving [1. times 2.]	59.1	38.2	17.5
Mean annual amount per recipient ($)	3,322	3,060	1,888

Source: Census Bureau (1993: table 6; 1991a: table C).
Notes: "Separated" includes a small number of women with spouse absent for reasons other than marital discord. Age, education, and employment status of mother are as of March 1992. The denominator for the percentage in 2. under "Child Support in 1989" is those who have an award (or agreement) and were supposed to receive support in 1989.

children with never-married, divorced, and separated mothers. Never-married mothers are young: 30 percent of children with a never-married mother live with a parent under age 25 compared with 9 percent of those with a separated parent and 4 percent of those with a divorced mother.

Never-married mothers are also less well-educated than divorced mothers because unmarried childbearing often occurs before young women finish school (Hofferth and Moore 1979). Only 59 percent of children with a never-married mother live with a high school graduate, compared with 82 percent of those with a divorced mother. Consequently, only 38 percent of children with a never-married mother live with a parent who is employed, compared with 69 percent of those with a divorced mother (table 4.2). The end result is that the median income provided to children in never-married mother-child families is one-half that provided to children living with a divorced mother. Two-thirds of children with a never-married mother live in poverty.

In addition to their own low levels of educational attainment and unemployment, never-married mothers' ability to garner income from the fathers of their children is much lower than among women who are formerly married. According to April 1989 Current Population Survey data shown in table 4.2, only about one-quarter of never-married mothers with own children under 21 have an agreement or court award of child support from the absent father, compared with about one-half of separated mothers and three-quarters of divorced mothers. Approximately 18 percent of never-married mothers with a co-resident child under age 21 received at least some child support income in 1989, compared with 38 percent of separated mothers and 59 percent of divorced mothers (table 4.2).[6] The average annual amount of child support received by never-married mothers was considerably lower than for divorced or separated mothers who received support (table 4.2) (Census Bureau 1991a: table C). This in part reflects the lower economic status—and resulting inability to provide (adequate) financial support to children—of the fathers of children with never-married mothers as compared with divorced mothers.

Most would agree that the growth in mother-child families is related to poverty among children because children in these households enjoy dramatically less financial security, on average, than children who live with two parents. If the proportion of children in mother-only families had remained constant after 1960, other things being equal, poverty would have been lower by the late 1980s than it actually was (Eggebeen and Lichter 1991; Hernandez 1993; Lichter and Eggebeen 1993; McNeil 1992; Ryscavage, Green, and Welniak 1992).

But how important was the growth in mother-child families in explaining the high incidence of childhood poverty during the 1980s? Economic analyses have tended to discount the role of shifts in family structure (Blank 1991: table 9; Cutler and Katz 1992: table 4). In the late 1970s and early 1980s poverty among children in two-parent families also began to increase because of the decline in earnings of the primary earner (usually the father in two-parent households) (Bane and Ellwood 1989; Fuchs and Reklis 1992).

Estimates of the significance of shifting family structure for child poverty have been derived by demographers who asked: What if the distribution of children across family types was unchanged between two points? How many fewer (or more) children would be in poverty at any given point in time? Eggebeen and Lichter (1991) have suggested that one-half of the increase in the number of children in poverty between 1979 and 1988 can be attributed to a shift in family structure. Hernandez's (1993) recalculation of the figures used by Eggebeen and Lichter suggests that the estimate of one-half is probably too high, but that perhaps one-quarter to one-third fewer children might have been in poverty if the distribution across family types had not changed during the 1980s. Ryscavage and colleagues (1992) showed that shifts in family structure were more important in accounting for income change during the 1970s, but that the movement away from two-parent families continued to exert a downward pressure on family income, it exacerbated income inequality, and it increased poverty (by about 20 percent according to Ryscavage et al.'s estimates) during the 1980s.

Changing family structure during the 1980s was intertwined with increased poverty among children in at least two ways. First, although the *rate* of increase in mother-only families slowed considerably during the 1980s, the number of mother-child families continued to grow (Census Bureau 1992b: table F). In addition, the increase was dominated by the poorest single-parent families, those headed by a never-married mother. Hence, more children started and ended the decade in poor mother-only families (Census Bureau 1992a: table 2; 1992e: table 4; Bianchi 1990: tables 3, 5). Because the upward trend in formation of mother-child families was greater among blacks than whites, the reduction in poverty that might have occurred had family structure remained unchanged was larger for blacks than for whites (Eggebeen and Lichter 1991; McNeil 1992).[7]

The second aspect of the family structure shift was the increasing number of children in households with only one (or no) earner, usually their mother. Since women's earnings continue to be far less than men's, this has contributed to increasing inequality of the primary earner in families with children. Whether this should be considered a family composition effect, or a gender effect, or purely an economic/earnings inequality effect is partly semantics, but the reality for children was that many children moved into the more precarious earnings situation of a one-parent, one-earner family. That one earner was usually female, and in 1989, 45 percent of white, 50 percent of black, and 59 percent of Hispanic working female householders with children under age 18 had earnings below that necessary to lift a family above poverty (Census Bureau 1992g). The increased proportion of children living in families relying on a sole female earner meant significantly more children in poverty by the early 1990s than would otherwise have been the case.

GOVERNMENT INCOME TRANSFERS AND TAXATION

In addition to broad macroeconomic conditions and changing family structure, government transfers and taxes affect the income situation of children's families in absolute terms and relative to households without children. Sawhill (1988), among others, has discussed the role of cash transfers in reducing poverty, and Danziger and Stern (1990) have documented how trends in transfers and taxes have affected children's families.

Most researchers make the distinction between social insurance programs—programs in which the aim "is to prevent poverty by replacing income lost through unemployment, disability, retirement, or death of a family breadwinner"—and public assistance, or means-tested programs—programs in which the purpose "is to assist those who are already poor" (Sawhill 1988: 1098). Major examples of social insurance programs are Social Security, Medicare, and unemployment compensation. Public assistance programs, often referred to as welfare, include cash programs, the most important of which is Aid to Families with Dependent Children (AFDC), and in-kind programs, the largest of which are Medicaid and Food Stamps.

Danziger and Stern (1990) demonstrated that cash transfers per household increased dramatically until the mid-1970s. Growth continued after that, but it was almost all in social insurance programs and not in public assistance programs, the latter of which disproportionately benefit children. "Most of the increased Federal social spending over the past 25 years is accounted for by the expansion and indexation of social security benefits and the introduction and expansion of Medicare, Medicaid, and the Supplemental Security Income program, all of which provide benefits disproportionately to the elderly" (Danziger and Stern 1990: 13). Danziger and Stern noted that between the late 1970s and late 1980s, federal program expenditures targeted on children declined by 4 percent, whereas those for the elderly increased by 52 percent.

Danziger and Weinberg (1992: table 7) assessed the antipoverty impact of government transfers in families with children for the 1967–90 period. Their estimates were derived by subtracting cash public transfers from pretax family income and relating this measure of income to the official poverty thresholds. Currently, about 37 percent of those who would be poor without government transfers are moved above the poverty line by cash transfers.[8] In families with a male breadwinner, most of which are two-parent families, about 13 percent of those poor before social insurance and public assistance cash payments were removed from the official count of the poor by government cash transfers in 1967. This proportion increased to 25 percent in 1973 but subsequently declined to 18 percent in 1990. In 1990, cash social insurance payments were about twice as important as public assistance in removing families with a male breadwinner from poverty, and the official poverty rate was 9.3 percent for these families, about two points lower than it would have been without government cash assistance.

Government transfers removed about 17 percent of mother-only families from poverty in 1967. This proportion increased to 23 percent in 1973 but subsequently declined to only 11 percent in 1990. Social insurance and public assistance payments played an equal role in reducing poverty in these families. In 1990, 48 percent of mother-only families with children were among those counted as poor after government cash transfers, about 6 percentage points lower than if no cash government assistance had been received (Danziger and Weinberg 1992: table 7).

What has happened over time to program benefits for children? Cash public assistance benefits, such as AFDC, were eroded by high inflation during the 1970s. State legislatures, those responsible for setting AFDC benefit levels, failed to index benefits for inflation, so real benefits declined (Danziger and Stern 1990; Moffitt 1992). However, between 1965 and the mid-1970s, total benefits continued to rise dramatically because of the introduction of Medicaid and expansion of the Food Stamp program (Moffitt 1992: figure 1). Public assistance benefits leveled off during the latter 1970s and declined in the 1980s as program rule changes and budget cuts, implemented in the early 1980s under the Reagan administration, made it more difficult for the unemployed to receive unemployment benefits and more difficult for welfare recipients to receive benefits if they worked (Danziger and Stern 1990).

Danziger and Stern (1990) have also pointed out that taxes on a family with income at the poverty line increased between the mid-1970s and 1986, the year in which the Tax Reform Act eliminated federal income taxes for most poor families with children. Even after 1986, however, state taxes continued to reduce the disposable income of many working poor families, and Social Security (payroll) taxes rose throughout the 1980s.

FACTORS THAT DECREASED CHILDHOOD POVERTY

Not all changes have been in the direction of increasing poverty among children. At least three factors have worked to mediate growing earnings inequality, changing family structure, and declining public assistance.

First, the average number of children per family has declined. Both mother-only and two-parent families now have fewer children, on average, than two decades ago (Bianchi 1990: table 5). Hence, after adjusting for inflation, a given family income goes to support fewer children in the 1990s than in earlier decades, and the per capita well-being of children has been enhanced because of this.

Second, rising parental educational attainment is a positive trend for children because more-educated parents are, on average, better able to provide an adequate family income. Between 1970 and 1990, the percentage of children who lived with a parent who had completed college increased from 15 to 24 percent (Bianchi 1990: table 5; Census Bureau 1992a: table 6). The average educational level of parents in both single-parent and two-parent families improved (Bianchi 1990: table 5).

The percentage of children with a parent who was a high school graduate increased even more dramatically, from 62 percent to 83 percent between 1970 and 1990 (Bianchi 1990: table 5; Census Bureau 1992a: table 6). Unfortunately, however, as mentioned earlier, as the high school graduation rate of parents increased, the ability of that high school diploma to ensure a life above poverty for children was diminishing in the 1980s. The proportion of high school graduates, working full time, year-round, who had annual earnings *below* the poverty level for a family of four increased from 13 percent to 22 percent between 1979 and 1989 (U.S. Bureau of the Census 1992g: table F).

The increased likelihood that a child's mother will work outside the home is a third factor that has improved the income situation of children. Of course, this trend may mean greater opportunity for single parenting, and employment outside the home may take mothers away from providing care for their own children. But there is little question that the dramatic increase in employed mothers has enhanced the money income available to children, particularly in two-parent families (Bianchi 1990; Bianchi and Spain 1986; Macunovich and Easterlin 1990).

For children in married-couple families, the rapid increase in labor force participation of wives has helped to counterbalance the lack of wage growth of husbands. Hernandez (1993) has examined the role of mother's income in reducing poverty during the 1939 to 1988 period. He calculated a poverty rate for two-parent families with mother's earnings subtracted from family income and then compared this hypothetical with the actual poverty rate to estimate the effect of mothers' earnings on the poverty situation of children. He concluded that the increase in income from children's mothers sped the poverty decline until 1969 and then slowed the subsequent increase by offsetting about two-thirds of the decline in income that fathers were able to provide in two-parent families.

These "good news" factors for children have been more than offset, however, by poverty-enhancing trends. Hernandez (1993: 329) concludes from his analysis of the 1939–88 period that changes in "available fathers' income can account for much of the post-Depression decline and subsequent increase in childhood relative poverty." The decline in "available fathers' income" has two aspects. One aspect is the decline in real wages of less-educated fathers and the declining ability of a father's income alone to keep children in two-parent families out of poverty. The other aspect is the disappearance altogether of a father's income from a growing proportion of children's families. The growth in mother-child families has resulted in more children without adequate support. Absent fathers do not always support their children, government transfers fail to lift these children out of poverty, and the composition of poor mothers has shifted toward young, never-married mothers who have limited access to support from absent fathers and face a job market increasingly unfavorable to the unskilled.

URBAN GHETTO POVERTY AND THE RURAL POOR

Much of the discussion of poverty in recent years has focused on the urban underclass, or inner-city ghetto poverty areas. The U.S. population is an urbanized population, and the majority of the poor (75 percent in 1991) live in metropolitan areas (Census Bureau 1992e: xiii). Only a minority of the poor in urban areas are concentrated in inner-city areas, but the urban poor did seem to become more geographically concentrated in the 1970s. There is also preliminary evidence that this trend continued, and perhaps even accelerated, in the 1980s (Mincy, Sawhill, and Wolfe 1990; Ricketts and Sawhill 1988).

Among the ghetto poor, racial and ethnic residential segregation constrains economic opportunity (Massey 1990; Massey and Eggers 1990; Massey, Gross, and Eggers 1991; Wilson 1987). A constellation of risk factors is detrimental to the life chances of children growing up in the ghetto—low income, family disruption, poor schools, drugs, crime, and lack of adequate medical attention.

Excessive attention focused on the "urban underclass" or "ghetto poor" may have produced an urban bias in research and policy discussions on poverty, however (O'Hare 1988; O'Hare and Curry-White 1992). Poverty rates for children living in nonmetropolitan areas are higher than for children in metropolitan areas (though not higher than for children in central cities of metropolitan areas) (Rogers 1991). The factors implicated in rural poverty are somewhat different than for the urban inner-city poor. For example, poor rural children are more often living in two-parent families, and their use of welfare, such as AFDC, is lower than in urban poverty ghettos (Jensen 1989).

The lack of jobs with wage rates high enough to keep a family out of poverty is a major problem for both the concentrated poor in large cities and the dispersed poor in less-urban settings. Both populations also lack the education and skills necessary to compete for jobs that might provide financial security (Jensen and McLaughlin 1992; Wilson 1987). And, although living in a mother-only family is less common for children in nonmetropolitan than metropolitan areas, the percentage is increasing (Rogers 1991). Hence, it is not only the wage-earning difficulties of fathers but also of mothers, in particular single mothers, that adversely affects child well-being in both rural and urban settings.

ANTIPOVERTY PROGRAMS: CAUSE OR CURE OF POVERTY?

To some extent, the United States does not have any explicit antipoverty policy. The government has an official poverty threshold and a number of means-tested programs that come under the general umbrella term *welfare*, but there is no explicit policy that all persons, or all children, should be assisted when family income is below the official standard. Hence, some who are not defined as poor by the official measure, which relies on annual pretax income, meet the eligibility criteria for specific programs—for example, Food Stamps.

Conversely, and more frequently, many who receive welfare support such as AFDC have income that remains below the poverty level even after the addition of government assistance.

The conservative critique of the welfare system, exemplified by Charles Murray's (1984) Losing Ground: American Social Policy, 1950–1980, argues that the availability of welfare breeds dependency, discourages fathers from financially supporting their children, and fosters marital breakup and out-of-wedlock childbearing, all of which have generated more poverty among children. In this view, the very programs set up to alleviate poverty cause more, not less, poverty, because they undermine the two-parent family in which mothers and fathers take responsibility for nurturing and providing for their children.

The liberal response (Wilson 1987) has been to focus on economic opportunity and income inequality as the root problems. The argument here is that there are more mother-child families today, as well as less financial support from children's absent fathers, because poor economic conditions for those at the bottom of the income distribution have undermined fathers' ability to support their children and have increased marital disruption or discouraged marriage altogether, particularly among blacks. In this view, poverty breeds family disruption, and the welfare system has been a bit player in the larger drama of economic restructuring, regressive payroll taxes and tax breaks for the rich, and massive trade and budget deficits that have hurt the American working and middle classes and have led to the formation of more mother-child families and, in turn, more poverty.

Before effective policies to assist children in poverty can be designed, the question of whether the current welfare system has caused the breakup of the family must be addressed. A growing body of research indicates that the availability of welfare may have been a factor influencing the growth in mother-only families, but that the "welfare effect" cannot account for most of the growth in mother-child families during the past few decades (Garfinkel and McLanahan 1986; Hernandez 1993; Moffitt 1992; Sawhill 1988).

First, the increase in single parenting was widespread, not just a trend among lower-income individuals. Hence, it is hard to argue that welfare was a primary motivation for the increase in mother-only families (Garfinkel and McLanahan 1986). Second, the time interval that provides most of the evidence for lay discussions of welfare causing family breakup is the 1965 to 1975 period when real welfare benefits (AFDC plus Food Stamps and Medicaid) available to single-parent families rose dramatically, coinciding with a dramatic rise in the number of mother-only families (Moffitt 1992: figure 1). However, real benefits leveled off in the latter part of the 1970s and declined in the 1980s as the number of mother-child families continued to increase, albeit at a slower rate than previously.

Moffitt (1992:31) noted that no study has found welfare effects large enough to explain the rapid increase in mother-child families in the 1960s and early 1970s. Garfinkel and McLanahan (1986) reviewed several studies of the effect of AFDC on the increased prevalence of mother-child families and reported that the "welfare effect" that can be derived from reputable studies ranges from negative (Minarik and Goldfarb 1976) to zero (Cutright and Scanzoni 1973; Honig 1973: 1970 estimates) to a high of 42 percent among blacks (Honig 1973: 1960 estimates). Relying on the studies they consider most comprehensive and methodologically sophisticated (Ellwood and Bane 1985; Danziger et al. 1982), Garfinkel and McLanahan (1986) estimated that the increase in government benefits may have led to a 9–14 percent increase in mother-child families between 1960 and 1975.

Studies suggest that welfare may impede remarriage and foster marital breakup, but that the effect is modest (Danziger et al. 1982; Ellwood and Bane 1985; Hoffman and Duncan 1988; Moffitt 1990; see Moffitt 1992 and Sawhill 1988 for reviews of this literature). Evidence supporting the assertion that welfare increases out-of-wedlock childbearing remains mixed and unconvincing (Duncan and Hoffman 1990; Ellwood and Bane 1985; Moore and Caldwell 1976, 1977; Plotnick 1990), but welfare availability does appear to result in somewhat more independent household formation once an out-of-wedlock birth occurs (Ellwood and Bane 1985; Hutchens, Jakubson, and Schwartz 1989).

A second related issue is whether the availability of welfare has eroded the work ethic of the poor. Does the availability of welfare discourage labor force participation? Research conducted prior to 1980 and reviewed in Danziger, Haveman, and Plotnick (1981) provided evidence that the AFDC program did discourage work among participants. As Moffitt (1992: 56) noted, this was "not surprising given that the average benefit is approximately equal to the earnings a woman would receive if she worked full-time at a minimum wage job."

However, there is little evidence that single mothers who are ineligible for AFDC because their income is too high subsequently lower the amount they work to meet AFDC program requirements (Moffitt 1992: 17). Also, female labor supply is not easily influenced up or down by program changes. For example, adjusting benefit levels or benefit reduction rates (the amount the AFDC benefit is reduced for each dollar earned) affects work effort of single mothers a little, but not significantly.

There has been relatively little empirical research on the potential work disincentives associated with in-kind programs such as Food Stamps or Medicaid. There is the presumption that loss of health benefits under Medicaid, for example, offers a strong disincentive to exit welfare for work. To date, the research findings are mixed. Blank (1989) found no effect of state variation in Medicaid benefits on AFDC participation, Winkler (1991) found Medicaid to have a disincentive on female labor supply, and Moffitt and Wolfe (1992) found that Medicaid benefits significantly reduced employment rates and increased AFDC participation but that the relationship depended upon the health status of family members.

What has been the role of welfare, if any, in discouraging fathers from financially supporting their children? Is an unmarried or divorced father's sense of financial obligation to his children—indeed, perhaps his determination to work at all or to work enough to earn a living that would support not only himself but dependents—undermined by his knowledge that his children can receive at least a minimal level of support through the welfare system? There is not much research on this topic, in part because the connection between welfare and male labor force behavior is difficult to make empirically, and hence, difficult to study. Some would point to the increase in nonparticipation of young males in the labor force, particularly among young, less-educated black males, as support for this welfare effect. However, as with increased mother-child families and welfare, is it availability of welfare that is causing young fathers not to work, marry, and support their children or is it the inability of these young men to find jobs offering a wage high enough to make them feel able to marry and to be viewed as desirable marriage partners by the mother of their children?

Studies to date have tied only a fraction of the secular decline in black marriage rates to the declining labor market status of black men (Hoffman, Duncan, and Mincy 1991; Mare and Winship 1991). If a welfare effect could be shown, as with the determinants of the increase in mother-only families, it would likely account for only a small part of the failure of fathers to support children in poverty. The reality (as shown earlier in table 4.2) is that many fathers, not just fathers of poor children, are not very responsive to the financial needs of their children when they no longer (or never did) reside with them (Census Bureau 1991a; Hill 1992; Seltzer 1991; Teachman 1991).

Finally, what do we know about long-term welfare dependency and intergenerational transmission of characteristics that make the next generation likely to be dependent on welfare? Gottschalk, McLanahan, and Sandefur (1992: 13) have provided evidence that the majority of welfare spells are short, lasting less than two years, and that "only a small percentage of children grow up in a family that is persistently poor or dependent on welfare for extended periods of time."[9] Further, only a small percentage of the small group of individuals exposed to persistent poverty and welfare dependence as children become persistently poor or welfare dependent as adults, which suggests that poverty and welfare dependence are not frequently passed on from one generation to the next. Hence, although there may be a causal relationship between welfare and dependency, no research to date convincingly shows that effect to be large.

CHALLENGES FOR PUBLIC POLICY

Achieving an understanding of the causes of poverty is obviously not easy, and translating such insight into programs that alleviate poverty is a large additional step. One lesson learned over the years is the need to carefully consider possible negative or unintended consequences of direct policy intervention, such as the apparent work disincentive of AFDC, while also paying attention to the indirect consequences for the poor of policies, such as tax policies, in which the primary aim is something other than alleviating poverty.

What has existed in the United States, at least since the depression and, some would argue, since the founding of this nation, is national sentiment in favor of the "deserving poor"; that is, that those who "through no fault of their own" fall on hard times should have assistance in getting on their feet again. Thus, social insurance should exist so that a worker who loses a job when his plant closes is able to keep feeding his family while he looks for another job. Similarly, surviving spouses and their dependents should not be left destitute when a breadwinner dies. And elderly adults who have been productive citizens throughout their lives should not have to live in poverty during old age.

Over time, however, skepticism has grown as to just how "deserving" many of those receiving public assistance really are. Most would classify children as among the "deserving poor," since their economic circumstances are not of their own doing. But there is growing concern that some of the adults upon whom poor children depend are not so "deserving." Growth in welfare caseloads, economic conditions, and the political climate have all contributed to the skepticism about the efficacy of welfare.

For example, the AFDC caseload increased dramatically (270 percent) between 1965 and 1985, and expenditures, particularly for programs initiated or expanded in the 1960s, skyrocketed (U.S. Social Security Administration 1966, 1988, cited in Moffitt 1992: table 1 and figure 1). As noted in the previous section, the task of disentangling cause and effect in the growth of welfare caseloads and expenditures has engendered intense debate.

At the same time, family income inequality has grown, the wage-earning capacity of less-skilled workers has deteriorated, and taxation on wages has increased, all of which have led to a growing sense on the part of those in the middle of the income distribution that they must work harder and harder just to stay in place (Levy 1987). So long as the economy was expanding and the average well-being of the population was improving, as it was during the 1960s, less concern about those receiving welfare was evident. But once productivity slowed, wages stagnated, and family incomes were maintained or increased only by more work effort on the part of wives, generosity to the poor seemed to many to be unfair and unnecessary.

It is against this backdrop—skepticism about welfare and a feeling on the part of the nonpoor of being squeezed economically—that proposals for how best to alleviate the current and future situation of poor children will be evaluated. Add to this the fact that the United States has a massive federal deficit, the reduction of which many feel should be the number one national priority, and it is clear that moving forward on the many fronts that are needed to assist poor children will not be easy.

What emerges from the discussion of causes of poverty is that the first, and foremost, need of poor children is to have parents—fathers and mothers—whose jobs earn them enough to keep their families above poverty. Failure to achieve this will mean that our nation's children remain in grave jeopardy. The need for jobs was recognized both in the Clinton administration's economic stimulus package and in the longer-term investment proposals put before Congress in February 1993 (Clinton 1993), but there continues to be disagreement as to what the United States can afford, given the federal deficit, and what mix of private and public investment will yield the most jobs for U.S. workers.

To date, much attention has been given to the declining wage-earning potential of men, but gender inequality in wage-earning capacity is equally as deserving of our focus. Ideally, children should be supported by both parents. When they are not, it seems reasonable to direct attention to enhancing the earnings capacity of the parent (or parent surrogate) who is supporting and caring for them. Increasingly, children are being supported solely by their mothers, and one way to help these children is to assist their mothers in the labor market.

Of course, policies that enhance the wage-earning capabilities of women may have the consequence of creating yet more single-parent families. Gender equality in the market would, if anything, make women more economically independent. In fact, gains by women in the labor force have occurred along with the increase in independent living and marital breakup (Bianchi and Spain 1986; Cherlin 1992). As with the availability of welfare, market equality would make a choice to raise children without the assistance of the father less difficult.

An additional way to assist children whose parents are attempting to support them through work but who have low earnings is to use the tax system to provide relief. For example, the Earned Income Tax Credit (EITC), a refundable tax credit targeted on low-income families with children, is an income-support measure that is not "antiwork" and is available to two-parent as well as single-parent families with low earnings. The EITC has been effective in alleviating the economic hardship of the poor (Danziger and Stern 1990; McLanahan and Garfinkel 1992; Sawhill 1992). The presumption is that expanding the program would do even more to eliminate poverty, and indeed, the broad outline of the welfare reform plan of the Clinton administration includes expansion of the EITC as one of the components (Clinton 1993).

In addition, Danziger and Stern (1990) have advocated raising the Dependent Care Credit—the tax credit for child care expenses of working parents—and making it refundable like the EITC. This would assist working-poor, two-parent families as well as single-parent families. If the credit were more appropriately targeted on low-income families, a refundable credit might be paid for by phasing out the credit at higher-income levels. Currently, all households with children of working parents are eligible for the Dependent Care Credit.

Over the longer term, upgrading of the educational attainment and job skills of parents, particularly young parents, is needed. Increasingly, those at the bottom of the income distribution are there because they do not have the skills to get and keep a job that pays enough to keep them and their dependents out of poverty. Given the need to ensure that young adults have the requisite skills to secure good jobs, the increase in family formation among young, never-married women complicates an already difficult situation. To move these women toward self-sufficiency, it is no longer enough to concentrate solely on education and training. A young mother needs child care to be able to obtain skills, find a job, and hold that job.

There is increasing recognition that the availability and cost of child care constrain market work, particularly for single mothers. The Family Support Act of 1988 provides for increased federal spending for job training and day care but also relies heavily on states to cover the costs of these services (McLanahan and Garfinkel 1992). Effective welfare-to-work programs are expensive to initiate and sustain. And unless the transition to work leads to a job that pays relatively well, partial reliance on public support must continue if there is to be any reduction in poverty.

In addition to jobs and job training for their parents, a second approach to improving the well-being of children is to better ensure that they are supported by both parents, regardless of the marital decisions their parents make. The child support issue is a complex one, however. Better child support enforcement has widespread support because it seems, a priori, well directed toward requiring absent parents to provide economic support for their own children. But Moffitt (1992) has pointed out that increasing child support, especially if a percentage of an absent parent's income is assessed and collected, may have the unintended consequence of reducing the labor force participation of the absent parent. This may not be a large problem, given recent evidence from the Wisconsin child support demonstration project that an absent father's income tends to rise substantially in the years following separation from his child (Phillips and Garfinkel 1992). But it serves as a reminder that seemingly optimal solutions to the problem of child poverty can have unintended consequences that subvert the original goal of legislation or policy changes.

The Family Support Act of 1988 includes provisions to facilitate the establishment of paternity and improve collection of child support from absent fathers. The Clinton administration's welfare reform proposals also include provisions to strengthen the child support collection system (Clinton 1993).[10] However, the United States has no minimum child support guarantee for children living with one parent (Danziger and Stern 1990), and existing research shows that a sizable group of poor children will not be reached even with better child support enforcement (Hill 1992). In the absence of a minimum child support assurance, many nonpoor children may be helped dramatically, but the benefit to children at the bottom of the income distribution may be much more modest (Garfinkel 1992). Child support enforcement alone will be far from sufficient to ensure adequate income in poor single-parent families.

A third approach for helping improve the material condition of poor children is through programs targeted on specific health and educational outcomes. For example, the Special Supplemental Food Program for Women, Infants, and Children (WIC), which provides nutritional assistance to poor pregnant mothers and young children, has been shown to be cost-effective but serves only 40 percent of the eligible (Danziger and Stern 1990; Sawhill 1992). It has been argued that expanding coverage and funding for such programs, and for immunizations and preventive health care for young children, would be a particularly cost-effective use of the public dollar (Klerman 1991; Sawhill 1992). President Clinton's budget and economic plan, submitted to Congress in February 1993, proposed new funding for childhood immunizations and WIC and set a goal of full funding for the WIC program by 1996 (Clinton 1993).

There is also recognition of the need for pregnancy prevention and better access to family planning services for teens, a group with high levels of unintended childbearing. This seems particularly important, given the increase in family formation among young, never-married mothers. One suggestion has been to increase funding of school- or community-based services. However, opposition to such proposals is substantial because it is feared that such programs undermine the family and impart knowledge that increases early sexual activity. In the end the threat of AIDS may do more to garner support for such interventions than arguments about improving the well-being of U.S. youth.

Finally, although it is questionable whether positive effects can be sustained without follow-up in later years, there is widespread agreement that early childhood educational programs, such as Head Start, help poor children. Sawhill (1992) and Danziger and Stern (1990) have argued that Head Start, which serves about 30 percent of the eligible, should be expanded to serve all eligible children and should be made full-day, year-round programs to help working parents. The Clinton administration's long-term investment plan includes increased funding for Head Start, with the goal of sufficient funding to serve all eligible children by 1999. Also included are requests for funding for meals and medical coverage of enrolled children (Clinton 1993). In addition, Sawhill (forthcoming) has argued that improving teacher quality, increasing parental involvement, and conducting follow-up studies after children enter elementary school would enhance the effectiveness of the program.

SUMMARY AND CONCLUSION

To summarize the main points of this chapter, the poverty situation of children is affected by macroeconomic conditions, but during the 1980s economic growth did not "trickle down" to the poor to the extent it had during the 1960s. A major culprit in this failure was the increase in earnings inequality, and in particular, the declining ability of young, less-educated parents to earn enough to keep a family above the poverty level. Also, diminished public spending on the poor provided less of a buffer against poverty in the late 1970s and 1980s.

Over the longer term (though perhaps less so in the 1980s), the shift toward more single parenting has been an additional factor that has harmed children financially. A disturbing trend of the 1980s was the increased share of mother-only families headed by a young, less-educated, often unemployed, never-married mother.

The plight of children might have been even worse had not family size continued to decline in the 1970s and 1980s, had not the average educational attainment of parents improved, and had not mothers, especially in two-parent families, gone to work in ever greater numbers in the 1970s and 1980s. Although differences exist in the causes of poverty in rural and urban ghetto areas, the most important factors increasing the poverty of children in both settings are the lack of jobs providing enough earnings to keep a family out of poverty and the lack of education and job skills on the part of young parents.

There is some merit to the argument that the current welfare system is antiwork and that the availability of welfare indirectly causes more poverty by increasing the number of mother-child households. But a review of the existing research literature leads to the conclusion that the availability of welfare cannot explain the majority of the increase in mother-child families, an increase that has occurred throughout the population, not just among the poor. Nor can welfare serve as the explanation for one of the most prominent factors associated with the poverty of children in the 1980s: the declining earnings of the unskilled.

The challenges for public policy are many, especially given the public skepticism about the efficacy of welfare, the economic constraints that affect the nonpoor as well as the poor, and the massive federal deficit. Still, if one accepts that a nation as affluent as the United States should not have one in five children living below the poverty line, and if one accepts that the most basic physical, educational, and social-psychological needs are not being adequately met for a sizable minority of U.S. children, then there is much to be done.

The greatest needs of poor children are, in some sense, the same as those of poor adults. Children need to be able to learn and develop a variety of skills. Children need adequate medical care and health insurance coverage. They need to be cared for and supported by both parents. Finally, and perhaps most important, children need parents who have jobs that can support a family, adequate child care while their parents work, and income support in cases where their parents are disabled or unable to work.

Several of President Clinton's recent proposals indicate that the needs of poor children are beginning to receive public attention (Clinton 1993). There appears to be growing awareness of the dimensions of the task ahead, as well as an appreciation of the need to anticipate the unintended when designing proposals to alleviate child poverty. Liberals as well as conservatives seem increasingly sensitive to the need to bolster, not undermine, individual responsibility and initiative and parental commitment to the rearing of their children.

There are many paths to the same destination, as a recent international analysis of gender inequality in poverty illustrates (Casper, McLanahan, and Garfinkel 1993). Italy has little gender inequality in poverty because of high rates of marital stability, Sweden has taken the path of equalizing work roles of men and women, and Holland and Germany have generous public assurances for all citizens, which creates a floor below which all adults (and children) do not drop. The challenge is to figure out what mix of private incentives and public expenditures best fills the needs of U.S. children. The goal is to determine the level of child well-being for which it is realistic and desirable to strive, given what the United States can and should be able to afford for its citizens, and then to move toward ensuring that level of well-being for all children.

Notes

The comments of several individuals have helped me clarify the points made in this chapter. I wish to thank William Butz, Judith Chafel, Donald Hernandez, Larry Long, Martha Riche, Paul Ryscavage, Kathleen Short, William Scarbrough, Daniel Weinberg, and two anonymous reviewers. Of course, I remain solely responsible for the views expressed. The interpretation of the research on causes of poverty is my own and not that of the U.S. Bureau of the Census.

1. These poverty thresholds were originally developed at the U.S. Social Security Administration (Orshansky 1965) and were last revised in 1981 by an interagency committee (U.S. Bureau of the Census 1992: A-7). They are currently undergoing scrutiny again by a panel of experts convened by the National Academy of Sciences.

2. For a discussion of how the 1939 and 1949 estimates were derived, see Hernandez (1993: chap. 7). Smolensky, Danziger, and Gottschalk (1988) and Ross, Danziger, and Smolensky (1987) derived similar estimates from the 1940 and 1950 Censuses.

3. For an extensive treatment of the shortcomings of the official poverty measure, see Ruggles (1990). For a summary and overview of the measurement issues, see Sawhill (1988: 1075–82).

4. The official poverty rate for the total population reached an all-time low in 1973, but the rate among children reached its lowest point in 1969 (U.S. Bureau of the Census, 1992e: tables 2, 3).

5. The base year of 1983 is used because methodological changes that improved the Census Bureau's count of children with never-married mothers were fully in place by that year. Prior to that time, there was an undercount of children living with their mother when the mother was not living independently. Since the incidence of living with other relatives is higher for never-married than other single parents, prior to 1983 there was a sizable undercount of children living with their never-married mother.

6. These figures are derived by multiplying the percentage of mothers with court awards by the percentage (of those with awards and who were supposed to receive in 1989) who actually received child support income in 1989.

7. The issue of the interrelationship among race, family structure, and poverty is complicated and highly politicized. Much of the debate goes back to the mid-1960s when Daniel Patrick Moynihan (1965) pointed out the large differences in economic well-being between the black and white populations that were in some sense attributable to family structure differences. Although Moynihan cited the lack of employment opportunities for black males as a cause of the racial differences in family structure, for the next 15 years it became virtually taboo to discuss racial differences in family structure as a factor related to racial economic inequality. Owing to the work of black sociologists, in particular William Julius Wilson (1987), it has become more acceptable to address the issue of family structure in discussions of race and poverty, but racial differences in family structure remains a sensitive topic (see Cherlin 1992: chap. 4 for a recent discussion of the issue).

8. If the official poverty rate is adjusted to reflect noncash benefits and taxes, the reduction in pretransfer poor is estimated to be even greater—as much as 44 percent in 1990.

9. From the perspective of the AFDC caseload at any given time, a relatively large number of cases are long-term dependent cases, however (Gottschalk, McLanahan, and Sandefur 1992).

10. Proposals to "toughen child support collection" include: streamlining paternity establishment, collection of "seriously delinquent" accounts by the Internal Revenue Service (IRS), a national registry to track "deadbeat" parents, requiring employees to report child support obligations on IRS W-4 forms, and increasing absent parents' support for the medical care of their children (Clinton 1993: 101).

References

Acs, Gregory, and Sheldon Danziger. 1990. "Educational Attainment, Industrial Structure, and Male Earnings, 1973–87." Population Studies Center Research Report 90-189. Ann Arbor, Mich.: University of Michigan.

Bane, Mary Jo, and David Ellwood. 1989. "One Fifth of the Nation's Children: Why Are They Poor?" *Science* 245 (Sept. 8): 1047–1053.

Bianchi, Suzanne M. 1990. "America's Children: Mixed Prospects." *Population Bulletin* 45 (1). Washington, D.C.: U.S. Government Printing Office.

————. Forthcoming. "The Changing Demographic and Socioeconomic Character of Single-Parent Families." *Marriage and Family Review* 22 (1/2, Spring/Summer).

Bianchi, Suzanne M., and Daphne Spain. 1986. *American Women in Transition.* New York: Russell Sage.

Blackburn, McKinley L., David E. Bloom, and Richard B. Freeman. 1991. "Changes in Earnings Differentials in the 1980s: Concordance, Convergence, Causes, and Consequences." NBER Working Paper 3901. Cambridge, Mass.: National Bureau of Economic Research.

Blank, Rebecca M. 1989. "The Effect of Medical Need and Medicaid on AFDC Participation." *Journal of Human Resources* 24 (1, Winter): 54–87.

————. 1991. "Why Were Poverty Rates So High in the 1980s?" NBER Working Paper 3878. Cambridge, Mass.: National Bureau of Economic Research.

Borjas, George, Jr., Richard B. Freeman, and Lawrence F. Katz. 1992. "On the Labor Market Effects of Immigration and Trade." In *The Economic Effects of Immigration in Source and Receiving Countries,* edited by George Borjas and Richard Freedman. Chicago: University of Chicago Press.

Bound, John, and Harry J. Holzer. 1991. "Industrial Shifts, Skill Levels, and the Labor Market for White and Black Males." Population Studies Center Research Report 91-211. Ann Arbor, Mich.: University of Michigan.

Bound, John, and George Johnson. 1992. "Changes in the Structure of Wages during the 1980s: An Evaluation of Alternative Explanations." *American Economic Review,* 82 (3 June): 371–392.

Casper, Lynne M., Sara McLanahan, and Irwin Garfinkel. 1993. "The Gender Poverty Gap: What Can We Learn from Other Countries?" Paper presented at annual meeting of the Population Association of America, Cincinnati, Apr. 1–3.

Census Bureau. See U.S. Bureau of the Census.

Cherlin, Andrew. 1992. Marriage, Divorce, Remarriage, revised and expanded ed. Cambridge, Mass.: Harvard University Press.

Clinton, William. 1993. A Vision of Change for America. Address to the Joint Sessions of Congress, February 17. Washington, D.C.: U.S. Government Printing Office.

Cutler, David M., and Lawrence F. Katz. 1991. "Macroeconomic Performance and the Disadvantaged." Brookings Papers on Economic Activity, no. 2 (1–74). Washington, D.C.: Brookings Institution.

Cutright, Phillips, and John Scanzoni. 1973. "Income Supplements and the American Family." In Studies in Public Welfare, Joint Economic Committee, Paper 12 (45–49). Washington, D.C.: U.S. Government Printing Office.

Danziger, Sheldon, and Jonathan Stern. 1990. "The Causes and Consequences of Child Poverty in the United States." Innocenti Occasional Papers, Number 10. Florence: UNICEF International Child Development Centre, November.

Danziger, Sheldon H., and Daniel H. Weinberg. 1992. "Market Income, Income Transfers, and the Trend in Poverty." IRP Conference Paper, "Poverty and Public Policy: What Do We Know? What Should We Do?" Madison: University of Wisconsin, Institute for Research on Poverty.

Danziger, Sheldon, Robert Haveman, and Robert Plotnick. 1981. "How Income Transfers Affect Work, Savings, and the Income Distribution: A Critical Review." Journal of Economic Literature 19 (3, Sept.): 975–1028.

Danziger, Sheldon, George Jakubsen, Saul Schwartz, and Eugene Smolensky. 1982. "Work and Welfare as Determinants of Female Poverty and Household Headship." Quarterly Journal of Economics 97 (3, August): 519–34.

Davis, Steven J., and John Haltiwanger. 1991. "Wage Dispersion between and within U.S. Manufacturing Plants, 1963–87." Brookings Papers on Economic Activity: Microeconomics (115–80). Washington, D.C.: Brookings Institution.

Duncan, Greg J., and Saul Hoffman. 1990. "Welfare Benefits, Economic Opportunities, and Out-of-Wedlock Births among Black Teenage Girls." Demography 27 (4, November): 519–35.

Duncan, Greg J., and Willard Rodgers. 1991. "Has Children's Poverty Become More Persistent?" American Sociological Review 56 (August): 538–50.

Eggebeen, David J., and Daniel T. Lichter. 1991. "Race, Family Structure, and Changing Poverty among American Children." American Sociological Review 56 (December): 801–17.

Ellwood, David T., and Mary Jo Bane. 1985. "The Impact of AFDC on Family Structure and Living Arrangements." In *Research in Labor Economics*, vol. 7, edited by Ronald Ehrenberg. Greenwich, Conn.: JAI Press.

Ellwood, David T., and Lawrence H. Summers. 1986. "Poverty in America: Is Welfare the Answer or the Problem?" In *Fighting Poverty*, edited by Sheldon H. Danziger and Daniel H. Weinberg (78–105). Cambridge, Mass.: Harvard University Press.

Farley, Reynolds, and Suzanne M. Bianchi. 1991. "The Growing Racial Difference in Marriage and Family Patterns." In *The Black Family: Essays and Studies*, 4th ed., edited by Robert Staples. Belmont, Calif.: Wadsworth.

Fuchs, Victor R., and Diane M. Reklis. 1992. "America's Children: Economic Perspectives and Policy Options." *Science* 255 (January 3): 41–46.

Garfinkel, Irwin. 1992. *Assuring Child Support*. New York: Russell Sage.

Garfinkel, Irwin, and Sara McLanahan. 1986. *Single Mothers and Their Children*. Washington, D.C.: Urban Institute Press.

Gottschalk, Peter, Sara McLanahan, and Gary Sandefur. 1992. "The Dynamics and Intergenerational Transmission of Poverty and Welfare Dependence." IRP Conference Paper for "Poverty and Public Policy: What Do We Know? What Should We Do?" Madison: University of Wisconsin, Institute for Research on Poverty.

Hernandez, Donald J. 1993. *America's Children: Resources from Family, Government, and the Economy*. New York: Russell Sage.

Hill, Martha S. 1992. "The Role of Economic Resources and Remarriage in Financial Assistance for Children of Divorce." *Journal of Family Issues* 13 (2, June): 158–78.

Hofferth, Sandra L., and Kristen A. Moore. 1979. "Early Childbearing and Later Economic Well-Being." *American Sociological Review* 44 (October): 784–815.

Hoffman, Saul, and Greg J. Duncan. 1988. "A Comparison of Choice-Based Multinomial and Nested Logit Models: The Family Structure and Welfare Use Decisions of Divorced or Separated Women." *Journal of Human Resources* 23 (4, Fall): 550–62.

Hoffman, Saul D., Greg J. Duncan, and Ronald B. Mincy. 1991. "Marriage and Welfare Use among Young Women: Do Labor Market, Welfare, and Neighborhood Factors Account for Declining Rates of Marriage among Black and White Women?" Paper presented at the annual meeting of the American Economic Association, New Orleans, December.

Honig, Marjorie. 1973. "The Impact of AFDC Income, Recipient Rates, and Family Dissolution." *Journal of Human Resources* 9: 303–22.

Hutchens, Robert M., George Jakubson, and Saul Schwartz. 1989. "AFDC and the Formation of Subfamilies." *Journal of Human Resources* 24 (4, Fall): 599–628.

Jensen, Leif. 1989. "Rural-Urban Differences in the Utilization and Ameliorative Effects of Welfare Programs." *Policy Studies Review* 7 (4): 782–794.

Jensen, Leif, and Diane K. McLaughlin. 1992. "Human Capital and Nonmetropolitan Poverty." In *Investing in People: The Human Capital Needs of Rural America*, edited by L. J. Beaulieu and D. Mulkey. Boulder, Colo.: Westview Press.

Karoly, Lynn A. 1990. "The Trend in Inequality among Families, Individuals, and Workers in the United States: A Twenty-Five Year Perspective." RAND Corporation Working Paper. Santa Monica, Calif.: RAND Corp.

Katz, Lawrence F., and Kevin M. Murphy. 1992. "Changes in Relative Wages, 1963–87: Supply and Demand Factors." *Quarterly Journal of Economics* 107 (February): 35–78.

Klerman, Lorraine. 1991. *Alive and Well: A Research and Policy Review of Health Programs for Poor Young Children*. New York: National Center for Children in Poverty.

Krueger, A. B. 1991. "How Computers Have Changed the Wage Structure: Evidence from Microdata, 1984–89." Paper presented at the National Bureau of Economic Research Summer Labor Workshop, Cambridge, MA.

Levy, Frank. 1987. *Dollars and Dreams: The Changing American Income Distribution*. New York: Russell Sage.

Levy, Frank, and Richard J. Murnane. 1992. "U.S. Earnings Levels and Earnings Inequality: A Review of Recent Trends and Proposed Explanations." *Journal of Economic Literature* 30 (September): 1333–81.

Lichter, Daniel, and David J. Eggebeen. 1993. "Rich Kids, Poor Kids: Changing Income Inequality among American Children." *Social Forces* 71 (March): 761–80.

Macunovich, Diane J., and Richard A. Easterlin. 1990. "How Parents Have Coped: The Effect of Life Cycle Demographic Decisions on the Economic Status of Pre-School Age Children, 1964–87." *Population and Development Review* 16: 301–25.

Mare, Robert D., and Christopher Winship. 1991. "Socioeconomic Change and the Decline of Marriage for Blacks and Whites." In *The Urban Underclass*, edited by Christopher Jencks and Paul E. Peterson. Washington, D.C.: Brookings Institution Press.

Massey, Douglas. 1990. "American Apartheid: Segregation and the Making of the Underclass," *American Journal of Sociology* 96 (2, September): 329–357.

Massey, Douglas, and Mitchell Eggers. 1990. "The Ecology of Inequality: Minorities and the Concentration of Poverty, 1970–80." *American Journal of Sociology* 95 (5, March): 1153–88.

Massey, Douglas S., Andrew B. Gross, and Mitchell L. Eggers. 1991. "Segregation, the Concentration of Poverty, and the Life Chances of Individuals." *Social Science Research* 20: 397–420.

McLanahan, Sara, and Irwin Garfinkel. 1992. "Single Motherhood in the United States: Growth, Problems, and Policies." Conference draft prepared for the Research and Policy Workshop on the Single Parent Family, Lake Louise, Mar. 18–21.

McNeil, John. 1992. "Results of an Exercise: Hypothetical Estimates of the Relative Income Status of Children under 6 under the Assumption of No Change in the Percent Living in Married Couple Families." Memorandum prepared at the request of the U.S. Senate, Mar. 30.

Minarik, Joseph, and Robert Goldfarb. 1976. "AFDC Income, Recipient Rates, and Family Dissolution: A Comment." *Journal of Human Resources* 9 (Spring): 243–57.

Mincer, Jacob. 1991. "Human Capital, Technology, and the Wage Structure: What Do Time Series Show?" NBER Working Paper 3581. Cambridge, Mass.: National Bureau of Economic Research.

Mincy, Ronald B. 1992. "The Underclass: Concept, Controversy, and Evidence." IRP Conference Paper for "Poverty and Public Policy: What Do We Know? What Should We Do?" Madison: University of Wisconsin, Institute for Research on Poverty.

Mincy, Ronald B., Isabel V. Sawhill, and Douglas A. Wolfe. 1990. "The Underclass: Definition and Measurement." *Science* 248 (Apr. 27): 450–53.

Moffitt, Robert. 1990. "The Effect of the U.S. Welfare System on Marital Status." *Journal of Public Economics* 41 (1, February): 101–24.

———. 1992. "Incentive Effects of the U.S. Welfare System: A Review." *Journal of Economic Literature* 30 (March): 1–61.

Moffitt, Robert, and Barbara Wolfe. 1992. "The Effect of the Medicaid Program on Welfare Participation and Labor Supply." *Review of Economics and Statistics* 74 (4, Nov.): 615–626.

Moore, Kristen, and Steven Caldwell. 1976. *Out-of-Wedlock Pregnancy and Childbearing*. Washington, D.C.: Urban Institute Press.

———. 1977. "The Effect of Government Policies on Out-of-Wedlock Sex and Pregnancy." *Family Planning Perspectives* 9 (4): 164–69.

Moynihan, Daniel Patrick. 1965. *The Negro Family: The Case for National Action*. Washington, D.C.: U.S. Department of Labor.

Murphy, Kevin, and Finis Welch. 1992. "The Role of International Trade in Wage Differentials." In *Workers and Their Wages*, edited by M. Kosters (39–69). Washington, D.C.: AEI Press.

Murray, Charles. 1984. *Losing Ground: American Social Policy: 1950–80*. New York: Basic Books.

National Center for Health Statistics. 1992. "Annual Summary of Births, Marriages, Divorces, and Deaths: United States, 1991." *Monthly Vital Statistics Report* 40 (13, September). Hyattsville, Md.: Public Health Service.

O'Hare, William P. 1988. "The Rise of Poverty in Rural America." *Population Trends and Public Policy*, vol. 15 (July). Washington, D.C.: Population Reference Bureau.

O'Hare, William P., and Brenda Curry-White. 1992. "The Rural Underclass: Examination of Multiple-Problem Populations in Urban and Rural Settings." Staff Working Papers. Washington, D.C.: Population Reference Bureau.

Orshansky, Mollie. 1965. "Counting the Poor: Another Look at the Poverty Profile." *Social Security Bulletin* 42 (June): 387–406.

Phillips, Elizabeth, and Irwin Garfinkel. 1992. "Changes over Time in the Incomes of Nonresident Fathers in Wisconsin." Institute for Research on Poverty Discussion Paper 967-92. Madison: University of Wisconsin.

Plotnick, Robert. 1990. "Welfare and Out-of-Wedlock Childbearing: Evidence from the 1980s." *Journal of Marriage and the Family* 52 (3, August): 735–746.

Ricketts, E. R., and Isabel V. Sawhill. 1988. "Defining and Measuring the Underclass." *Journal of Policy Analysis and Management* 7 (2, Winter): 316–325.

Rogers, Carolyn C. 1991. "The Economic Well-Being of Nonmetro Children." *Rural Development Research Report* 82. Washington, D.C.: U.S. Department of Agriculture, Economic Research Service.

Ross, Christine, Sheldon Danziger, and Eugene Smolensky. 1987. "The Level and Trend of Poverty in the United States, 1939–79." *Demography* 24 (November) 587–600.

Ruggles, Patricia. 1990. *Drawing the Line.* Washington, D.C.: The Urban Institute Press.

Ryscavage, Paul, and Peter Henle. 1990. "Earnings Inequality in the 1980s." *Monthly Labor Review* 113 (December): 3–16.

Ryscavage, Paul, Gordon Green, and Edward Welniak. 1992. "The Impact of Demographic, Social, and Economic Change on the Distribution of Income." In *Studies in the Distribution of Income* (11–30). U.S. Bureau of the Census, *Current Population Reports*, ser. P-60, no. 183. Washington, D.C.: U.S. Government Printing Office.

Sawhill, Isabel V. 1988. "Poverty in the U.S.: Why Is It So Persistent?" *Journal of Economic Literature* 26 (September): 1073–1119.

————. 1992. "Young Children and Their Families." In *Setting Domestic Priorities: What Can Government Do?* edited by H. J. Aaron and C. Schulze. Washington, D.C.: Brookings Institution Press.

Seltzer, Judith A. 1991. "Relationships between Fathers and Children Who Live Apart: The Father's Role after Separation." *Journal of Marriage and the Family* 53 (1, February): 79–101.

Smolensky, Eugene, Sheldon Danziger, and Peter Gottschalk. 1988. "The Declining Significance of Age in the United States: Trends in the Well-Being of Children and the Elderly since 1939." In *The Vulnerable,* edited by John L. Palmer, Timothy Smeeding, and Barbara Boyle Torrey. Washington, D.C.: Urban Institute Press.

Teachman, Jay. 1991. "Who Pays? Receipt of Child Support in the United States." *Journal of Marriage and the Family* 53 (3, August): 759–72.

U.S. Bureau of the Census. 1984. "Marital Status and Living Arrangements: March 1983," by Arlene F. Saluter. *Current Population Reports,* ser. P-20, no. 389. Washington, D.C.: U.S. Government Printing Office.

_____. 1991a. "Child Support and Alimony: 1989," by Gordon H. Lester. *Current Population Reports*, ser. P-60, no. 173. Washington, D.C.: U.S. Government Printing Office.

_____. 1991b. "Trends in Relative Income: 1964 to 1989," by John McNeil. *Current Population Reports*, ser. P-60, no. 177. Washington, D.C.: U.S. Government Printing Office.

_____. 1992a. "Household and Family Characteristics: March 1991," by Steve W. Rawlings. *Current Population Reports*, ser. P-20, no. 458. Washington, D.C.: U.S. Government Printing Office.

_____. 1992b. "Marital Status and Living Arrangements: March 1991," by Arlene F. Saluter. *Current Population Reports*, ser. P-20, no. 461. Washington, D.C.: U.S. Government Printing Office.

_____. 1992c. "Measuring the Effect of Benefits and Taxes on Income and Poverty: 1979 to 1991," by John McNeil. *Current Population Reports*, ser. P-60, no. 182-RD. Washington, D.C.: U.S. Government Printing Office.

_____. 1992d. "Money Income of Households, Families, and Persons in the United States: 1991," by Carmen DeNavas and Edward J. Welniak, Jr. *Current Population Reports*, P-60, no. 180. Washington, D.C.: U.S. Government Printing Office.

_____. 1992e. "Poverty in the United States: 1991," by Eleanor Baugher and Martina Shea. *Current Population Reports*, ser. P-60, no. 175. Washington, D.C.: U.S. Government Printing Office.

_____. 1992f. "Studies in the Distribution of Income," by Paul Ryscavage, Gordon Green, Edward Welniak, and John Coder. *Current Population Reports*, ser. P-60, no. 183. Washington, D.C.: U.S. Government Printing Office.

_____. 1992g. "Workers with Low Earnings: 1964 to 1990," by John McNeil. *Current Population Reports*, ser. P-60, no. 178 (issued March).

_____. 1993. "Marital Status and Living Arrangements: March 1992," by Arlene F. Saluter. *Current Population Reports*, series P20-468. Washington, D.C.: U.S. Government Printing Office.

U.S. Social Security Administration. 1966. *Social Security Bulletin: Annual Statistical Supplement, 1966*. Washington, D.C.: U.S. Government Printing Office.

_____. 1988. *Social Security Bulletin: Annual Statistical Supplement, 1988*. Washington, D.C.: U.S. Government Printing Office.

Wilson, William J. 1987. *The Truly Disadvantaged: The Inner City, The Underclass, and Public Policy*. Chicago: University of Chicago Press.

Winkler, Anne. 1991. "The Incentive Effects of Medicaid on Women's Labor Supply." *Journal of Human Resources* 26 (2, Spring): 308–37.

Wojtkiewicz, Roger A., Sara S. McLanahan, and Irwin Garfinkel. 1990. "The Growth of Families Headed by Women: 1950–1980." *Demography* 27 (1, February): 19–30.

Chapter Five

CHILDHOOD POVERTY AND CHILD MALTREATMENT

Joan I. Vondra

A single mother of three, living on welfare with her own mother, angrily ignores her hungry two-year-old's whining cries, then hits him when he tries to gag himself. The child is hospitalized two weeks later for failure to thrive. The mother was hospitalized earlier for severe depression.

An unemployed father beats his eight-year-old son unconscious after the boy's teacher sends home a note about his behavior problems in school. The boy had earlier witnessed his father attack his mother physically and/or verbally on several occasions, often over some small economy she had tried to institute.

The question of how and to what extent family poverty and child maltreatment are related has been under debate for decades. Linkages between the two exist at the empirical, theoretical, service, and policy levels. For example, any professional widely involved with families suspected of, reported for, or documented as having committed child maltreatment is likely to note an overrepresentation of economically disadvantaged families in this population, a finding well replicated in the research literature (Garbarino 1976, 1977; National Center for Child Abuse and Neglect [henceforth, NCCAN] 1988a; Straus and Gelles 1986). On the other hand, economically disadvantaged families are considerably more likely to have contact with public officials who report to Child Protective Services regarding observed or suspected childrearing practices or circumstances that deviate from white, middle-class norms and/or appear problematic. These family contacts range from visits to the welfare office or WIC (Special Supplemental Food Program for Women, Infant, and Children) office and reliance on hospital emergency room or public health clinic services, to experience of more frequent police patrols or raids in low-income and/or high crime neighborhoods. Is it possible to disentangle increased opportunities for reporting child maltreatment from a higher actual incidence of child maltreatment for families in poverty? Increasingly, researchers argue yes.

In 1978, Leroy Pelton summarized data on the relation between family poverty and child maltreatment and pointed to several converging findings that indicated a positive relationship between socioeconomic status (SES) and child abuse and neglect, after taking into account differences in reporting rates. These findings include not only a disproportionate amount of abuse and neglect among lower-class families but also more maltreatment and more severe cases of maltreatment among the poorest of lower-class families (Gil 1970, 1971). Changing rates of child abuse and neglect have been linked to rates of unemployment and/or size of the work force (Steinberg, Catalano, and Dooley 1981; Straus, Gelles and Steinmetz 1980), and can be predicted across different communities on the basis of family income, presence of single-parent households, transience of residents, and number of working mothers with young children (Garbarino and Crouter 1978; Garbarino and Sherman 1980).

In their summary of 1986 national child maltreatment reporting data, the American Humane Association (in NCCAN 1988a) noted that family poverty was most clearly associated with reports of child neglect, and that child neglect ("deprivation of necessities") represented over half of all cases of reported maltreatment. Whereas 29 percent of families reported for physical abuse included an unemployed caregiver and 25 percent were headed by a single female, 42 percent of families reported for neglect included an unemployed caretaker and 51 percent were headed by a single female. Neglect was also more likely than physical or sexual abuse to be perpetrated by a female and by a black, both of whom are more likely to be poor and to experience economic and social discrimination.

It is not, however, the case that child maltreatment within the family is entirely, or even primarily, a poverty phenomenon. It is, rather, a more *concealed* phenomenon among middle- and upper-class families with the resources to maintain family privacy (for example, a suburban home, private physicians and counselors) and the social status to ensure some measure of silence on the part of suspecting individuals (for example, school personnel, friends, and neighbors). The relative rarity of public exposure in cases of middle-class child maltreatment is evidenced by the extensive media attention devoted to them (for example, the 1989 Lisa Steinberg murder case in New York City [*Time*, Feb. 13, 1989]). Nevertheless, rates, severity, and chronicity of child maltreatment consistently appear worse among those at greatest individual and contextual risk, and poverty is perhaps the single most predictable risk factor for child maltreatment. Maltreatment occurs across the entire economic continuum, but is most heavily concentrated among families in poverty. It is one thing to identify family poverty as a risk factor for child maltreatment but quite another thing to understand the processes by which poverty interacts with other stressors to undermine parental care—in the extreme, to the point of abuse or neglect. Considerable attention by researchers to the determinants of both "normative" differences in parental care and the extremes of caregiving represented by maltreatment, however, has helped to illuminate the complex interplay of parent, child, and contextual factors that appear to mediate the relation between poverty and maltreatment. The sections following summarize this work and discuss some of its implications for public policy. Limitations of existing data with respect to policy development are considered next, followed by recommendations for potential collaboration on practical solutions. Challenges for public policy are presented in the subsequent section, followed by conclusions about the significance of links between family poverty, child maltreatment, and criminal behavior.

MAJOR FINDINGS ON CHILD MALTREATMENT

Definitions of child maltreatment vary from state to state and across different professions. In most cases, however, a key component of the definition is actual or impending harm to a child. Studies of child functioning and child development indicate that constellations of social and emotional problems can be linked to experiences of maltreatment. These include disturbances in affect, disorganization of the parent-child attachment relationship, troubled peer relations, problems with behavioral self-regulation, poorer school performance and need for special education services, juvenile delinquency, and adjustment problems in adulthood, including higher risk of perpetrating child maltreatment (Egeland, Jacobvitz, and Papatola 1987; Garbarino and Plantz 1986; Youngblade and Belsky 1990). Although seen more frequently among children from poverty backgrounds, these problems can be directly linked to abuse and neglect in childhood and/or adolescence.

For the purposes of this chapter, a broad definition of child maltreatment is most useful: acts of omission (neglect) or commission (abuse) by a parent or guardian that jeopardize a child's social, emotional, physical, and/or cognitive functioning. Understanding the causes of child maltreatment requires consideration of broad and interacting sets of factors that contribute to isolated instances of abusive behavior or, more commonly, a pattern of chronic emotional maltreatment and neglect of the physical and/or psychological needs of the developing infant, child, or adolescent. These factors arise from within *and* outside the family, converging to create a family situation characterized by both extreme need and an inability to develop or maintain the external supports that could help bolster this fragile system. Of great importance to public policy is the fact that recurrent maltreatment is *not* the outcome of any single factor, whether the pathology of the parent, the difficultness of the child, the absence of adequate social supports, the cultural milieu, or economic hardship and deprivation (see Belsky and Vondra 1989; Vondra 1990a). Cicchetti and Rizley (1981) helped to clarify this by categorizing maltreatment risks into "enduring" (chronic) and "transient" (acute) stressors and "potentiating" versus "compensatory" factors. Family poverty must be considered within this broader framework if appropriate conclusions are to be drawn with respect to public policy.

Poverty as Risk

At its most fundamental level, poverty can, in fact, be considered a broad and generic "risk" for child maltreatment in the sense that it increases the experience of both chronic and acute stressors known to act cumulatively in undermining parental care (see Vondra 1986). In truth, financial hardship affects family functioning at every level, from individual distress and substance abuse, to strained marital and parent-child relations, to changes in the balance of family power and altered family beliefs (Elder, Liker, and Cross 1984; Komorovsky 1940; Moen, Kain, and Elder 1983). As Pelton (1978) pointed out, whereas a middle-class parent can, literally, "afford" some irresponsibility or carelessness with money, equivalent behavior on the part of an impoverished parent may well jeopardize, at least temporarily, his or her ability to provide for a child's basic needs. At the same time, financial hardship typically implies such long-term stressors as inadequate housing, residence in a dangerous and/or resourceless neighborhood, inability to pay for practical and human services, and lack of transportation to access affordable resources.

   Acute stressors associated with family poverty may best be characterized as discrete events that further imperil family livelihood by precipitating financial crises. Examples include the loss of whatever low-paying job a family member may have held, a medical problem that suddenly requires (uninsured) professional attention, or even the loss (through conflict or death) of a financially supportive relationship. In each case, a marginally functioning family economy may be strained to the breaking point.

Parental Psychology as Risk

Although the stresses associated with poverty undoubtedly undermine parental functioning, there is no clear evidence that financial deprivation in and of itself causes child maltreatment. In those cases where economic hardship co-occurs with actual abuse or neglect, there is typically evidence of other risk factors in and outside the home, most commonly factors related to social functioning and interpersonal relationships. Indeed, it has been argued that attachment issues—unconscious feelings of insecurity derived from and regarding relationships—form the crux of the maltreating family's frequent interpersonal problems (Crittenden and Ainsworth 1989; DeLozier 1982; Vondra 1990b; see also Mayseless 1991). Common findings in the research on determinants of child maltreatment include problematic relationships at many levels: the marital or cohabiting relationships of the parent, broader social network support, and both current and past relations with the family of origin. Maltreating adults appear to share a common history of insecure, unstable, and/or pathological relations with their parents and, ultimately, with other adults as well.

What makes these adult psychological issues relevant to a poverty analysis is the role played by parents either in garnering resources for themselves and their families or in creating and maintaining stress. An adult who has experienced highly problematic relations with his or her own parents from childhood seems to be at greater risk for problematic intimate relationships in adulthood, characterized by greater conflict, instability, and/or poor interpersonal skills (see Vondra and Belsky 1992, for a review). When these interpersonal difficulties exist in a setting with multiple social and economic buffers, the consequences for parenting—or at least child development—may be minimized. However, when they occur in the context of socioeconomic stress, hardship, and deprivation, these difficulties appear to lay the groundwork for child neglect, child battering, and child exploitation. In their comparison of low-income mothers providing good-quality versus inadequate child care, Egeland and Brunnquell (1979) observed that "both groups of mothers experienced a considerable amount of stress, but the good [care] mothers seemed better able to cope with problems and frustrations. . . . The inadequate [care] mothers seemed to expect and accept problems without doing much about them" (227–28).

At the same time, a parent who lacks social skills, secure intimate relationships, and the self-esteem or ego-strength that such relationships nourish, may be more likely to suffer socioeconomic hardships. In the most obvious example, such a parent (particularly a woman, who is more often dependent upon a partner for financial support) may suffer economically because he or she has greater difficulty establishing and maintaining a stable relationship with an emotionally *and* financially supportive partner. He or she is also likely to have difficulty in creating and using effectively a social network of supportive friends, relatives, and neighbors. Patricia Crittenden (1985) described two problematic social network patterns among parents who mistreat their children. Neglecting parents seem especially likely to report social isolation: having few friends, friendships that last a shorter period of time, and dissatisfying relations with kin (see also Polansky et al. 1981). In contrast, abusing parents seem more likely to describe conflicted, enmeshed relationships with family and friends that may alternate from over- to underinvolvement. In either case, these are parents who are most likely to find themselves without emotional or financial support from their network in times of special need. They are also among those *least* likely to reach out for professional help. It should come as no surprise that child maltreatment is associated with increased rates of depression and substance abuse (Famularo, Kinscherff, and Fenton 1992; Kotelchuck 1982), given the links between these failures in coping and both interpersonal difficulties and economic hardship.

Finally, interpersonal problems may strain employment relations, limit opportunities for advancement, and even compromise job security. Self-worth, self-confidence, autonomy, and social competence are all aspects of personal functioning relevant to job success that have been associated with attachment security and supportive intimate relationships (Eysenck 1980; Kobak and Sceery 1988). Without these individual resources, advancement in job status may be difficult during periods of economic growth, and simply maintaining job status may be problematic during periods of economic stagnation and retrenchment. Prior to establishing an adult employment history, serious family relationship problems and troubled peer relations during the teenage years may jeopardize later job status through their association with school failure, dropping out of school, and adolescent pregnancy (Garbarino and Asp 1981).

Parental personal resources and interpersonal functioning—both of which stem, in part, from developmental and family relationship history—thus appear to play a critical role in minimizing or exacerbating the stresses of poverty on family well-being. Although central to the model of determinants of child maltreatment, parental attachment history, interpersonal relations, and self-esteem are by no means the only personal resources relevant to this analysis, however. Parental intelligence, for example, is another factor that may mediate the relationship between poverty and maltreatment. Neglecting parents, in particular, appear to have a greater probability than expected of functioning in the low-normal to retarded range of intelligence (Crittenden 1988; Tymchuk and Andron 1990).

Psychologically, lower intelligence may make it especially *unlikely* that destructive childhood and adolescent experiences are worked through or processed cognitively. Evidence is accumulating that an adult who has not reevaluated his or her own experiences of abuse or neglect is at greater risk of perpetuating an intergenerational legacy of child maltreatment (Egeland, Jacobvitz, and Sroufe 1988; Hunter and Kilstrom 1979; Main and Goldwyn 1984). Pragmatically, lower intelligence sets limits on educational attainment, employment options, and the ability to generate creative responses to complex social and economic difficulties. Managing the family budget and allocating resources effectively is never more challenging cognitively and emotionally than when finances are scarce. Still, intellectual limitations are most likely to contribute to active maltreatment only when past and current relationship issues already interfere with the quality of parent-child relations. The stresses of poverty become simply a catalyst for more extreme parental behavior and reactions.

A recent investigation of the relationship between poverty and child maltreatment indicates that as the stresses of poverty *decrease*, parental psychological risk factors become increasingly apparent in cases of maltreatment (Trickett et al. 1991). Among working-class families, substantiated child maltreatment was associated with parental reports of family conflict, fewer family outings and activities, negative feelings about the child, perceptions of the child as a behavior problem, and less support for child independence. Among lower-class families, these associations with maltreatment were either weaker or nonexistent. In some cases, this was because *both* maltreating and comparison families in the lower class exhibited the same risk factors, presumably a consequence, in part, of socialization in poverty. In other cases, deviant parental attitudes or behaviors were simply more prominent among parents who, though not stressed by the same degree of poverty, nevertheless maltreated their children. This investigation suggests that parental risk factors may play a more singular role in the etiology of maltreatment when there are relatively fewer environmental stressors. But when environmental stressors are great (e.g., in more extreme poverty), parental risk factors then exacerbate conditions already ripe for maltreatment.

Community Resources and Societal Values as Risk

It would be misleading to focus this entire analysis at the level of the individual parent and family. Obviously, broader social, cultural, and economic influences ultimately are played out at the level of the *family*. But differences at the level of the community and society in which each family functions ultimately shape individual and inter-personal behavior in ways significant for this discussion.

With respect to the neighborhood or community, factors that predict child maltreatment rates *other* than socioeconomic and demographic characteristics include level of community morale, social integration, and availability of resources for children and families within the neighborhood (Garbarino and Crouter 1978; Garbarino and Kostelny 1992; Garbarino and Sherman 1980). In communities with *higher* than expected rates of maltreatment, community leaders in human service agencies "knew less about what other community services and agencies were available, and demonstrated little evidence of a network or support system, either formal or informal" (Garbarino and Kostelny 1992: 461). In contrast, leaders in communities with *lower* than expected rates of maltreatment reported more available services, were more informed about these services, described important formal and informal social support networks, and noted strong political leadership from a local leader. Garbarino and Kostelny's community-level analyses clearly support their conclusion that "child maltreatment is a symptom of not just individual or family trouble, but neighborhood and community trouble as well. It is a *social* as well as a *psychological* indicator" (1992:463). When quality of neighborhood life is poor—indicated by unavailability of either high-quality child care or of educational, public transportation and recreational facilities, and by a lack of organization and participation by community members—families are further undermined in their care and protection of children.

Beyond the level of community, both culture and society dictate attitudes about children, parenting, and family values. Urie Bronfenbrenner (1977) coined the term "macrolevel" effects to describe societal influences on the family and the individual in his model of the ecology of human development. With respect to child maltreatment, many have argued cogently about the deleterious macrolevel effects of societal attitudes regarding violence, the privacy of the family, and family "ownership" of children (Garbarino 1977; Garbarino, Stocking, and Associates 1980; Gil 1970; Zigler 1981).

The United States is notorious in the developed world as a violent culture, with images of violence and violent solutions to conflict pervasively and prominently displayed in all forms of media. These images reinforce cultural acceptance of and support for physically coercive responses to conflict and both physical and verbal interpersonal aggression. At the same time, there is a deeply rooted tradition in American culture for parents to have "ownership" of their children and the right to rear them as they see fit, in the privacy of their home. The combination of a zealous defense of family privacy, the tradition of "ownership" of children by their parents, and a culture of violence is, however, literally a lethal one for children. In the context of a family history of troubled relationships, multiple stresses relating to poverty, and/or power-coercive parenting, this sociocultural backdrop encourages a problematic parent-child relationship to become a maltreating one.

The relative lack of societal support for family functioning represents another macrolevel effect in the United States. The Children's Defense Fund (1990) has provided compelling statistical comparisons (based on data collected by UNICEF, the Urban Institute, and the federal government) between the United States and other, comparable nations illustrating just how unsupportive our well-to-do society (second-highest-ranked gross national product [GNP] in the world) is vis-à-vis our children and families. Relevant statistics include the disturbing percentage of children living in poverty; the teenage pregnancy rate; the infant mortality rate; the proportion of gross national product invested in child health; the absence of universal health coverage, child care and parental leave for children and parents; and the number of school children for every teacher. In most cases, the U.S. performance ranks between 15th and 25th among industrialized nations. In practical terms, this means more children in America will grow up with preventable health problems, in poor families, and with parents who lack important resources for parenting. In sociocultural terms, this means U.S. children are valued—at least politically—less than they are in other nations. Ultimately, these statistics and the messages they convey mean that more children in America will be abused or neglected than might otherwise have been. For policy implications, certainly, it is unwise to ignore the contributions made at the societal level both to rates of poverty and to rates of child maltreatment.

Sociocultural Considerations

Some important caveats are in order when discussion of child maltreatment shifts to society-level effects and sociocultural influences. Attitudes, values, and practices relating to the family and to childrearing differ by both social class and ethnic/sociocultural context. These differences, in and of themselves, can complicate understanding of not only the processes and dynamics of child maltreatment but even the definition of maltreatment. Religious differences in the use of medical treatments for childhood illnesses, social class differences in reliance on child labor to supplement family income, and cultural differences in beliefs about appropriate child disciplinary techniques, for example, require some degree of flexibility in criteria for defining parental behavior as abusive or neglectful. This is not to say that minimal standards for protecting the welfare and development of children cannot be established. But understanding (1) what constitutes "acceptable" but atypical variation in parental care, (2) how the dynamics of sociocultural differences are played out in cases of maltreatment, and (3) when (and how) it is appropriate for public officials to intervene becomes, if anything, less straightforward (Chestang 1978; Ishisaka 1978).

The fact that poverty is confounded with social class and, in many cases, with ethnicity as well further complicates the picture. Sociocultural differences in attitudes, values, and practices relating to family functioning within the United States can represent, in part, necessary adaptations on the part of groups of people socially and economically subordinated through castelike status by the majority culture (Ogbu 1978). In her ethnographic study of kinship patterns and practices among low-income blacks living in an urban housing project, for example, Carol Stack (1974) illustrated how family form and function had been adapted to meet the survival needs of economically impoverished adults and children. At the same time, Ogbu has claimed that painful awareness of discrimination and subordination reinforces minority culture efforts to affirm cultural uniqueness, in part by "regarding certain forms of behavior, events, symbols, and meanings as inappropriate because they are characteristic of White Americans . . . and claiming other (often the opposite) forms of behavior, events, symbols, and meanings as appropriate because these are not White ways" (1988:23). Ogbu concluded that, as a consequence:

What is appropriate or even legitimate for in-group members is defined in opposition to the preferences and practices of White Americans in selected domains of life. This results in a kind of coexistence of two opposing cultural frames of reference, one appropriate for the minorities and the other for White Americans. (1988:23).

The implications of these cultural differences with respect to child-rearing have immediate relevance to definitional issues about what constitutes unacceptable and/or inappropriate care.

Socialization goals differ as a function of both social class and culture/ethnicity, so that strategies considered "optimal" or simply "acceptable" to middle-class, white Americans sometimes differ dramatically from those considered optimal or acceptable to low-income whites, blacks, Native Americans, or Hispanics (Harrison et al. 1990). As an illustration, the authoritative childrearing pattern emphasizing rational, democratic parenting and respect for the rights of both parent and child, appears especially suited to the socialization goals and societal opportunities of middle-class, white America. However, this pattern is not particularly suited to the socialization goals and societal experiences of many low-income, black families, especially those living in urban poverty areas. In this case, the authoritarian pattern emphasizing conformity and obedience from children appears more suitable. Indeed, data on competence and resiliency among children from poor families living in high-risk neighborhoods suggest that the strict rules, unquestioned obedience, and punitive responses to child transgressions characteristic of authoritarian parenting, when combined with strong family ties and religious commitment, may represent an important protective factor for children's competent development (Baldwin, Baldwin, and Cole 1990).

The role of the kin network can also differ dramatically for a child from a poor and/or ethnic minority family (Hill 1972; Wilson 1989). "Child keeping," as Stack (1974) termed it, has been an integral part of childrearing for black families in poverty who have not had sufficient food, housing, or intimate emotional support to provide adequate care for their children at all times. Thus, children have been "fostered" out in times of physical or emotional difficulty to real or fictive kin who have previously demonstrated some investment in these children. As a result, the "foster" parents have gained some say, at least temporarily, in subsequent childrearing decisions regarding them. Other extended kin ties—whether on the mother's or father's side—have been of similar importance in family functioning, particularly in cases of single or teen parenthood. Indeed, parenting by a single or a teen mother—with the support of one or more extended kin—was not uncommon. Despite near-universal poverty and disadvantage, then, instrumental and emotional assistance of some sort have been mobilized in times of need through a small, but dense network of cooperative relationships, and reliance on help systems outside the kin network has, to some extent, been minimized.

To a white, middle-class service provider, one picture painted by the childrearing strategies just described might be of a child suffering emotionally from a harsh and overburdened parent who abruptly leaves him (with his two younger sisters) in the care of his maternal aunt for a period of six months (while trying to make up differences with a boyfriend searching for work in another city). On the one hand, ethnic differences in strategies of childrearing and in the use of social ties separate the parent and the service provider. Poverty, an important contributing factor to this scenario, further separates the experience and viewpoint of these two individuals.

Thus, the answer to the question of whether child maltreatment is occurring can vary considerably according to sociocultural interpretation. Community, cultural, and social class norms for child care and family functioning need special attention within legal, policy, and service initiatives. Nevertheless, the very existence of social class differences in rates of child maltreatment also points to the role that economic stressors play in family dysfunction. As this discussion of empirical findings has indicated, financial hardship evolves in part from individual and familial factors that, themselves, place children at risk for abuse and neglect. However, financial hardship not only exacerbates already-existing problems (relationship conflict and instability, adjustment problems and poor coping skills, lack of nurturing models for effective parental behavior, etc.), but it also creates new problems that contribute further to the risk of maltreatment, including poor housing, residence in a high-crime community, day-to-day stress and hardship, and medical risk. Explicating the multiple roles poverty plays in the wider genesis of child maltreatment is relevant to the question of whether intervention is called for and, if so, what that intervention should be. Is "fixing" the parent, "fixing" the neighborhood, or "fixing" the poverty the issue here (Whittaker 1983)? It is increasingly clear that intervention needs to address contributing factors at all three levels of risk. Intervention is addressed in more detail in the section following, in terms of public policy.

IMPLICATIONS FOR PUBLIC POLICY

Knowledge about the multiple personal, situational, social, and economic factors that contribute to child maltreatment can and should be used to create and modify social policy relating to children and families. Understanding the ways in which culture and ethnicity alter family and community dynamics should also inform the policies that are implemented to support families and/or to protect children. This section examines policy implications that reflect these considerations.

Prevention or Intervention?

A continuum of opportunity exists for helping children and families who might otherwise fall victim to maltreatment. Along this continuum there is an inverse relation between level of risk and both breadth and intensity of services needed to be effective. As the risk of child abuse and neglect increases, the necessary range and strength of an array of necessary services increases and, given limited public funds, the number of children and families who can be served adequately decreases accordingly. This is true whether child maltreatment is considered a problem at the level of the individual family or at the level of the community.

At the low-risk end of the continuum, families are at no specific risk of child maltreatment, and services represent efforts to enhance family functioning. At the middle of the continuum, families are at broad risk for child maltreatment, according to socioeconomic and/ or demographic indicators, and services represent preventive efforts to support and maintain effective family functioning. At the high-risk end of the continuum, families are at specific risk of child maltreatment, either because of converging individual and familial risk indicators or because maltreatment has occurred in the past. In the latter case, services reflect intervention efforts to change current and/ or family functioning. The following subsections outline the range of service orientations and raises relevant questions about implementing services.

WIDE-SCALE PREVENTION

It has been argued that the most effective societal approach to preventing child maltreatment involves broad-based family support policies that: (1) aim at assisting all families to function more effectively, (2) operate *before* there has been opportunity for parenting breakdown, and (3) avoid stigmatizing families that are at greater risk of problems (Belsky and Vondra 1987; Cohn 1983; Garbarino, Stocking, and Associates 1980; Pecora, Whittaker, and Maluccio 1992). National "agendas" for children and families proposed by the Children's Defense Fund (1990), the National Commission on Children (1991), and other child advocacy organizations reflect this broad-based perspective (see also Shore 1988). In every case, recognition of the fundamental importance of providing all families with the economic foundations for adequate functioning is central to the policies proposed. Employment training and opportunities, family and medical leave policies, flexible work scheduling alternatives, availability of affordable, high-quality child care, pro-family tax reform and tax credits for low-income workers with children, child support enforcement and insured child support benefits, and universal health insurance are examples of policies proposed to accomplish this.

However, in no case is it assumed that economic support for families is sufficient in and of itself to prevent child maltreatment. Consistent with the growing body of theory and research on the determinants of maltreatment, a wide-scale prevention effort must recognize the roles of individual, familial, and social influences on child abuse and neglect. In the spirit of *universal* (and culturally relevant) support versus identification (and stigmatization) of individuals and families at risk, this means parent and family support services that fit naturally into the "ecology" of family and community life. Normative points of contact between families and organizations such as hospitals (especially at birth), clinics (childhood medical checkups), child care programs, schools (particularly during the early years when parental involvement is expected and encouraged), churches, and community agencies and gathering places are ideal settings for outreach programs that routinely serve *all* parents and families that use them (Belsky and Vondra 1987).

Prenatal and postnatal support and education programs for new parents; early childhood screening and treatment programs for health and developmental problems; basic and life skills programs for children, adolescents, and young adults; community-run self-help groups (e.g., neighborhood redevelopment, child care, parent support, foster grandparent programs, Big Brother/Sister programs); and central information sources to publicize programs and services could and should be embedded in routine contacts between families and each of the community organizations just described (Cohn 1983; Garbarino, Stocking, and Associates 1980). The critical feature here is conveying to families that stress and difficulty are normative, but so too is openness to support, assistance, and guidance from others. To be effective, this approach requires multiple, simultaneous efforts by all segments of the community—the sort of neighborhood mobilization that Garbarino and Kostelny (1992) call for. Without both neighborhood commitment and at least some measure of broader governmental support, the ideal represented by this approach is unlikely to be achieved. The fact that there *are* communities that function in this manner, however, testifies to the potential for its implementation and effectiveness (Garbarino and Kostelny 1992; Garbarino and Sherman 1980).

NARROW-SCALE PREVENTION

When prevention or any other kind of service is limited to only a subset of the population, it is immediately clear to policymakers, service providers, the families being served, and the wider community that only individuals or families with some level of "problems" get help. This is especially true of after-the-fact intervention, but often characterizes prevention programs as well. Families that do not define themselves as having a problem, or define the problem differently (an employment problem, a crowding problem, a child "discipline" problem, a family member who "spoils," etc.) are often targeted for services they neither requested nor perceive themselves as needing. In essence, families that are seen as "needing" services become stigmatized, or perceive themselves as stigmatized, for failing in some way. This is the immediate drawback of limiting services to those in need (as defined by "risk" status), the approach requiring the fewest dollars "up front." Voluntary involvement and level of commitment by families both decline as a result. Nevertheless, the notion of early screening for health, developmental, or parenting problems, often included in a wide-scale prevention/enhancement agenda, implies subsequent prevention or intervention services targeted specifically for families experiencing difficulty.

One factor that may help predict successful narrow-scale prevention, however, is the social (and cultural) "embeddedness" of the program (Garbarino, Stocking, and Associates 1980). Fitting programs within the social and developmental context of day-to-day family functioning, rather than expecting families to step out of their routine and circumstances to seek help, can represent a more effective way to reach out to families and mobilize resources that are both immediate to and of potentially longstanding availability for the family (Whittaker 1983). It is extremely rare that a program of short-term "inoculation" from an outside service agency can demonstrate any long-term effect, since the ecology of the family—the social, economic, and physical context of daily family life—has not been changed in any fundamental way. As Whittaker (1983) pointed out, individual psychosocial improvement from intensive residential treatment programs tends to depend far more on continuity and support of treatment gains after discharge than on either initial functioning or improvement over the course of treatment.

Olds (1983) and Olds and Henderson (1989), for example, established the efficacy of a visiting nurse program for poor, unmarried, teenage mothers recruited from prenatal clinics. Two features that may have been instrumental in the program's success are (1) the multifaceted service orientation focusing on parent education, the involvement of family and friends in the transition to parenthood, *and* the linkage of family members with other formal health and human services and (2) the program's emphasis on strengthening normative, already-existing links between mother and hospital staff through home visitation. As Olds and Henderson (1989) pointed out, the home visitation program:

> provides a means of reaching out to parents who lack self confidence and trust in formal service providers—those least likely to show up for other services, such as parent-group meetings. . . . It has been our experience that the special attention provided by one caring, nonjudgmental professional can eventually bolster parents' self-confidence to the point where seeking other formal services and attending meetings are no longer threatening. . . . Another significant advantage is that the home-visitor can acquire a more accurate and complete understanding of all of the factors in the home and family that interfere with parents' efforts to create optimal conditions for pregnancy and early childrearing. (p. 742)

Olds's program illustrates the potential for the success of combining the strengths of professional expertise with the strengths of already-existing social network resources in working to establish a *long-term* supportive environment for parents and children. It also illustrates the efficacy of an *early* prevention orientation for families at broad risk of parenting dysfunction. In fact, Olds and Henderson (1989) concluded from their own and from similar intervention work that initiating the program during pregnancy for first-time mothers may have helped to ensure its success.

On the other hand, Olds pointed out several limitations in his program's efficacy that are relevant to this chapter's consideration of the multiple determinants of child maltreatment. For those mothers at more specific risk of maltreatment due to their own experiences of parenting trauma in childhood, comprehensive therapy was called for *in addition to* the parenting support services of the nurse home visitor. The program was not powerful enough, in and of itself, to compensate for such experiences. Furthermore, for those mothers living in higher-risk communities—communities with high rates of unemployment, drug abuse, and other risk conditions for family functioning—broader, neighborhood-wide change was needed. Without public policies to increase educational and occupational opportunities and decrease racial and gender discrimination, whatever personal accomplishments mothers could be helped to achieve were undermined by the stress and hardship engendered by community life (Olds and Henderson 1989). Thus, by selecting individuals and families already defined to be at some risk, narrow-scale prevention by its very nature ultimately identifies families and circumstances that represent much greater, more specific risk of child maltreatment. In this case, the more intensive services implied in intervention are called for to ameliorate existing problems. These are discussed next.

WIDE-SCALE INTERVENTION

Programmatic efforts to intervene in cases of dysfunctional parenting on a broad scale are probably best represented by the current Child Protective Services (CPS) system. With mandated reporting by professionals of suspected instances of child maltreatment, the number of cases that the CPS is legally required to investigate and, where indicated, intervene increased dramatically across the 1980s (NCCAN 1988a, b). Interventions resulting from substantiation of maltreatment reports range from a variety of counseling and surveillance services by CPS workers to purchased parent, child, or family therapy, and from temporary removal of children from dangerous situations at home to legal termination of parental rights.

Funds for assessment, legal, and service interventions, however, have never kept pace with reporting rates. Thus the current program struggles to provide minimally adequate follow-up to the more serious reports of child maltreatment, with neither the staff, time, nor resources to do so. As a result, only those cases judged most compelling are generally pursued at length, and only those factors considered pivotal in family dysfunction are generally given much attention. It is notably difficult to deal with the complex interaction of individual, familial, environmental, and *cultural* factors—different for each case—that together set the stage for abuse or neglect. To accomplish this on the scope required of child protective services is a formidable task, indeed, and one that is open to criticism. The disproportionate number of ethnic minority families comprising the child welfare system, for example, has provoked real concern about the sensitivity of the reporting, investigating, and intervention process to cultural differences (Chestang 1978; U.S. Children's Bureau 1977).

To some extent, however, CPS should be seen as coordinator and supervisor of a host of smaller intervention efforts that can be somewhat more readily tailored to the unique needs of families experiencing different kinds and levels of dysfunction. It is at this level that intervention appears to have some modicum of success, not simply in protecting the welfare of the child but in helping a dysfunctioning family or perhaps a family in dysfunctional circumstances to function more adequately.

NARROW-SCALE INTERVENTION

A discouraging number of maltreatment intervention programs fail to demonstrate stable, long-term improvement in parent-child relations and child welfare outcomes relative to comparison groups (Berkeley Planning Associates 1977; Cohn 1979; Pardeck 1989; Pecora et al. 1992). A critical review of these programs suggests that, in general, intervention was not comprehensive enough or not enduring enough to effect anything more than transient improvement in parental or family functioning. In view of the multiple, spiraling, destructive circumstances that precipitated the maltreatment, many of which may have evolved over years, it can hardly be expected that even an intensive intervention focusing on just one or two risk factors (parental relationship problems, child behavior problems, economic hardship, social isolation, etc.) for a period of perhaps 6 to 18 or even 24 months is likely to support lasting change.

When interventions do produce change that is still apparent at a delayed follow-up (*if* any follow-up is undertaken), certain features appear in common. First, the intervention program is comprehensive.

Therapeutic (whether behavioral or psychological) needs of both parent(s) and child(ren) who now share a history of relationship problems are addressed; referrals and linkages to special services for substance abuse, spousal violence, and/or legal or medical problems are made; daily stressors associated with unemployment, economic impoverishment, child care, child disciplinary problems, and lack of transportation are dealt with; parent education—whether formal (literacy training, general equivalency diploma [G.E.D.] program, etc.) or informal (knowledge about child development, learning to run a household or balance a budget)—is promoted; and improvement in social support for and social integration of parents and family is undertaken.

Second, the program involves visits to the family home. Whether these visits are periodic counseling or support sessions from a social worker or visiting nurse, or intensive in-home services through a home-based family preservation program, there is evidence that an in-home component significantly increases an intervention program's chance of success (Cohn 1983). In describing innovative service programs that combine formal and informal services to prevent out-of-home placement, Bryce and Lloyd (1981) asserted that:

> the first and greatest resource investment is made in the care and treatment of children in their own homes. . . . The service setting is primarily the home, but includes problem-solving efforts in the family's ecological system (i.e., where the family interfaces with community systems). There is maximum utilization of family resources, extended family, and community. (p. 7)

Finally, there are active efforts to strengthen and energize the social network within which the family functions, usually through a combination of professional and more informal mechanisms. This is the critical "linking up" process: getting needed services to families but, perhaps more importantly, supporting parents in engaging the social systems around them. Helping families toward supportive social integration is, in essence, working to establish a fundamental and long-term change in the ecology of family life. This implies not only professional services provided *to* families, but active family participation in self-help groups, regular contact with community volunteers and lay therapists, use of local support services (including crisis nurseries, hot lines, parent aides), and involvement of extended family in support of parents (Cohn 1983; Whittaker 1983). Here the aim is to improve the social "embeddedness" of the families themselves.

Fraiberg (1980), Greenspan and colleagues (1987), and Kinney and colleagues (1977) have offered descriptions and case illustrations of the kinds of intensive, comprehensive interventions needed to change the circumstances and dynamics of families experiencing a breakdown of parenting. Each of the three critical factors—multifaceted services, home visits, and activation of social support—is typically present in these programs. Indeed, the reader is invariably impressed by the *intensity* of the intervention program needed to ensure long-term change in the families involved. In relation to the prevention efforts described previously, it is clear from the challenges of intervention that the longer a risk/problem situation is left to deteriorate, the more difficult is the possibility of creating enduring, positive change. As Cohn (1983:12) noted, "The later intervention occurs . . . . the lower are the odds of success. Similarly the more broadly based and comprehensive the intervention, the better its chances of succeeding." Whether the issue is prevention or intervention, an understanding of the ecology of parenting certainly suggests that this is so.

When to Intervene?

The relation between level of risk and service needs certainly argues, both from a psychological perspective and an economic one, for a preventive social policy approach in the area of child maltreatment. And if policy reflected research and theory in the field, two primary foci for prevention would be economic support/opportunities for families who might otherwise slip below the poverty line and extended relationship therapy for children and adolescents who have been maltreated or experienced other breakdowns in care. The former helps alleviate a complex of stresses that undermine parental functioning at many levels; the latter helps to ensure that a legacy of disturbed social relationships is not passed down from one generation to the next. A preventive approach shifts U.S. policy from the crisis/pathology orientation currently reflected in the child welfare system to an etiological orientation that addresses risk and opportunity *before* problems have become so widespread and entrenched that even the most intensive interventions are limited in their potential for producing change.

To the extent that a preventive approach strives to enhance the conditions of family life for all families, sociocultural differences in what constitutes "problem" functioning become less critical for deciding whom and when to serve. However, differences in what puts a family at "risk" for child maltreatment among varying popula-tions, as well as differences in the most effective strategies to enhance family functioning, remain critical issues for serving families opti-mally—the "when" and "how" of prevention. And ultimately, because prevention can only decrease but not eliminate the occur-rence of maltreatment, definitions of what constitutes maltreatment remain a sociocultural concern. These issues are discussed further in the upcoming section on future research.

Goals of Intervention

An area of debate within the current child welfare system—and at issue for public policy—is the *purpose* of intervention. The ecological orientation adopted in this chapter emphasizes family functioning within the wider social context of family life. Thus, intervention implies changing family functioning directly by working with family members and/or the family unit and also indirectly by altering the context in which that family is embedded. This is the parent/family support perspective adopted by leaders in the child welfare field and by the federal government in the Adoption Assistance and Child Welfare Act of 1980. This act dictated that states provide services that "prevent unnecessary separation of children from their families by identifying family problems, assisting families in resolving their problems, and preventing breakup of the family where the prevention of child removal is desirable and possible" (PL 96-272 1980:519). The logic underlying this philosophy is social-psychological in nature: merely removing a child (permanently) from a dysfunctional family does not guarantee either psychological well-being for the child, the safety or well-being for other children in the same family, or proper concern and assistance for a family in need of help.

The real, but unintended, ramifications of this approach, however, have been a vastly overburdened child foster care system, a subset of children who are victimized by a series of unsuccessful (occasionally harmful), temporary placements, and cases of further maltreatment and even death after return of the child to a "treated" family. One response to these policy sequelae has been the "child rescue" per-spective (e.g., Gelles, forthcoming; Goldstein, Freud, and Solnit 1973, 1979; Solnit, Nordhaus, and Lord 1992). The logic underlying this alternative philosophy is developmental in nature: understanding of and respect for children's developmental needs argues for early and immediate removal of young children from maltreating homes for permanent, legal placement in functional, adoptive families.

Although theoretically appealing from an individual child vantage point, this approach ignores the needs of the family, of other children in the family, and the potential for collaboration between family, community, and government in the protection and care of children (Garbarino et al. 1982). Furthermore, if critics are accurate in perceiving a tradition of ethnic bias in the child welfare system—resulting in disproportionate designation of minority children as dependents of the state (Billingsley and Giovannoni 1972; Chestang 1978; Ishisaka 1978)—the child rescue approach further victimizes disadvantaged minority families.

A critical point raised by this perspective, however, is that exclusive services for maltreating parents or, less commonly, for the family as a whole also ignore the very real needs of the maltreated child, who not only may contribute to family dysfunction with reactive behavior (Gaensbauer and Sands 1979; Trickett and Kuczynski 1986) but is also now at social, psychological, and behavioral risk in a number of developmental ways (Egeland and Erickson 1987; Erickson, Egeland, and Pianta 1989; Youngblade and Belsky 1990). In other words, knowledge about the determinants of parenting and the ecology of family functioning that can be used to inform intervention must be supplemented by understanding of child development needs and-processes that are also critical to intervention and long-term prevention.

Any policy of intervention after maltreatment has occurred must acknowledge both the systemwide problems that interfere with adequate family functioning and the psychological disturbances that maltreatment produces in children. Merely stabilizing family functioning (no easy feat itself) in no way ensures adequate "healing" for the child, who is at risk, among other things, of contributing to the creation of another maltreating family in the next generation. The multiple levels of need, then, represented by the substantiation of child maltreatment are sobering, indeed. And attempts to "minimize" the cost of repairing damaged psyches, damaged relationships, and anchoring a family floundering without needed resources and supports run the serious risk of "fixing" the immediate problem while engineering long-term damage.

So where does this leave public policy for child maltreatment? From what we know about the multiple determinants of maltreatment, the multiple needs of maltreating families, and the multiple risks of providing insufficient intervention when maltreatment has occurred, the wisest course of action would appear to be a two-tiered approach: (1) invest fully in prevention to promote family functioning at every level of risk and to decrease substantially the incidence of child maltreatment; and (2) coordinate an entire network of professional and lay, as well as formal and informal, services to support and redirect both family and child when maltreatment does occur. In each case, a critical goal for cost-effectiveness is to identify the best *combination* of services for helping families with different needs along the full continuum of risk. This means attending not only to the individual, family, and contextual factors that undermine effective parenting but also taking into account the sociocultural milieu in which each family functions. There remains considerable work to be done if we seek to tailor policy and practice to the specific needs of individual families. Some of this work is detailed in the next section, which considers the policy-relevant research that still needs to be done.

POLICY QUESTIONS FOR FUTURE RESEARCH

The most fundamental questions for public policy in child maltreatment still to be resolved concern definitions of risk and maltreatment, the extensiveness of services required, and the ability to demonstrate cost-effectiveness. Each of these questions has a direct impact on how policy is developed and implemented, and each draws on a body of research needing further extension and refinement. All three questions are briefly outlined and discussed in this section.

Agreeing on Definitions

Although there has come to be some consensus regarding acts of physical or sexual abuse and neglect, there is still enough variability in state definitions of child maltreatment that, for example, parents are prosecuted for criminal behavior in one state but not in another under very similar circumstances. Even greater variability exists when it comes to psychological or emotional maltreatment, for which some states lack any definition whatever (Corson and Davidson 1987). There is inconsistency across the nation—typically in the less extreme cases—in what reports are investigated, who is served, when legal intervention is instituted, and how likely it is that parents will lose custody of their children. This inconsistency occurs across court jurisdictions and county lines as well as across states.

There is also variability in definitions used for legal, for clinical, and for research purposes (Vondra, Kolar, and Radigan 1992). Legal definitions tend to be extremely narrow (though often noticeably vague), based on observable damage to the child (most often physical) that can be related to the care received. Clinical definitions emphasize current or impending damage to the child (often psychological) related to parenting practices and/or family dynamics. Research definitions include either measurable patterns of destructive parent-child interaction or measurable damage (physical or psychological) to the child, usually emphasizing the developmental needs of the child.

It should be apparent from these descriptions that there are sometimes critical discrepancies—whether across geographic regions or professional disciplines—about what constitutes child maltreatment. Clinical, empirical, and legal or political understanding of the origins of maltreatment will differ if definitions of maltreatment differ. Thus, understanding of what constitutes risk will also differ across disciplines. Forging links, then, between disciplines is already problematic. What can researchers do to help bridge these gaps?

One of the keys to conducting research that will help inform policy and practice is careful selection and specification of the samples used in research studies. On the one hand, limiting (noncomparison) sample recruitment to families with legally substantiated (i.e., by Child Protective Services [CPS]) occurrences of maltreatment provides data of more immediate relevance to the system currently in practice (at least in those states with similar legal definitions). At the same time, exploring family functioning, contextual stresses and supports, and child development outcomes among families who may or may not appear at risk but do not have substantiated reports of maltreatment can help to clarify how current definitions and practices related to these definitions may need to be altered. When parenting "risk" or dysfunction that is not officially declared maltreatment is the focus of inquiry, it is critical for policy implications that the researchers precisely measure and describe the criteria for inclusion in the sample. Whether legal maltreatment or more general parenting dysfunction is the basis for sample selection, the more diverse the sample, the fewer conclusions and generalizations are likely to be possible. Instead, careful efforts to identify and study families representing particular patterns of background, functioning, or context are needed to begin to make risk assessment and service delivery specifically suited to unique patterns of need in different families. For example, research on patterns of abuse versus neglect among children of migrant farmer families (Larson, Doris, and Alvarez 1990) and on differences in mother-child interaction in low-income families where physical abuse only, physical neglect only, abuse and neglect, or emotional unavailability has been documented (Crittenden 1988; Egeland and Erickson 1987) begins to delineate more specifically the nature of the problem in diverse family circumstances and to point to more specific foci for intervention.

Especially lacking in the research literature are data on well-functioning black, Hispanic, or Native American families, and (comparative) studies focusing on the etiology, dynamics, and treatment of child maltreatment within any of those populations. Comparative data on families reported for neglect versus abuse or sexual abuse, and for combinations of these dysfunctions, are also needed, both from majority and minority populations. Systematic sampling for other potentially significant demographic characteristics, including family structure (e.g., single parent, multigenerational, changing form), socioeconomic status (upper class, working class, welfare-dependent), and age of maltreated child (infant/toddler, school-age, adolescent), may mean the difference between discerning underlying patterns of commonality or failing to detect systematic differences with comparison families.

Until attention is paid to untangling some of the complexity that less systematic sampling contributes to research findings, policy may reflect only dynamics that are attributable to the families and cultures most represented in the current child protective service system or in studies of diverse white (and occasionally black), low-income families at risk (without regard to potentially significant subsample distinctions). Although such studies may tell us something about average risk (i.e., teen parenthood, welfare dependency, maltreatment in the family of origin, substance abuse, social isolation) and typical functioning (i.e., power-assertive parenting, interparental conflict or separation, poor coping skills), they tend to be limited in helping to modify the system in ways that are more responsive to individual family needs, whether in terms of prevention or intervention services.

Setting the Scope of Intervention

Given descriptive data on carefully delineated subsets of families and well-specified definitions of maltreatment, "risk," or dysfunction, insights may be gained about those areas of greatest need within and outside different kinds of families. Current research on the determinants of parenting and child maltreatment has made initial progress in achieving this, though more attention to family diversity is warranted. Much less work has been done, however, on studying effective *combinations* of troubled families and supportive services. This sort of study is more challenging from a pragmatic standpoint and is also academically unfashionable. Yet it is exactly the sort of research with the most direct implications for policy.

Even when families are similar in terms of level of risk, parent-child dynamics, or sociocultural context, they may differ in their responsiveness to particular forms or levels of prevention or intervention services. It is also not expected that the same service strategies or service delivery will have equal efficacy for families that differ in risk, dynamics, or context. Thus, the issue of sampling family "types" for research on parenting and child maltreatment is further complicated by the additional need to sample *service* "types" for research on prevention or intervention. "How big?" and "How long?" are questions that must reflect both the form and delivery of services and the diversity of families served. This point has been well established in the general literature on psychotherapy (Barton, Alexander, and Sanders 1985; Gurman, Kniskern, and Pinsof 1986), but remains to be operationalized in the field of maltreatment intervention.

Generally lacking in evaluation studies (when such studies can be found) is examination of *graduated* services and their efficacy with particular subsets of families. A notable exception to this is work by Olds (1983) and Olds and Henderson (1989), described earlier. As an example of the kinds of interaction effects that are likely to occur, Olds reported that nurse visitation during pregnancy was less powerful in affecting mother and infant functioning, including the incidence of maltreatment, than nurse visitation that continued throughout infancy. However, these effects were only consistently significant for poor, unmarried teen mothers. Some effects were observable for teen mothers in general, but the only effects observed for older mothers were in terms of finding employment for poor, unmarried mothers after the infant's birth. The extensive prevention program, in other words, had little demonstrated usefulness for mothers who were married, were not poor, and/or were at least 19 years old at the time of their infant's birth. Furthermore, only first-time mothers were included in the study, with the rationale that they would be more receptive to professional support and guidance (i.e., mothers with other children would be less responsive to the treatment). Until treatment evaluation work is conducted on a wider scale in the area of parenting dysfunction, and until this work systematically reflects the complexity of treatment by client interactions, it is hard to imagine how either maltreatment prevention or intervention can have maximum efficacy *or* efficiency. This is a critical issue from the standpoint of cost-effectiveness, discussed in the next section.

Demonstrating Cost-Effectiveness

The research needs addressed so far deal essentially with substantive and methodological issues. Who is at risk? When do we call dysfunction maltreatment? How do we match families with services? But many would argue that by far the more pressing concern is ability to demonstrate cost-effectiveness, ultimately a political issue. Without societal and governmental support for the necessary identification, assessment, and treatment services, what good is it to know which families are at risk and how best to help them? Cost-effectiveness has, more and more, become the core issue in gaining social, political, and financial acceptance for national human service initiatives.

The issue of cost-effectiveness demands a very different emphasis in research studies. In addition to demonstrating *treatment* (whether preventive or interventive) efficacy, it is now necessary to document a savings, not only in social-psychological but also in monetary terms. Although researchers have generally been reluctant to acknowledge and act on this imperative, important lessons have been gained from experiences with Head Start research (McKey et al. 1985; Washington and Oyemade 1987) and with research on the Homebuilders program (Kinney et al. 1977; Whittaker 1986). In both instances, governmental support has hinged on successful documentation of program cost-effectiveness. This documentation has highlighted key components for establishing a favorable cost-benefit ratio.

The most persuasive case can be made when it is possible to demonstrate convincingly the cost of social services saved when a family (child, client, etc.) is responsive to treatment. For Head Start, this was the cost of having a child repeat a grade and/or receive special education services. For the Homebuilders program, this was the cost of placing a child in the care of the state. To furnish data like these, it must be possible to produce figures on the percentage of socioeconomically and geographically comparable families who receive particular social services with and without treatment. Consequently, service use and service costs at multiple levels must be carefully documented.

Whether the focus is on subsequent (social) service costs or simply quality of functioning, longitudinal, follow-up data are essential.

This has been perhaps the weakest aspect of most evaluation research. In the case of cost-effectiveness, it is especially critical to document long-term functioning differences and/or differential use of (social) services. There may be small "treatment" effects—not necessarily the effects targeted for study—at the time of service delivery that accumulate or intensify over time (for example, stemming from a couple's new willingness to get their child enrolled in a local enrichment program, or a parent's new willingness to become involved in a local church program).

Although the risk of finding no discernible long-term effects is a very real one, it is likely to provide testimony to the need for a more expanded, extended, and/or intensive service network at the time of the prevention/intervention efforts. Evaluation research must be conducted more systematically if negative results are to inform future treatment efforts rather than jeopardize the entire prevention and/or intervention enterprise. And for such systematic assessment of treatment, there clearly must be greater dialogue and collaboration between federal/state government, research institutions, and service agencies. This is the topic of the next section.

FOSTERING COLLABORATION ON SOLUTIONS

Conducting systematic applied research, particularly treatment evaluation research, attracting competent researchers to conduct such research, and acquiring the kinds of data that make this research useful for policy all require collaboration between policymakers, practitioners, and researchers. Disseminating applied research findings, clarifying their relevance to policy formation and modification, and creating policies that reflect theoretical and empirical advances also necessitate collaboration between these experts. This section suggests ways in which more systematic collaboration could occur for the benefit of research, policy, and practice relating to child maltreatment.

In the United States, Child Protective Services (CPS) represents the umbrella agency for coordinating identification, assessment, and intervention in cases of child maltreatment. As a result, CPS has access to a vast quantity of data—some collected systematically, some unsystematically—of great potential value to research and policy. To the extent that CPS referrals and cases could furnish the foundation of a systematic database on long-term case management, development, and outcome, a wealth of applied research could be undertaken that is currently feasible in only very limited ways. Drawing upon subsets of data that represent families of different background and functioning, following different courses of treatment, and involvement with different legal interventions allows researchers to make carefully controlled case comparisons, gain critical background information on families currently participating in more-intensive research investigations, and/or gather outcome data relevant to prevention research. It is even conceivable that CPS could serve as a repository of data gathered through independent research on families having contact with the agency.

Given not only current funding and staffing shortages but the absence of national guidelines for the use of CPS data for research purposes and the lack of facilities and procedures for collecting and storing more detailed case data, this vision of a potential role for CPS is untenable at present. Clearly, a cadre of data management staff, possibly funded through a separate mechanism, would be required as a first step in making this strong link between research and practice feasible. Such individuals would be needed to train CPS staff to develop case record-keeping into systematic data collection, to supervise data entry, to serve as liaisons with external researchers, and to ensure confidentiality of all CPS data. The relative inaccessibility, unreliability, and idiosyncracy of the data currently collected on families served by CPS represent an *obstacle* to rather than a resource for high-quality research. So long as this continues to be the case, collaboration of this sort will remain difficult to achieve.

To some extent, the court system may be considered another relatively untapped resource for fostering collaboration among research, policy, and practice. Data from court records on criminal charges and prosecution of cases with bearing on child maltreatment can represent valuable follow-up information about groups of high-risk children and families. Links established in research between, for example, child maltreatment and subsequent juvenile delinquency (Brown 1984; Garbarino 1989; Lewis, Mallouh, and Webb 1989) suggest that court records are relevant to examination of long-term program cost-effectiveness. Once again, however, this requires cooperation on the part of court officials and procedures for ensuring case confidentiality. At present, this resource is only rarely tapped, given legal and procedural constraints, for research on child maltreatment.

Universities and other research organizations represent the obvious source for qualified researchers committed to policy-relevant applied research. However, the research establishment has implicitly discouraged its members from conducting such research or from training qualified students in applied methods. This is the result of a number of related circumstances. First, opportunities to conduct well-controlled, rigorous investigations of applied topics in applied settings have consistently been limited. Partly as a result, what little applied research has been conducted tends to be flawed by a number of methodological weaknesses, tends not to be published in respected scholarly journals, and tends not to garner funding for further investigations. Thus, it is usually impractical for younger scholars who may be at their peak of research productivity but are under pressure to establish a research record and publish data relatively quickly. In addition, results of these investigations—indeed, results of even very rigorous research—can often be misrepresented to and/or misinterpreted by either policymakers or the general public, and have been used inappropriately to support unsubstantiated political or policy initiatives. Although there are some obvious efforts by professional research organizations to establish official channels for the dissemination and interpretation of research findings, these can only begin to address the need for more systematic communication and collaboration between science and practice.

Financial support for routine, systematic collection of detailed (i.e., high-quality) data in key applied settings; funding incentives and rigorous methodological review to attract and support investigators engaged in both practically and scientifically valuable research; emphasis on collaborative research that includes multiple investigators and multiple settings; and standardized mechanisms and guidelines for disseminating study results outside the scientific community are all critical elements in raising the scholarly quality and status of applied research. As with the current potential of Child Protective Services for data collection and storage, operationalizing these elements requires more than the efforts of any individual agency or several agencies, and more than just changes or accommodations within the research community. Guidelines, incentives, and support at the governmental level set the foundation for collaboration across professional arenas concerned with child maltreatment.

Governmental policies and practices can serve as catalysts for professional collaboration through a number of different mechanisms. Governmental mandates—with accompanying funds—for outcome and cost-effectiveness data from every governmentally sponsored prevention/intervention project can help establish a tradition of longitudinal follow-up to treatment efforts. Governmental support for collaborative research can be used to promote *comparative* research on innovative service alternatives for families with different needs, in effect minimizing the need to "prove" the value of any one service project. Finally, governmental guidelines for sharing data from confidential case records and for disseminating results and interpretations of research investigations can help set standards for linking research and practice. These efforts, however, cannot be inaugurated in opposition to or in competition with existing or forthcoming intervention initiatives. Rather, separate but parallel mechanisms for proposal development, evaluation, and funding must exist to ensure maximum support for and protection of critically needed resources for intervention.

To some extent, the dialogue between research, policy, and practice regarding Head Start programming is one example of how government, academia, and local service agencies can collaborate. Initial governmental support for early education service models and accompanying evaluation research created public demand for services as well as some empirical support for different program elements (e.g., parental involvement). Increased government funding became, in part, dependent upon empirical evidence of program efficacy, including long-term outcomes. Over the decades, evaluation research on Head Start programs has become more extensive, more sophisticated, and more compelling in its presentation of results as well as qualifications to the findings. There is evidence that research on infant day care may be moving in this direction, as research, practice, and public investment provide joint impetus for governmental support of collaborative study. With public and governmental commitment to collaborative efforts in the field of child maltreatment, significant, policy-relevant progress could be achieved.

CHALLENGES FOR PUBLIC POLICY

Understanding the multiple determinants of child maltreatment, recognizing the limitations of research on the problem, and addressing the obstacles to collaboration across professions together pose significant challenges for public policy. There is, on the one hand, a fundamental economic basis for community impoverishment, family dysfunction, substance abuse, and child maltreatment. But in some measure, economics merely exacerbates adjustment problems and interpersonal difficulties among those individuals who are already at risk due to their own troubled histories (the "brittle bone" model proposed by Youngblade and Belsky 1990). Thus, public policy can afford to ignore neither the family and communities of poverty nor the need for significant numbers of individuals to be "reparented." Neither can it afford to ignore broader societal images of violence, children, and the family. Yet each of these problems represents potentially enormous expenditures of time, effort, and resources.

At the same time, there is a constant tension between the need to take a long-term perspective and develop policies of prevention and the need to deal with the vast numbers of families that have already passed the boundary from marginally adequate or inadequate child care to active maltreatment and broader dysfunction. In other words, a two-pronged prevention/intervention approach is the only strategy that confronts both current demands and future needs. At present, however, governmental policy appears to lean toward short-term remediation for those families in direct need, with more limited support for isolated program models of prevention. Meanwhile, the problem of child maltreatment is, if anything, growing in scope (Donnelly 1991).

Finally, these service concerns are, themselves, embedded in a poorly coordinated system of research, policy, and practice that is not oriented toward systematic inquiry into improving strategies of family service. Definitions of need and risk, attention to community and sociocultural differences that have an impact on service delivery, tailoring services to individual family needs, tracking child and family outcomes longitudinally, and documenting indices of cost effectiveness are all critical needs still to be addressed adequately in research, policy, and practice. Yet collaboration across these disciplines faces a number of obstacles arising from, in some cases, severe financial restrictions (for policy and practice), incompatible priorities and incentives (in research and policy arenas), and the absence of guidelines and standards for linking expertise across disciplines.

These challenges may be summarized in three broad statements of policy need within the field of child maltreatment:

1. Risk and need within the family must be operationalized along a continuum from prevention for those at no or low risk to intervention for those at immediate, high risk. Standards for need and risk should reflect the full range of research on family and community functioning and should be sensitive to the diversity of families and communities within the United States, but should also show some measure of consistency across political and geographic regions.

2. Risk and need within the family and the community should be matched with a carefully derived menu of services that reflect systematic inquiry into treatment efficacy and cost-effectiveness. Priorities for service provision should be carefully established and acknowledged, and there should be governmental commitment to fund priority matches between need and services fully.
3. To accomplish these goals, there should be a system of guidelines, incentives, and evaluation set in place to promote coordination of services both within the community and within the public and private sectors, and collaboration across governmental, academic, legal, and human service professions.

To the extent that research, policy, and practice in child maltreatment remain piecemeal and unsystematic, neither prevention nor intervention can or will demonstrate widespread success in combatting the problem either in this or future generations.

CONCLUSION

Much of this chapter has been devoted to considering the multiple ways in which society, the economy, the community, family dynamics, and parents themselves contribute to child maltreatment. Almost no attention has been given to the significant *outcomes* of child maltreatment for society more broadly. Obviously, the occurrence of maltreatment itself denotes features of a society—or at the very least of a community and/or a family—at risk. But the societal implications of child maltreatment extend far beyond that. Children raised in dysfunctional and, particularly, maltreating families represent a generation at risk for a number of health, psychological, school, and social problems.

Children raised with abuse or neglect are likely to confront later parenting with significant disadvantages that range from disturbed attachment models, adjustment problems, and/or troubled marital relations to a substantially greater risk of perpetrating maltreatment themselves. Mention has already been made of the links between child (or adolescent) maltreatment, juvenile delinquency, and substance abuse. Children who are victimized have learned what can be a lifelong role of victimization, whether that role is acted out against themselves, as in substance abuse, prostitution, or suicide, or acted out against others, as in spouse abuse, drug-related violence, or other violent crimes.

As noted earlier, our society has an unenviable reputation among developed nations for its level of violence. It is a society in the throes of drug-related dysfunction and crime, a society struggling to manage prisons that cannot hold the number of criminals it engenders, and, in sobering ways, a society where punishment takes precedence over prevention. When all is said and done, the ultimate policy question is how long a crisis-focused social system such as this can endure. Accelerating rates of child poverty, child homelessness, child abandonment at birth, and child maltreatment would appear to speak directly to this question. It remains to be seen whether enough commitment for change can be generated before the patterns become irreversible.

References

Baldwin, A., C. Baldwin, and R. Cole. 1990. "Stress-Resistant Families and Stress-Resistant Children." In Risk and Protective Factors in the Development of Psychopathology, edited by J. Rolf, A. Masten, D. Cicchetti, K. Neuchterlin, and S. Weintraub. New York: Cambridge University Press.

Barton, C., J. F. Alexander, and J. D. Sanders. 1985. "Research in Family Therapy." In The Handbook of Family Psychology and Therapy, edited by L. L'Abate (pp. 1073–1106). Homewood, IL: The Dorsey Press.

Belsky, J., and J. Vondra. 1987. "Child Maltreatment: Prevalence, Consequences, Causes, and Interventions." In Childhood Aggression and Violence: Sources of Influence, Prevention, and Control, edited by D. H. Crowell, I. M. Evans, and C. R. O'Donnell. New York: Plenum Press.

————. 1989. "Lessons from Child Abuse: The Determinants of Parenting." In Child Maltreatment: Theory and Research on the Causes and Consequences of Abuse and Neglect, edited by D. Cicchetti and V. K. Carlson (153–202). New York: Cambridge University Press.

Berkeley Planning Associates. 1977. Adult Client Impact. Vol. 3 in Evaluation of Child Abuse and Neglect Demonstration Projects, 1974–1977. Hyattsville, Md.: National Center for Health Services Research.

Billingsley, A., and J. Giovannoni. 1972. Children of the Storm. New York: Harcourt Brace.

Bronfenbrenner, U. 1977. "Toward an Experimental Ecology of Human Development." *American Psychologist* 32: 513–30.

Brown, S. E. 1984. "Social Class, Child Maltreatment, and Delinquent Behavior." *Criminology* 22: 259–78.

Bryce, M., and J. C. Lloyd, eds. 1981. *Treating Families in the Home.* Springfield, Ill.: Charles C Thomas.

Chestang, L. W. 1978. "The Delivery of Child Welfare Services to Minority Group Children and Their Families." In *Child Welfare Strategy in the Coming Years.* Washington, D.C.: U.S. Children's Bureau.

Children's Defense Fund. 1990. *Children, 1990: A Report Card, Briefing Book, and Action Primer.* Washington, D.C.: Children's Defense Fund.

Cicchetti, D., and R. Rizley. 1981. "Developmental Perspectives on the Etiology, Intergenerational Transmission, and Sequelae of Child Maltreatment." In *Developmental Perspectives on Child Maltreatment,* edited by R. Rizley and D. Cicchetti. New Directions for Child Development, no. 11. San Francisco: Jossey-Bass, Publishers.

Cohn, A. H. 1979. "Effective Treatment of Child Abuse and Neglect." *Social Work* 24: 513–19.

————. 1983. *An Approach to Preventing Child Abuse.* Chicago: National Committee for Prevention of Child Abuse.

Corson, J., and H. Davidson. 1987. "Emotional Abuse and the Law." In *Psychological Maltreatment of Children and Youth,* edited by M. J. Brassard, R. Germain, and S. N. Hart (185–202). New York: Pergamon Press.

Crittenden, P. M. 1985. "Social Networks, Quality of Childrearing, and Child Development." *Child Development* 56: 1299–1313.

————. 1988. "Relationships at Risk." In *Clinical Implications of Attachment,* edited by J. Belsky and T. Nezworski (136–74).

Crittenden, P. M., and M. D. S. Ainsworth. 1989. "Attachment and Child Abuse." In *Child Maltreatment: Theory and Research on the Causes and Consequences of Abuse and Neglect,* edited by D. Cicchetti and V. K. Carlson. New York: Cambridge University Press.

DeLozier, P. P. 1982. "Attachment Theory and Child Abuse." In *The Place of Attachment in Human Behavior,* edited by C. M. Parkes and J. Stevenson-Hinde (95–117). New York: Basic Books.

Donnelly, A. H. C. 1991. "What We Have Learned about Prevention: What We Should Do about It." *Child Abuse and Neglect* 15: 99–106.

Egeland, B., and D. Brunnquell. 1979. "An At-risk Approach to the Study of Child Abuse." *Journal of the American Academy of Child Psychiatry* 18: 219–35.

Egeland, B., and M. F. Erickson. 1987. "Psychologically Unavailable Caregiving." In *Psychological Maltreatment of Children and Youth* edited by M. R. Brassard, R. Germain, and S. N. Hart (110–20). New York: Pergamon Press.

Egeland, B., D. Jacobvitz, and K. Papatola. 1987. "Intergenerational Continuity of Abuse." In *Child Abuse and Neglect: Biosocial Dimensions,* edited by R. Gelles and J. Lancaster (255–76). New York: Aldine Publishing Co.

Egeland, B., D. Jacobvitz, and L. A. Stroufe. 1988. "Breaking the Cycle of Abuse." *Child Development* 59: 1080–88.

Elder, G. H., Jr., J. K. Liker, and C. E. Cross. 1984. "Parent-Child Behavior in the Great Depression: Life Course and Intergenerational Influences." In *Life-span Development and Behavior*, vol. 6, edited by P. B. Baltes and O. G. Brim, Jr. (109–58). New York: Academic Press.

Erickson, M., B. Egeland, and R. Pianta. 1989. "The Effects of Maltreatment on the Development of Children." In *Child Maltreatment: Theory and Research on the Causes and Consequences of Child Abuse and Neglect,* edited by D. Cicchetti and V. K. Carlson (647–784). New York: Cambridge University Press.

Eysenck, H. 1980. "Personality, Marital Satisfaction, and Divorce." *Psychological Reports* 47: 1235–1238.

Famularo, R., R. Kinscherff, and T. Fenton. 1992. "Parental Substance Abuse and the Nature of Child Maltreatment." *Child Abuse and Neglect* 16: 475–83.

Fraiberg, S., ed. 1980. *Clinical Studies in Infant Mental Health.* New York: Basic Books.

Gaensbauer, T. J., and K. Sands. 1979. "Distorted Affective Communications in Abused/Neglected Infants and Their Potential Impact on Caregivers." *Journal of the American Academy of Child Psychiatry* 18: 236–50.

Garbarino, J. 1976. "A Preliminary Study of Some Ecological Correlates of Child Abuse: The Impact of Socioeconomic Stress on Mothers." *Child Development* 47: 178–85.

————. 1977. "The Human Ecology of Child Maltreatment: A Conceptual Model for Research." *Journal of Marriage and the Family* 39: 721–32.

————. 1982. *Children and Families in the Social Environment.* New York: Aldine Publishing Co.

————. 1989. "Troubled Youth, Troubled Families: The Dynamics of Adolescent Maltreatment." In *Child Maltreatment: Theory and Research on the Causes and Consequences of Child Abuse and Neglect,* edited by D. Cicchetti and V. K. Carlson (685–706). New York: Cambridge University Press.

Garbarino, J., and C. Asp. 1981. *Successful Schools and Competent Students.* Lexington, Mass.: Lexington Books.

Garbarino, J., and A. Crouter. 1978. "Defining the Community Context for Parent-Child Relations: The Correlates of Child Maltreatment." *Child Development* 49: 604–16.

Garbarino, J., and K. Kostelny. 1992. "Child Maltreatment as a Community Problem." *Child Abuse and Neglect* 16: 455–64.

Garbarino, J., and M. C. Plantz. 1986. "Child Abuse and Juvenile Delinquency: What Are the Links?" In *Troubled Youth, Troubled Families: Understanding Families At Risk for Adolescent Maltreatment,* edited by J. Garbarino, C. J. Schellenbach, and J. Sebes (27–39). New York: Aldine Publishing Co.

Garbarino, J., and D. Sherman. 1980. "High-Risk Neighborhoods and High-Risk Families: The Human Ecology of Child Maltreatment." *Child Development* 51: 188–98.

Garbarino, J., S. H. Stocking, and Associates. 1980. *Protecting Children from Abuse and Neglect: Developing and Maintaining Effective Support Systems for Families.* San Francisco: Jossey-Bass, Publishers.

Garbarino, J., M. T. Gaboury, F. Long, P. Grandjean, and E. Asp. 1982. "Who Owns the Children? An Ecological Perspective on Public Policy Affecting Children." *Child and Youth Services Review* 5: 41–61.

Gelles, R. Forthcoming. *Out of Harm's Way: Creating a Safe World for Children.* New York: Free Press.

Gil, D. 1970. *Violence against Children: Physical Child Abuse in the United States.* Cambridge, Mass.: Harvard University Press.

————. 1971. "Violence against Children." *Journal of Marriage and the Family* 33: 639–48.

Goldstein, J., A. Freud, and A. J. Solnit. 1973. *Beyond the Best Interests of the Child.* New York: Free Press.

————. 1979. *Before the Best Interests of the Child.* New York: Free Press.

Greenspan, S. I., S. Wieder, R. Nover, A. Lieberman, R. Lourie, and M. Robinson, eds. 1987. *Infants in Multirisk Families.* New York: International Universities Press.

Gurman, A. S., D. P. Kniskern, and W. M. Pinsof. 1986. "Research on the Process and Outcome of Marital and Family Therapy." In *Handbook of Psychotherapy and Behavior Change,* edited by S. L. Garfield and A. E. Bergin (565–624).

Harrison, A. O., M. N. Wilson, C. J. Pine, S. Q. Chan, and R. Buriel. 1990. "Family Ecologies of Ethnic Minority Children." *Child Development* 61: 347–62.

Hill, R. S. 1972. *The Strengths of Black Families.* New York: Emerson Hall.

Hunter, R., and N. Kilstrom. 1979. "Breaking the Cycle in Abusive Families." *American Journal of Psychiatry* 136: 1320–22.

Ishisaka, A. 1978. "American Indians and Foster Care: Cultural Factors and Separation." *Child Welfare* 57: 299–308.

Kinney, J., B. Madsen, T. Fleming, and D. Haapala. 1977. "Homebuilders: Keeping Families Together." *Journal of Consulting and Clinical Psychology* 45: 667–73.

Kobak, R. R., and A. Sceery. 1988. "Attachment in Later Adolescence: Working Models, Affect Regulation, and Representations of Self and Other." *Child Development* 59: 135–146.

Komarovsky, M. 1940. *The Unemployed Man and His Family.* New York: Dryden Press.

Kotelchuck, M. 1982. "Child Abuse and Neglect: Prediction and Misclassification." In Child Abuse Prediction, edited by R. H. Starr, Jr. (66–90). Cambridge, Mass.: Ballinger Publishing.

Larson, O. W., J. Doris, and W. F. Alvarez. 1990. "Migrants and Maltreatment: Comparative Evidence from Central Register Data." Child Abuse and Neglect 14: 375–85.

Lewis, D. O., C. Mallouh, and V. Webb. 1989. "Child Abuse, Delinquency, and Violent Criminality." In Child Maltreatment: Theory and Research on the Causes and Consequences of Child Abuse and Neglect, edited by D. Cicchetti and V. K. Carlson (707–21). New York: Cambridge University Press.

Main, M., and R. Goldwyn. 1984. "Predicting Rejection of Her Infant from Mother's Representation of Her Own Experience: Implications for the Abused-Abusing Intergenerational Cycle." Child Abuse and Neglect 8: 203–17.

Mayseless, O. 1991. "Adult Attachment Patterns and Courtship Violence." Family Relations 40: 21–28.

McKey, R. H., L. Condelli, H. Ganson, B. Barrett, C. McConkey, and M. Plantz. 1985. The Impact of Head Start on Children, Families, and Communities (Final Report of the Head Start Evaluation, Synthesis, and Utilization Project). Washington, D.C.: CSR Inc.

Moen, P., E. Kain, and G. H. Elder, Jr. 1983. "Economic Conditions and Family Life: Contemporary and Historical Perspectives." In American Families and the Economy, edited by R. Nelson and F. Skidmore (213–53). Washington, D.C.: National Academy Press.

National Center for Child Abuse and Neglect. 1988a. Highlights of Official Child Neglect and Abuse Reporting, 1986. Denver: American Humane Association.

————. 1988b. Study of National Incidence and Prevalence of Child Abuse and Neglect, 1986. Washington, D.C.: U.S. Department of Health and Human Services.

National Commission on Children. 1991. Beyond Rhetoric: A New American Agenda for Children and Families. Final Report of the National Commission on Children. Washington, D.C.: U.S. Government Printing Office.

NCCAN. See National Center for Child Abuse and Neglect.

Ogbu, J. U. 1978. Minority Education and Caste: The American System in Cross-Cultural Perspective. San Diego: Academic Press.

————. 1988. "Cultural Diversity and Human Development." In Black Children and Poverty: A Developmental Perspective, edited by D. T. Slaughter. New Directions for Child Development, no. 42. San Francisco: Jossey-Bass, Publishers.

Olds, D. L. 1983. "An Intervention Program for High-Risk Families." In Minimizing High-Risk Parenting, edited by R. Hoekelman. Media, Pa.: Harwal Publishing Co.

Olds, D. L., and C. R. Henderson. 1989. "The Prevention of Maltreatment." In *Child Maltreatment: Theory and Research on the Causes and Consequences of Abuse and Neglect*, edited by D. Cicchetti and V. K. Carlson (722–63). New York: Cambridge University Press.

Pardeck, J. T. 1989. "Child Abuse and Neglect: Theory, Research, and Practice." In *Child Abuse and Neglect: Theory, Research, and Practice*, edited by J. T. Pardeck (1–8). New York: Gordon and Breach Science Publishers.

Pecora, P. J., J. K. Whittaker, and A. N. Maluccio. 1992. *The Child Welfare Challenge: Policy, Practice, and Research*. New York: Walter de Gruyter.

Pelton, L. 1978. "Child Abuse and Neglect: The Myth of Classlessness." *American Journal of Orthopsychiatry* 48: 608–17.

PL 96-272. Adoption Assistance and Child Welfare Act of 1980. 1980. Washington, D.C.: U.S. Government Printing Office.

Polansky, N., M. A. Chalmers, E. Buttenweiser, and D. P. Williams. 1981. *Damaged Parents*. Chicago: University of Chicago Press.

Shore, L. 1988. *Within Our Reach: Breaking the Cycle of Disadvantage*. New York: Anchor Press/Doubleday.

Solnit, A., B. Nordhaus, and R. Lord. 1992. *When Home Is No Haven*. New Haven, Conn.: Yale University Press.

Stack, C. B. 1974. *All Our Kin: Strategies for Survival in a Black Community*. New York: Harper.

Steinberg, L. D., R. Catalano, and D. Dooley. 1981. "Economic Antecedents of Child Abuse and Neglect." *Child Development* 52: 975–85.

Straus, M. A., and R. J. Gelles. 1986. "Societal Change and Change in Family Violence from 1975 to 1985 as Revealed in Two National Surveys." *Journal of Marriage and the Family* 48: 465–79.

Straus, M. A., R. J. Gelles, and S. K. Steinmetz. 1980. *Behind Closed Doors: Violence in the American Family*. New York: Anchor/Doubleday.

Trickett, P. K., and L. Kuczynski. 1986. "Children's Misbehaviors and Parental Discipline Strategies in Abusive and Non-abusive Families." *Developmental Psychology* 22: 115–23.

Trickett, P. K., J. L. Aber, V. Carlson, and D. Cicchetti. 1991. "The Relationship of Socioeconomic Status to the Etiology and Developmental Sequelae of Physical Child Abuse." *Developmental Psychology* 27: 148–58.

Tymchuk, A. J., and L. Andron. 1990. "Mothers with Mental Retardation Who Do or Do Not Abuse or Neglect Their Children." *Child Abuse and Neglect* 14: 313–23.

U.S. Children's Bureau. 1977. *Migrant Child Welfare*. Washington, D.C.: U.S. Children's Bureau.

Vondra, J. I. 1986. "Socioeconomic Considerations: The Family Economy." In *Troubled Youth, Troubled Families*, edited by J. Garbarino and Associates. New York: Aldine Publishing Co.

————. 1990a. "The Community Context of Child Abuse and Neglect." *Marriage and Family Review* 15: 19–38.

————. 1990b. "Sociological and Ecological Factors." In *Children at Risk: An Evaluation of Factors Contributing to Child Abuse and Neglect,* edited by R. T. Ammerman and M. Hersen (149–70). New York: Plenum Press.

Vondra, J., and J. Belsky. 1992. "Developmental Origins of Parenting: Personality and Relationship Factors." In *Parenting: An Ecological Perspective,* edited by T. Luster and L. Okagaki. Hillsdale, N.J.: Lawrence Erlbaum.

Vondra, J. I., A. B. Kolar, and B. L. Radigan. 1992. "Psychological Maltreatment of Children." In *Assessment of Family Violence: A Clinical and Legal Sourcebook,* edited by R. T. Ammerman and M. Hersen (253–90). New York: John Wiley & Sons.

Washington, V. and U. J. Oyemade. 1987. *Project Head Start: Past, Present, and Future Trends in the Context of Family Needs.* New York: Garland.

Whittaker, J. K. 1983. "Social Support Networks in Child Welfare." In *Social Support Networks: Informal Helping in the Human Services,* edited by J. K. Whittaker and J. Garbarino. New York: Aldine Publishing Co.

————. 1986. *Improving Practice Technology for Work with High-Risk Families: Lessons from the "Homebuilders" Social Work Education Project.* Seattle, Wash.: University of Washington.

Wilson, M. N. 1989. "Child Development in the Context of the Black Extended Family." *American Psychologist* 44, 380–85.

Youngblade, L. M., and J. Belsky. 1990. "The Social and Emotional Consequences of Child Maltreatment." In *Children at Risk: An Evaluation of Factors Contributing to Child Abuse and Neglect,* edited by R. T. Ammerman and M. Hersen (109–46). New York: Plenum Press.

Zigler, E. 1981. "Controlling Child Abuse: Do We Have the Knowledge or the Will?" In *Child Abuse: An Agenda for Action,* edited by G. Gerbner, K. Ross, and E. Zigler. New York: Oxford University Press.

Chapter Six

THE CHILD OF POVERTY: ENDURING IMAGES AND CHANGING INTERPRETATIONS

Elsie G. J. Moore

The Civil Rights movement and other social movements of the 1960s focused national attention on the alarming rate of apparent intergenerational poverty in large segments of American society. The questions of how the poverty cycle was perpetuated and what could be done to ameliorate it stimulated considerable policy debate, culminating in 1964, in a rather amorphous federal plan known as the "War on Poverty" (Ellwood 1988; Harrington 1982). Hindsight reveals that the hastily conceived strategies to significantly diminish, if not eliminate, poverty in America grew out of political demands for a "quick fix" of the problem (see Gallagher 1991). In other words, the "War on Poverty" was projected to be a short one. To this end, considerable federal funding was made available for research and program development to address poverty nationwide. Logically, poor children became a major target of research and intervention programs. On the one hand, they were the most vulnerable victims of poverty in view of the dependent nature of childhood; and, on the other hand, they appeared a reasonable point of intervention to quickly break the cycle of intergenerational poverty, or what Duncan and Rodgers (1991: 549) have recently referred to as "permanent poverty."

During the 1960s, the consistently observed positive intercorrelations between educational attainment, occupational status, and income led social scientists, educators, and policymakers to assume that support for poor children's educational achievement was a key factor in empowering them to escape poverty in their adult lives. This analysis of the problem is evident in the 1968 assertions of social scientists Martin Deutsch and Irwin Ktaz that

> perhaps the most fundamental domestic problem of latter twentieth century America is the persistence of gross inequalities in the life opportunities of youth from different social classes and racial groups. A

critical component of the problem is the failure of most poor children
to master the basic knowledge and skills that are necessary for
assimilation into a highly technical and industrialized economy. The
scholastic achievement gap that separates pupils in slums from those in
affluent neighborhoods remains tragically wide. . . . (p. 1)

This "critical component" of the problem of intergenerational poverty generated a substantial amount of basic and applied research
designed to inform understanding of why poor children were not
developing necessary knowledge and skills at the same rate as their
more economically advantaged peers, and what could be done to
facilitate their development in this area (Hilgard 1968).

Almost 30 years after the War on Poverty was launched, the percentage of children living in poverty has risen steadily since 1970.
In 1988, children comprised 40 percent of the poor in America, with
one in every five American children living in poverty (U.S. Congress,
Select Committee on Children, Youth, and Families [henceforth, U.S.
Congress, Select Committee] 1989). An additional 25 percent live
just above the poverty line in conditions nearly identical to those of
the officially identified poor (Ropers 1991). As a result of the increase
in the proportion of American children living in poverty or near-
poverty circumstances, it is estimated that today one child in five
is experiencing poor nutrition, inadequate or nonexistent primary/
preventive health care, and substandard housing (Baumeister, Kupstas, and Klindworth 1991).

Historically in the United States a disproportionate number of
ethnic minority children have lived in poverty. Currently, the nationwide rate of poverty among children in the two largest ethnic minority
populations, that is, African-Americans and Hispanics, is twice as
high as the average for American children in general (U.S. Congress,
Select Committee 1989). African-American children are also more
likely than white children to experience persistent poverty. Ellwood's (1988) analyses of the Panel Study of Income Dynamics (PSID)
survey data indicated that among children born between 1967 and
1973, the majority of African-American children (56 percent) experienced 4 to 10 years of poverty from birth to age 10, compared to
8 percent of the white children. Duncan and Rodgers (1988) also
presented analyses of the PSID survey data indicating that the prevalence of poverty among African-American children living in continuously two-parent families is similar to that observed for white children who live continuously in one-parent families.

It is apparent from a consideration of these trends in child poverty that the War on Poverty has yet to be won. In fact, the problem of intergenerational poverty appears to have evolved into a more virulent form in view of contemporary correlated issues such as increases in adolescent childbearing (Osofsky 1990), child physical abuse in the home (Daniel, Hampton, and Newberger 1983), violent crime in poor urban neighborhoods (Baumeister et al. 1990), homelessness (U.S. Congress, Select Committee 1989), alcohol and drug misuse (Rogers 1990), and maternal and infant HIV infection (Joseph 1990).

Although significant gains have been made in the educational attainments of African-American youths, at least in the proportion who complete high school and attain some postsecondary education, their average literacy and numeracy skill levels as measured by standardized test performance are significantly lower than the average for white youths (Bock and Moore 1986; Ellwood 1988). In the case of Hispanic youths, there has also been some improvement in the proportion who complete high school. However, the high school dropout rate among Hispanic 18- to 24-year-olds (approximately 31 percent) is more than twice that for whites in this age range (approximately 13 percent), and the number of Hispanics who complete college has actually shown a decline since 1985 (U.S. Department of Education, Office of Educational Research and Improvement 1988).

These trends should signal concern about America's future in view of projections by economic and business analysts indicating that our economic growth and competitiveness in the global economy will depend upon a "high-skill, high-wage work force" (Wheelock 1992: 14). However, as we look forward to the 21st century, we face a shrinking youth cohort, many of whom are growing up in persistent poverty and are vulnerable to the negative developmental outcomes correlated with poverty. Ethnic minority children, who are disproportionately represented among the poor and undereducated, are projected to comprise one-third of all young people entering the work force by the year 2000, and about one-half of all American school-age children by the year 2020 (Commission on Minority Participation in Education and American Life 1988; Hamburg 1992).

Clearly, America's future economic growth and competitiveness, and our general quality of life, are dependent upon effectively addressing the developmental needs of poor children. It is axiomatic that continuities and change in the various facets of a society are effected through the shaping of each generation in accordance with the particular society's needs, demands, and expectations (see Levine 1973). This process (i.e., socialization) begins in the family at birth and continues subsequently in the various institutions beyond the family that are responsible for preparing children for adult roles in society (e.g., schools). The success or failure of families and other institutions in this regard is significantly affected by the quality of interactions between these primary institutions (e.g., involvement of parents in the formal education of their children, and with the larger social ecology in which they are embedded; and economic trends that directly and indirectly affect the quality of experiences provided for children) (see Bronfenbrenner 1979, 1986). Therefore, it is reasonable to conclude that we can change the negative social patterns in our society that threaten our future by improving the quality of experiences available to poor children.

The question of what needs to be done to improve the life experiences of poor children and prepare them for productive adult lives evokes a myriad of responses from child advocates, social scientists, educators, and policy analysts. Certainly, there is consensus that basic needs must first be satisfied; that is, adequate health care (including prenatal care), nutrition, housing, and physical safety must be provided (see Hamburg 1992; Rogers and Ginzburg 1990). However, whether we effectively facilitate poor children's development of skills, motivation, and attitudes required for participation in the work force of the 21st century depends upon the image of poor children that is advanced in policy discussions. If the child of poverty is seen as deprived and lacking in skills, then a reasonable response would be to develop interventions to compensate for the deprivation if compensation is deemed possible. If the child of poverty is viewed as able and competent, then a reasonable response would be to reform the education system, which has, historically, demonstrated a pattern of undereducation of poor children.

This chapter critically examines various conceptualizations of poor children's development and their relation to interventions designed to facilitate their scholastic achievement and educational attainment. Although some theorists and investigators (e.g., Ginsburg 1972; Valentine 1971) have argued that poor children are able and competent, the dominant view, over time, is that poor children are deprived and lacking in skills (e.g., Jensen 1969). The latter perspective has been modified somewhat in recent conceptualizations of poor children, which describe them as "at risk" or "vulnerable" in the process of "normal" development, but still imply what I choose to term the deficient child perspective. The following section reviews the conceptual and research bases of the deficient child perspective and the interventions suggested by this view.

DEFICIENT CHILD PERSPECTIVE

Most of the early research on poor children focused on their cognitive and language development. Poor children consistently achieved significantly lower average IQ test scores, aptitude test scores, language test scores, and achievement test scores than their more economically advantaged peers (see Deutsch 1973). The lower average test scores observed for poor children were interpreted as evidence of deficits in their cognitive and language skill development. Since an extensive empirical literature already existed demonstrating a significant positive correlation between performance on such tests and scholastic achievement (see Anastasi 1964, 1982), investigators believed they had identified the critical link between poverty and scholastic difficulties: poor children lacked basic skills required for successful school performance at the point of school entry. However, there were highly divergent views of the source of these deficiencies. Some posited environmental sources, whereas others advanced genetic deficiency arguments. These two perspectives and the social policy response each perspective implies are explored next.

Deficient Environment Equals Deficient Development Perspective

The view that poor children's assumed deficient cognitive and linguistic development resulted from deficient home environments (see Deutsch 1973) was encouraged, in part, by ethnographic research that examined life in communities characterized by social isolation from mainstream American life and concentrated poverty (e.g., Banfield 1960; Clark 1965; Lewis 1966; and Moynihan 1965). This work suggested the existence of what came to be known as the "culture of poverty," a hypothesis describing poor communities as distinct social systems within American society characterized by unstable and disorganized family structures, patterns of inadequate childrearing, maladaptive values, and personal maladjustment that undermine the preparedness of adults and children for participation in mainstream America. Specifically, the hypothesis posits that families in the culture of poverty demonstrate values and attitudes (e.g., inability to delay gratification, lack of impulse control, feelings of marginality and dependency) that function to perpetuate the cycle of poverty. Whether the observations made by these investigators are appropriately interpreted as evidence of a culture of poverty or as situational responses to poverty that would likely change if the conditions of poverty were relieved continues to be debated (see Duncan and Rodgers 1991; Ellwood 1988: 195–99; Jencks 1992).

Consistent with the "culture of poverty" hypothesis, researchers came to view poverty status as an efficient index of the occurrence of a complex of stimulation and experiences insufficient to support "normal" development of cognitive, socioemotional, and linguistic functioning (see, for example, Bereiter and Engelman 1966; Deutsch 1965; Hess 1970; Zigler, Abelson and Seitz 1973). Consequently, researchers who subscribed to this perspective on the nature of poor children's developmental problems began to engage in more qualitative research (e.g., in-home observations of mother-child interactions designed to specify the complexity of cause-and-effect relations, which mediated the correlations between economic status indicators and variables such as language complexity, vocabulary, scholastic achievement, and IQ).

This line of research provided evidence of differences in the home environments of poor and middle-class children in the amount, variety, and complexity of animate and inanimate stimulation provided to children (see, for example, Dave 1963; Whiteman and Deutsch 1968); differences in the styles of interaction in the home, especially as related to language behavior (see, for example, Bee et al. 1969; Bernstein 1961; Hess 1970); and differences in the patterning of stimulation to organize information for the child (e.g., how parents teach their children [see, for example, Hess and Shipman 1965]).

Results of this sort were used to support the deficit perspective on poor children's development, as well as to provide insights into the cause of the children's developmental deficiencies: environmental deprivation. Poor children were variously described as culturally deprived, socially disadvantaged, culturally disadvantaged, or socially and culturally disadvantaged. However, regardless of the label used, the assumption of deficient development prevailed.

Of particular importance for this conceptualization of the nature of poor children's scholastic difficulties was the inference that since the assumed deficiencies were environmentally caused, they could be remediated, even prevented, through environmental intervention (Deutsch 1973). This represented a significant departure from social scientists' traditional view that IQ tests measured fixed intellectual potential (Deutsch 1973; Zigler and Valentine 1979).

Another "insight" was revealed in research related to IQ test score stability and change that proved exceedingly important in the development of programs to remediate poor children's assumed cognitive deficiencies. Bloom (1964) presented results from analyses of cross-sectional and longitudinal data that he interpreted to indicate that *50 percent of development* of intelligence measured at age 17 occurs between birth and age 4. This finding suggested that the preschool years are a kind of "critical period" for the development of IQ. It also suggested to some theorists that preschool-age children were maximally responsive to remediation aimed at redirecting their negative developmental trajectories. According to Zigler and Valentine (1979), the prevailing view was that "the young child was plastic material to be molded *quickly and permanently* [emphasis mine] by the proper school environment. . . ." (p. 9).

All of these "insights" about poor children's deficient development and the developmental course of IQ suggested a "quick fix" strategy to address poor children's developmental problems: early childhood education. Thus, in 1965, the first large-scale, national intervention program was implemented: Project Head Start. Head Start was designed to facilitate poor children's intellectual, social, and emotional development; to help meet their health and nutritional needs; and, to involve their parents in helping them to learn (see Clarke, 1984). Ultimately, the goal was to launch poor children on the road to educational and occupational success.

PROJECT HEAD START: SUCCESS OR FAILURE?

Despite the fanfare with which Head Start was launched, it is now clear that the well-intentioned social scientists and educators who entered the intervention arena did not sufficiently understand poor children's development to effect the long-term goals they set. Some have claimed that the decision to implement Project Head Start was primarily determined by political urgings rather than scientific insights (see Zigler and Valentine 1979). Recently, Gallagher (1991: 435) concluded that the "quick fix" approach to intervention served the interests of its political sponsors well because their "self-interest depends on great and immediate success of the programs they endorse." Gallagher noted that in the late summer of 1965, President Lyndon Johnson proudly announced that " 'as a result of the summer program of Head Start, 250,000 children have been taken off the welfare roles and placed on the work roles. . . .' " (1991: 434).

In the midst of the hopefulness and excitement of this period, Edmund Gordon (1968) cautioned that

if the flood of interest and activity currently being poured into work with the disadvantaged were based more on substantial research findings or reflected considered, empirically-derived evidence, one could have greater hope that this effort would result in greatly improved life chances for the target populations. Although one must appreciate the fact that human and material resources are being directed at this long neglected problem, we simply will be helping to compound the disadvantaged status and to reinforce old prejudices if we fail to recognize the limitations of these efforts. Given the present level of knowledge and work, five or ten years from now many of our disadvantaged youngsters may still be at the bottom of the academic heap. Such a result could give renewed popularity to the now more dormant concepts of inherent inadequacy. This retreat to a theory of innate deficiency would be defended on the grounds that during the sixties this nation poured resources into helping these children and achieved relatively little despite all efforts. It may not readily be remembered that enriched diet did little to conquer tuberculosis, not because this measure was applied with insufficient diligence, but because the inappropriateness of this treatment modality was less evident before the nature of the disease was better understood. (pp. 405–6)

Gordon's observations proved prophetic. In 1969, just four years after Project Head Start was implemented, Arthur Jensen published his famous *Harvard Educational Review* article, "How Much Can We Boost IQ and Scholastic Achievement?" which questioned the effectiveness of the interventions in achieving their stated goals. Although some of the programs included under Project Head Start had succeeded in significantly increasing the IQ test scores of poor children, the data indicated that these increments "washed out" after a few years of public school attendance. Jensen posited that the failure of the intervention programs to produce permanent changes in the children's IQ scores and educational achievement was due to genetically determined deficiencies in the intellectual potential of the children. As Gordon (1968: 406) had predicted, the early results did give rise to "dormant concepts of inherent inadequacy."

As discussed later in this chapter, there were effective empirical and conceptual rebuttals to Jensen's "inherent inadequacy" hypothesis. However, as Spencer, Brookins, and Allen (1985: xvii) observed, Jensen's hypothesis appears to have "caused politicians and academicians to seriously question the feasibility of government funded 'enrichment' programs for the 'disadvantaged'. . . ." Consistent with this view of the effect of Jensen's analysis on politicians, Gallagher (1991) shared a personal experience while in the U.S. Department of Health, Education and Welfare in 1970. Gallagher recounted that during an interagency meeting to discuss the fate of Head Start, one

of the "bright young men from the White House" announced that
" 'we know that Head Start was a failure' " (p. 435). Apparently, the
"bright young [man] from the White House" had accepted the idea
that significant lasting change in IQ scores represented a reasonable
basis for determining the success of Head Start. It appears that policymakers over the past two decades have implicitly judged Head Start
less than successful in view of the fact that the program has never
been funded sufficiently to serve all children who are eligible. Brooks-
Gunn (1990) has reported that Head Start serves one-fifth to one-
quarter of eligible children.

Clarke (1984) concluded that the original planning, development,
and outcome projections for Head Start were based on four largely
unsubstantiated assumptions. The first was that the preschool years
are a critical period for intellectual development as measured by IQ
tests, and that, therefore, intervention in these early years could
permanently boost intellectual development so measured. Clarke
asserted that Bloom's (1964) use of the phrase "percent of development" rather than "percent of variance accounted for" was "responsible for the exaggerated claims for the alleged importance of the early
years" (p. 129).

The second assumption was that a short-term intervention was
sufficient to produce long-term effects on poor children's educational
achievement and attainment. This assumption was also derived from
Bloom's (1964) conclusions about the "percent of development" that
occurs in the preschool years.

The third assumption, closely related to the second, was that the
home environments of poor children, which had caused the presumed deficiencies in the children, would no longer affect their
development after successful intervention had occurred, that is, after
their IQ scores had been raised. However, even if Bloom's (1964)
conclusion that 50 percent of development occurs before age 4 is
accurate, 50 percent of growth remains after age 4. As Clarke (1984)
pointed out, this represents ample opportunity for the forces of poverty to take their toll on poor children's IQ, motivation, and attitudes
toward school-related learning when they return to the routines of
their family life and community schools.

Finally, Clarke (1984) questioned the assumption that IQ causes
educational achievement. Contrary to traditionally held views of IQ
tests, they are as much a measure of achievement as any formally
designated achievement test. The major difference between IQ tests
and other achievement tests is that the former assess a wider range
of specific skills than do the latter. Clarke further posited that the

observed positive correlation between IQ scores and school achievement measures does not necessarily indicate that IQ causes achievement: a plausible alternative interpretation of the correlation is that two-way interactions occur between the measures. Clarke cited the work of Crano, Kenny, and Campbell (1972) as supporting this alternative interpretation of the relationship between IQ scores and scholastic achievement indices.

Crano et al. (1972) attempted to empirically determine the causal direction of the IQ-achievement correlation. Specifically, these investigators questioned whether the acquisition of concrete mental skills (e.g., reading and arithmetic) causes later development of higher-order organizational rules (i.e., intelligence), or whether intelligence causes increased capacity for acquisition of concrete mental skills. Using the cross-lag panel correlation technique with IQ and the Iowa Test of Basic Skills data available for 5,495 poor and middle-class students for both fourth and sixth grades, these investigators explored the direction of causality between IQ and school achievement. Crano et al. (1972) interpreted their results to indicate that in the case of middle-class students, IQ appears to cause more rapid acquisition of specific skills. In the case of poor children, increases in specific skills appear to cause an increase in IQ.

In view of the Crano et al. (1972) results, one may conclude that the home experiences of middle-class children provide opportunities for the development of specific academic skills sufficient for them to demonstrate their capacity for higher-order organizational rules on IQ tests. In the case of poor children, it may be that home experiences do not provide the opportunity for development of the specific skills required to demonstrate their development of higher-order organizational rules on such tests.

If we accept Clarke's (1984) hypothesis of a two-way interaction between IQ and achievement, then Head Start must be judged a success on the basis of the initial IQ gains. The program demonstrated that the relatively brief exposure of poor children to the skills utilized in IQ testing was sufficient for them to show their higher-order cognitive development, which suggests that they came to Head Start as intellectually competent children who simply lacked some specific knowledge. It would seem reasonable to question not the value of early intervention for promoting scholastic achievement, but why public schools are so ineffective at sustaining the specific skills Head Start demonstrates poor children to be capable of achieving in a relatively short period of time.

Head Start should also be judged successful on the basis of long-term effects on poor children's educational progress that have been demonstrated in follow-up studies. Children who participated in these programs, compared to control group peers, were less likely to be placed in special education classes, and their school attendance was better (McKey et al. 1985). In the case of children who participated in smaller scale, longer-term intervention programs such as those included in the Consortium for Longitudinal Studies, follow-up studies revealed that these children, compared to control children, were less likely to be retained in grade or placed in special education classes, and showed higher average mathematics achievement (Lazar and Darlington 1982).

Still, it remains the case that Arthur Jensen and other hereditarians viewed Head Start and other preschool intervention programs as failures because sustained increases in IQ were not obtained by the interventions. The hereditarian perspective, and related conclusions about Head Start and intervention in general, are examined next.

Low IQ Equals Hereditary Inadequacy Perspective

The hereditarian view of poverty has a long history in American society. Lewis Terman, a pioneer in the U.S. IQ testing movement, concluded that "the social class to which the family belongs depends less on chance than on parents' native qualities of intellect and character" (1916: 115). Herrnstein (1971) advanced a similar argument regarding the basis of socioeconomic stratification.

The historical confluence of race/ethnicity and poverty in American society served to lend credibility to Jenson's (1969) "hereditary inadequacy" hypothesis of the failure of various intervention programs to produce sustained increments in the IQ scores of the target children. Obvious physical differences in the appearance of African-Americans versus individuals of European ancestry, which are clearly genetically determined, have been focused upon at various points in American history to advance genetic inferiority analyses of African-Americans and to justify their position in the American socioeconomic structure (see, for example, analyses by Gould 1981).

Although most researchers in child poverty at the time viewed poverty as the critical variable in the determination of various deficiencies they assumed characterized the children who were their research subjects, it was also the case that many of the children were poor African-Americans. Jensen (1969) focused on the significant difference in the average IQ scores of African-American and white children within various socioeconomic strata to support his genetic hypothesis of between-group differences in IQ and scholastic achievement. At the time, this was not a new observation. As early as 1960, McQueen and Browning had reported IQ and school achievement differences between African-American and white students "matched" for socioeconomic status. However, prior to 1969, the observation was not considered a salient issue in mainstream social science research, for at least two reasons.

First, the idea of a "match" between the two groups on socioeconomic indicators was considered, implicitly if not explicitly, a ludicrous notion. The historical social isolation of African-Americans from mainstream culture and American life made the idea untenable that similar ratings for African-Americans on indicators of socioeconomic status such as family income and parental education would index the same patterns of environmental transactions observed in white homes. Trotman's (1977) analysis of African-American and white homes, similarly identified as middle-class, for what was termed the *intellectuality* of home environment revealed significant differences on this dimension favoring the white rearing environment. Similarly, Moore (1986) presented a comparative analysis of dimensions of childrearing thought to be relevant to children's IQ test performance based on data derived from middle-class adoptive white and African-American mothers. In this study, both groups of mothers had adopted African-American children. The results revealed significant differences in facets of their childrearing that were investigated, favoring the white mothers, and the differences were significantly related to their adopted African-American children's IQ test performance.

A second reason for ignoring the finding of between-group differences in IQ test performance within social class designations as possible evidence of genetic difference between the populations has to do with the concept of heritability. As Bock and Moore (1986) have observed,

> Standard models of quantitative genetics deal exclusively with variation *within* [emphasis mine] populations; intergroup comparisons of behavioral traits are problematic because, insofar as there is any environmental component in the trait variation, there is no basis for inferring the quantitative effect of environmental influences on the population mean. Jensen . . . violates this principle of genetic analysis when he extrapolates models of genetic variability and transmission derived from analysis of within-group variation of the trait (IQ score) to account for between-group differences in the population means. (p. 82)

Other efforts to test Jensen's inherited inadequacy hypothesis of the nature of IQ score differences between African-American and white children have failed to confirm it. For example, Scarr and colleagues (1977) tested Jensen's (1973) hypothesis that there is a correlation of about .50 between degree of white ancestry and IQ test scores based on his estimates of the effects of genetic variation between African-Americans and whites for these scores. Scarr and colleagues estimated the degree of white ancestry in a large sample of African-American and white children using blood group markers. They correlated these estimates with obtained IQ test scores for the sample. The results revealed no significant correlations between the estimates of white ancestry and the children's test scores. In fact, the highest correlation observed between the two measures was .13.

However, even if Jensen had not been in error, his hereditarian analysis of the observed between-group differences in IQ test scores did not preclude the potential for effective intervention to support poor African-American children's success in school as well as IQ test performance. Unfortunately, there is a tendency among social scientists, educators, policymakers, and the American public in general to assume that if a characteristic is linked to genes, environmental factors cannot have an effect on developmental outcomes. This is clearly not the case. Bock (1974) demonstrated the critical importance of environmental factors in the determination of traits that are known to be strongly genetically determined, using the case of average stature difference between European, American, and Asian populations. He noted that in two generations, all three groups have increased in average stature by nearly one standard deviation, and the increase in average Japanese stature has increased even more dramatically since World War II. Bock contended that environmental factors, specifically better nutrition in the case of stature, can substantially change the mean of a highly heritable quantitative trait. Bock concludes that nothing known about general verbal ability, which is what most IQ tests really measure (Anastasi 1982) "should induce us to rule out a similar trend in the average ability of the U.S. black minority as it moves out of years of segregated life and into the majority educational, linguistic, and cultural environment of the United States" (1974: 595).

Similarly, even Jensen (1981) admitted that if intelligence as measured by an IQ test is highly heritable, in the range of .70 to .80, the potential for environmental effects remains remarkably substantial. He posited that with this high heritability estimate, assuming existing environmental influences on IQ test scores is normally distributed, the total range of environmental influences would be about 45 IQ test points. This represents considerable potential gain from well-developed environmental intervention.

Recently, Scarr (1992), in her presidential address to the biennial meetings of the Society for Research in Child Development, advanced a hereditarian view of developmental differences between children that implies far less potential for intervention strategies to succeed in facilitating children's optimal development than did Jensen. Scarr presented behavioral genetics research in support of the construct "genotype-environment correlation" as a way of conceptualizing the effects of children's rearing environments on developmental outcomes such as personality traits, school achievement, and IQ.

Genotype-environment correlation is a construct borrowed from evolutionary theory that posits that each species is genetically preprogrammed to respond to specific aspects of the environment while ignoring others (Tooby and Cosmides 1990). Genotype-environment correlation is essentially implied by the idea of ecological niche. However, Scarr (1992) has generalized this species-level construct to individual-level developmental processes to argue that, owing to individual differences in genotype, children create different environments for themselves within the same family by focusing on certain features and ignoring others.

Scarr (1992) has further argued that, to the extent child developmentalists and other social scientists observe correlations between parental behavior, rearing environment characteristics, and child development measures, these relations are due to shared genes between biological parents and their offsprings. That is, observed relations between children's characteristics such as IQ, scholastic achievement, and home environment features are due to the covariance of genotypes and environments. In other words, the home environment different parents provide their children—socioemotionally and materially—is largely a reflection of parental genotypes that are also shared with biological children. For example, Scarr (see Scarr-Salapatek 1975) observed that bright parents are likely to have children with above-average IQs and to provide advantaged environments to their children, whereas parents with retardation may have "less bright children under any environmental circumstances but also may supply those children with educationally deprived environments" (p. 30).

Scarr (1992) pointed out that the inferences she has advanced regarding the salience of individual-level genotype-environment correlation in the determination of individual differences in developmental outcomes are based on heritability estimates for measures of intelligence, specific cognitive abilities, personality, and psychopathology derived from North American and European populations. However, her extended discussion of evidence supporting the hypothesis of pervasive effects of presumed genotype-environment correlations on child development does not reflect a careful delimitation to North American and European populations. Instead, Scarr, in effect, generalizes her conclusions to all children, regardless of racial/ethnic background.

Scarr (1992) concluded that so long as children are reared in "average expectable environments," genetically determined developmental trajectories will not be altered. What constitutes an "average expectable environment" is described in very general terms allowing for tremendous variation, but specifically excludes violent, abusive, and neglectful family behavior. To exemplify the point, Scarr (1992) stated:

> . . . . it is not easy to intervene deliberately in children's lives to change their development, unless their environments are outside the normal species range . . . . for children whose development is on a predictable but undesirable trajectory and whose parents are providing a supportive environment, interventions [emphasis mine] have only temporary and limited effects. . . . Feeding a below average-intellect more and more information will not make her brilliant. Exposing a shy child to socially demanding events will not make him feel less shy. The child with below-average intelligence and the shy child may gain some specific skills and helpful knowledge of how to behave in specific situations, but their enduring intellectual and personality characteristics will not be changed. (pp. 16–17)

Clearly, Scarr's (1992) interpretation of the nature of individual differences in child developmental outcomes suggests that specific social policy designed to support the optimal development of children reared in poverty, unless the children are in abusive, violent, and/or neglectful homes, is likely to produce only modest, superficial changes in areas of development typically targeted (e.g., IQ, scholastic achievement, socioemotional well-being). However, Scarr is premature in drawing this conclusion.

Even if we allow that genotype-environment correlation is a major source of individual differences in development, the idea that wide variations in environments within the range of "average expectable environments" presents "functional equivalent" opportunities for "normal development" ignores the well-established constructs of "genomic repertoire" and "reaction range." Genomic repertoire refers to the "potential for a particular genotype to develop into any one of a number of phenotypes," and reaction range refers to "the quantitatively different phenotypes that can develop from the same genotype under varying environmental conditions" ranging from restricted to enriched (Scarr-Salapatek 1975: 15). Therefore, one cannot conclude that wide variation within "average expectable environments" presents "functional equivalent" opportunities for normal development. Actually, we have no idea of the *potential* for "normal" development of a given child until the child has been provided a favorable environment from which to construct his or her own experiences.

The gains in IQ test scores, specific skill development, and academic motivation observed for poor and ethnic minority children at the time of their completion of compensatory education programs suggest the importance of the reaction range construct in relation to variations in environments. There is reason to believe that if these children had been exposed to continuously enriched educational environments for the duration of their elementary and secondary school experience, the positive effects on their personal development and scholastic achievement might have been dramatic (Gallagher 1991). Indeed, a number of investigators have posited that deficiencies in the K–12 schools that poor and ethnic minority children attend, not the children, cause the achievement difficulties they experience. These investigators advance a cultural difference perspective on development among poor and ethnic minority children. This hypothesis and related research findings are examined next.

CULTURALLY DIFFERENT CHILD PERSPECTIVE

The analyses of poor and ethnic minority children's academic achievement problems advanced by both the environmentalists and hereditarians converged in that both schools of thought assumed that deficiencies in requisite cognitive skills undermined the children's educational progress. However, as the disciplines represented by researchers at work on the issue became more diverse, significant challenges emerged to the deficit perspective. Cultural anthropologists, cognitive psychologists, and sociolinguists advanced the construct of cultural relativism in interpreting the meaning of socioeconomic status and ethnic group differences in standardized test performance and scholastic achievement.

This hypothesis, referred to here as the "culturally different child perspective," asserted the existence of a significant interaction between poverty and culture in determining disparities in outcome measures observed between various social class and ethnic groups. It also questioned the assumption of functional equivalence of measures of behavior and meaning of behavior, such as IQ test scores, derived from groups facing different cultural realities that, presumably, result in different forms of behavior in both quality and quantity. In contrast to the traditional environmentalist position, investigators guided by the cultural difference perspective interpreted between-group variations in IQ test performance and specific measures of language as artifacts of cultural differences between groups rather than as indicators of cognitive ability differences (Baratz and Baratz 1970; Cole and Bruner 1971; Labov 1970, 1972).

A conceptual basis for postulating culturally determined differences in behavior patterns between socially isolated ethnic groups in the United States has been provided by the vast anthropological literature. Herskovits (1958) presented evidence of possible links between certain characteristic behaviors of African-Americans and their African origins. Reissman (1962) posited that certain ethnic minority groups in America had developed distinctive behavior patterns, or cultures, in response to the poverty that had characterized their experiences in the United States. However, Blauner (1970), although advancing a similar conceptualization of behavioral discontinuities between different groups in America, claimed the existence of a "black culture" distinct from the generalized "culture of poverty" suggested by Reissman. Blauner reasoned that many of the characteristic behaviors of African-Americans represent this ethnic group's unique response to a history of racism and discrimination in America.

Psychologists reported differences in the patterns of mental abilities of children from different ethnic groups, suggesting a possible connection between subcultural experiences and cognitive performance. For example, Lesser, Fifer, and Clark (1965) investigated the level and pattern of mental abilities of African-American, Chinese-American, Jewish, and Puerto Rican first-grade children from middle- and lower-socioeconomic status backgrounds in New York City. The children were administered verbal, numerical, spatial, and reasoning tests. The findings indicated significant ethnic group differences in overall level of performance as well as differences in the pattern of performance among the groups. Socioeconomic status affected the level of performance within each ethnic group, but not the pattern of performance.

Stodolsky and Lesser (1967) replicated Lesser and colleagues' (1965) study in Boston, but added a fifth ethnic group to the design: Irish-Catholic children. This study yielded results similar to those of the earlier study for African-American, Chinese-American, Jewish, and Puerto Rican children. However, no distinctive pattern of performance or socioeconomic status effects emerged for the Irish-Catholic children.

Investigators who subscribe to the cultural difference perspective questioned two major assumptions underlying the use of IQ tests in this area of research: first, IQ test scores reliably and validly convey meaningful information about the ability of individuals to learn from and adapt to their environment; and, second, IQ test scores reflect genetically determined differences in cognitive potential. It is argued that there is a fundamental distinction between a child's performance on IQ tests and his or her intelligence or competence. That is, some groups of children may consistently achieve lower average scores on intelligence tests, but it cannot be concluded that such children are less competent or less skilled than their higher-scoring peers. From this perspective, IQ tests measure performance; they do not necessarily assess children's fundamental cognitive ability (Cole and Bruner 1971; Mercer 1971).

A number of investigators who subscribed to the cultural difference perspective advanced the argument that IQ tests are biased in favor of middle-class white children. Three major areas of bias have been identified. First, such tests demand specific information and manipulations from children that are more representative of everyday experiences of middle-class white children than of nonwhite and/or poor children (Cole and Hall 1974; Williams 1972). The tests also favor standard English-speaking children over children for whom English is not their first language and children who speak a dialectical form of English. Lack of proficiency in standard English skills can affect test performance because children so characterized may have difficulty determining what is expected of them and/or generating an appropriate response (Labov 1970; Stewart 1970). Finally, children from different ethnic groups enter the test situation with not only a different (not deficit) set of skills but also different attitudes and strategies for negotiating the situation, creating a considerable mismatch between test demands and the resources they bring to the testing situation. This mismatch is conceptualized as the major source of variance in average scores observed for middle-class white children and nonwhite and/or poor children (Cole and Bruner 1971).

Ginsburg (1972) approached the issue of the meaning of within- and between-group differences in IQ test performance from the perspective of Piaget's (1952) theory of cognitive development. Ginsburg argued that intelligence tests, by focusing on the number of correct responses to sets of questions, assess only superficial or surface differences in children's cognitive processes. However, from a Piagetian perspective, to conclude that a particular child or group of children is deficient in cognitive ability, assessment of cognitive competence requires an intelligence test that taps the reasoning or mental operations employed by children. Ginsburg's research demonstrated no ethnic or social class differences in physically healthy children's abilities to organize and adapt to the world. In other words, all children are similar in the development of cognitive universals: modes of language and thought.

From this perspective, environments may vary in specific characteristics or features; however, the development of cognitive universals requires only that the environment provide a sufficient variety of experiences for the child's natural processes to act upon. Differences in specific characteristics of environments or specific experiences provided by the environment may affect the content of thought and children's patterning of thought, but not the basic categories of cognition such as space, time, causality, equivalence, seriation, or the reasoning processes underlying such concepts that all children ultimately achieve (Ginsburg 1972: 12–139).

The work of other cognitive psychologists generally supports Ginsburg's conclusions (see Mermelstein and Schulman 1967; Gaudia 1972; Ginsburg and Russell 1981). It is also the case that no significant socioeconomic status or ethnic group differences in children's performance are observed on infant intelligence scales, which measure abilities such as sensory perception, large and fine motor skills, adaptability to social situations, attention span, and reactivity (Thomas 1970)—the bases of the development of intellectual competencies according to Piaget. Researchers also report no significant relation between home environment measures and infants' performance on the infant scales (Elardo, Bradley, and Caldwell 1975). However, between-group differences appear in children's performance on IQ tests when the tests begin to emphasize language and demand specific information. It is also at this point that significant correlations are observed between home environments and IQ test scores (Elardo et al. 1975).

Cultural differences are also thought to contribute to the low academic achievement and educational attainment of poor and/or nonwhite children. Due to discontinuities between the knowledge, skills, and behaviors with which the children enter school and those that are expected (which are similar to the expectations of IQ test settings), teachers assume that the children cannot learn. Consequently, the children are relegated to lower placements in the school curriculum, where they are not provided the same level of exposure to educational materials or required to demonstrate as high a level of mastery as children considered more capable (Cole and Bruner 1971; Haskins, Walden, and Ramey 1983; Rist 1973; Shade 1982).

Baratz and Baratz (1970) asserted the need for investigators to begin to develop research strategies to discover the different forms of ethnic group behaviors, because "then and only then can programs be created that utilize the child's differences as a means of helping him acculturate to the mainstream while maintaining individual identity and cultural heritage" (p. 47). However, this call has gone essentially unheeded by the majority of mainstream social scientists. The training of a relatively small cadre of ethnic minority scholars during the 1960s and 1970s has resulted in a growing body of literature that is specifically focused on explicating minority child development from cultural/ecological perspectives (see, for example, Spencer et al. 1985; and *Child Development: Special Issue on Minority Children,* April 1990, edited by Spencer and McLoyd).

Although supportive of research guided by the cultural difference perspective, Ogbu (1978, 1982, 1985), a cultural anthropologist, has cautioned that African-Americans, Native Americans, and Mexican-Americans are a special type of minority: a castelike minority. Ogbu has posited that castelike stratification is different from stratification by social class and has significantly different implications. A castelike minority group is described as one that is "incorporated into a society involuntarily and permanently, and whose only means of escape from this forced subjugation is through 'passing' or immigration—routes that are not always open" (1982: 125).

Among the significant personal consequences of membership in a castelike minority group is the job ceiling—"that is, highly consistent pressures and obstacles that selectively assign blacks and similar minority groups to jobs at the lowest level status, power, dignity and income while allowing members of the dominant white group to compete more easily for more desirable jobs above that ceiling" (Ogbu 1982: 125). Ogbu concluded that African-American children and children from the other castelike minority groups perform less well in school than noncastelike minorities and whites because of their early recognition of this job ceiling. Therefore, interventions suggested by insights developed from the cultural difference perspective on child development are not likely to boost African-American children's school performance as dramatically as one might expect until the perceived social structural barriers to their occupational goals are removed.

Ogbu's (1982) conceptualization specifies an ecological variable that social scientists have been reluctant to focus upon in their analysis of significant factors affecting developmental outcomes among poor ethnic minority children: institutional racism/ethnocentrism and related discrimination in American society. However, it is the case that compensatory education programs have effected modest gains in the educational achievement of poor ethnic minority children, in spite of their castelike minority status. Changes in K–12 public school education that are now being advocated could function to post more substantial gains in the specific skill development of poor and ethnic minority children. This issue is elaborated upon in subsequent sections of this chapter. But, first, an examination of today's most prevalent image of poor children: the at-risk/vulnerable child.

THE AT-RISK/VULNERABLE CHILD: DEFICIENT CHILD REVISITED

The at-risk/vulnerable child conceptual framework is now the most prevalent perspective from which poor children's development is researched and analyzed. Superficially, this perspective avoids the controversy and debate of the late 1960s and 1970s over the meaningfulness and appropriateness of the deficit conceptualization of poor children's development that underpinned research and policy formation during this time. It is a rather neutral descriptor that, unlike the original deficient child perspective, implies the possibility of negative developmental outcomes such as school achievement difficulties rather than the near inevitability of such outcomes. Brooks-Gunn (1990) described the at-risk/vulnerable child perspective as follows: "Vulnerability implies that a particular child or group of children who are at risk in a probabilistic sense for manifesting a certain behavior or set of behaviors are susceptible to decrements in well-being" (p. 104). Well-being in children is further elaborated by Brooks-Gunn (1990) to include cognitive and academic domains (e.g., IQ, language, academic performance), the health domain (e.g., physical, cognitive and mental health, low birthweight, and chronic illness), the emotional domain (e.g., emotional self-regulation, psychopathology, behavior problems, and self-esteem), and the social domain (e.g., parental and peer relationships, perceptions of competence, and internal motivational factors).

A careful reading of the literature on at-risk/vulnerable children reveals an underlying deficient child perspective. When investigators conceptualize the risk factors and how they function to place children at risk, what is unmasked is a child presumed deficient in cognitive, socioemotional, and/or linguistic development on the basis of indicators traditionally used to document deficiencies in poor children (e.g., IQ, language test scores, and academic achievement difficulties). Essentially what the at-risk/vulnerable child perspective does is to embed the issues earlier identified with poor children, including the assumed cognitive difficiencies, in a broader context of children experiencing developmental challenges (e.g., psychopathology, conduct disorders, and chronic illness).

As currently used in the social science and policy literature, the at-risk/vulnerable child construct is so inclusive in the specification of risk factors that the majority of American children may be considered at risk to a greater or lesser degree, even when the presence of multiple risk factors is used as the criterion for at-risk designation. For example, while poverty, minority status, neglect, and abuse are viewed as risk factors, so, too, are anxious attachment in infancy, rejection by peers in childhood, low parental education, low child IQ, large family size, parental conflict, divorce of parents, remarriage of parents, serious illness, or accidents in the immediate family (Farrington et al. 1990; Goldstein 1990; Sameroff and Fiese 1989; Sroufe 1989). Consequently, the application of the concept of the at-risk/vulnerable child to poor children may function to obscure the unique developmental challenges associated with the confluence of chronic poverty and other risk factors such as minority status (see McLoyd 1990; Spencer and Markstrom-Adams 1990).

Indeed, Brooks-Gunn (1990) concluded that one strategy employed to screen for at-risk children (i.e., birth certificate information: mother's education, age, and race) would designate the majority of children in some poor neighborhoods as at risk. This observation suggests that poor children are disproportionately represented among the at-risk population; however, specific focus on the meaning and consequences of their at-risk status relative to nonpoor at-risk children is generally not addressed in this paradigm. The effect of the at-risk/vulnerable child perspective has been to dilute, if not eliminate, a specific policy and research focus on poor children. Yet, they remain our most at-risk children.

In the future, policy analysts and researchers should separate poor children from the broadly conceived at-risk/vulnerable child category. The developmental supports required for a child in a poor urban neighborhood permeated by crime, unemployment, drug use, violence, and general hopelessness, whose mother gave birth to him or her at age 15 and never completed high school are necessarily different from those required by an affluent child in a serene neighborhood with good schools, who lives with his or her recently remarried mother and her husband, and whose other major risk factors are that his or her school achievement is discordant with ability test results, and there are indicators of low self-esteem and difficulty in forming friendships. The point here is not that the latter child is not at risk, only that there is probably a significant quantitative and qualitative difference in what the two children need to be supported into healthy adulthood.

Gross (1990) has presented results from a large multisite randomized clinical trial of an intensive early intervention project with low birthweight infants and their mothers that suggest the need for a specific focus on poor children in policy development. The eight medical institutions that participated in the project were the University of Arkansas for Medical Sciences; Albert Einstein College of Medicine; Harvard Medical School; University of Miami School of Medicine; University of Pennsylvania School of Medicine; University of Texas Health Science Center at Dallas; University of Washington School of Medicine; and Yale University School of Medicine. Higher IQ scores were obtained in the study for intervention infants compared to control infants except at the Harvard site. Gross speculated that the lack of observed intervention effects at this site "may be related to its relatively large proportion of college-educated mothers and abundant community services" (p. 156).

Gross (1990) also reported a significant intervention by maternal education effect in parental reports of child behavior problems. There was no difference in the number of child behavior problems reported by college-educated mothers in the intervention and control group. However, among mothers with less education, those in the intervention group reported fewer child behavior problems than the mothers in the control group. Gross speculated that this interaction effect was due to less-educated mothers in the intervention group becoming better informed about age-appropriate behaviors, and "consequently report[ing] fewer problems" (p. 157); and/or their having learned more effective behavior management techniques through the intervention program; or the intervention could have actually altered their children's behavior. These results indicate that although all the infants were at risk, the benefits of intervention may have accrued disproportionately to the less-educated mothers and their children.

A positive effect of the at-risk/vulnerable child conceptualization of poor children is that it has facilitated a broader consideration of environmental factors that affect child developmental outcomes. That is, much of the earlier research focused on home environment correlates of IQ and scholastic achievement or the intellectuality of the rearing environment (e.g., language use and maternal teaching styles). However, the at-risk conceptualization emphasizes environmental factors that affect the whole child, including cognitive, physical, behavioral and emotional well-being, and the interaction effects among these aspects of child development. For example, this line of research reveals that poor expectant mothers are less likely to receive timely and adequate health care, which often results in harmful effects on their unborn children. Poor maternal nutrition, infection, and maternal stress, to name a few of the treatable problems during pregnancy, can negatively impact upon poor children's development prenatally (Baumeister et al. 1991). These conditions can result in low birthweight or prematurity, and subsequent neurodevelopmental dysfunction and chronic health problems, all of which have implications for the efficiency with which children can develop the social and cognitive skills required for success in school and adult roles.

Of course, not all children reared in poverty demonstrate significant developmental problems. Garmezy (1976) termed such children "invulnerable" (1976) or "resilient" (1991) and suggested an important direction for research designed to specify processes by which poverty negatively influences child development. Garmezy reasoned that research comparing the psychosocial experiences of children similarly classified as poor, but who also demonstrated significant differences on various measures of developmental outcomes such as school achievement and socioemotional adjustment, could help identify the processes that mediate the correlation between poverty and adverse development among children. This search for what are termed "protective factors," that is, circumstances that promote or maintain healthy development in children at risk for negative development (Rutter 1979), has resulted in some insights. Garmezy (1991) identified three variables that appear to function as protective factors for poor children: temperament, such as "activity level, reflectiveness

in meeting new situations, cognitive skills and positive responsiveness to others"; family contexts characterized by "warmth, cohesion
and the presence of some caring adult (such as a grandparent) in the
absence of a responsive parent or in the presence of marital discord";
and, the "presence of external support, such as a strong maternal
substitute, a kind and concerned teacher or the presence of an institutional structure such as a caring agency or a church that fosters ties
to the larger community" (p. 421). Continuing research on protective
factors and how they function (e.g., Werner and Smith 1992) holds
promise for the identification of intervention strategies that may be
quite economical, such as the use of volunteer mentors and grandparents.

It is reasonable to conclude that the most enduring image of the
poor child is that of the deprived child lacking in specific skills
and basic intellectual competence. The reason for the poor child's
assumed deficiencies remains a point of debate among some theorists
and investigators and is ignored by many others. So far in this chapter's discussion, only those investigators who subscribe to the cultural difference perspective of poor children's lower average performance on cognitive, linguistic, and language tests have asserted that
poor children are able and competent. However, some researchers
in the sociology of education have also advanced the view that poor
children are skilled and able. In the view of these theorists, the
deficient child perspective on poor children is a social construction
designed to perpetuate the existing economic stratification and social
inequalities. This perspective is examined in greater detail in the
following section.

DEFICIENT CHILD PERSPECTIVE:
MYTH IN SERVICE OF INEQUALITY

Most Americans believe that compulsory education extends opportunities for socioeconomic upward mobility to all children, regardless
of economic status or ethnicity. The relative success individual children experience in educational achievement and attainment is presumed to result from differences in their ability, motivation, and
effort. The significant positive correlation between IQ and educational achievement is interpreted as evidence that the opportunity
structure is open to all, such that poor children who are competent
and motivated have the same chance for success through education

as middle-class children who are competent and motivated. Those least competent, regardless of family social status, will also be least successful in the competition for educational and occupational status.

Although many poor people escape poverty through educational success, some sociologists have argued that many more who could do not because the function of public schools is to maintain the prevailing social structure by reallocating the majority of each successive generation of youth to their original social status (Bowles and Gintis 1973; Persell 1977). According to this perspective, the correlation between social class and IQ, and the lower average performance on IQ tests observed for certain ethnic minority children, are artifactual of the test content that is intentionally biased to favor white middle-class children. Because middle-class children tend to achieve high average scores, their higher educational and occupational success are justified by the ability factor (Persell 1977).

Bowles and Gintis (1974) have conducted analyses of the effects of family-of-origin social class on the status attainment of individuals with the same IQ score. The results indicate that these individuals show no significant change in their adult status from their beginning status. Findings of this sort have led these investigators to conclude that social class origin is a much stronger predictor of educational and occupational attainment than IQ. However, Jencks (1992) reported that educational attainment among African-Americans became less dependent on family background between 1940 and 1980, resulting in better educational prospects (in terms of years of school completed) for "disadvantaged" children from this ethnic group. In the case of white children, there was little change in the effects of family background after 1970 (Jencks 1992: 200). However, measures of specific skill development still show white advantage.

Oakes (1992) has posited that measured intellectual ability is a social construction like race and gender that makes no real contribution to variations in how much children learn. However, such scores are used "fraudently" to claim that ability grouping and tracking are appropriate responses to differences in children's capacities and motivations (p. x). However, the ability group or track placement of individual pupils does make a difference in how much children learn because it determines how much they are allowed to learn, the way they are taught, and teachers' expectations of their performance.

The stigmas of poverty—that is, the perception that poor children are lacking in skills and the expectation that they will not succeed—appear to affect classroom teachers' responses to them as people and the way they are taught. Research indicates that in the early years of school, poor children are not provided the same level of exposure to new materials, are not encouraged in independent exploration, and are not required to demonstrate mastery at the same level as their middle-class peers (see Haskins et al. 1983; Hupp 1991). Good and Brophy (1987) reported from classroom observations that teachers' perceptions of children's ability affect the quality and quantity of classroom interaction with individual children. Children who are perceived as low achievers are asked fewer questions, are given less time to respond to teacher questions, and experience less supportive and motivating interactions with teachers than those perceived as high achievers. Bock and Moore (1986) have presented data to indicate that the differences between the scholastic achievement of poor and nonpoor youths, and between white and ethnic minority youths, tend to be negligible at eighth grade, but that the gap in the group's performance grows through the high school years.

The literature generally suggests that processes related to school, not the ability of poor children, significantly impact children's academic achievement and educational attainment. Ability grouping and tracking appear to play a significant role in the undereducation of poor children. It is this concern that has led a number of child advocacy and civil rights groups to call for an end to tracking and ability grouping in the public schools (see Wheelock 1992). Although tracking and ability grouping are thought to facilitate children's motivation to learn and the development of skills, research indicates that the practice has the opposite effect. The negative effects of tracking fall disproportionately to poor and ethnic minority children. Wheelock (1992) has called for an untracking of the schools and a new emphasis on "releasing intelligence rather than quantifying it and nurturing effort rather than defining ability" (p. 7).

CHALLENGES FOR SOCIAL POLICY

This chapter's discussion underscores a number of challenges for social policy. First, we must find a way to provide for the basic needs of poor children, particularly of those likely to spend most of their childhood in poverty. That is, adequate health care (including prenatal care), nutrition, housing, and physical safety must be made available. Children's physical well-being is a prerequisite for efforts to promote positive developmental outcomes in other domains of their functioning.

Second, the available research examining the effects of Head Start, and especially of carefully planned preschool intervention programs such as those included in the Consortium for Longitudinal Studies, attests to the developmental benefits of preschool education for poor children, particularly of those experiencing persistent poverty. We need to make quality preschool programs available to all poor children at risk of spending most of their childhood in poverty.

Third, school reform is critical to successful education of poor children, especially those from ethnic minority groups. Eliminating ability grouping in the lower grades and eliminating tracking in the junior high, middle schools, and high schools would be important steps. A large body of evidence indicates that ability grouping and tracking do nothing except guarantee and justify the undereducation of poor children. However, school reform must also entail changes in the way teachers facilitate learning (i.e., more cooperative and individualized goal structures and less competitive drill and recall) and the curriculum resources used. Accompanying such changes, school class sizes should decrease at all levels. This will afford teachers and students the opportunity to know one another better as people, and should help teachers to better plan learning experiences consistent with the needs and interests of their students.

Fourth, Ogbu's (1978, 1982, 1985) ideas about castelike minorities and the effect of this minority status on poor ethnic minority children's impetus to achieve and commitment to education should be explored through research. If Ogbu's hypotheses are correct, finding ways to address this issue through school reform or community programs could significantly affect success in engaging children in the learning process.

Fifth, the issues of children of poverty should be separated from the at-risk focus of current social policy. Certainly, poor children reared in persistent poverty are at risk for negative development in many areas. However, the uniqueness of the interaction of risk factors in the case of poor children must be recognized and examined through research focused specifically on them.

CONCLUSIONS

Our national interests are inextricably linked to facilitating the physical, emotional, social, and academic development of poor children.

Their numbers as a proportion of the shrinking youth population are growing. We can ill-afford to continue to debate whether the children are competent or lacking in skills. Sufficient evidence has accrued from Head Start and other intervention programs that have provided optimum learning environments for poor children indicating that such children can develop scholastic skills in relatively short periods of time, regardless of IQ scores. In children who show no evidence of neurodevelopmental dysfunction, there is every reason to believe that they can learn the skills and master the knowledge bases our society requires of them in their adult roles. If there is neurodevelopmental dysfunction in the case of some children, the specific problem can be identified and appropriate intervention provided so that these children are empowered to effectively pursue the educational process.

Americans can no longer allow the talent and potential represented in poor communities to go undeveloped or underdeveloped. Probably the most critical factor in efforts to increase the scholastic achievement and educational attainment of poor youths is the identification of effective educational processes and curricula to engage them in the learning process.

References

Anastasi, A. 1982. *Psychological Testing*. New York: MacMillan Publishing Co., Inc.

Banfield, E. 1960. *The Unheavenly City*. Boston: Little, Brown Publishing Co., Inc.

Baratz, S. and J. Baratz. 1970. "Early Childhood Intervention: The Social Science Base of Institutional Racism." *Harvard Educational Review* 40: 29–50.

Baumeister, A., F. D. Kupstas, and L. M. Klindworth. 1991. "The New Morbidity: A National Plan of Action." *American Behavioral Scientist* 34(4): 468–500.

Bee, H. L., L. F. Van Egeren, A. P. Streissguth, B. A. Nyman, and M. S. Leckie. 1969. "Social Class Differences in Maternal Teaching Strategies and Speech Patterns." *Developmental Psychology* 1: 726–34.

Bereiter, C., and S. Engelman. 1966. *Teaching Disadvantaged Children in Preschool*. Englewood Cliffs, N.J.: Prentice-Hall.

Bernstein, B. 1961. "Social Class and Linguistic Development." In *Education, Economy and Society*, edited by A. J. Halsey, J. Floud, and C. A. Anderson. New York: Free Press.

Blauner, R. 1970. "Black Culture: Myth or Reality?" In Americans from Africa: Old Memories, New Moods, edited by P. Rose. New York: Atherton Press.

Bloom, B. 1964. Stability and Change in Human Characteristics. New York: John Wiley & Sons.

Bock, R. D. 1974. Book Review of Educability and Group Differences, B. A. R. Jensen. Perspectives in Biology and Medicine 17: 594–97.

Bock, R. D., and E. G. J. Moore. 1986. Advantage and Disadvantage: A Profile of American Youth. Hillsdale, N.J.: Lawrence Erlbaum Associates.

Bowles, S. and H. Gintis. 1973. "IQ and the U.S. Class Structure." Social Policy, 3: 65–96.

Bronfenbrenner, U. 1979. The Ecology of Human Development. Cambridge, Massachusetts: Harvard University Press.

————. 1986. "Ecology of the Family as a Context for Human Development: Research Perspectives." Developmental Psychology 22(6): 723–42.

Brooks-Gunn, J. 1990. "Identifying the Vulnerable Child." In Improving the Life Chances of Children at Risk, edited by D. E. Rogers and E. Ginzberg. San Francisco: Westview Press.

Clark, K. E. 1965. Dark Ghetto. New York: Harper and Row.

Clarke, A. M. 1984. "Early Experience and Cognitive Development." In Review of Research in Education, 11, edited by E. W. Gordon. Washington, D.C.: American Educational Research Association.

Cole, M., and J. Bruner. 1971. "Cultural Differences and Inferences about Psychological Processes." American Psychologist 26: 867–76.

Cole, M., and W. S. Hall. 1974. "The Social Context of Psychoeducational Research." Paper presented in Series on Public Policy, Center for Urban Studies, Harvard University, Cambridge, Mass., May.

Coll, C. T. G. 1990. "Developmental Outcomes of Minority Infants: A Process-Oriented Look into Our Beginnings." Child Development 61(2): 270–89.

Commission on Minority Participation in Education and American Life. 1988. One-Third of a Nation. Washington, D.C.: American Council on Education, May.

Crano, W. D., D. A. Kenny, and D. T. Campbell. 1972. "Does Intelligence Cause Achievement?" Journal of Educational Psychology 63: 258–75.

Daniel, J., R. Hampton, and E. Newberger. 1983. "Child Abuse and Accidents in Black Families: A Controlled Comparative Study." American Journal of Orthopsychiatry 53: 645–53.

Darlington, R. B., J. M. Royce, A. S. Snipper, H. W. Murray, and I. Lazar. 1980. "Preschool Programs and Later Competence of Children from Low-Income Families." Science 208: 202–4.

Dave, R. H. 1963. "The Identification and Measurement of Environmental Variables that Are Related to Educational Achievement." Ph.D. dissertation, University of Chicago.

Deutsch, C. 1973. "Social Class and Child Development." In *Review of Child Development Research*, edited by B. M. Caldwell and H. Ricciuti. Chicago: University of Chicago Press.

Deutsch, M. 1965. "The Role of Social Class in Language Development and Cognition." *American Journal of Orthopsychiatry* 36: 78–88.

Deutsch, M., and I. Katz. 1968. "Introduction." In *Social Class, Race, and Psychological Processes*, by M. Deutsch, I. Katz, and A. Jensen. San Francisco: Holt, Reinhart & Winston.

Duncan, G. J., and W. Rodgers. 1991. "Has Children's Poverty Become More Persistent?" *American Sociological Review* 56: 538-50.

————. 1988. "Longitudinal Aspects of Childhood Poverty." *Journal of Marriage and the Family* 50: 1007–21.

Elardo, R., R. H. Bradley, and B. M. Caldwell. 1975. "The Relation of Infants' Home Environments to Mental Test Performance from Six to Thirty-Six Months: A Longitudinal Analysis." *Child Development* 46: 71–76.

Ellwood, T. T. 1988. *Poor Support.* New York: Basic Books.

Farrington, D., R. Loeber, D. Elliot, D. Hawkins, D. Kandel, M. Klein, J. McCord, D. Rowe, and R. Tremblay. 1990. "Advancing Knowledge about the Onset of Delinquency and Crime." In *Advances in Clinical Psychology*, vol. 13, edited by B. Lahey and A. Kazdin. New York: Plenum Press.

Gallagher, J. J. 1991. "Longitudinal Interventions: Virtues and Limitations." *American Behavioral Scientist* 34(4): 431–39.

Garmezy, N. 1976. "Vulnerable and Invulnerable Children: Theory, Research, and Intervention." Abstracted in *JSAS Catalog of Selected Documents in Psychology* 6: 96 (ms. 1337).

————. 1991. "Resiliency and Vulnerability to Adverse Developmental Outcomes Associated with Poverty." *American Behavioral Scientist* 34(4): 416–30.

Gaudia, G. 1972. "Race, Social Class and Age of Achievement of Conservation on Piaget's Tasks." *Developmental Psychology* 6: 158–65.

Ginsburg, H. 1972. *The Myth of the Deprived Child.* Englewood Cliffs, N.J.: Prentice-Hall.

Ginsburg, H. and R. Russell. 1981. "Social Class and Racial Influences on Early Mathematical Thinking." *Monographs of the Society for Research in Child Development.* 6: 46.

Goldstein, M. 1990. "Family Relations as Risk Factors for the Onset and Course of Schizophrenia." In *Risk and Protective Factors in the Development of Psychopathology*, edited by J. Rolf, A. Masten, D. Cicchetti, K. Neuchterlein, and S. Weintraub. New York: Cambridge University Press.

Good, T. L. and J. E. Brophy. 1987. *Looking in Classrooms.* New York: Harper and Row.

Gordon, E. W. 1968. "Programs of Compensatory Education." In *Social Class, Race, and Psychological Development*, edited by M. Deutsch, I. Katz, and A. Jensen. San Francisco: Holt, Rhinehart & Winston.

Gould, S. 1981. *Mismeasure of Man.* New York: W. W. Norton & Co.

Gross, R. T. 1990. "Multisite Randomized Intervention Trial for Premature, Low Birthweight Infants: The Infants Health and Development Program." In *Improving the Life Chances of Children at Risk,* edited by D. E. Rogers and E. Ginzberg. San Francisco: Westview Press.

Hamburg, D. A. 1992. *Today's Children.* New York: Times Books.

Harrington, M. 1982. *The Other America.* New York: Penguin Books.

Haskins, R., T. Walden, and C. T. Ramey. 1983. "Teacher and Student Behavior in High and Low Ability Groups." *Journal of Educational Psychology* 75: 965–76.

Hernstein, R. 1971. "I.Q." *Atlantic Monthly* 228: 44–64.

Herskovits, M. 1958. *The Myth of the Negro Past.* Boston: Beacon Press.

Hess, R. 1970. "Social Class and Ethnic Influences on Socialization." In *Carmichael's Manual of Child Development,* 3rd ed., vol. 2, edited by P. H. Mussen. New York: John Wiley & Sons.

Hess, R., and V. Shipman. 1965. "Early Experience and the Socialization of Cognitive Modes in Children." *Child Development* 34: 869–86.

Hilgard, E. R. 1968. "Preface." In *Social Class, Race, and Psychological Development,* edited by M. Deutsch, I. Katz, and A. Jensen, New York: Holt, Rinehart and Winston, Inc.

Hupp, S. C. 1991. "Promoting Cognitive Competence in Children at Risk." *American Behavioral Scientist* 34: 454–67.

Jencks, C. 1992. *Rethinking Social Policy: Race, Poverty, and the Underclass.* Cambridge, Mass.: Harvard University Press.

Jensen, A. R. 1969. "How Much Can We Boost I.Q. and Scholastic Achievement?" *Harvard Educational Review* 39:1–123.

———. 1973. *Educability and Group Differences.* New York: Harper and Row.

———. 1981. "Raising the IQ: The Ramey and Haskins Study." *Intelligence* 5: 29–40.

Joseph, S. C. 1990. "Focusing on Effective Measures for Saving Children." In *Improving the Life Chances of Children at Risk,* edited by D. E. Rogers and E. Ginzberg (162–67). San Francisco: Westview Press.

Labov, W. 1970. "The Logic of Nonstandard English." In *Language and Poverty,* edited by F. Williams. Chicago: Markham Press.

———. 1972. "Academic Ignorance and Black Intelligence." *Atlantic Monthly,* 229.

Lazar, I., and R. Darlington. 1982. "Lasting Effects of Early Education: A Report from the Consortium for Longitudinal Studies." *Monographs of the Society for Research in Child Development* 47 (entire issues, nos. 2, 3).

Lesser, G., G. Fifer, and D. Clark. 1965. "Mental Abilities of Children from Different Social Class and Ethnic Groups." *Monographs of the Society for Research in Child Development* 30: 1–115.

Levine, R. A. 1973. "Culture, Personality, and Socialization." In *Handbook of Socialization Theory and Research,* edited by D. A. Goslin. Chicago: Rand McNally.

Lewis, O. 1966. "The Culture of Poverty." *Scientific American* 215: 19–25.

McKey, R. H., L. Candelli, H. Ganson, B. J. Barrett, C. McConkey, and M. C. Plantz. *The Impact of Head Start on Children, Families and Communities: Final Report of Head Start Evaluation, Synthesis, and Utilization Project* (DHHS no. 85-31193). Washington, D.C.: U.S. Department of Health and Human Services.

McLoyd, V. C. 1990. "The Impact of Economic Hardship on Black Families and Children: Psychological Distress, Parenting, and Socioemotional Development." *Child Development* 61(2): 311–46.

McQueen, R., and C. Browning. 1960. "The Intelligence and Educational Achievement of a Matched Sample of White and Negro Students." *School and Society* 88: 327–29.

Mercer, J. 1971. "Institutionalized Anglocentrism: Labeling Mental Retardates in Public Schools." In *Race, Change, and Urban Society*, edited by P. Orleans and W. Russell, Jr. Los Angeles: Sage Publications.

Mermelstein, E., and L. Schulman. 1967. "Lack of Formal Schooling and the Acquisition of Conservation." *Child Development* 38: 39–51.

Moore, E. G. J. 1986. "Family Socialization and the IQ Test Performance of Traditionally and Transracially Adopted Black Children." *Child Development* 22(3): 317–26.

Moynihan, Daniel Patrick. 1965. *The Negro Family: The Case for National Action*. Washington, D.C.: U.S. Department of Labor.

Oakes, J. 1992. "Preface." In *Crossing the Tracks*, by A. Wheelock. New York: New Press.

Ogbu, J. 1978. *Minority Education and Caste*. New York: Academic Press.

————. 1982. "Societal Forces as a Context of Ghetto Children's School Failure." In *The Language of Children Reared in Poverty*, edited by L. Feagans and D. Farran. New York: Academic Press.

————. 1985. "The Cultural Ecology of Competence among Inner-City Blacks." In *Beginnings: The Social and Affective Development of Black Children*, edited by M. Spencer, G. Brookins, and W. Allen. Hillsdale, N.J.: Lawrence Erlbaum Associates.

Osofsky, J. 1990. "Risk and Protective Factors for Teenage Mothers and their Infants." *SRCD Newsletter* (Winter): 1–2.

Persell, C. H. 1977. *Education and Inequality*. New York: Free Press.

Piaget, J. 1952. *The Origins of Intelligence in Children*. (M. Cook, trans.) New York: International University Press.

Reissman, F. 1962. *The Culturally Deprived Child*. New York: Harper & Row.

Rist, R. C. 1973. *The Urban School as a Factory for Failure*. Cambridge, Mass.: M.I.T. Press.

Rogers, D. E. 1990. "Introduction." In *Improving Life Chances of Children at Risk*, edited by D. E. Rogers and E. Ginzberg, Boulder, Colorado: Westview Press.

Rogers, D. E., and Ginzberg, eds. 1990. *Improving the Life Chances of Children at Risk*. Boulder, Colorado: Westview Press.

Ropers, R. H. 1991. *Persistent Poverty.* New York: Plenum Press.

Rutter, M. 1979. "Protective Factors in Children's Responses to Stress and Disadvantage." In *Primary Prevention of Psychopathology,* edited by M. Kent and J. Rolf. Hanover, New Hampshire: University Press of New England.

Sameroff, A., and B. Fiese. 1989. "Transactional Regulation and Early Intervention." In *Early Intervention: A Handbook of Theory, Practice, and Analysis,* edited by S. J. Meisels and J. Shonkoff. New York: Cambridge University Press.

Scarr, S. 1992. "Developmental Theories for the 1990s: Development and Individual Differences." *Child Development* 63: 1–19.

Scarr-Salapatek, S. 1975. "Genetics and the Development of Intelligence." In *Review of Child Development Research,* vol. 4, edited by F. D. Horowitz. Chicago: University of Chicago Press.

Scarr, S., A. Pakstis, S. Katz, and W. Barker. 1977. "The Absence of a Relationship between Degree of White Ancestry and Intellectual Skills within the Black Population." *Human Genetics* 39: 69–86.

Scott-Jones, D. 1984. "Family Influences on Cognitive Development and School Achievement." In *Review of Research in Education,* edited by E. W. Gordon. Washington, D.C.: American Educational Research Association.

Shade, B. 1982. "Afro-American Cognitive Style: A Variable in School Success." *Review of Educational Research* 52: 219–44.

Spencer, M. B., and C. Markstrom-Adams. 1990. "Identity Processes among Racial and Ethnic Minority Children in America." *Child Development* 61(2): 290–310.

Spencer, M. B., G. K. Brookins, and W. Allen. 1985. *Beginnings: The Social and Affective Development of Black Children.* Hillsdale, N.J.: Lawrence Erlbaum Associates.

Spencer, M. B., and V. C. McLoyd (editors). 1990. *Child Development: Special Issue on Minority Children* 61(2): 263–592.

Sroufe, A. 1989. "Pathways to Adaptation and Maladaptation: Psychopathology as Developmental Deviation." In *Rochester Symposium on Developmental Psychopathology,* vol. 1, edited by D. Cicchetti. Hillsdale, N.J.: Lawrence Erlbaum Associates.

Stewart, W. A. 1970. "Towards a History of American Negro Dialect." In *Language and Poverty,* edited by F. Williams. Chicago: Markham Press.

Stodolsky, S., and G. Lesser. 1967. "Learning Patterns in the Disadvantaged." *Harvard Educational Review* 37: 546–93.

Terman, L. M. 1916. *The Measurement of Intelligence.* New York: Houghton Mifflin Co.

Thomas, H. 1970. "Psychological Assessment Instruments for Use with Human Infants." *Merrill Palmer Quarterly,* 16: 179–223.

Tooby, J., and Cosmides, L. 1990. "On the Universality of Human Nature and the Uniqueness of the Individual: The Role of Genetics and Adaptation." *Journal of Personality*, 58(1): 17–67.

Trotman, F. 1977. "Race, IQ, and the Middle Class." *Journal of Educational Psychology*, 69(3): 266–73.

U. S. Congress, Select Committee on Children, Youth, and Families, U.S. House of Representatives. 1989. *U.S. Children and Their Families: Current Conditions*. Washington, D.C.: U.S. Government Printing Office.

U.S. Department of Education, Office of Educational Research and Improvement. 1988. *Youth Indicators 1988: Trends in the Well-Being of American Youth*. Washington, D.C.: U.S. Government Printing Office.

Valentine, C. A. 1971. "Deficit, Difference and Bicultural Models of Afro-American Behavior." *Harvard Educational Review* 41: 137–57.

Werner, E. E., and R. S. Smith. 1992. *Overcoming the Odds: High Risk Children from Birth to Adulthood*. Ithaca, New York: Cornell University Press.

Wheelock, A. 1992. *Crossing the Tracks*. New York: New Press.

Whiteman, M., and M. Deutsch. 1968. "Social Disadvantages as Related to Intellective and Language Development." In *Social Class, Race, and Psychological Development*, edited by M. Deutsch, I. Katz, and A. Jensen. New York: Holt, Rhinehart & Winston.

Williams, R. L. 1972. "The BITCH—100: A Culture-Specific Test Paper" presented at the 80th Annual Convention of the American Psychological Association, Honolulu, Hawaii, September.

Zigler, E., and E. Butterfield. 1968. "Motivational Aspects of Changes in IQ Performance of Culturally Deprived Nursery School Children." *Child Development* 39: 1–14.

Zigler, E., and J. Valentine (Eds.). 1979. *Project Head Start: A Legacy of the War on Poverty*. New York: Free Press.

Zigler, E., W. Abelson, and V. Seitz. 1973. "Motivational Factors in the Performance of Economically Disadvantaged Children on the Peabody Picture Vocabulary Tests." *Child Development* 44: 294–303.

Chapter Seven

THE 101ST CONGRESS: AN EMERGING AGENDA FOR CHILDREN IN POVERTY

Sandra L. Hofferth

The 101st Congress has been labeled the "Children's Congress" because it passed major children's legislation such as the Head Start reauthorization, expansion of Medicaid, the Family and Medical Leave Act, and the Child Care and Development Block Grant (National Association for the Education of Young Children [henceforth, NAEYC] 1990). After almost two decades of effort, major legislation affecting children and families was signed into law in 1990. The issues that led to the passage of this legislation and the particular policies involved, as well as a number of continuing unresolved questions, are the focus of this chapter. Events are reviewed from the perspectives of low-income children and their families.

THE ISSUES: LOW-INCOME CHILDREN AND THEIR FAMILIES

Low-income families and children have historically been a focus of public attention for two reasons: first, the present public burden of financial support if families are not economically self-sufficient; and second, the future burden on society if children do not grow up to become healthy and productive citizens.

Self-Sufficiency

It has been in the federal government's interest to promote or maintain adult productivity—for example, by providing jobs and job training for the unemployed; providing child care to enable women to work in wartime factories; and providing child care for welfare mothers so that they can work or attend job training (Phillips 1991). From the establishment of Aid to Dependent Children in 1935 to the Aid to Families with Dependent Children (AFDC) program of the mid-1980s, there was a gradual shift in thinking about welfare, from supporting widowed mothers to stay home and raise children to preparing divorced and never-married mothers for employment. Since a majority of all mothers were employed outside the home by the mid-1980s, it had become less justifiable to support poor mothers to stay home and care for their children than to provide them with employment and training. This shift was supported by a broad consensus from both the left and right, and occurred rather gradually, starting with the Work Incentive Program (WIN) in 1967.

Since the mid-1960s, a program of incentives to place welfare mothers in job training and employment has been in place. However, exemptions for mothers of preschool-age children reduced the need for child care services and the proportion of mothers who could benefit (Nelson, Jr. 1982; Phillips 1991). The movement of middle-class mothers with preschool children into the work force in the 1970s reduced the justification for exempting mothers with preschool children. Moreover, research found that young unmarried women who entered AFDC with young children were at greatest risk of becoming long-term recipients (Gueron and Pauly 1990). Although some voluntary efforts had taken place earlier, and several states were experimenting with "workfare" programs, the change in philosophy had never been fully implemented. With the passage of the Family Support Act of 1988, this shift was enacted into law. The goal of welfare became that of temporary assistance, with a focus on preparing mothers with children age three and older for self-sufficiency through employment in a job training and education program appropriately called "JOBS" (Job Opportunities and Basic Skills).

Although the Family Support Act of 1988 clearly directed public efforts toward assisting low-income parents to become self-sufficient, it was recognized that the transition between welfare and work would have to be gradual, or the incentive to leave would be small (Primus 1989). The additional expenses mothers would incur after leaving AFDC, such as child care and medical care, could make self-sufficiency unaffordable. Thus, the Family Support Act included a one-year transition period in which mothers' child care could be paid on a sliding fee scale and families would retain medicaid coverage.

Child Health and Development

It has long been feared that poverty not only harms the present lives of families but that it negatively affects the next generation, as children who grew up in disadvantaged households fail in school, have children at a young age, and repeat their parents' history of dependence on public assistance, thus remaining trapped in poverty (Duncan, Hill, and Hoffman 1988). An alternative strategy for breaking the cycle of poverty focuses attention on the child by providing high-quality compensatory education to low-income children to help offset their disadvantaged environments. This approach is based upon theories of development that identify the preschool years as critical for social and cognitive growth, as well as research that demonstrates that high-quality preschool intervention programs can reduce school retention and increase school completion among disadvantaged children (Berreuta-Clement et al. 1984; Phillips 1991). In the late 1980s, proponents of this strategy were relieved that, finally, increased attention was being paid to ensuring that children get a healthy start in life, not only physically but emotionally and intellectually.

The placement of child health and development on the legislative agenda can be attributed to both a set of demographic changes, including increased migration, an increased proportion of children raised in single-parent families, and the reduced well-being of children and their families; and economic changes, including declining wages, federal budget deficits, and worldwide economic problems such as recession and trade deficits. Evidence of effective programs to help children, particularly through early intervention in the health and education of parent and child, provided support for a set of policies that were gradually being eroded by federal budget cuts.

Both issues—parental self-sufficiency and the quality of child health and development—met in the 101st Congress. In this "two-generation approach" the two strategies came to be viewed as complements, albeit ill-coordinated, rather than substitutes (Smith, Blank, and Bond 1990).

Window of Opportunity

The "window of opportunity" that presented itself was the 1988 presidential election, pitting moderate Republican Vice President George Bush against liberal Democrat Michael Dukakis. President Ronald Reagan had successfully cut taxes on the wealthy and social programs for the poor in his term of office (Primus 1989). The additional money held by wealthy Americans did not trickle down to the rest; rather, the economic situation of the poorest Americans deteriorated while that of the richest improved. Welfare rolls continued to increase, and the proportion of children in poor families was rising (U.S. Congress, House Committee on Ways and Means 1985). Partly to combat the image of hardheartedness leveled against him by liberal activists, presidential candidate Bush promised a kinder, gentler society and, to back up his rhetoric, made a campaign promise to pass new child care legislation and to fund Head Start for all four-year-olds (Kosterlitz 1988). With both presidential candidates promising child and family legislation, the time had come. What would be proposed and eventually passed differed; however, as discussed in the next section, the origins are evident in the long debates over the two decades preceding 1990.

EVOLUTION OF CHILD CARE LEGISLATION

In his book *Agendas, Alternatives, and Public Policies* (1987), John Kingdon argued that legislation results when problem, policy, and political streams converge in a "window of opportunity." This section of the chapter focuses on setting the agenda for action, preparation of policy alternatives, and their resolution through the political process.

Setting the Agenda

As mentioned previously, concern over the well-being of children in the late 1980s stemmed partly from demographic changes, which produced a large number of births as the baby boom babies entered their peak childbearing years, and economic and social changes—such as rising female education and declining male wages—which led to increased employment of mothers with young children (Levy and Michel 1991). Contributing factors included technological changes such as the introduction of oral contraceptives, which increased female control over the timing and number of births, and social changes such as the women's movement, which fostered the idea that a woman could have a career while raising a family. In addition, parents came to view enrollment in early childhood programs as important for their children's socialization and preparation for school, regardless of maternal employment status.

The effect of these changes, a major rise in the demand for early childhood care and education, was felt as far back as the late 1960s and resulted in several unsuccessful attempts to pass comprehensive child care legislation at that time. However, a number of important events predated even these early attempts at comprehensive legislation.

FEDERAL SUPPORT FOR CHILD CARE FOR EMPLOYED MOTHERS

Probably the first federal program to subsidize care of children occurred in the 1930s during the Great Depression, when nurseries were established under the Work Projects Administration for children of participants and under the Farm Security Administration for children of migrant workers (Nelson, Jr. 1982). During World War II, the largest federal program to that point was instituted. As women entered factory work in large numbers, there was a huge demand for child care and a tremendous outcry over children being left without supervision while their mothers worked. Under the Lanham Act, the government spent $52 million to care for more than 100,000 children in day care centers. This funding ended with the war's end in 1945 (Nelson, Jr. 1982; Ribar 1991).

In 1971, Senator Walter Mondale and Representative John Brademas sponsored a bill to provide a $2 billion package of comprehensive services for children in day care. Services would have been free of charge for the poor and available on a graduated fee schedule for middle-income families. This bill passed Congress but was vetoed by President Richard Nixon for a variety of reasons, including its cost and administrative problems. However, the most publicized objections were that the program would "Sovietize" child care by taking children from the care of their mothers and placing them into the care of the state (Nelson, Jr. 1982).

This reasoning was ironic, since prior to this new legislation and since 1954 the most extensive program for assisting families with child care had been the Child Care Deduction in the federal income tax code, which became the Child and Dependent Care Tax Credit in 1976. Child care was considered a necessary work expense (Nelson and Warring 1982). Low- to moderate-income working mothers in two-parent families and single parents could deduct their child care expenses up to $600 per year. This deduction amounted to $18 million in 1954 (Nelson, Jr., and Warring 1982). In 1976 the income ceiling was dropped and the deduction was transformed into a 20 percent tax credit on care-related expenses up to $2,000 for one and $4,000 for two or more dependents. In 1976, $548 million of expenses were claimed under the credit (U.S. Congress, House of Representatives 1992).

Several other attempts to pass child care legislation were made in the mid 1970s; however, objections such as those that killed the 1971 legislation prevented passage (Phillips and Zigler 1987). The only major legislation in this regard passed during the 1970s was the consolidation of federal social services with funds specifically targeted for child care under President Gerald Ford in 1975 and 1976 (Title XX of the Social Security Act) (Phillips and Zigler 1987).

Ronald Reagan became president in 1980 on a platform of reducing federal intervention. One of the first acts of his administration was to change the status of federal assistance to states from categorical problems with specified funding amounts to block grants with more state discretion over how the money would be spent and fewer reporting requirements. Title XX, one of the major sources of direct federal funds for child care, was renamed the Social Services Block Grant, its funding was cut, and federal provisions regarding eligibility, reporting, state matching funds, and regulation were dropped. All provisions for setting aside a portion for child care were also dropped, leaving to state discretion how the funds would be used. For the next several years federal child care policy consisted of dismantling direct federal involvement, including the collection and dissemination of information. At the federal level, contracts to collect and analyze child care data were canceled, federal offices had "Child Care" removed from their titles, and staff were assigned other duties. Some states (e.g., Maryland) dismantled the system of centers that had been funded by contracts from state offices, while others (e.g., California) invested state funds. A few states (e.g., Massachusetts) began testing alternative means of providing vouchers to parents who would select their own arrangements.

As a consequence of the change in approach to child care funding—from contracts with providers to funds going directly to parents through the Child and Dependent Care Tax Credit—a large proportion of federal child care subsidies shifted from low-income to middle- and upper-income families. Low-income families were less likely to pay for care and, if they did, they were less likely to benefit from the Child and Dependent Care Tax Credit, since it could only be taken against taxes owed, and low-income families incurred little tax liability (Barnes 1988; Steuerle 1990). To redress this perceived imbalance, several individuals and organizations in the mid-1980s proposed making the tax credit refundable (see, for example, Robins 1988). However, the cost of refundability and widespread opposition to paying for such changes by reducing benefits to upper-income families precluded altering the existing tax credit; hence new programs were needed. In 1988, two-thirds ($3.813 billion) of all federal funds for child care ($5.809 billion) were spent in the form of tax credits (table 7.1).[1]

In fiscal year (FY) 1988, federal child care funds other than those spent through the tax credit were distributed through some 46 separate federal programs, the largest of which were the Social Services Block Grant ($660 million) and the Child Care Food Program ($586 million) (U.S. General Accounting Office 1989a). These programs provided assistance primarily to low-income families.

FEDERAL SUPPORT FOR INVESTMENT IN CHILD HEALTH AND DEVELOPMENT

Another strand of the picture is increased demand for early childhood programs for children's socialization and preparation for school, regardless of maternal employment status. The origin of programs such as Head Start can be found in the social reform movements of the late 1800s and early 1900s and in the nursery school movement of the 1920s (Cahan 1989; Nelson, Jr. 1982). In the 1920s social workers founded settlement houses, which provided for the health, care, education, and moral development of children of the poor. The goal of the nursery school movement, on the other hand, was to énhance the psychological development of the child. Such programs catered mainly to middle-class children and their families. Head Start, designed to enhance the psychological development of poor children, was begun in 1965 by the U.S. Office of Economic Opportunity as a small pilot summer project (Nelson, Jr. 1982). In 1992 it served more than 600,000 three-, four-, and five-year old children in a part-day, school-year program at a cost of about $2.2 billion. The success of Head Start attests to the bipartisan consensus over the value of early investments in the health and education of children. This consensus reflects the hard work of child advocacy groups over the past two decades.

Political interest in children of the poor declined dramatically in the 1960s after the War on Poverty ended and control of the White House passed to the Republicans. In the mid-1970s there was a push for reform of the juvenile justice and child welfare systems (Kosterlitz 1988). The movement changed radically when President Reagan came into office in 1980. His first budget radically scaled back programs for children of the poor, including Medicaid, AFDC, Maternal and Child Health, and various block grants that included social service funding. The result of these cutbacks was the mobilization and

Table 7.1 MAJOR FEDERAL PROGRAMS SUPPORTING EARLY EDUCATION, CHILD CARE, AND RELATED SERVICES

Program	Estimated Funding (nominal $ in millions)							
	FY 1980	FY 1988	FY 1989	FY 1990	FY 1991	FY 1992	FY 1993	FY 1994
Child and Dependent Care Tax Credit	956	3,813	2,442[a]	2,554[a]	2,650[b]	2,756[b]	2,860[b]	2,860[b]
Social Services Block Grant	446	660[a]	660[a]	660[a]	660[a]	660[b]	660[b]	660[b]
Head Start	735	1,206	1,235	1,552	1,952	2,202	2,776[b]	4,150[b]
Child and Adult Care Food Program	216	586	646	720	900	1,200	1,273	1,528[b]
State Dependent Care Development Grants	—	—	13	13	13	13	13	13[b]
Child Care Licensing & Improvement Grants	—	—	—	13	13	13	13	13[b]
Child Care and Development Block Grants	—	—	—	—	732	825	893	933[b]
At-Risk Child Care Program	—	—	—	—	300	300	300	300[b]
AFDC/Transitional Child Care	—	—	—	40	321	415	480	545
Other Child Care-Related Programs	700[a]	750[a]	750[a]	750[a]	750[a]	750[a]	750[b]	750[b]
Total	3,053	7,015	5,746	6,302	8,291	9,121	10,018	11,752
Earned Income Tax Credit	1,986	5,940	6,595[a]	6,929[b]	8,806[b]	10,697[b]	11,914[b]	11,914[b]

Sources: U.S. General Accounting Office, 1989a; U.S. Congress, House of Representatives 1992; Executive Office of the President, 1993a.
a. Estimated.
b. Projected.

unification of new advocacy groups for children around the country. National groups such as the Children's Defense Fund started state chapters, began building state alliances, and launched a "Child Watch" to monitor the impact of budget cuts in 80 communities. Children's advocates grew in sophistication, learning about the budget process and mounting public education efforts on children's issues though an annual Children's Defense Fund Budget and other reports (Children's Defense Fund 1989; Kosterlitz 1988).

The U.S. Congress also played an active part in identifying the impact of declining resources invested in poor children and their families and bringing it to the public's attention (Primus 1989). The House Select Committee on Children, Youth, and Families was launched in 1982 by those concerned with providing both a knowledge base and a forum in which to discuss these issues. The House Committee on Ways and Means issued detailed analyses both of trends in public spending on children (e.g., the Green Book [U.S. Congress, House of Representatives 1992]) and of trends in child poverty and the income security of families (U.S. Congress, House Committee on Ways and Means 1985). Whereas some reports focused on identifying the problems, others focused on solutions. An influential report from the Select Committee on Children, Youth, and Families (U.S. Congress, House Select Committee 1985) provided cost and benefit data for seven successful programs: nutrition for pregnant women (the Special Supplemental Food Program for Women, Infants, and Children [WIC]), preschool programs for disadvantaged children, compensatory education, childhood immunization, Medicaid, education for the handicapped, and youth employment and training.

State governments also began taking an interest in these issues, including the then-governor of Arkansas, Bill Clinton, who was active in children's issues and chairman of the National Governors' Association. Several states launched major education initiatives. State government interest in poor children and their families laid the groundwork for the federal welfare reform legislation and, later, for child care legislation. "Concern for better education broadened into a concern for human development" (Governor Bill Clinton, in Kosterlitz 1988: 2939).

Business leaders were concerned about productivity. They arrived at the same realization that new labor force entrants were not adequately prepared and that this was contributing to productivity declines. The growth of the share of the population who came from disadvantaged homes was alarming. An early report of the Committee on Economic Development (CED), an association of business and corporate leaders, focused on educational reform. However, CED members were recognizing that problems started much earlier. They were impressed by findings of tangible payoffs to children later on from investment in early childhood programs. A subsequent CED report, *Children in Need: Investment Strategies for the Educationally Disadvantaged,* (Committee for Economic Development 1987), placed business fully behind increased public and private investment in programs for disadvantaged children and youth. The CED's interest continues with the release of two recent major reports on investment in early childhood care and education (Galinsky and Friedman 1993; Committee for Economic Development 1993).

PROGRAM QUALITY AND THE BATTLE OVER REGULATIONS

The preceding two issues—employment-related child care and investments in child health and development—met head-on in the great standards battle of the 1970s. Proponents of providing child care services for maternal employment, welfare reform, and self-sufficiency wanted to offer child care at the lowest possible cost to serve as many as possible. Proponents of the early intervention model insisted that the quality remain at a high level to preserve its effectiveness. They saw regulation as one of the most important tools to maintain the quality of programs. Opponents of regulation argued that tightening regulation would lead to higher costs and lower supply, thus serving fewer children (see Phillips, Lande, and Goldberg 1990; Phillips and Zigler 1987).

The first attempt at regulating child care at the national level occurred around 1900 and dealt primarily with 24-hour care, such as in orphanages (Nelson 1982). Its purpose was that of health and safety, since there was concern about higher infant mortality in such settings. During World War II a first set of standards for child day care was developed and recommended to the states (though it was not mandated). A 1962 Welfare Reform package that included provisions for child care for employed welfare mothers stipulated that federal funds could only be used in state-licensed facilities (Nelson, Jr. 1982). This further moved the issue of licensing and regulation onto the federal agenda.

Several sets of federal standards for child care were developed in the late 1960s and 1970s, but were never implemented. The first of these, the Federal Interagency Day Care Requirements, was drafted in 1968 but never fully enforced. When the passage of Title XX legislation in 1974 mandated that centers receiving federal funds comply with federal regulations, the question of the effect on supply of enforcing regulation was raised. A research study was undertaken in the mid-1970s by the U.S. Department of Health, Education & Welfare (HEW) to provide the necessary scientific basis for regulation (Ruopp et al. 1979). Subsequently, a revised set of standards was developed at the end of the 1970s and signed by the secretary of HEW in March 1980, but these standards were nullified when Title XX was converted into the Social Services Block Grant in the early 1980s (Nelson, Jr. 1982; Phillips and Zigler 1987).

As a result, while each state has its own set of standards, and there are many similarities, there is enormous variation among states (Phillips et al. 1987). For example, Maryland requires one staff member for every three infants in centers, whereas South Carolina requires one for every eight (Morgan 1987). The issue of federal standards remained unresolved.

Although earlier policies assisted all employed parents, and recent welfare reform has supported employment activities of low-income parents, a third set of legislative proposals designed to promote parental choice and to assist families with one parent remaining home to care for children emerged during the debates.

PARENTAL CHOICE

Parental choice was an important buzzword for conservatives during the late 1980s, a term that became synonymous with loosening federal regulation. A substantial proportion of parents were using relatives and other informal arrangements for the care of their children. Increasing parental choice meant permitting parents to use public funds for whatever arrangements they chose, including a relative. This struck a blow at the formal system, since some arrangements, such as providers caring only for related children, would be exempt from public regulation. Advocates were concerned that unrestricted choice would reduce the quality of care children received. What was not known was the extent to which parents' choices reflected true preferences rather than financial and other constraints.

What constraints do parents, particularly low-income parents, face in choosing child care? First, parents confront a limited selection of arrangements in their communities. Although the quality of some early childhood programs is high (Kisker et al. 1991), the quality of others has been found to range from poor to mediocre (Whitebook, Howes, and Phillips 1989). Even if the programs available to low-income families do not differ in quality by income (Kisker et al.

1991), a poor-quality program may be a more serious problem for low- than for high-income children, who experience a richer home environment. Second, characteristics of the parents, such as access to relatives, location, availability of transportation, income, work hours, information, preferences, and values, may constrain their choices. Research shows that low-income parents are more likely than other parents to depend on a relative for child care. Although parents may prefer a nonrelative, they may not have that choice because relative care is most affordable. In addition, whereas parents are aware of and cite quality as important in choosing a provider, research consistently shows that price is also one of the most important considerations (Hofferth and Wissoker 1992). While fees overall do not seem unreasonably high (many low-income families do not have to pay anything), child care can still take a big chunk out of the budget. Low-income parents who pay for care spend an average of about 24 percent of family income on child care, compared with an average of 10 percent for all families and an average of only 6 percent for high-income families (Hofferth et al. 1991). Low-income parents may also need care for nonstandard hours such as during the evening or on a weekend, which may eliminate options such as child care centers and family day care homes, few of which provide care other than during prime work days and hours (Willer et al. 1991). Finally, it is also likely that low-income families lack information about how to access and pay for child care. Recent research on participants in the JOBS program suggests that low-income parents are often not fully informed of all their options by their case workers (Mitchell, Cooperstein, and Larner 1992). In other cases it is clear that even with full information many parents will be suspicious of nonfamily child care, and that it requires extensive discussion and information to convince parents otherwise (Kisker and Silverberg 1991).

FEDERAL SUBSIDIES FOR PROGRAMS SPONSORED BY RELIGIOUS ORGANIZATIONS

Advocates of parental choice argue that since a substantial proportion of children are enrolled in child care programs located in religious buildings, parents should also have the option of selecting a program in a religious setting. A 1982 study by the National Council of Churches identified some 14,500 early childhood programs located in church buildings nationwide (Lindner, Mattis, and Rogers 1983). Although not all of these centers are actually sponsored by the church (many just rent space), this represents a substantial proportion of centers. About 30 percent of centers and one-quarter of parents said that one of the goals of their program was to provide some religious instruction, though fewer than 5 percent said that this was their program's main goal (Hofferth et al. 1991; Kisker et al. 1991). However, the separation of church and state prohibits providing federal funds for religious education, and public education groups have consistently opposed any efforts to do so. Because churches often subsidize programs indirectly through free space or minimal rent (Culkin, Morris, and Helburn 1991), without such programs the cost of child care would be substantially higher and parents would have substantially less choice.

PARENTAL CHOICE TO CARE FOR CHILDREN THEMSELVES

The issue is not just choice of child care type by employed mothers. Low-income parents may prefer that one parent stay home and care for their children; however, if they do, they are denied tax credits that are available to higher-income, two-parent, two-earner families who pay for child care. The Bush administration and conservative groups advocating maternal care for children argued that existing programs encouraged mothers in two-parent families to work rather than to stay home with their children. Two-parent families in which mothers remain home to care for their children forgo the additional income and standard of living that they would enjoy if the mother worked outside the home, and this is a form of expenditure (Rovner 1989b). Should one-earner two-parent families be taxed to subsidize child care expenses for otherwise similar families in which the mother is employed? The question is that of equity between families with and without children, rather than between families with and without child care expenditures (Steuerle 1990). If parents have sufficient funds, they can choose the best child care for their children without additional support, whether it be one parent staying home, unpaid relative care, or paid care in a formal institution. Children's advocates, on the other hand, argued that tax credits neither provided enough money to parents to purchase care nor ensured quality and supply. Low-income families generally do not have the choice for the mother to stay home and raise the children—the mother must work.

FEDERALLY SUPPORTED HEALTH CARE FOR WELFARE FAMILIES

The Family Support Act of 1988 promoted the self-sufficiency of low-income parents. The act stipulated that mothers receiving assis-

tance who had children aged three and above were required to participate in training, schooling, or work if child care was available. However, they had to be exempted if child care was not available. There
was no cap on federal matching expenditure for child care, so long
as states could come up with their share (from 20 percent to 50
percent, depending on the state) (U.S. Congress, House of Representatives 1992). States were permitted to provide child care with vouchers
and contracts, as well as through disregarding income spent on child
care (the earned income disregard), which has been standard practice.
Besides assistance while in schooling or training, states were required
to provide continued assistance for one additional year to any recipient who left welfare due to increased earnings. This transitional
assistance included subsidies for child care (transitional child care)
and continued coverage under Medicaid.

Receipt of Medicaid has traditionally been tied to the receipt of
other subsidies such as AFDC. Beginning in 1987, Congress has
required states to extend Medicaid to pregnant women and children
under age 6 with family incomes below 133 percent of the federal
poverty income guidelines. Since 1991, states are required to cover
all children under age 19 born after September 30, 1983, and whose
family income is below 100 percent of the federal poverty level (U.S.
Congress, House of Representatives 1992: 1642). In 1993, states are
required to cover children up to age 10. They are permitted to extend
eligibility to pregnant women and infants under 1 year old with
household incomes up to 185 percent of poverty. As of 1993, a majority of states had extended coverage above the minimum required
(National Governor's Association 1993).

FOCUS ON LOW-INCOME FAMILIES

Finally, the budget deficit precluded any efforts to expand federal
assistance to middle-income families. Given consensus about who
most needed additional child care assistance and the constraint of
the budget deficit, debate quickly focused on ways to assist low-
income working families.

Summary

It became clear throughout the 1980s that there were multiple concerns about the care and education of children (increasing maternal
employment, furthering the development of children, and equity
between parents and nonparents) and that these needs were not

totally compatible. Children's advocates argued that conditions in child care were poor and that children's health and development would suffer if quality were not raised through direct subsidies to providers (grants and contracts) or through regulation. The Reagan and Bush administrations argued that requiring stricter standards would increase the cost and reduce the supply of child care. Instead, they favored making the existing Child and Dependent Care tax credit refundable and, thus, of benefit to low-income families. Conservative proponents of maternal care for children argued for maximizing parental choice: increasing family incomes directly through the Earned Income Tax Credit (EITC) rather than through either the Child and Dependent Care Tax Credit or through grants and contracts to providers. Children's advocates argued that the Child and Dependent Care Tax Credit neither provided enough money to parents to purchase care nor ensured quality and supply. Although the EITC was helpful because it increased the incomes of poor families, it would not necessarily be used to purchase child care.

LEGISLATIVE HISTORY OF CHILD CARE AND EARLY EDUCATION PROVISIONS IN OMNIBUS BUDGET RECONCILIATION ACT OF 1990

Although there was a growing consensus in the mid-1980s that a child care bill was needed, issues that had surfaced in previous years remained major concerns in developing specific policies. As cited by the House Committee on Ways and Means (U.S. Congress, House of Representatives 1992: 948), these issues included:

> 1) the type of subsidy (tax credits, vouchers, contracts) that should be made available and for whom, 2) whether or not the federal government should set national child care standards, 3) conditions under which religious child care providers could receive federal funds, and 4) how best to assure optimal choice for parents in selecting child arrangements for their children, including options that allow a mother to stay home.

Early Phase: Writing the ABC Bill and Forming the Alliance

In the spring of 1986, Representative Nancy Johnson (R.-Conn.) introduced a bill that would provide $300 million in grants to states for vouchers (see table 7.2 for child care legislative history during this period). These vouchers could be used for any form of child care, including unregulated family day care. The child care community opposed the bill because they were against permitting federal funds to be used for unregulated care and because they believed they could get a better package and more money. The Democrats in Congress had begun to think about recapturing the family as a symbol in a way that differed from the Republican emphasis on "family values"— which generally meant a set of morally conservative values (Kosterlitz 1990)—and child care fit into that agenda as a focal issue that united families across class and party lines. They did not want to cede control over the issue to the Republicans.

That summer (1986), the Children's Defense Fund (CDF) and a range of national groups—including the National Association for the Education of Young Children (NAEYC), the National Women's Law Center, the National Conference of Jewish Women, the Association of State, Federal, County and Municipal Employees, women's organizations, religious groups, the Association of Junior Leagues, and the Child Welfare League—formed a National Child Care Alliance. A group of key national child care leaders met with representatives of the alliance that July and agreed on a basic outline for a child care bill, called "the Act for Better Child Care," or "ABC." The ABC bill provided federal funds to states to help lower- and middle-income families pay for child care through either vouchers or direct subsidies to providers, to expand existing programs into full-day and year-round programs, and to increase the availability and improve the quality of child care through enforcing state licensing policies, establishing resource and referral programs, and providing a minimum amount of annual training for providers. In fall 1986, a steering committee of about 35 groups from the alliance was formed; eventually the alliance would grow to 135 national groups in support of the ABC bill.

In November 1986, the CDF again assembled about 50 child care leaders for their second meeting on the ABC. The CDF and the alliance sponsored a series of working groups in Washington, D.C., in winter and spring of 1987. The first meeting focused on welfare reform and child care. The group's recommendation to require states to subsidize child care directly and to move away from dependence upon the more indirect funding mechanism of an income "disregard"[2] was enacted in the 1988 welfare reform legislation (the Family Support Act of 1988). The other meetings of the CDF and the alliance covered salaries, standards, infant care, and schools and child care.

Table 7.2 MAJOR EVENTS IN PASSAGE OF 1990 CHILD CARE LEGISLATION

Date		Person/Organization	Event
1986	Spring	Rep. Nancy Johnson	Proposed $300 million to states for vouchers
1986–1987	Summer–Winter	Children's Defense Fund (CDF) and others	Formed National Child Care Alliance for ABC[a] bill
1987	Spring	Sen. Christopher Dodd	Hearings on ABC
	Fall	CDF and others	Grass-roots organizing effort
	November	House of Representatives/ Senate	ABC introduced
1988	November		George Bush reelected over Michael Dukakis
	Winter	Rep. Dale Kildee	Formal hearings on ABC
1989	January	Sens. Dodd and Orin Hatch	ABC bill reintroduced
	January	Rep. Augustus Hawkins	Introduced HR 3, an alternative to ABC
	March	Senate	"Marked-up" ABC
	March	President George Bush	Introduced Working Family Child Care Assistance Act
	Fall	Reps. Thomas Downey and George Miller	Introduced their own child care bill
	Fall	House	Could not reconcile two House versions
1990	Spring	House	Passed Downey/Miller child care bill
	Summer	House/Senate	Began conferencing
	Summer	CDF and others	Media campaign to keep issue alive
	Fall	Congress/White House	Negotiated budget agreement with child care
	November 3	Congress/White House	Hawkins Human Services Reauthorization Act signed
	November 5	Congress/White House	Omnibus Budget Reconciliation Act signed

a. ABC, Act for Better Child Care.

A draft ABC bill was completed in early 1987, and alliance members began to seek cosponsors on Capitol Hill. Helen Blank, of the Children's Defense Fund, who spearheaded the alliance, worked with congressional committee staffs to garner members' support. Democrats saw family and, particularly, children's issues as a means to unite the party and eventually win the White House back from the Republicans (Kosterlitz 1990). In 1987 Representative Augustus Hawkins (D.-Calif., chair, House Committee on Education and Labor) agreed to sponsor the bill in the House of Representatives, though he eventually ceded sponsorship to Representative Dale Kildee (D.-Mich., chair, House Subcommittee on Human Resources). Christopher Dodd (D.-Conn.) eagerly sought to sponsor it in the Senate and held preliminary hearings in March and June of 1987. The Act for Better Child Care was introduced in November 1987 at a bipartisan press conference with a request for $2.5 billion in federal funds for direct child care services, federally mandated child care standards for states which would be created by a child care commission, and set-asides to strengthen the quality of child care.

Garnering Support

During fall 1987 the CDF and the alliance began an intensive grass-roots effort to gain support for passage of child care legislation. Amy Wilkins of the CDF was the primary organizer at the state level, visiting nearly 35 states to build early and sustained support for child care legislation. This involved setting up state offices and building state alliances so that the CDF could mobilize support locally and thereby pressure their elected representatives in Congress.

As the ABC bill began to move forward, the House held its first formal hearing in February 1988, under the leadership of Dale Kildee. The Senate held formal hearings that March and June. The new bill was reported out of the Senate and House committees and was then revised (called a "markup") by the respective chambers in August (Senate) and September (House) 1988. Although Senator Orin Hatch (R.-Utah) had introduced his own bill, in a surprise move at the end of the summer Hatch agreed to support the ABC bill if some changes were made to loosen federal requirements regarding minimum health and safety standards (Rovner 1989a: 585). This was an important breakthrough, since the backing of Hatch, a conservative and ranking Republican on the Senate Labor and Human Resources Committee, hinted at bipartisan agreement on child care.

It was an election year. Reagan's second term was expiring and the race between Massachusetts Governor Michael Dukakis and Vice President Bush would be decided in November. Both candidates talked about new and expanded health and social welfare programs for disadvantaged children and federal support for child care. The Democratic leadership met in spring 1988 at the Greenbrier resort in West Virginia and agreed to bring family and children's issues to the top of their agendas (Kosterlitz 1990). However, neither child care nor the family and medical leave legislation was taken to the floor in 1988. Action on these bills had so far been an attempt on the part of the Democrats to show that the Republicans were not serious about family issues, rather than a serious attempt at passage. The differences among the approaches had not been ironed out, and partisan posturing in a presidential election year prevented any compromise over unresolved issues such as federal standards in the ABC bill and a family leave mandate in the Family and Medical Leave Act.

Middle Phase: Compromise, Division, and Defeat

The next phase, January to November of 1989, was, to borrow Kingdon's (1987) language, the "political phase." It involved reconciling interests of many different groups—churches and religious groups, states, stay-at-home mothers, for-profit child care providers, education organizations, and congressional committees. Standards, church-state issues, and the form of assistance would all require negotiation.

STANDARDS

Child care standards had been an important issue for advocates early on. However, as time passed, it became clear that the consensus in the field was that getting a bill passed was of paramount concern. Given that the National Governors' Association opposed standards, not enough votes could be mustered to pass a bill that included them (Cammisa 1992). Consequently, that section of the ABC bill was redrafted in June 1989. States were required to have standards in key areas (e.g., health and safety, child/staff ratios, training), but specifics of the standards were left to state discretion (Rovner 1989c: 1476). Advocates felt that this still represented some progress toward better-quality child care, since many states did not have any standards at all in these key areas (e.g., group size). A subcommittee of the alliance worked with Senator Dodd's staff, who negotiated the compromise language on standards with the NGA.

CHURCH-STATE

A main sticking point was how to allow funding to go to child care services provided by religious institutions, a prerequisite for Republican support. Religious groups wanted to give hiring and placement preference to their own members, while education and civil liberties groups were concerned about discrimination and separation of church and state. Restrictive language to prevent significant child care funds from going to church-sponsored programs (added in 1988) had provoked substantial opposition. To pass the bill, the language had to be revised. In spring 1989 an agreement was reached between education and religious groups. The new language prevented programs that received 80 percent or more of their funds from government sources from discriminating on the basis of religion. Programs receiving less than 80 percent of their funding from government sources were prevented from discriminating on the basis of religion in admitting children whose care was paid for with federal funds, but for other slots could give preference to children of church-affiliated parents (Rovner 1989a: 587). Similarly, in hiring of staff, programs could give preference to church members. However, the Catholic Conference continued to lobby for support for child care that included a religious education component. After it was thought that an agreement had been reached, the U.S. Catholic Conference sought an amendment to allow the use of vouchers for religious education. To avoid a potentially devisive amendment, Senate leadership revised the ABC's language so that vouchers could be used for religious education (Rovner 1989c: 1476; 1989e: 3070). That move split the alliance; the National Education Association and the National Council of Jewish Women, among others, left because of their categorical opposition to funding for religious programs. This was the first major split in the alliance.

TAX CREDITS VERSUS GRANTS, CONTRACTS, AND VOUCHERS

The debate over whether families would be best helped through direct payments to their care providers or through tax credits and deductions intensified. As time passed, agreement grew for a dual approach, although the specification of that mix was still undecided. Representatives of the National Governors' Association and the

National Association of Counties argued for a mix of tax credits and direct federal resources (Rovner 1989b: 902).

THE SENATE

The Senate ABC bill was reintroduced in January 1989 by Senator Dodd at a hearing and press conference, with Senator Orin Hatch as the prime Republican sponsor. The Senate took the lead and marked up ABC in March 1989. In the campaign, Bush had committed himself to passing a child care bill. The Senate markup of its own bill forced Bush to introduce his own agenda or face vetoing a child care bill with which he disagreed, an unthinkable prospect given his campaign commitment. In March, Bush introduced his own bill, the Working Family Child Care Assistance Act, which consisted of refundable tax credits for low-income families and a refundable Child and Dependent Care Tax Credit, two of the four programs he had proposed in his FY 1990 budget. He also introduced the Head Start Amendments of 1989, which authorized increased levels for Head Start, the third of his 1990 initiatives. Regardless, the ABC bill passed the Senate by a voice vote after a week of debate in June 1989, and President Bush threatened a veto.

THE HOUSE

Largely because he wanted a substantial proportion of money to fund child care provided through the public school system, Representative Hawkins of the Education and Labor Committee once again became involved and introduced both the ABC bill and an alternative to ABC in January 1989. The new proposal, HR 3, distributed funds among three programs: public school-based child care, expansion of Head Start to a full-day, full-year program so that poor working parents could enroll their children, and an ABC-like grant program (Rovner 1989e: 3070). Hawkins held several hearings. A fourth program to help states coordinate their child care activities was added when the House Education and Labor Committee marked up the bill in June 1989.

In fall 1989, after the Senate had passed the ABC, the House Ways and Means Subcommittee on Human Resources (led by Representative Thomas Downey [D.-N.Y.]), which, with the Education and Labor Committee, had joint jurisdiction on child care because of its jurisdiction over tax legislation, marked up its version. The version favored by Downey and his coauthor, Representative George Miller (D.-Calif.), kept the public school-based child care and Head Start funding in the Hawkins bill but proposed to earmark additional funds for child care in an expanded Social Services Block Grant (SSBG), instead of following the ABC approach of creating an entirely new program. The Social Services Block Grant was a (capped) entitlement that did not require an annual appropriation like the ABC approach. Downey and Miller argued that funding would be more secure under this existing entitlement legislation than under a new grant which required an annual appropriation. Their approach was opposed, however, by child advocates who thought less money would be forthcoming as an earmark under the block grant. Title XX funding levels had been the same for several years, whereas funding for Head Start was increasing. The goal was to achieve the same visibility for child care as for Head Start. The other difference between the Hawkins and Downey-Miller bills was that the latter bill proposed expanding and adjusting the Earned Income Tax Credit (EITC) for family size. The House leadership was unable to resolve the differences between the two bills as to how new funding sould be channeled to the states, so it brought both versions to the floor and included them in the 1989 budget reconciliation bill (Rovner 1989d: 2565).

OUTCOME

The House and Senate could not resolve their differences, largely because the House could not decide between its two versions. Faced with strong presidential opposition to *both* the ABC and the SSBG set-aside, the budget bill was enacted without a child care component. This killed child care for the year. Although Speaker Thomas Foley blamed it on lack of time to resolve differences and promised to give child care a high priority in 1990, advocates were bitterly disappointed (Rovner 1989f: 3162). Victory had seemed so close.

The Final Push—Holding Public Attention and Making Compromises

At the end of March 1990 after much debate, the House passed a new bill earmarking funding for child care in an expanded Social Services Block Grant as a substitute for ABC. The House and Senate began conferencing in summer 1990. As a substitute for the Social Services Block Grant earmark proposed by Downey and Miller, the Senate Finance Committee offered a new program under Title IV-A of the Social Security Act for families at risk of going on welfare. However, there were still substantial differences to resolve between

House and Senate versions, and the bill appeared stalled as the summer ended.

Meanwhile, advocates, fearing that the issue had peaked, worked to keep child care in the news. Led by the Children's Defense Fund, advocates across the country made paper chains that were flown between cities. Rallies were held across the country, including one in Washington, D.C., in June 1990. Early in July, the CDF and the alliance organized a press conference on the steps of the Capitol featuring key leaders of children's organizations, women's groups, religious groups, and governors. An event a week was held during the first three weeks of September 1990, culminating in a press event in which paper chains were stretched from the White House to the Capitol and then hung on the doors of congressional leaders.

In the fall, Congress started negotiating the 1990 budget agreement. The administration wanted child care tax credits, the centerpiece of President Bush's proposed plan; Senate leaders insisted on a grant program, the centerpiece of which was the ABC. The Senate negotiated a compromise agreement with the White House. The White House accepted a grant program it had opposed (now called the Child Care and Development Block Grant), the Senate had to drop funds for upgrading quality, Hawkins had to give up the requirement that money be passed through schools, and Downey and Miller gave up their effort to channel money through the Social Services Block Grant. After a conference with the House, a three-pronged compromise was reached: (1) authorization for child care grants to states through a new grant program, (2) a capped entitlement program within Title IV of the Social Security Act, and (3) addition of expanded tax credits for low-income working families to the Omnibus Budget Reconciliation Act of 1990. This compromise bill (PL 101-964) passed both Houses on October 27, 1990, and was signed by President Bush into law on November 5, 1990. Head Start was also expanded as part of PL 101-501, the Augustus F. Hawkins Human Services Reauthorization Act, and signed into law on November 3, 1990. This authorization permits spending to rise by 1994 to a level that would provide funds for all eligible children to be covered, a significant accomplishment.

CHILD CARE AND EARLY EDUCATION LEGISLATION PASSED BY 101ST CONGRESS

The 1990 legislation (U.S. Congress 1990; Gebhardt 1990; Golonka and Ooms 1991; Morse and Steisel 1990) contained the following major components:

1. Expansion of the Earned Income Tax Credit (EITC), and two new credits, which are expected to total $18 billion to low-income working families between 1990 and 1995. Projected expenditures are $11.9 billion dollars in FY 1993.

2. A new child care grant program, the Child Care and Development Block Grant, which is expected to amount to $2.5 billion between 1991 and 1993. In FY 1991, $732 million (of $750 million authorized) was appropriated, in FY 1992, $825 million (as authorized) was appropriated, and in FY 1993, $893 was appropriated, a cut of 8 percent over the authorized level.

3. A new entitlement program that expands child care assistance under title IV-A for families "at risk" of welfare dependency, and which is expected to amount to $1.5 billion between 1990 and 1995, at $300 million per year.

4. Authorization for the Child Care Improvement Grants program was increased from $13 million to $50 million, though annual appropriations remained at $13 million.

5. Expansion of Head Start's authorization level from $1.95 billion in FY 1991 to as much as $7.6 billion by FY 1994. Actual appropriations amounted to $1.95 billion in FY 1991, $2.2 billion in FY 1992, and $2.7 billion in FY 1993.

6. A small ($60 million) program to integrate and coordinate programs for children and youth (Coordinated Services for Children, Youth, and Families) was authorized.

[These components are discussed in the subsections following.]

Expansion of Tax Credits

The Earned Income Tax Credit (EITC) was first enacted in 1975 as a means of targeting tax relief to low-income working taxpayers with children. In 1990, before the new legislation was passed, the maximum credit was $953 (14 percent of the first $6,810 of earned income, reduced by 10 cents for each dollar of adjusted gross income in excess of $10,730). Between 1991 and 1994 the new legislation gradually increases the basic EITC and adjusts it for family size. In 1991 the basic EITC increased from $953 to $1,192 for families with one child and to $1,235 for families with two or more children (U.S. Congress, House of Representatives 1992). By 1994, the maximum will be $1,860 for families with one child and $2,025 for families with two or more children.[3] The EITC will no longer count as income in determining eligibility for benefits for federal means-tested programs.

The new legislation adds two new credits: a "wee tot" credit and a health insurance credit. The purpose of the "wee tot" credit is to provide additional assistance to poor working families with children under one year of age by refunding an additional 5 percent of earned income. Families claiming this credit can no longer claim the Child and Dependent Care Tax Credit. Consequently, since the Child and Dependent Care Tax Credit is worth more to working families, the "wee tot" credit was designed to be used primarily by families with a mother who cares for her infant at home. It may also be claimed by families with an employed mother who cannot claim the credit for other reasons (use of nonpaid care, use of nonregulated provider). The cost of this credit is expected to be $700 million over five years.[4]

The second new credit is designed to help low-income families with children whose employers provide health insurance for the worker, but not for dependents. The maximum amount of the credit is $428 per year. Few EITC families will qualify for this program because so few purchase their own health insurance privately. The total cost is expected to amount to $5.2 billion between 1991 and 1995.[5]

Child Care and Development Block Grant

Seventy-five percent of the funds under the Child Care and Development Block Grant (CCDBG) are to provide child care services to eligible children on a sliding scale fee basis and to improve the availability (90 percent) and quality of care (no more than 10 percent). States are required to give priority to low-income and special needs children, although all chidren under age 13 in a family with incomes under 75 percent of the state median income are eligible. These funds do not require a state match. This is a significant expansion of federal funds for child care for low-income families.

The remaining 25 percent of Block Grant funds are to be spent as follows: 5 percent for quality improvement activities; 18.75 percent to establish, expand, or conduct early childhood education and before- and after-school programs; and 1.25 percent either for quality improvement activities or for early childhood development and before- and after-school services.

States are required to offer qualifying parents the option of either enrolling their child with a provider who has a grant or contract to provide services, or receiving a child care certificate to be used as payment by the parents for child care services for any eligible provider of their choice. This grant addresses issues of parent choice by expanding the definition of provider. Eligible providers include family members such as grandparents as well as center-based, group home, or family day care providers that meet state requirements. Providers are required to meet applicable state and local regulatory standards, including health and safety standards, to receive funds (NAEYC 1992). Permissible quality improvements include training providers and increasing staff salaries.

"At-Risk" Child Care Program

Title IV-A child care assistance authorized under the Family Support Act JOBS program was expanded to provide child care assistance to "low-income, non-AFDC families that need such care in order to work and would otherwise be at risk of becoming dependent upon AFDC" (U.S. Congress, 1992a). This program requires a state contribution ranging from 20 percent to 50 percent, depending on the particular state. Funding of $300 million per year was provided for five years beginning in FY 1991.

Child Care Improvement Grants

The Child Care Improvement Grants program was a small program intended to improve licensing, registration, and training of providers. The new legislation increased authorization levels for the program from $13 million to $50 million for FY 1992–94. Congress deleted funds for this program in the FY 1992 Department of Health and Human Services (DHHS) appropriations bill when funding became tight, and former President Bush initially recommended no funding in his FY 1993 budget. Advocates considered this program to be critical for quality improvements, especially given the restrictions on use of CCDBG funds for such purposes, and funding was restored in the 1993 budget.

Head Start

Under Title I of the Augustus F. Hawkins Human Services Reauthorization Act of 1990, the Head Start Program was reauthorized with a large increase. Authorization for FY 1991 was $2.4 billion, though only $1.95 billion was appropriated. The intent of Congress was to provide coverage for all eligible three- to five-year-old children by

FY 1994. However, the actual number of children served depends upon the level and intensity of services provided. Head Start programs were not designed to provide child care for the children of employed mothers; rather, their purpose is to compensate for the effects of social and economic disadvantage by providing a high-quality educational program. They typically operate part-day for part of the year, although some programs have shown an interest in helping families obtain wraparound care (for the remainder of the working day) from other funding sources. Although this is helpful to those whose mothers are not employed, it may not serve the needs of children of employed mothers. Recent research shows that low-income employed parents piece together several arrangements in order to enroll their children in Head Start, and others may simply not be able to enroll their children in Head Start programs at all (Hofferth 1992a). Thus, many low-income children may lose the advantage of this high-quality preschool program and may not benefit from other superior child care programs because of cutbacks in the funds that can be used for quality improvements in the CCDBG.

Policymakers have, in the past, made the decision to serve more children rather than to provide increased and improved services for those enrolled. The Clinton administration's goal is to serve 90% of all eligible three- and four-year-old children. Exactly how to do so and with what services is still undecided. Unfortunately, the Head Start appropriation amounted to $2.76 billion in FY 1993 (compared with an authorized level of $5.9 billion), considerably less than what full-funding was estimated to cost ($8 billion).

Coordinated Services for Children, Youth, and Families

Under the same Human Services Reauthorization Act, $60 million was authorized for integrating and coordinating federal, state, and local programs for children and teenagers. The program included the Young Americans Act (grants to states to coordinate services to children and encourage greater coordination at the federal level); a national clearinghouse of family resources and support programs and grants to expand such programs in local communities; the Primary Pediatric Outreach and Care Program, which funds outreach and primary health care for disadvantaged children; and a demonstration grant to help pregnant women and children establish Medicaid eligibility (Morse and Steisel 1990).

CHILD CARE AND EARLY EDUCATION LEGISLATION PASSED BY 102ND CONGRESS

Four pieces of legislation affecting children passed the 102nd Congress: the Ready to Learn Television Act; the Head Start Quality Improvement Act; Family Resource Centers; and technical amendments to the Child Care and Development Block Grant (NAEYC 1992).

Ready to Learn Television Act

The Ready to Learn Television Act would provide support for the development and dissemination of educational programming and materials for preschool and elementary school children. It would also support the development of training materials for care providers and parents. The purpose is to promote school readiness of children and to enhance the skills of parents and providers. Although $25 million was authorized, no funds were appropriated for FY 1993.

Head Start Quality Improvement Act

The Head Start Quality Improvement Act authorizes Head Start funds to be used to purchase facilities instead of renting them and to extend health care services to younger siblings of Head Start children. The legislation requires Head Start to provide parents with training in literacy and parenting skills, thus strengthening its commitment to parent involvement. The act also requries the DHHS to provide guidelines for transportation to and from Head Start programs.

Family Resource Centers

The 1993 appropriation includes $5 million for Family Resource Centers created under the 1990 Augustus F. Hawkins Human Services Reauthorization discussed earlier but which had received no funding. This funding provides support for model Family Resource Centers in 3 states. These community-based centers provide integrated services such as parenting classes, child care resource and referral, and social services, and linkages to schools, health care, and legal services.

Technical Amendments to Child Care and Development Block Grant

The technical amendments, included in other legislation, ensure that funds received under the CCDBG will not be counted as income in determining eligibility for other federal programs that are income-conditioned. In addition, they assure that states have two years to spend their CCDBG funds, which is necessary given that the funds are released at the end of each fiscal year.

Summary

During the 1980s children's issues came of age, a consequence of major social changes in the 1960s and 1970s as well as retrenchment on social policy and social programs in the 1980s. Interest groups led a major campaign to place social issues affecting the well-being of children in the forefront of the conscience of the American people, and, finally, at the doorstep of Congress. States, social welfare groups, and even the business community complained and then mobilized. Their well-timed strategies and coalition-building plus a Democratic strategy that placed child and family issues high on the agenda resulted in a Congress primed and ready to act. Almost 20 years after President Nixon said that child care legislation would "Sovietize" American children, the U.S. Congress passed major child care legislation.

As a result of the 1990 legislative changes, federal expenditures on child care programs will be substantially raised. It is estimated that total federal expenditures on child care increased by about $2 billion dollars in FY 1991 and that expenditures on the EITC alone will increase by about $18 billion between 1991 and 1995 (Golonka and Ooms 1991). For families, these programs provide substantial new funding to assist with the cost of childrearing and child care. The lion's share of the new funding is targeted at low-income families with either a nonemployed mother (through the EITC) or an employed mother (through the CCDBG). Child care benefits accruing to middle- and upper-income parents were not affected by the new legislation, since no changes were made to the Child and Dependent Care Tax Credit, the major program benefiting them. Middle-income families may benefit from the small proportion of the Block Grant funds that support quality initiatives, such as an increase in Resource and Referral programs that help families find child care.

Financial restraints were important considerations in the passage of the new legislation. Although the impact of these new laws on the budget will be to increase federal outlays, increased expenditures on low-income families were rationalized, in part, as offsetting new taxes on gas, alcohol, and cigarettes, which fall more heavily on low-income families. In addition, to the extent that the outlays help families remain self-sufficient, they were argued to be cost-effective. The new legislation addresses all of the objectives and purposes outlined earlier. Support for maternal employment is expanded through additional funding for child care for mothers who work outside the home (CCDBG). New money is being made available to expand programs for the health and development of children from low-income families (Head Start, Medicaid expansion). Expansion of the EITC and the introduction of the two new tax credits are efforts to ease the financial burden of raising children regardless of whether the mother is employed outside the home. These new laws also preserve parental choice in two ways: (1) by allowing families to use tax credits to pay for child care or to partially offset the cost of having one parent remain home to care for the children, and (2) by allowing parents to use vouchers to pay for a provider of their choice. Targeting funding for quality improvements (including resource and referral programs, assistance in meeting state and local standards, monitoring of compliance with licensing and regulatory requirements, training, and improving salaries) and requiring providers to meet minimum standards for health and safety will, it is hoped, improve the quality of care.

Although these measures will be invaluable in improving the quality of care, they do not begin to address the financial burden of bringing the quality of average child care programs up to a standard comparable to the high-quality preschool program that child developmental psychologists and advocates agree is necessary (Hayes, Palmer, and Zaslow 1990; U.S. General Accounting Office 1989b; Willer 1990). Thus, these advances are not likely to substantially improve the outcomes for low-income children.

CHALLENGES FOR PUBLIC POLICY AND CLINTON ADMINISTRATION

Challenge of Quality

A major concern of children's advocates and developmental psychologists alike is that low-income children will have the worst of both worlds—that is, children will neither be cared for by their mothers (because mothers are required to work), nor will they receive adequate care and attention by a substitute care provider. Thus, advocates have placed improving the quality of substitute care at the top of their agenda for the future. Public health officials are also concerned with issues of health and safety in programs. Children in group care provide an opportunity not only for educational intervention but also for intervention in health—screening and testing with appropriate treatment for those who need it.

Although all providers must meet state health and safety requirements to receive funds under the CCDBG, unfortunately, the regulations that implement the new legislation continue to both restrict the use of funds for quality improvements in child care services and restrict the extent to which states may pay differential rates for different types of services (Blank and Lockner 1992; NAEYC 1992; National Governor's Association 1992; U.S. Congress 1992a, b).

What constitutes high-quality child care is not completely agreed upon. Reports from the National Academy of Sciences and the U.S. General Accounting office suggest that the annual cost of care per child that meets standards recommended by professional associations such as the National Association for the Education of Young Children is in the magnitude of $6,000, compared with the $3,000 that parents currently pay (Hayes et al. 1990; U.S. General Accounting Office 1989b). These standards are based on research conducted in the late 1970s by Abt Associates for the federal government (Ruopp et al. 1979). Costs are calculated on the basis of parental and program expenditures in the late 1980s. How each of the proposed standards affects outcomes for children and the effect of marginal changes both on the cost of care and outcomes for children is also unknown. What are the trade-offs among different components of quality? For example, can highly trained teachers provide quality care for larger groups of children?

The Clinton administration proposes expansion of the Earned Income Tax Credit to raise families above poverty and the phasing out of welfare after two years. How do current child care programs interact with such proposed changes in the EITC? Will the quality of programs be affected if more money goes directly to parents? Will they spend the money on better programs?

What Are the Priorities for Head Start and Other Federal Programs?

Since not all eligible children are currently served, a major issue is whether it is more appropriate to spend additional funds to serve children more intensively—more hours and more services—or to serve more children (Chafel 1992; Rovner 1990). In "A Vision of Change for America," President Clinton proposes full funding of the Head Start program. To do so the administration has proposed to increase funding for Head Start in 1997 by $3.2 billion over previous levels, a total of $8 billion more over four years, which is to achieve full funding for an estimated 1.4 million eligible disadvantaged children by 1999 (Executive Office of the President 1993b). This is based upon covering 90 percent of eligible three- and four-year old children with incomes below the poverty line. Along with bringing more children into Head Start, the administration proposes increased funds for the child care food program and for Medicaid to feed and cover the medical expenses of these new entrants, and increased funds for parenting and family support services. Questions about the ability of programs to absorb these new funds, as well as about the trade-off between quantity and quality in Head Start, will be hotly debated over the coming years.

Challenges of Coordination

A primary concern in implementing the new legislation passed in 1990 is that of coordination and integration, so that eligible parents find out about and receive the services they need and for which they are eligible. The legislation directs states to coordinate and integrate these new programs, but does not create specific mechanisms or target resources for these purposes (except for the Coordinated Services Program under the Head Start reauthorization). Given that there are nearly four dozen federal child care assistance programs administered at the state level by a variety of agencies, an increasing number of state-funded preschool programs administered by school boards, and Head Start, administered at the federal level, coordination will be a major challenge. If the Clinton administration's efforts are to be successful, coordination is key.

Challenge of State Implementation

Increasingly, states are responsible for designing and implementing a variety of programs. All states were responsible for submitting state plans to obtain CCDBG funding, and almost all have had their plans reviewed and approved. States are currently engaged in the crucial process of implementing the new legislation (Blank 1991). Since its passage in 1988, the implementation of JOBS child care and transition benefits has been slow. According to recent data, roughly one out of three JOBS participants received JOBS child care, and fewer received transition benefits upon leaving AFDC for employment (Children's Defense Fund 1992; Mitchell, Cooperstein, and Larner 1992). There are several possible reasons for lower-than-expected use, including limited access to JOBS, low payment rates for child care, little information provided to parents about availability of child care benefits, limited time to seek child care, and confusing implementation of transitional benefits.

Parental Leave

Prior to 1993, the United States, in contrast to almost all developed Western nations (Kamerman and Kahn 1991), had no provision for parental leave from employment (other than medical leave to recuperate) following the birth of a child. Parental leave provides the missing piece, since it gives parents the option to care for infants themselves without losing their jobs and health benefits. This is particularly important for low-income parents, since child care for infants is difficult to find and expensive. Since 1986, 23 states have passed maternity/parental leave provisions, indicating broad popular support for the measure. The Family and Medical Leave Act, which mandates that 12 weeks of unpaid parental leave be provided by all employers with 50 or more employees, was passed by both houses in the 101st Congress, then vetoed by President Bush in 1990. In the 102nd Congress, it again passed both houses, only to be vetoed by President Bush a second time. Reintroduced in the early days of the 103rd Congress, it was signed by President Clinton on February 5, 1993. Although a milestone, the legislation that passed the 103rd Congress will not solve all the problems of infant care because the leave is unpaid. Although low-income mothers will no longer be at risk of losing their jobs and health benefits if they have a child, it is unlikely that they will be able to afford to remain off the job for the maximum of 12 weeks allowed. In addition, because so many low-income parents work for small employers, they may not be eligible for this new benefit. This issue is still unresolved.

SUMMARY AND CONCLUSIONS

In the legislation it considered and passed into law, the 101st Congress helped to illuminate an agenda for children in poverty. This chapter has reviewed the roots and evolution of recent children's legislation, its torturous route to passage in the 101st Congress, additional accomplishments in the 102nd and 103rd Congresses, and unresolved issues. Because there were several goals, there could be no single solution. The different pieces of legislation address three major objectives: (1) supporting maternal employment, (2) providing high-quality preschool programs for low-income children, and (3) providing families assistance in raising children as they choose. What has been accomplished so far? A substantial amount of additional money has become available for the care and education of low-income children. Beyond that, advocates have gained valuable knowledge and experience in working for children's issues and have won the support of important constituencies such as state governors and business leaders.

Major pieces of the agenda remain unexecuted, however, including four principal issues: raising the quality of early education and care, setting priorities in expanding Head Start, facilitating the implementation of these diverse pieces of legislation, and coordinating an even larger and more complex set of federal programs to assist families to care for and educate their children. A final unresolved issue is that of parental leave. Even though the Family and Medical Leave Act was finally passed into law in the early days of the Clinton administration, the issues of extending it to small employers and providing at least partial income replacement are likely to be raised in the future.

Implementation

Because of the emphasis on parental choice, parents have both a greater opportunity and a greater responsibility to make choices than they had before. For parents to have a true choice they must, first, have alternatives to choose from and, second, the information on which to make the best choice for themselves and their children (see Hofferth 1992b, for a discussion of issues in choice). After adequate funding, the issue of information is one of the most important for low-income parents.

What are the solutions? Several national organizations (for example, the Center on Budget and Policy Priorities, Children's Defense Fund, National Women's Law Center) are working to disseminate information to parents on eligibility for expanded tax credits. Several organizations have mounted a campaign to inform parents and others about what is meant by high-quality care (NAEYC, Child Care Action Campaign, National Child Care Resource and Referral Association).

Similar leadership is needed for welfare parents. Recent evidence from implementation of welfare reform suggests that welfare clients are not receiving information about the child care options available to them either while on welfare or after they leave it (Children's Defense Fund 1992; Mitchell et al. 1992). Consequently, utilization of JOBS Child Care and the Transitional Child Care program is low. Child care resource and referral networks are a potential source of information and training of providers. Unfortunately, Child Care Improvement Grants, which fund child care resource and referral agencies, received no funding in FY 1992. Although funds have apparently been appropriated for 1993, it is important to remain vigilant regarding the funding of small but important programs.

Coordination

Table 7.1 describes eight major child care programs (excluding the Child and Dependent Care Tax Credit). States must coordinate these major programs, and other smaller ones, each of which has its own administrative mechanism, regulations, and eligibility requirements, so that clients receive appropriate services. State coordination strategies have included, first, identifying the various programs, amount of funding, and the administering agency. Second, some states have assigned administrative responsibility for several programs to a single agency or have established offices for children charged with coordinating these programs (National Governors' Association 1992). Alternatively, states have moved child care programs into community organizations such as child care resource and referral agencies, which then are charged with providing or brokering services to eligible clients. In many states these agencies also recruit child care providers, provide technical assistance and training. Third, states have established common payment rates, sliding scale fees, and a single application for multiple programs. Several states (Arkansas, Illinois, and Texas), have established computerized eligibility and management systems for tracking various funding sources. Other coordination efforts include using CCDBG funds to provide before- and after-school care for Head Start programs, helping child care and Head Start centers obtain Medicaid funds for child health programs, funding health care coordinators in centers, providing funding for a child care coordinator within the Department of Education to coordinate state preschool programs with child care programs, and linking family day care providers in local networks whereby they can communicate with one another and obtain the assistance they need (National Governors' Association 1992).

Quality

Although the issue of national standards appears closed for now, the issue of quality has not been resolved. Given the budget deficit, advocates will have to present a strong case for increasing investments in program quality. Although many European nations have long made high-quality programs for children a national priority, the United States has not come to such a consensus. Thus, more studies are needed to evaluate the relationships among standards, expenditures, and the quality of programs for children in cost-benefit terms.

Conclusion

Substantial research indicates that high-quality programs at an early age go a long way toward increasing (low-income) children's chances of success later on. Yet, more work remains to be done before widespread societal support for these initial investments in the young can be assumed. Adequate reimbursement of parental expenditures is critical. But it is not just a matter of funding. Parents need to be educated and informed as to what constitutes high-quality care and education and how to get it. Providers need to be seen as partners as well. As a society we need to move from a situation of conflict between the interests of parents, children, and providers to one of agreement that the well-being of all three groups and the society are linked.

Notes

I am grateful to Helen Blank for her taped recollections about the development and passage of the 1990 child care legislation. Comments from Judith Chafel, William Gormley, Deborah Phillips, Wendell Primus, Ann Stewart, and Joan Vondra were quite helpful. The contributions of Sharon Deich in summarizing recent child care legislation and Mitchell Tobin for research assistance are also gratefully acknowledged.

1. Because Head Start is a part-day, part-year program, it cannot serve the needs of children for care while the parents are working. Thus, Head Start is not considered a child care program, and the $1.2 billion in expenditures for it in fiscal year 1989 are not included here.

2. Family expenditures on child care up to a maximum amount per month ($160) can be disregarded as income for the purpose of calculating AFDC benefits. This was the primary means of subsidizing child care for AFDC families prior to the passage of the Family Support Act in 1988.

3. The Omnibus Budget Reconciliation Act (OBRA) of 1993 (U.S. Congress, 1993) revised the maximum credit in 1994 to $2,038 for one qualifying child and to $2,527 for two qualifying children with additional increases in 1995. The rate of reduction as income rises was also increased.

4. In the 1993 OBRA, both the supplemental young child credit and the supplemental health insurance credit were repealed.

References

Barnes, R. 1988. "The Distributional Effects of Alternative Child Care Proposals." Paper presented at the annual meeting of the Association for Public Policy Analysis and Management, Seattle, October 27–29.

Berrueta-Clement, Lawrence J. Schweinhart, W. Steven Barnett, Ann Epstein, and David Weikart. 1984. *Changed Lives: The Effects of the Perry Preschool Program on Youths through Age 19.* Ypsilanti, Mich.: High/Scope Press.

Besharov, Douglas, and Paul Tremantozzi. 1988. "The Costs of Federal Child Care Assistance." AEI Occasional Papers. Washington, D.C.: American Enterprise Institute for Public Policy Research.

Blank, Helen. 1991. The Child Care and Development Block Grant and Child Care Grants to States under Title IV-A of the Social Security Act: A Description of Major Provisions and Issues to Consider in Implementation. Washington, D.C.: The Children's Defense Fund, January 14.

Blank, Helen, and Sherrie Lockner. 1992. "Final Child Care Regulations for the 'At-Risk' Child Care Program and the Child Care and Development Block Grant." Memorandum. Washington, D.C.: Children's Defense Fund.

Cahan, Emily D. 1989. *Past Caring: A History of U.S. Preschool Care and Education for the Poor, 1820–1965.* New York, N.Y.: National Center for Children in Poverty.

Cammisa, Anne Marie. 1992. *Intergovernmental Lobbying: State and Local Governments as Interest Groups.* Ph.D. dissertation. Washington, D.C.: Georgetown University.

Chafel, Judith. 1992. Funding Head Start: What Are the Issues? *American Journal of OrthoPsychiatry* 62(January): 9–21.

Children's Defense Fund. 1989. *A Vision for America's Future. An Agenda for the 1990s: A Children's Defense Budget.* Washington, D.C.: Author.

―――――. 1992. Child Care under the Family Support Act: Early Lessons from the States. Washington, D.C.: Author.

Committee for Economic Development. 1987. Children in Need: Investment Strategies for the Educationally Disadvantaged. New York: Committee for Economic Development.

―――――. 1993. Why Child Care Matters: Preparing Young Children for a More Productive America. New York: Committee for Economic Development.

Culkin, Mary, John R. Morris, and Suzanne W. Helburn. 1991. "Quality and the True Cost of Child Care." Journal of Social Issues 47(2): 71–86.

Duncan, Greg J., Martha S. Hill, and Saul D. Hoffman. 1988. "Welfare Dependence within and across Generations." Science 239(29, January): 467–71.

Executive Office of the President. 1993a. The Budget of the United States. Washington, D.C.: U.S. Government Printing Office.

―――――. 1993b. A Vision of Change for America. Washington, D.C.: U.S. Government Printing Office.

Galinsky, Ellen, and Dana Friedman. 1993. Education before School: Investing in Quality Child Care. New York: Scholastic.

Gebhardt, Joell. 1990. "The Augustus F. Hawkins Human Services Reauthorization Act of 1990." State-Federal Issue Brief 3(6, November): 1–9.

Golonka, Susan, and Theodora Ooms. 1991. "Child Care in the 101st Congress: What Was Achieved and How Will it Work?" Background Briefing Report and Meeting Highlights. Washington, D.C.: Family Impact Seminar.

Gueron, Judith M., and E. Pauly. 1990. The Effects of Welfare-to-Work Programs: A Synthesis of Recent Experimental Research. New York: Manpower Demonstration Research Corp.

Hayes, Cheryl D., John L. Palmer, and Martha J. Zaslow. 1990. Who Cares for America's Children? Child Care Policy for the 1990s. Washington, D.C.: National Academy Press.

Hofferth, Sandra. 1992a. "At the Margin: Managing Work and Family Life at the Poverty Line." Paper presented at the annual meeting of the American Sociological Association, Pittsburgh, Aug. 21.

―――――. 1992b. "How Do Parents Make Child Care Choices? Do Models of Parent Choice Bear Any Resemblance to Reality?" Paper presented at the Ninth Annual Symposium of the A. L. Mailman Family Foundation on The Shifting Contexts of Parent Choice in Early Childhood Education, Rye, N.Y., June 29.

Hofferth, Sandra, and Douglas Wissoker. 1992. "Price, Quality, and Income in Child Care Choice." Journal of Human Resources 27(1): 70–111.

Hofferth, Sandra, April Brayfield, Sharon Deich, and Pamela Holcomb. 1991. National Child Care Survey, 1990. Washington, D.C.: Urban Institute.

Kamerman, Sheila B., and Alfred J. Kahn. 1991. Child Care, Parental Leave, and the Under 3's: Policy Innovation in Europe. Westport, Conn.: Auburn House.

Kingdon, John. 1987. Agendas, Alternatives, and Public Policies. Glenview, Ill.: Scott, Foresman & Co.

Kisker, Ellen, and Marsha Silverberg. 1991. "Child Care Utilization by Disadvantaged Teenage Mothers." Journal of Social Issues 47(2): 159–77.

Kisker, Ellen, Sandra Hofferth, Deborah Phillips, and Elizabeth Farquhar. 1991. A Profile of Child Care Settings: Early Education and Care in 1990. Washington, D.C.: U.S. Government Printing Office.

Kosterlitz, Julie. 1988. "Not Just Kid Stuff." National Journal 20(47, Nov. 19): 2934–39.

_____. 1990. "Family Fights." National Journal 22(22, June 2): 1333–37.

Levy, Frank, and Richard C. Michel. 1991. The Economic Future of American Families: Income and Wealth Trends. Washington, D.C.: Urban Institute Press.

Lindner, Eileen, Mary C. Mattis, and June R. Rogers. 1983. When Churches Mind the Children: A Study of Day Care in Local Parishes. Ypsilanti, Mich.: High/Scope Press.

Mitchell, Anne, Emily Cooperstein, and Mary Larner. 1992. Child Care Choices, Consumer Education, and Low-Income Families. New York: National Center for Children in Poverty.

Morgan, Gwen. 1987. The National State of Child Care Regulation, 1986. Watertown, Mass.: Work/Family Directions.

Morse, Ann, and Sheri Steisel. 1990. "Child Care: A Summary and Analysis of New Federal Programs and Tax Credits." State-Federal Issue Brief 3(8 December): 1–16.

NAEYC. See National Association for the Education of Young Children.

National Association for the Education of Young Children. 1992. "Final Child Care Regulations Issued." Public Affairs Alert. Washington, D.C.: Author.

_____. 1990. "101st Congress: The Children's Congress." Early Childhood Advocate 2(1): 1.

_____. 1992. "Major Early Childhood Accomplishments Achieved in the 102nd Congress." Early Childhood Advocate (Fall, conference ed.): 1–3.

National Governors' Association. 1992. "Child Care: Creating Quality Seamless Systems." In Brief: Employment and Social Services Policy Studies, Sept. 21.

_____. 1993. "State Coverage of Pregnant Women and Children—January 1993." MCH Update. Washington, D.C.: National Governor's Association.

Nelson, John R., Jr. 1982. "The Federal Interagency Day Care Requirements." In Making Policies for Children: A Study of the Federal Process, edited by Cheryl Hayes (151–205). Washington, D.C.: National Academy Press.

Nelson, John R., Jr., and Wendy E. Warring. 1982. "The Child Care Tax Deduction Credit." In *Making Policies for Children: A Study of the Federal Process*, edited by Cheryl Hayes (206–65). Washington, D.C.: National Academy Press.

Peirce, Neal R. 1990. "Bush's New Head Start Budget Is Just a Start." *National Journal* 22(6, Feb. 10): 345.

Phillips, Deborah. 1991. "With a Little Help: Children in Poverty and Child Care." In *Children in Poverty: Child Development and Public Policy*, edited by A. Huston (158–89). New York: Cambridge University Press.

Phillips, Deborah, and Edward Zigler. 1987. "The Checkered History of Federal Child Care Regulation." In *Review of Research in Education*, vol. 14, edited by E. Rothkopf. Washington, D.C.: American Educational Research Association.

Phillips, Deborah, Jeff Lande, and Marc Goldberg. 1990. "The State of Child Care Regulation: A Comparative Analysis." *Early Childhood Research Quarterly* 5:151–79.

Primus, Wendell E. 1989. "Children in Poverty: A Committee Prepares for an Informed Debate." *Journal of Policy Analysis and Management* 8(1): 23–34.

Ribar, David C. 1991. *Federal Child Care Assistance Takes its First Steps: 1933–1946*. Working Paper 2-91-2. University Park, Pa.: Pennsylvania State University Department of Economics.

Robins, Philip. 1988. "Federal Support for Child Care: Current Policies and a Proposed New System." *Focus* 11(2): 1–9.

Rovner, Julie. 1989a. "Child-Care Debate Intensifies as ABC bill Is Approved." *Congressional Quarterly Weekly Report*, 47(11, Mar. 18): 585–87.

———. 1989b. "Consensus Grows on Dual Path to Boosting Child-Care Aid." *Congressional Quarterly Weekly Report* 47(16, Apr. 22): 902.

———. 1989c. "Partisan Lines Drawn in Senate as Child-Care Debate Opens." *Congressional Quarterly Weekly Report* 47(24, June 17): 1475–77.

———. 1989d. "House Braced for Floor Fight over Child-Care Proposals." *Congressional Quarterly Weekly Report* 47(39, Sept. 30): 2565.

———. 1989e. "House-Senate Conferees Agree on New Child-Care Program." *Congressional Quarterly Weekly Report* 47(45, Nov. 11): 3070.

———. 1989f. "Delay on Child-Care Measure Prompts Angry Criticism." *Congressional Quarterly Weekly Report* 47(46, Nov. 18): 3162.

———. 1990. "Head Start Is One Program Everyone Wants to Help." *Congressional Quarterly Weekly Report* 48(16, Apr. 21): 1191–95.

Ruopp, Richard, Jeffrey Travers, Frederic Glantz, and Craig Coelen. 1979. *Children at the Center*. Cambridge, Mass.: Abt Associates.

Smith, Sheila, Susan Blank, and James T. Bond. 1990. *One Program, Two Generations*. New York: Foundation for Child Development.

Steuerle, C. Eugene. 1990. "Tax Credits for Low-Income Workers with Children." *Journal of Economic Perspectives* 4(Summer): 201–12.

U.S. Congress. 1990. "Omnibus Budget Reconciliation Act of 1990." Public Law 101-508. Washington, D.C.: U.S. Government Printing Office.

————. 1992a. "Aid to Families with Dependent Children At-Risk Child Care Program." Final rule. *Federal Register* 57(150, Aug. 4): 34434–63. Washington, D.C.: U.S. Government Printing Office.

————. 1992b. "Child Care and Development Block Grant." Final rule. *Federal Register* 57(150, Aug. 4): 34352–431.

U.S. Congress, House of Representatives, Committee on Ways and Means. 1985. *Children in Poverty*. Washington, D.C.: U.S. Government Printing Office.

————. 1992. *1992 Green Book: Overview of Entitlement Programs*. Washington, D.C.: U.S. Government Printing Office.

U.S. Congress, House of Representatives, Select Committee on Children, Youth, and Families. 1985. *Opportunities for Success: Cost-Effective Programs for Children*. Washington, D.C.: U.S. Government Printing Office.

U.S. General Accounting Office. 1989a. *Child Care: Government Funding Sources, Coordination, and Service Availability*. Washington, D.C.: U.S. General Accounting Office.

————. 1989b. *Early Childhood Education: Information on Costs and Services at High-Quality Centers*. Washington, D.C.: U.S. General Accounting Office.

Whitebook, Marcy, Carolee Howes, and Deborah Phillips. 1989. *Who Cares? Child Care Teachers and the Quality of Care in America*. Final Report: The National Child Care Staffing Study. Oakland, Calif.: Child Care Employee Project.

Willer, B. 1990. *Reaching the Full Cost of Quality*. Washington, D.C.: National Association for the Education of Young Children.

Willer, Barbara, Sandra Hofferth, Ellen Kisker, Patricia Divine-Hawkins, Elizabeth Farquhar, and Frederic Glantz. 1991. *The Demand and Supply of Child Care in 1990: Joint Findings from the National Child Care Survey, 1990, and A Profile of Child Care Settings*. Washington, D.C.: National Association for the Education of Young Children.

Chapter Eight

HUMAN CAPITAL: THE BIGGEST DEFICIT

Harold Watts

The outcomes of thwarted personal development and outright damage that are the likely consequences of child poverty are bad enough
to stir altruistic motives in almost anyone. These outcomes have been
detailed earlier in this volume. My concern in this chapter is with
the added impetus of self-interest that comes from the realization
that children living in poverty in the United States today will be a
major part of the available work force as our country, and its capacity
to produce, moves into the 21st century. Unless we, as a society,
manage to equip each child with the basic skills, and capacity to
adapt, that are necessary for continuing the generational cycle, we
can expect not only our material living standards but our self-esteem
to deteriorate. As Frank Knight put it, eloquently, more than 70 years
ago, we live in "a world where individuals are born naked, destitute,
helpless, ignorant and untrained, and must spend a third of their
lives acquiring the prerequisites of a free contractual existence"
(1921: 374–5). This is still true, with perhaps some extension of life
spans, and it underscores the crucial role of child development in
determining the possible futures for our nation's people.

Considerable ink and rhetoric have been devoted to the problem
of the "twin deficits," that is, the federal budget deficit that adds to
the public debt and the trade deficit that increases debts of U.S.
nationals to parties abroad. Concern about those deficits and debts
is entirely proper, but only if they are viewed in the context of other
deficits and debts. Deficits that reflect underspending on the real
determinants of productive capacity are not so readily measured in
dollar terms as are those represented by documents of indebtedness,
but they are much more directly and critically related to how well
we can live in the future and what our incomes (or pensions) will
be able to buy. I argue in this chapter that a balanced approach to
the economic and social problems we face would put first priority
on the real foundations of our well-being, that is, the vigor and

productivity of our citizens, and would then address the financial implications of "doing the right thing," both morally and economically.

A recurrent theme in this chapter's discussion is the need to pierce the "veil of money" to see more clearly the real resources and products that are the stuff on which our well-being primarily depends. A modern, complex, market-based economy like ours uses money and other financial instruments and institutions in the process of guiding the production and distribution of the shoes, steaks, and superbowls that comprise our collective market basket. It is simpler to think of the dollar totals of income, saving, consumption, and so on, measured in a common monetary unit than of the amounts and peculiarities of a myriad of individual items. But in taking that shortcut one must not forget that the prices used to combine "apples and oranges" are always subject to change, and, indeed, depend on the supplies of real goods and the number of dollars offered for them. No less than in a primitive money-less society, the amount of goods and services we will find available for apportioning in the future will depend on the number and capacities of active adults as well as on the tools and infrastructure with which they work.

The children now alive and those to be born in the rest of this decade will form the core of our labor force in the first third of the next century. The previous chapters leave little doubt that child poverty and poor institutions are creating a large deficit in the productive capacities of a great many of those future workers. That deficit must be closed if our nation expects to redeem the promises made to the workers who will be retiring over the next 30 years. It is uniquely appropriate that the cost of the needed investment in our human resources be given first claim on the saving now being accumulated in the Social Security Trust Fund. That accumulation was planned to provide the financial basis for paying retirement benefits to the bulge of retirees projected for the future (Kusserow 1988). It is now necessary to develop the basis of real resources if those dollars are to find an adequate supply of consumer products at that time (Aschauer 1991). It is proposed below to allocate the trust fund saving to investments in the nation's children and thereby close the deficit that is the most direct threat to our future well-being. Those investments must both eliminate the poverty of families rearing children and strengthen and augment the other institutions that affect child development.

The sections following first introduce the basic concept of human capital and its properties and then interpret the developmental deficits discussed in earlier chapters in terms of the human investment process. Additional evidence of neglect and failure in that investment process is then reviewed. Consideration of the implications of those deficits for meeting future needs and commitments follows, with particular emphasis on the demands of the "baby boom" cohorts as they enter their retirement years. The last sections discuss, first, the attempts of the trustees of the Social Security system to anticipate the demographic "dependency bulge" by building up trust fund reserves, and then make the case that unless those trust funds are invested in some form of capital that promises a payoff of productivity when the reserves are called on, the purchasing power of the benefits will be a serious disappointment to the retired population. Finally, the policy of giving first priority to human capital investment by earmarking the planned Social Security Trust Fund surplus accumulation for family support and child development activities is proposed. The Social Security surplus, which is beginning to swell considerably, is now simply used to reduce the deficit in the federal budget. The case made here is that those surplus revenues should not be merged with all other net receipts of the government, but should be invested in a responsible manner that can deliver the goods when the time comes to cash in those reserves. Failure to do so will incur real and irreversible costs in the future that are much more serious than those associated with increases in the public debt. Once the *real* deficit in our human capital is under control, attention can properly be turned to the problem of the *financial* deficit.

The bottom line of this chapter is an appeal to self-interest on behalf of ending child poverty. Our nation is paying a high and growing penalty for neglect of this issue, and much of the burden is likely to fall on the retired population of the early 21st century. It is neither too late to stop the senseless waste of human potential that is the sure result of child poverty, nor perhaps to recover some of the lost opportunities already evident in our youth cohorts.

WHAT IS HUMAN CAPITAL?

Human capital is a concept used by economists to refer to the capacity of individuals to perform functions that are of value to themselves or others. Those capacities are a result of the many influences or factors that bear on human development in its broadest sense. Human capital is not just the strength, knowledge, and skills used, for example, to earn a wage or salary or to operate a successful business. It also includes the skills and wisdom used to produce the elements of home and family life, as well as those that enable persons to be effective in the social and political institutions of the broader community.[1]

Some may find the capital metaphor much too commercial and materialistic for the full range of useful human capacities. But the analogy is really quite close. Human capital is built up by the productive efforts of others, it can be destroyed by lack of maintenance and misuse, it can assume a great many different forms. As with a piece of equipment, the value of any specific human capital depends on the demand for its particular productive service, and specific human capital can become obsolete just like a machine. The capital that represents the capacity to seek and absorb new experiences and learn from them is especially important for development of more specialized forms of human capital, and it has a clear counterpart in the tools that produce more tools in the realm of physical capital. Finally, both the nonhuman and human wealth of a person (or a nation) depend on the amount and value of the productive services obtainable by use of the capital goods and human capital that the person (or nation) possesses (Watts 1977).

Investments in human capital, then, are no less essential for a nation's continued ability to produce a high and possibly growing standard of living than investments in factories, equipment, and infrastructure. Again, to borrow from Knight (1921: 375) "Besides the torch of life itself, the material wealth of the world, a technological system of vast and increasing intricacy and the habituations which fit men for social life must be carried forward to new individuals born devoid of all things as older individuals pass out."

Child development is an alternative, and more widely recognized, name for the human capital investment that precedes the threshold of adulthood. That investment is produced, with active participation of the child that increases with maturity, by the efforts of parents, other family members, teachers, clergy, and neighbors, and augmented as needed and if possible by doctors, counselors, and social service personnel. The effectiveness of those efforts depends in turn on the human and material wealth that is available to that large cast of participants in the development process.

Human development certainly continues beyond childhood, but choices about those investment activities are made by the adult person and are heavily influenced and circumscribed by the human capital acquired as a child. Human capital of the most specific kinds is typically acquired on the job, and may or may not be useful in a different firm or different set of tasks. But to get the on-the-job experience, one has to get the job! That often requires convincing evidence of a well-developed capacity to learn, together with the socialization appropriate for getting along with co-workers, and the motivation to pursue goals that are reasonably within reach.

Both the importance of human capital and the pivotal influence of the foundations of that capital acquired in early childhood have been emphasized in the preceding chapters. Poverty itself is obviously related to the human capital of the potential earners in a child's family—most prominently, one or both parents. If the job-oriented capital is there, then the poverty problem facing public policymakers is one of maintaining an adequate level of demand in the market—not an easy problem to solve, but not one of inadequate human investment. But as Bianchi, in chapter 4 of this volume, indicates, the recent divergence of pay rates between those with higher qualifications and those with minimal ones is evidence that too many young are entering adulthood without the human capital to compete successfully for the better-paying jobs. Consequently, the pay for the scarce, "capital-rich" workers is bid up and the pay for the "capital-poor" is driven down by oversupply. It is not clear that a lower overall unemployment rate would reduce those disparities (though it might convert some unemployed poor into working poor). Hence, we see that the shortage of human capital among current childrearing adults is a root cause of poverty itself. Indeed, the effect of that poverty on the development of children's capital is the main concern of this volume.

But another part of parents' human capital is their capacity to function as parents. Musick (chapter 2, in this volume) emphasizes the critical necessity of strong parenting skills among poor parents to meet the many challenges and hazards that confront them in typically unfriendly environments. She argues persuasively that such parents need to be truly heroic in both capacity and effort to bring children into productive adulthood. Moreover, states Musick, among the hazards that may befall female children (and not only in poor environments) are sexual abuse and exploitation that "make early childbearing almost inevitable for them." That result commonly leads to incomplete development not only of the child's crucial parenting capacities, but of her livelihood capacities, which tends to perpetuate the problems.

The levels and disheartening trends in poverty among children are well chronicled by Scarbrough in chapter 3 of this volume. The growth in childhood poverty since the mid 1970s and its increasing concentration among racial and ethnic minorities testify to a miserable performance in achieving the lofty goals of alleviating poverty that have been repeatedly enunciated by our nation's leaders (CEA 1992, White House Conference on Families 1980). Scarbrough also indicates the difference in poverty incidence among different groups of children defined by urbanization and regional categories. Poor children and their parents in these varied environments also face different obstacles to development of human capital and different institutional supports in meeting those challenges.

Scarbrough furthermore reminds us of distinctions that need to be made in terms of the severity of poverty and its duration as a proportion of childhood years. Clearly the most extreme cases of foregone and frustrated human capital investment exist among young persons and parents in areas of concentrated, severe, and persistent poverty in our largest metropolitan areas. This segment of the poor population, labeled by many researchers as belonging to the "underclass," does not appear to be growing at an alarming rate; yet, it seems relatively impervious to the improvements we generally expect when the economy picks up momentum and reduces general unemployment rates (Jencks and Peterson 1991).

Scarbrough criticizes the measure of poverty that is used for our official indicators, but indicates that correcting the faults of the measure would generally make the situation of poor children seem worse. That is correct, but it is worth noting that the use of a relative measure, such as half the median, may produce different movements in the distributions of nominal poverty among racial and ethnic groups. Based on recent tabulations by the U.S. Census from the Current Population Survey, the incidence of relative poverty for children at 50 percent of the median increased from around 20 percent in the 1960s to nearly 30 percent by 1989 (U.S. Bureau of the Census [henceforth, Census Bureau] 1991).[2] If we examine how the share of that relative poverty among children is divided among racial groups over the period 1964–89, we see that black children represent a declining portion of poor children, from 35 percent to 30 percent, even though their incidence rates are high and have been growing since 1974. White and "other" racial groups show corresponding gains in their share of poverty over the period, with the white share reflecting a rapidly growing Hispanic share, up to 20 percent by 1989, and a slower decline among non-Hispanic whites. The "other" racial groups more than quadrupled in number over the whole 25-year period, largely from Asian and Pacific Islander immigration, and their children now represent around 5 percent of the relatively poor population, even though their incidence rates are well below those for black and Hispanic children. The different pattern for relative poverty, as compared to the official, "absolute" measure, is in large part due to the inclusion of more working poor families in the poor category when the thresholds are increased in pace with overall median income.

A more severe relative poverty standard at 25 percent of the median, which would certainly be regarded as very poor relative to the official thresholds, produces somewhat higher shares of poverty for black and Hispanic children. The changes through time are similar, however—modest declines for blacks and sharp increases for Hispanics. In terms of simple material deprivation, the 6.4 million children below the 25 percent standard in 1989 (more than half under six years of age) face dismal prospects for acquiring "the prerequisites of a free contractual existence."

The problem of maltreatment of children considered by Vondra, in chapter 5 of this volume, represents a sphere in which poverty and human capital, in the broad sense, may interact in passing the problem on between generations. If we consider the experiences of a child growing up in a socially isolated and abusive household as forming part of his or her capital for use during parenthood, there is a potential for maltreatment to be visited on the next generation. Whether that potential will be realized appears to depend on the amount and persistence of stressors, such as poverty-level income or the sorts of economic distress that may be felt by families with relatively high income when confronted with the unexpected loss of part of that income or of the sense of security provided by a steady job. A comprehensive approach to reducing maltreatment should consider both parts of the brew that produces it. Reducing the severe hardship causing stress among the very poor and reducing the sources of economic insecurity that stress the not-so-poor would reduce the abusiveness of many parents who are at risk because of the parenting capital they were endowed with. At the same time, early identification of maltreated children provides a chance to expose them to a wider range of learning experiences that will endow them with parenting capital that will enable them to handle stress less destructively. By one means or another, the acquisition of nonviolent ways of coping with the inevitable stresses of parenthood and life in general as part of the human capital endowment of new adults is our only hope for eliminating maltreatment as a major risk of childhood.

Moore's summation in chapter 6 of this volume, linking our

national interests to the development of poor children, speaks directly to the point emphasized in the current chapter. Moore discredits the arguments that some children—poor and/or minorities, to be specific—are unable or unwilling to acquire that fund of basic human capital that enables them to be fully participating adults and eventual parents. Some blame genetic differences, whereas others favor cultural ones as the source of handicap. Such misbegotten arguments, often claiming scientific certitude, have been used as excuses for neglecting the full development of the human potential of far too many children. Moore contends, and I hope to establish firmly, that continuation of that neglect is both unnecessary and expensive.

In summary, the chapters of this volume provide ample and compelling examples of the ways that the human capital of children is underdeveloped and impaired by growing up poor, in deprived environments, and/or reared by parents who themselves lack the human capital needed to provide the material, intellectual, and psychic nourishment that all children need. That some exceptionally robust children are able to escape these hazards with the help of extraordinary efforts of parents or mentors is undeniable, but of no comfort when we realize how many children do not escape. I consider now some measures of the size of the problem.

INDICATORS OF FAILURE AND NEGLECT OF HUMAN CAPITAL INVESTMENT

In 1991 more than one out of every seven persons in the 20–24-year age bracket lacked a high school diploma (and was not engaged in getting one) (Johnson 1993). That means that about a half-million young people are entering adulthood without that basic credential *each year.* How many of them will be able to enter a mainstream job and adapt to the steadily changing requirements for holding or progressing in that job over the next 40 years of their lives? How many will be prepared to provide the support and encouragement for their own children that is so important to the next generation's human capital endowment? It has been estimated that each year's class of dropouts costs, over their lifetime, $250 billion in lower wages and foregone tax payments (National Commission on Children 1993). This measure of how we are failing to develop our human capital summarizes for many an entire childhood of missed and botched chances to acquire the foundations of health, civility, confidence, and motivation that facilitate minimal success in school-based development. To do better we will have to go back to square one (or perhaps minus nine months), with the resolve that no child will fail to get the basic requirements of mainstream participation because of parental or societal neglect of his or her developmental needs (Hewlett 1991).

There are many aspects of education in this country that we can be proud of. In particular, the achievement of the top tenth of U.S. students is second to none internationally, and our graduate schools attract the best students from around the world. But the performance at the low end is a major embarrassment. Even as the fraction of the adult population with 12 or more years of education continues to increase, we are no longer confident that a high school diploma even indicates a usable level of literacy or the ability to make change for a simple money transaction (National Commission on Children 1993).

Besides the deficit in schooling, many of the same young people engage, as adolescents, "in behaviors that seriously threaten their own health and well-being, that of their families, and that of others in the community" (National Commission on Children 1993). Substance abuse, starting with tobacco and progressing to alcohol and illicit drugs, is one common form of risky behavior that may presage a failure to make a transition into responsible adulthood. Motor vehicle accidents are the most common cause of death among young people, and a large share of those are related to alcohol abuse. The suicide rate among teenagers has also been growing in recent years and is often associated with substance use and abuse (Census Bureau 1993).

In addition, unprotected sex introduces well-known disease hazards, both fatal and disabling, as well as pregnancies to young women in no way prepared to carry out the responsibilities of (single) parenthood. Ten percent of women under 20 years of age become pregnant every year, 4 percent have abortions, 1 percent miscarry, and the remainder give birth. Over a half-million babies started their childhood that way in 1989, and the numbers are still growing (Moore 1991; National Commission on Children 1993). The young mothers, of course, typically end, interrupt, or slow development of their own human capital.

Finally, delinquency, crime, and related violence are wasting the potential of a growing number of young men through death or incarceration. These hazards are more prevalent among minority youth and are often connected with traffic in illegal drugs, but the consequence for the human capital stock is disastrous regardless of the group or the specific crime involved. Teenage boys are more likely to die from gunshot wounds than from all other natural causes combined (National Commission on Children 1993). Murder and assault rates of and by juveniles have shot up since the mid 1980s. The prison population has more than doubled over the last decade, and at last count, nearly two out of seven prisoners were under 25 years of age (Census Bureau 1993).

Health and vitality are elements of human capital too, and once again there are indicators that we are doing less well than most of the civilized world and even worse than we have done in the past. More babies were born with late or no prenatal care in 1989 than in 1979 (National Commission on Children 1993). No progress in the incidence of low birthweight was made over that period, and the rate actually rose for black births (National Commission on Children 1993). These indicators are well known to increase the chance of future health problems for those children who survive the high infant mortality experience for those groups. Lowered rates of immunization for serious communicable diseases have led to many more outbreaks and continuing health complications. The increasing poverty rates among children over the last dozen years inevitably produce more nutritional problems ranging from inadequate nutrition of pregnant women to anemia and growth retardation among young children. Finally, access to medical attention for acute or chronic conditions is limited for many poor and near-poor children. This means that conditions that could have been remedied often result in a more permanent handicap.

In the end, it is hard to find even one aspect of human development where the indicators show improvement for poor and or minority children. Certainly the bottom quarter and probably the bottom half of children ranked by income or some other index of advantage seem likely to enter their adult years less well prepared for full and productive participation than previous generations. They will also be entering a labor market that places a higher relative value on "capital-rich" workers than was the case in earlier decades.

HUMAN CAPITAL INVESTMENT AND THE PARADE OF GENERATIONS

The growth and decline of real living standards in a society can be seen as a race between the total output of consumer goods and services and the number of persons who are to be fed, housed, educated, and so forth, from that total. In this discussion a broader concept of consumer goods and services than the one used in the national accounts is needed. We must recognize that a great deal of final consumption involves substantial productive activity within the household. Capital goods, supplies, and raw materials are acquired in the market and are combined with labor and human capital to produce meals, warm shelter, clean clothes, and so on. The level and quality of living standards is determined by productive activity in both the household and market sectors.

In any ongoing society there will be a nominally dependent part of the population consisting mainly of children, retired (or incapacitated) elders, and disabled adults who cannot support themselves. The remaining, active part of the population provides the labor and human capital inputs used in producing those goods and services. The ratio of such dependents to the total population, called the dependency ratio, is an important demographic determinant of living standards. Clearly the living level will be lower if two-thirds of the population is dependent on the output of the active third than it would be if the proportions were reversed. If birthrates, death rates, and disability hazards remain about the same, the dependency ratio will find a steady level. But changes in those rates and hazards will produce variations in the dependency ratio.

The famous post–World War II "baby boom" produced a sizable bulge in dependency while the "boomers" were children. When those same children moved into the active ages the dependency ratio dropped below the normal rate. The "baby bust" that was produced by later (and lesser) fertility among the "boomers" will contribute to an echo of high dependency as the "boomers" retire and reenter the dependent group in the 21st century. The rebound of dependency will not reach the levels experienced in the 1950s, but it will be composed of more elders and fewer children. Anticipation of that reentry inspired changes in the Social Security system, which are considered more closely later in this chapter.

Equally important for determining living standards, and more susceptible to change, is the productivity of the active part of the population. That productivity depends in turn on the quantity and quality of the capital that the active population has to work with. Physical capital, human capital, and social capital are each vitally important, and require constant replacement, repair, and updating to reflect new knowledge and needs.[3] But the processes that maintain and renew the three capital stocks are quite different.

Physical capital is itself produced by the same or similar means as consumer goods—we call them investment goods—and the gestation period for a new plant or piece of equipment is usually measured in months—two to three years at most. Once a private or public decision is reached to allocate current output toward a particular capital project, the job can be accomplished relatively quickly.

Human capital takes a little longer. The foundations on which a solid structure of human development can be built need to be formed in the earliest years, starting with conception and extending into the preschool years. Insults to and neglect of a child's physical, emotional, and cognitive health during these years may well be impossible to compensate for at a later time. The stimulation and socialization that are needed in the preschool years, and the development of basic language and numeracy skills in the early school years, are fundamental to the acquisition of further formal and informal learning that can produce a full participant in society. Individuals who have acquired the skills and dispositions needed to learn and adapt to changes in technology (in or out of the household) can renew and update their human capital in a relatively short time, but the entire process of developing a "fully franchised" adult occupies the whole period of childhood.

Social capital changes at a more glacial rate as institutions and traditions evolve. It is likely that the direction of such change is related to the nature and distribution of human capital, however. If human capital investment is directed more toward nonviolent ways of resolving conflicts, the institutions may rely more on self-control and less on overt police supervision. Inequality in the distribution of human capital and hence in the earning power and privileges that go with such capital can also contribute to the prejudice and mistrust that are unfortunate by-products of our social capital.

So, all three sorts of capital determine the productivity of the active part of the population and hence the upper bound on the goods and services that can be produced. The dependency ratio indicates roughly the proportion of output per active person that must be deducted to provide shares for the dependent ones. We know that the dependency ratio will increase as the baby boom enters retirement, a factor that would tend, by itself, to reduce living standards. What about the human capital of the generations that will be active at that point? Clearly quality can substitute for quantity in the active work force, but the facts just reviewed about deprivation and neglect among children are anything but hopeful in that regard. Our recent past has seen a steady deterioration in the quantity and quality of human development among poor and near-poor children that has left us with a large and growing deficit of human capital. That deficit, much more than the financial one, presents a major obstacle to recovering our international competitiveness and to meeting the needs and obligations of a technologically sophisticated *and* caring society as we confront the bulge in dependency looming in the next century.

SOCIAL SECURITY TRUST FUNDS—CAN WE TRUST THEM?

In 1983, following a careful study, amendments to the Social Security Act were adopted in recognition of the projected changes in the dependency ratio just mentioned. Where the program had been operated as a "pay-as-you-go" system, with a small trust fund used to smooth out small discrepancies between "contributions" (Social Security taxes) and benefit payments, provision was made to accumulate a more substantial fund to meet the high needs of baby boom retirees. As an indication of the size of the problem, in 1960 there were 5.1 workers contributing to the benefits of each eligible retiree. By 1990 there were only 3.2 workers per beneficiary. Current projections hold the figure steady at 3.3 through the year 2000, but see a drop to 2.4 by 2020 and further to 2.0 in 2040 (U.S. Congress, House of Representatives 1992).[4] Rates were adjusted to start building up the trust fund by raising the tax rates and contribution ceilings. The projections based on current plans build the fund to a maximum of $8 trillion in the year 2025, at which point the benefits will exceed contributions and the fund will be exhausted over the following 15–20 years. At present (mid-1993) the balance in the old age and survivors' account is over $400 billion and will soon be growing at $100 billion plus per year (U.S. Congress, House of Representatives 1992).

Those measures added considerably to both the equity and credibility of the system. It would not seem fair to keep the contributions low on the boomer generation while they were working and then raise the taxes to very high levels on their much-less-numerous successors. It is even doubtful that the required rates would have been politically supportable. But the measures taken deal only with the financial provisions needed to get 20th-century dollars into the hands of deserving 21st-century beneficiaries. We must now consider what will be available for those dollars to buy when the boomers get them.

This is where it is necessary to try to peer through the "veil of money" and see what is going on in the obscured reality.

What "really" happens when the Social Security system runs a surplus by requiring contributions in excess of current benefit payments? Quite simply, the excess, as with all federal trust funds, is placed at the disposal of the U.S. Treasury and an entry is made in a book (or computer) crediting the Social Security Trust Fund with the ownership of the appropriate amount of nonmarketable, interest-bearing federal securities.[5] In effect, the Treasury sells the trust fund a piece of the public debt. Given current accounting conventions, a Social Security surplus *reduces* the deficit since it reduces the amount of public debt that has to be sold to the public (or to foreign investors). So far, nothing real has happened to provide tangible goods in the year 2020 when the boomers really need them.

What really happens in the world of things that can be eaten, driven, worn, or worked with depends on further policy choices as well as on consumer and investor behavior—none of which can be predicted with much precision. If the Social Security surplus makes the federal deficit smaller or even turns it to a surplus, some political leaders might be inclined to cut other taxes and let the taxpayers (or at least some of them) have a break. Others might be encouraged by the relaxed budget position to indulge a bit more in exotic defense systems, or ever-more elaborate drug interdiction schemes, or more-generous subsidies for a favorite industrial or agricultural supplicant. However, anyone who supposes that many policymakers would entertain the idea of investing a part of that surplus in human capital that could pay off when the boomers really need the (geriatric) consumer goods must still be doing business with the tooth fairy. The pressures for immediate gratification of insistent petitioners are just too great.

The more fiscally responsible among our leaders would likely welcome the extra revenue and let the deficit be smaller and hence put less public debt on the market (or even retire some). That could have an effect on interest rates that would encourage consumers and investors to buy more capital equipment and would even improve the terms on which young people could choose to invest in their own human capital. This alternative is the slim reed of hope on which rests belief that the trust fund buildup will solve the problem of too many beneficiaries and too few workers that will occur in the 2010s. But even if the forced saving into the trust fund encourages human capital investment by way of interest rates or loan availability, very little of that is likely to be invested in poor or near-poor children.

The deficit in human investment is not located among those who can confidently project long horizon returns and find lenders willing to bet on their future prospects.

The real effect of the trust fund buildup, then, is reduced pressure on the federal budget, which could lead to tax cuts or more spending, with no recent experience suggesting that such spending or tax cutting will produce much investment in human capital. If those temptations are resisted, more investment could be encouraged, but that investment is not likely to be of the right kind to relieve the deficit in human capital.

What happens if the blind neglect continues? The real aspects of the nation's productive capacity in 2020 will look much the same as they would if no trust fund had been built to meet retirees' needs. This is because so much of the human potential in the active population at that time will remain undeveloped and/or maimed. Each Social Security beneficiary will still have at most 2.4 workers contributing to the trust fund, and the real output of a good share of those workers will be stunted because of the human capital deficit. Some, indeed, will have been added to the dependent rolls as single mothers or disabled adults because of that deficit. But, as planned, the Social Security beneficiaries will be getting more out of the large trust fund balance than the workers are paying in. In the absence of extra taxes of some other sort, this produces too much money chasing too few goods—a standard formula for inflationary pressure. Note, however, that the purchasing power of the beneficiaries would be maintained by existing escalator or cost-of-living adjustment (COLA) clauses, but that of most workers would not. Whether the promises underlying the buildup of the trust fund would be kept under those circumstances, at heavy cost to the most productive part of the active population, is highly questionable. In any case there would be a clear cause for bitter political conflict between the elders and the active population.

The fundamental problem is that putting away some dollar claims at the societal level does not automatically provide the future real goods and services the claimants will expect at redemption time. Perishable consumer goods and services cannot be stored and must either be produced or imported as needed. Unless the foundation of capital is there, both physical and human, the active population is going to come up short in satisfying everyone's expectations. Unless the advance saving in the form of a trust fund is paralleled by productive investment, the cupboard will be embarrassingly bare when we come to draw on those savings. There has not been parallel investment as a consequence of the first accumulation of the Social Security

Trust Fund, and there is no reason to expect, absent explicit policy, that subsequent accumulation will produce a different outcome.

It is supposed by some that a "fully funded" private retirement system would be more trustworthy than the pay-as-you-go Social Security system.[6] But the preceding discussion applies to full funding of a part of the future benefits, and as we have seen, unless the productive potential is there, those paper claims are likely to be at least partly dishonored. Full funding of totally private universal pensions would encounter the same problem when an unusually large (or small) cohort passes through the active and retired life stages, or when neglect of child development wastes the members' full potential. Unless the accumulation of financial claims is backed up by development of the human resources to redeem those claims in real goods and services, and there is no market mechanism that assures this, the real value of the final pensions will be eroded.

MATCHING THE SURPLUS WITH THE DEFICIT

Businesses make a sharp distinction between investments and current expenses of operation. They find that clear thinking about alternatives and wise, systematic planning for continued growth and survival are facilitated by the use of explicit capital accounts that keep track of investments. Those accounts record expenditures and other transactions involving facilities and equipment that will provide productive services over a lengthy future period. Financial provision for maintenance and replacement of capital items is allocated over the life of such investments, and annual amounts are entered as current expense along with current payrolls, supplies, and so forth. For a business to know whether it is operating at a profit (surplus) or loss (deficit) in its current operation, it is imperative that it keep separate accounts for capital investments (Clark, Hindelang, and Pritchard 1979). Otherwise, it will show a big spurious loss in periods when new machinery is acquired and equally misleading profits at other times. Government budgets can mislead in the same way.

Businesses do not impoverish themselves when they go into debt to purchase capital goods that will pay off over a number of years. If they are correct in their judgment of the prospective gains, deficit financing is entirely prudent. Of course, a business is courting disaster if it goes into debt to cover current expenses that are not being recovered in current sales revenues. That kind of deficit finance cannot long be sustained. Again, there is a close parallel with the federal government, and there should be no question about the nature of our recent deficits.

Numerous authorities have suggested that the federal budget would be a much more useful document for considering alternative programs and policies if it were cast in a framework that distinguishes capital investments from current expenditures (von Furstenberg 1980, Blejer and Cheasty 1991, Mazur 1992). Building and maintaining infrastructure; installing and dismantling weapon systems; maintaining park, forest, and range lands; and carrying on programs of research in health, agriculture, and physical science are all activities with long horizons of use and cost (National League of Cities 1983). It seems clear that both policymakers and the general public would better understand what the overall budget balance means if explicit capital accounts were presented. But so far this amount of added rationality has been firmly resisted at the federal level, even though capital budgeting is extremely common among state and local governments.

The case for a human capital account at the federal level is even stronger than for those more tangible capital items. Hardware and real properties are fairly easy to spot, and one can make allowance for extraordinary investment programs and acquisitions. But human capital, being intangible and hard to measure, is more easily lost track of. The items that can be considered investments in child development are scattered among many programs. Given the long gestation period and even longer period of active use for human capital, we need to keep records that say something about how much we are spending on this vitally important part of our productive capacity, and whether that investment is adequate to the task of providing full developmental opportunities for all children.

What is the source of funds for a human capital investment program? In the long run there must be a regular contribution from the current budget to a Human Capital Investment Budget which would support programs to ensure the preparation of *all* children to enter adulthood as full participants in our nation's economic, political, and social life. It is impossible to estimate how large such a provision would have to be if, and when, the nation reaches the goal where all new adults, and all new parents, enter those roles with a full complement of human capital. At that point, the need for supplementation and remediation efforts from the public sector will be much smaller than the need we now confront.

For the immediate future there is a better and more appropriate possibility. The Social Security Trust Fund, the real value of which is in clear danger of being eroded by the neglect of human capital investment, should be earmarked strictly for support of the Human Capital Investment Budget, as a source of funds for ending and, so far as possible, recovering from the neglect that has been documented in this volume. New and continuing appropriations, or parts of appropriations that are qualified as investments in human capital, should be charged against that budget and excluded from the current budget. This policy would dedicate the saving represented by the annual Social Security surpluses to appropriate investment uses and the existing accumulation in the trust fund would also be available for such uses if beneficial investments exceed the annual flow. In effect the Human Capital Investment Account would have exclusive rights to borrow from the Social Security Trust Fund, and those funds would no longer be available to finance current budget deficits. In this way it may yet be possible to redeem our obligations to the boomer and other generations now contributing to that trust fund.

A change in budget practice and presentation of this sort should be introduced by the Administration through the Office of Management and Budget. However, in order to maximize the commitment to follow this (or any other) budget, the new rules and conventions should be established with full participation of the Government Accounting Office, the Congressional Budget Office, both Congressional Budget Committees, Ways and Means, and the Senate Finance Committee. President Clinton and, especially his wife, have stressed the unmet needs of our nation's children. Directing the Office of Management and Budget to establish a Human Capital Account would be a valuable, and technically extremely straightforward, first step. Having established the Account, Clinton could then call on the relevant federal agencies to draw on it, developing new approaches and expanding and improving existing programs.

Is this just another facile justification for increased federal expenditures and consequent bigger deficits? The answer is no. The urgently needed increases in spending for developing human capital will increase the deficit unless offset elsewhere, but even so, borrowing to build future productivity (and both general and Social Security revenue) is entirely prudent. Segregating the trust fund surpluses and investing them in human capital will remove a source of finance for current government operations. The budget deficit on current account will be larger as a result and it will more accurately reflect true spending beyond current tax revenues. The trust fund surpluses were never intended to obscure fiscal recklessness on current account, and their dedication capital investments will end a major deception. If increased budgetary candor impels political leaders to bring current outlays and revenues back into long-run balance, so much the better. But the budget deficit cannot be accepted as sufficient reason to delay or forgo action to close the enormous deficit in human capital. That would compound one foolish policy choice with a second one.

Matching the nation's collective saving and borrowing activities with appropriations for meaningful policies and programs of future benefit—such as investment in human capital—is not a novel or radical idea. Business enterprises depend on such budgeting for their very survival in a changing world. State governments use capital budgets routinely to keep their current activities on an even keel while they invest in various facilities more sporadically. It is time the federal budgets reflected the difference between investment and current expense, for human capital if not for all kinds of investment.

A POLICY TO REDEEM OUR PROMISES

What, then, are possible components of a determined effort to bring every young person to the threshold of adulthood with the basic capacities to support self, form family, adapt to change, and nurture the next generation of new adults? How might that Human Capital Account be used? Recall that the Social Security Trust Fund now contains around $400 billion, which is about 6.67 percent of our $6 trillion gross domestic product, and is receiving surpluses of more than $100 billion each year. Federal expenditures that can be allocated to children totaled $75 billion in 1991, with income support and nutrition accounting for over half. Tax expenditures, mainly dependent exemptions and the Earned Income Tax Credit (EITC), amounted to another $29 billion (National Commission on Children 1993). Not all of those expenditures qualify as human capital investments, but, with the exception of the dependent exemptions, most are oriented toward poor or other at-risk children. Let us say the total currently being spent is $85 billion.[7] If that amount were charged against the Human Capital Account, it would leave $15 billion a year in the Account for additional human capital investment. The accumulated fund balance should also be considered available as a reserve for investment in promising experimental programs for both children and parenting adults. As with any investment decision, funding through the Account should be conditional on proven cost-effectiveness or, for experimental programs, on high potential.

The family is, of course, the locus of a child's first and generally most important investments, and a secure, stable level of disposable family income adequate to meet basic needs for food, shelter, clothing, transportation, and out-of-pocket medical costs is a cardinal necessity in any program to achieve the development goal stated previously. It is not argued that income above the poverty range is *sufficient* to assure that a family's children will get the material and human inputs to develop normally, but, rather, that it is beyond reason to see how a family could possibly meet those needs with only a third or a quarter of the wherewithal available to families at the median (who typically feel pretty hard-pressed themselves). For some families, income support may be sufficient and we should be grateful for that, because such help is much cheaper and easier to administer than the "expert intensive" services. But even in families where income support is not sufficient, it is *necessary* because learning, remediation, and image reinforcement therapies have a much better chance of success when parent(s) can spare some attention from the hunger, shame, and stress that are experienced at deprived levels of living. Programs to help parents rear success-bound children on almost no money should perhaps be tried out on the "middle class" before being inflicted on the poor.

Some families do not need income support, of course, because their income is above the range of poverty. But problems of violence, substance abuse, premature parenting, and plain ignorance about the developmental needs of children are encountered with discouraging frequency in nonpoor families. Here services directed toward the specific dysfunction can proceed without the distraction of poverty conditions, and may, of course, prevent the accumulation of problems that would end up in poverty.

The emphasis, then, is on a balance between income support and direct services. Both are necessary and neither is sufficient to achieve the development goals. Income to meet basic needs is essential for empowering the nurturing and developmental capacities possessed by parents, and services are essential for enhancing and supplementing those capacities. Unfortunately it is not yet clear whether *any* combination of income and services is sufficient to permit normal development of children in the almost inevitably dysfunctional families located in the most deprived and dangerous environments in our largest cities. If not, we may have to face the choice of giving up on some children or developing a new childrearing institution that can replace all or most of the parental influence.

Income supports are in need of improvement, and should be placed high on the list of new investment initiatives. The refundable EITC has proven to be a politically viable means of augmenting income of the working poor. Recent changes have complicated its administration, but it remains a promising vehicle for helping families with children and active low-wage earners. Raising the maximum benefit to the $3,000 to $4,000 range with a phaseout around the median would make it a more potent tool for this group. Provisions for making the benefit payments concurrent with low earnings, and also sensitive to variations in or sudden loss of earnings during a tax year, would further help many families. Replacement of the current child exemptions by a refundable tax credit of $1,000 per child as recommended by the National Commission on Children (1991), would also help the working poor, and in combination with a $3,000 EITC and the Child and Dependent Care Tax Credit, would go a long way toward assuring all full-time working parents a net disposable income above the poverty line. A refundable credit instead of an exemption also makes the income tax more progressive because it has the same dollar value to parents in all income tax brackets (even zero), while the exemption is worth more to a high-tax-bracket parent than to a low-bracket parent, and worthless to someone with no earned income.

One-parent families will also benefit from those provisions if they have jobs. Otherwise, they are mainly dependent on support from the noncustodial parent (or other relatives) and the Aid to Families with Dependent Children (AFDC)/Food Stamp/Medicaid complex of benefits, which is almost universally despised but is much in demand as a scapegoat for a long list of social ills. The Family Support Act of 1988 improved the collection of support from absent parents, and made it harder for unmarried fathers to avoid responsibility. However, it does not help when that absent parent has no or low income—perhaps because of a human capital deficit—or is dead or in prison. A further step, child support assurance, would ensure all children at least a minimal level of support when the noncustodial parent cannot meet that standard (Garfinkel 1992). Such a program would place many more mothers in a position to earn their family into independence from the welfare system.

The Clinton administration is committed to major reform of the welfare system. Early hints suggest that the reform will aim to convert the "welfare poor" into working poor both by improving incentives and facilitative supports such as child care and medicaid coverage and by limiting the period that a parent can remain on public assistance. Precisely how this carrot and stick approach will work, and what will be done with, for, or to the resistant residual remains to be seen. So far no one has mentioned sheltered workshops, although the National Commission on Children (1991) urged consideration of "community employment." Although there is hope that "workfare" will eventually reduce public expenditure on poor children, the immediate effect of "making work pay" for AFDC parents is sure to cost more, and will very likely add something to the income of those families.

On the income side then, a fattened EITC accompanied by a refundable tax credit and combined with Food Stamps would largely end poverty for families with one or more full-time workers. One-parent families would be given a more nearly even chance of self-sufficiency if child support assurance were adopted, and they would also be given help and strong encouragement to limit their dependence on means-tested public support. This array of improvements in the income support of childrearing families is feasible from the current savings deposited in the Human Capital Account and would do most of what is necessary to empower poor families who possess the competence, maturity, and motivation to rear similarly qualified new adults.

On the other side of the balance, services that enhance child development inside and outside the family must be augmented in both quantity and quality, and delivered in more coordinated and coherent packages to all children who need them. As examples: Health services for children and pregnant women urgently need reform and improvement in coverage; school readiness and child care services are inadequate in coverage and uneven in quality; Child Welfare and Fostering programs beg for reorientation; public schools seem to have lost their way, along with the confidence and trust of parents and students; and completing schooling and making the transition to adulthood is a trip that alarming numbers of young people are not making successfully.

In the case of health care, reform is under way, but the outcome is unknown. The needs for human capital investment and maintenance clearly require universal insurance coverage of some sort for the basic needs of all pregnant women and all children. But access to care will not improve in many areas even if financing is assured, and other means may be needed to get the right kinds of personnel and facilities in the right places. Finally, ready access is not enough in some cases, and more active outreach and screening will be needed to ensure that all mothers and children get needed medical attention when it can prevent disease and halt early conditions before they mature into lifelong handicaps and disabilities (Bell and Simkin 1993).

Medical service availability is not the same thing as health (Fuchs 1983). Healthy life-styles, including choice of food, exercise, and education regarding the dangers of using tobacco, alcohol, and other drugs are very important, as are community facilities for waste disposal, water supply, and food inspection. To ensure healthy children living in healthful home and community environments we must have the informed participation of parents who have acquired the human capital relevant for establishing and maintaining those environments. Health care can't do it all. Developing the knowledge and habits of healthful living is another high-priority investment need.

Our public schools must be helped to find a renewed commitment to a "no-lose" rather than a "no-fail" objective for *all* children in terms of basic competencies. But, in addition, we must consider using the school as an established locus of access to developing children in which other services may be provided or managed. We must not add more responsibilities to heavily stressed teachers, but additional personnel and resources may be highly effective in providing ancillary developmental services (Behrman 1992).

The one program for poor children between birth and kindergarten that almost everyone now regards as indispensable is Head Start. It has demonstrated important long-run benefits that exceed the costs (Donovan and Watts 1990). The problem is funding (and the appropriate human capital input in the form of teachers and aides) sufficient to serve all the children who are eligible for it. Maintaining and improving standards in some existing programs, while making the program available to all poor children, will call for improved staff salaries and higher per-child costs. Expanding part-day programs to full-day is another high priority to enable more parents to work without having to make additional care arrangements. This is a clear case for drawing on the Human Capital Account, with the caution that the expansion should not outrun our real capacity to upgrade some existing programs and maintain a high standard of personnel recruitment in the new ones.

Care of infants and toddlers—the zero to three-year-olds—is becoming more common among nonpoor parents and must be confronted directly as workfare programs move toward requiring mothers of younger children to work. There is no Head Start equivalent as yet, but the developmental importance of those years, beginning with the development of secure attachments to parents or other caregivers and continuing on to basic language and personality development, gives a high priority to the task of finding practical standards or models that will start and maintain healthy growth patterns.

For numerous specific problems, from teen pregnancy to family violence and many others, much has been learned in recent years from substantial program experience and systematic research. Through innovation and informal experimentation, various states and cities are searching for solutions to the old and new obstacles that children and parents encounter in their joint career of childrearing. This is the message that emerges loud and clear from Lisbeth Schorr's influential book, *Within Our Reach* (1988). It is now time to start a more systematic application of the lessons that have been learned (Schorr 1993; Larner, Halpern, and Harkavy 1992).

Several major themes emerge from the findings of research and experimentation. One theme is that programs for supporting families need to allow substantial room for local variation and initiative. The trick is to focus on accountability for the outcomes that really matter and allow freedom in finding the best way for particular people and places to achieve them. There is always room to learn more about how to engage parents and children in programs that require their active participation.

Another theme focuses on parental participation. Again and again in reports and evaluations of interventions to enhance children's progress toward adulthood, parents' participation is cited as almost imperative if lasting benefits are to be expected (Schorr 1993). A closely related finding is that programs dealing with serious dysfunctions are rarely successful unless they can coordinate the experts and agencies involved in making a concerted effort to deal with all the sources of stress and distress (Schorr 1993).

As previously mentioned, it is now time to start a more ambitious effort, using the lessons gained from field experience and research to reduce and, if possible, eliminate the enormous deficit in human capital that has resulted from years of neglect. No program should be cast in stone at this point. There is room for local autonomy and a strategy of "learning by doing" that enables programs to evaluate variations and evolve toward more effective models.

This is not the time to be intimidated by the size and persistence of the deficit in the federal budget. The human capital deficit has much more direct consequences for our future well-being, and it deserves first priority. We can substantially reduce child poverty and the waste of potential that has weakened our national strength and still be responsible from the point of view of economic balance and fiscal prudence.

Since the total currently being spent by the federal government on children and parenting is less than the annual surplus, setting up and using the Human Capital Account as I propose will increase the current deficit. If that deficit continues to be regarded as a serious threat to our economic health, the remedy is to cut less productive federal expenditures and/or raise taxes—not to use the surplus to cover up our real problems. The argument that we must continue to shortchange our investment in human capital until we get the fiscal balance in order simply piles another shortsighted error on top of the ones that produced the deficits during the past decade. We cannot expect to regain economic health by neglecting the maintenance and growth of our nation's most essential assets.

Notes

1. Nobel Laureate Gary Becker is the most authoritative developer and interpreter of the human capital concept (Becker 1975). Others who have contributed importantly to its origination and elaboration include Frank Knight, T. W. Schultz, and Jacob Mincer.

2. The statistics cited in this and the following paragraph have been calculated by me from the tables in the Census Bureau's report (Census Bureau 1991).

3. Human capital has been defined earlier here. Physical capital includes all the tangible tools—structures and infrastructure—regardless of whether they are public or private property. Social capital is less tangible and includes the many formal and informal institutions or traditions that enable family life, commerce, governance, and other forms of civil interaction to take place in safe environments and with mutual confidence and trust.

4. Clearly, estimates for 50 years in advance require uncertain assumptions about birth, death, immigration, and earnings rates. However, such calculations are carried out regularly to check on the short- and long-term health of the system.

5. This is well explained in the *Green Book* (U.S. Congress, House of Representatives 1992: 90ff).

6. Private retirement systems accept contributions from current workers and promise future money benefits (without cost-of-living adjustments). If they are "fully funded," those contributions are invested in various financial instruments, including U.S. debt obligations, just like the Social Security Trust Fund does, with the expectation that they will be liquidated when the contributor retires.

7. An additional $205 billion or so was spent in 1991 by state and local governments on primary and secondary education, and another $15 billion on child welfare, AFDC, and medicaid benefits for children (National Commission on Children 1993). Most of these expenditures would qualify as investments also, but this discussion is limited

to federal budgeting. The potential substitutional impact of changes in federal programs must be kept in mind, however.

References

Aschauer, David A. 1991. "The Third Deficit," The GAO Journal, No. 12, Spring.

Becker, Gary. 1975. Human Capital: A Theoretical and Empirical Analysis, with Special Reference to Education, 2nd ed. New York: Columbia University Press.

Behrman, Richard E., ed. 1992. School-Linked Services: The Future of Children, vol. 2, no. 1. Los Altos, Calif., David and Lucile Packard Foundation, Spring.

Bell, Karen N., and Linda S. Simkin. 1993. Caring Prescriptions: Comprehensive Health Care Strategies for Young Children in Poverty. New York: National Center for Children in Poverty, Columbia University.

Blejer, Mario I., and Adrienne Cheasty. 1991. "The Measurement of Fiscal Deficits: Analytical and Methodological Issues." Journal of Economic Literature. Vol. 24, no. 4 December.

Census Bureau. See U.S. Bureau of the Census.

Clark, John J., Thomas J. Hindelang, and Robert E. Pritchard. 1979. Capital Budgeting: Planning and Control of Capital Expenditures. Englewood Cliffs, N.J.: Prentice-Hall.

Council of Economic Advisors (CEA). 1992. Economic Report of the President, Washington, D.C.: U.S. Government Printing Office.

Donovan, Suzanne, and Harold Watts. 1990. "What Can Child Care Do for Human Capital?" Population Research and Policy Review 9(January): 5–23.

Fuchs, Victor R. 1983. How We Live. Cambridge, Mass.: Harvard University Press.

Garfinkel, Irwin. 1992. Assuring Child Support: An Extension of Social Security. New York: Russell Sage.

Hewlett, Sylvia Ann. 1991. When the Bough Breaks: The Cost of Neglecting Our Children. New York: Basic Books (Harper-Collins).

Jencks, Christopher, and Paul E. Peterson, eds. 1991. The Urban Underclass. Washington, D.C.: Brookings Institution.

Johnson, Otto, ed. 1993. The 1993 Information Please Almanac. Boston: Houghton Mifflin Co.

Knight, Frank H. 1921. Risk, Uncertainty, and Profit. Boston: Houghton Mifflin Co. Reprinted, New York, Harper and Row, 1965.

Kusserow, Richard P. 1988. "The Social Security Wild Card," The GAO Journal. No. 4, Winter.

Larner, Mary, Robert Halpern, and Oscar Harkavy, eds. 1992. *Fair Start for Children: Lessons Learned from Seven Demonstration Projects.* New Haven, Conn.: Yale University Press.

Mazur, Edward J. 1992. "The Vision for Improving Federal Financial Management," *Government Accountants Journal,* Fall.

Moore, Kristin A. 1991. *A State-by-State Look at Teenage Childbearing in the United States.* Flint, Mich.: Charles Stuart Mott Foundation.

National Commission on Children. 1991. *Beyond Rhetoric: A New American Agenda for Children and Families.* Final report. Washington, D.C.: Author.

————. 1993. *Just the Facts: A Summary of Recent Information on America's Children and Their Families.* Washington, D.C.: Author.

National League of Cities. 1983. *Capital Budgeting and Infrastructure in American Cities: An Initial Assessment.* Washington, D.C.: Author.

Schorr, Lisbeth B. 1993. "What Works: Applying What We Already Know about Successful Social Policy." *American Prospect,* no. 13 (Spring): 43–54.

Schorr, Lisbeth B., with Daniel Schorr. 1988. *Within Our Reach: Breaking the Cycle of Disadvantage.* New York: Anchor Press (Doubleday).

U.S. Bureau of the Census. 1991. *Trends in Relative Income: 1964–1989.* Current Population Reports, ser. P-60, no. 177. Washington, D.C.: U.S. Government Printing Office.

————. 1993. *Statistical Abstract of the United States: 1993.* 113th ed. Washington, D.C.: U.S. Government Printing Office.

U.S. Congress, House of Representatives, Committee on Ways and Means. 1992. *1992 Green Book: Overview of Entitlement Programs.* Washington, D.C.: U.S. Government Printing Office.

von Furstenberg, George M. 1980. *The Government and Capital Formation.* Cambridge, Mass.: Ballinger.

Watts, Harold W. 1977. "A Model of the Endowment of Human Wealth, or Let's Look at Social Policy through the Eyes of the 21st Century's Adults." In *Economic Progress, Private Values, and Public Policy,* edited by Bela Balassa and Richard Nelson (103–20). Amsterdam: North Holland.

White House Conference on Families. 1980. *Listening to America's Families: Action for the 80's,* Washington, D.C.: Author.

Chapter 1

ADVOCACY FOR CHILDREN IN POVERTY

Judith A. Chafel and Kevin Condit

Today, as the child poverty rate in the United States stands at 21.8 percent (Scarbrough, chapter 3, this volume), millions of children are disenfranchised economically and politically. Economically, children in poverty lack access to certain basics of life and, as a result, may suffer from numerous adverse outcomes.

Politically, children in poverty exemplify a powerless constituency neglected by society for a variety of reasons. First, because they are "nonvoters, noncampaigners, and nonlobbyists," the system has been indifferent to their cause (Roberts, Alexander, and Davis 1991; Segal and Gustavsson 1990; Steiner 1976: 242). Second, societal consensus is lacking about the wisdom of public intrusion into family life to ensure that children's basic needs are met. Third, no unifying point exists in government to energize federal responsibility for children's policies and programs (Hayes 1982). Finally, the poor have not particpated in the political process historically; some would say just the contrary: that is, that they have been excluded from it (Melton 1983).

Reports regularly appear in the media describing the plight of children in poverty (e.g., "Report Says Poor Children Grew Poorer in 1980s" 1992), but although such coverage is increasingly directing public attention to the problem, it has so far failed to inspire either policymakers or the American public to act. A rationale for doing so derives from the figures describing the incidence of child poverty, the risk factors associated with impoverishment, the absence of a viable domestic policy agenda for addressing the problem (Chafel 1990b; Kamerman 1989; Segal and Gustavsson 1990), and the fact that the afflicted represent a politically powerless group. All of these factors underscore the need for advocates to champion the cause of children in poverty.

This chapter addresses the concept of child advocacy from two perspectives: government and philanthropy. These two sectors of society are highlighted because they have been designed to serve the needs of the disenfranchised. By acting through government and philanthropy, advocates for children in poverty can prompt social action.

The chapter is intended for those who would like to be advocates for children in poverty but who require knowledge about how to do so effectively. Many academic disciplines concerned with children's issues (e.g., education, home economics, nursing) have not traditionally considered advocacy a formal aspect of their work, although increasingly they have come to do so. As a result, professionals whose areas of specialty focus on children (such as teachers, home economists, nurses) may lack specific advocacy strategies and techniques because their professional preparation and experiences have not cultivated such expertise.

The chapter begins with a brief discussion of the meaning of advocacy, including examples of advocacy activities and a description of advocacy styles and strategies. The chapter then analyzes domestic agenda-setting based upon Kingdon's (1984) theory and discusses specific strategies for influencing the legislative process. If advocates are to effect the design of social policy for children and families in poverty, they must be knowledgeable about how it is formed.

The next section of the chapter examines philanthropy as another sector of society upon which advocates can focus their energy. At a time when the number of children and families in poverty is escalating and the ability of government to respond to their needs is constrained by lack of resources and other priorities, pressure is mounting for the philanthropic sector to center more of its efforts on the poor (Ostrander 1989; Van Til 1990). Clearly, advocates need to know about philanthropy. The concept is defined here, its distinguishing functions are explained, and examples of "voluntary action for the public good" (Payton 1990: 179) are provided. The discussion then describes how various segments of the philanthropic community are uniting through coalition building to attain legislative support for children in need.

The final section of the chapter considers issues emanating from the previous discussion and suggests specific ways in which innovative modes of thinking about child poverty may be generated to effect social action. Four themes are developed: (1) pursuing research on advocacy; (2) reforming philanthropy; (3) coordinating policy on children's issues; and (4) training for advocacy. The discussion considers the problematic nature of each theme and offers a rationale for action.

Appendix 9.A at the end of the chapter describes national and state organizations engaged in research on child poverty and child policy as well as those performing child advocacy roles. The appendix has been compiled to assist advocates who may be unaware of the large number of private and public organizations dedicated to helping children and families in poverty. It is not an exhaustive compilation, but, rather, is intended as a starting point for readers.

Under the Clinton administration, prospects for the impoverished in our society are more promising than they have been for some time, and advocacy efforts may have a greater likelihood of payoff. President Clinton's commitment to investing in "human capital" by creating jobs and establishing health and education programs may cause a "policy window" to open for the poor ("Clinton Outlines His Plan" 1993). Challenges to be met are an American public perennially skeptical of "big government" and a soaring federal deficit that prohibits spending money for long-term social programs (Barnes 1993).

ADVOCACY: WHAT DOES IT MEAN?

Professional literature on advocacy is sparse. Although definitions of the term abound, relatively little is known about the styles, strategies, and methods that have been shown empirically to be most effective (Sosin and Caulum 1983). Sosin and Caulum's (1983) statement a decade ago that practitioners execute the role, yet lack a clear conceptual framework to guide them, is largely true today.

What is child advocacy? In general, an advocate may be defined as " 'one who argues for, defends, maintains, or recommends a cause or proposal, or one who pleads the cause of another' " (National Association of Social Workers Ad Hoc Committee on Advocacy 1969, quoted in Sosin and Caulum 1983: 12). Advocacy has been described as assuming "responsibility for promoting and protecting the developmental needs of both an individual child and children in general," with the former delineated as "case" advocacy and the latter as "class" advocacy (Westman 1979: 44). Although the two concepts are distinct, one type of advocacy may evolve into the other (Epstein 1981). Both forms are considered to comprise a comprehensive advocacy orientation (Kahn, Kamerman, and McGowan 1973).

Critical to an understanding of the concept of advocacy is the notion that an individual possesses rights and needs that require support to ensure access to "entitlements, benefits, and services"

(Kahn et al. 1973: 65). For the purposes of this chapter, then, child advocacy is defined as *acting on behalf of children to assure protection of their basic rights and needs.* The chapter focuses on class, as opposed to case, advocacy because the former is generalizable and, therefore, applicable to a variety of issues—and, as a result, has the potential for greatest impact.

So defined, class advocacy for children in poverty can take many forms: claiming newly conceptualized legal entitlements; seeking necessary services to address unmet needs; organizing the parents of disadvantaged (e.g., hearing impaired) children to become politically active; and, encouraging deprived community groups to organize (Kahn et al. 1973; Westman 1979), to mention a few. Advocacy efforts that focus on specific goals are more likely to be successful than those that target the more general one of "improving conditions for children" (Kahn et al. 1973: 104). Workable solutions must be offered for problems, and the issues must be well defined (Edelman 1987; Westman 1979).

Rickart and Bing (1989: 22–23) have described a typology of roles for advocates, ranging from "ivory-tower researchers" to "players working deep within the system" to "extremists." As they point out, no single style of advocacy is linked with effectiveness. Moreover, an advocate may assume different roles at various times (Rickart and Bing 1989). Activism can take place at local community, state, or national levels.

As agents of change, advocates may employ three types of strategies: normative, utilitarian, and coercive (Gamson 1968; cited in Rickart and Bing 1989). Normative strategies rely on persuasion: the advocate "mobilize[s] the public around widely shared normative sentiments as a means to reach consensus" (Rickart and Bing 1989: 70). The utilitarian strategy is based on bargaining. The advocate confers "with those who may not share the same sentiments or values, but who are willing to listen and eventually negotiate some aspects of the problem" (Rickart and Bing 1989: 70–71). The coercive strategy is fixed in conflict. The advocate bypasses normal procedures in "the absence of shared understandings, or even of willingness to listen" (Rickart and Bing 1989: 71).

NEEDED: A SOCIAL POLICY FOR CHILDREN IN POVERTY

Numerous proposals have been offered for solving the problem of child poverty (e.g., Danziger and Stern 1990; Fuchs and Reklis 1992;

National Center for Children in Poverty 1990; National Commission on Children 1991; U.S. Congress, House of Representatives 1985). While the proposals vary on specifics, any viable social policy for children and families in poverty should address several broad objectives (Congress of the United States and the Congressional Budget Office 1985; cited in Chafel 1990a). These objectives relate to the needs of children for access to certain "basics of life" (e.g., food, health care, shelter); for protection from the harmful effects of poverty on their development; and, for inclusion in families that are economically self-reliant. As the Committee for Economic Development (1987) has pointed out, substantial funding and governmental activity are requisite, if such purposes are to be achieved.

Within the purview of these broad objectives, advocates on behalf of children in poverty might promote the following specific goals: enlargement of the Special Supplemental Food Program for Women, Infants, and Children (WIC), a federally subsidized program that offers supplemental nourishment to low-income pregnant women, nursing mothers, and their children up to five years of age; enhanced funding for Head Start, the early intervention model, to make possible the enrollment of all eligible children; an elevation of the minimum wage; and, provision for the increased availability of low-cost, high-quality child care (Chafel 1990a, b), to cite but a few of many areas requiring governmental action.

DOMESTIC AGENDA-SETTING

If advocates are to have an impact on the design of social policy, they must be knowledgeable about how social policy is formed. Kingdon (1984), in analyzing how domestic issues become fixed on the national agenda, has explained that domestic agenda-setting entails three separate processes: individuals discerning problems, creating change proposals, and, finally, engaging in political activity (e.g., pressure group lobbying). Government, according to Kingdon, exemplifies an "organized anarchy." Cohen, March, and Olsen (1972: 2; cited in Kingdon 1984: 90) have described it as a "collection of choices looking for problems, issues . . . looking for decision situations . . . solutions looking for issues . . . and decision makers looking for work." Kingdon employs the metaphor of "a garbage can" to symbolize what he means by a "choice opportunity." Problems and solutions are tossed into the garbage can; what materializes is a function of the "mix" and how it is processed. The theory was advanced with respect to the federal level, but applies to state and local government, as well.

Kingdon's "garbage can model" negates the notion of rational decision making in policy formation. The three streams flowing through the system (that is, problems, policies, politics) function more or less autonomously, each evolving according to its own momentum. All three connect when a "policy window" opens, that is, as politically expedient occasions arise for pressing a problem or policy. Significant policy changes emanate as a result of the "coupling" of all three streams (Kingdon 1984: 93).

According to Kingdon's (1984) theory, then, it would be futile to search for generalizable principles on the origins of policy initiatives by analyzing a set of case studies because one instance would define the process one way and another would do so another way. Similarly, it would be pointless to attempt to discern conceptual patterns among case studies describing the "coupling" of the three streams (Kingdon 1984). The "climate in government" explains why an item appears on the national domestic agenda, not its origins. As Kingdon has said, "What made it take hold and grow" is fundamental to understanding policy change (p. 76). Hofferth (chapter 7, this volume) provides several examples of how a "policy window" opens.

Issues emerge on the national domestic agenda, then, as a result of a complex interplay of factors (Hayes 1982; Kingdon 1984). The next section of this chapter, by focusing on certain components belonging to what Kingdon (1984) has termed the "political stream," analyzes how advocates for children in poverty can influence the formation of social policy. These elements have been selected because agendas, as Kingdon has noted, are set, in part, by "politics." By recognizing when a "policy window" opens, that is, as politically expedient occasions arise for pressing a problem or policy, advocates can significantly advance their cause.

INFLUENCING THE LEGISLATIVE AGENDA FROM THE TOP DOWN AND THE BOTTOM UP

To influence the substance and direction of social policy for poor children and families, advocates must understand the political contexts in which policy is formed and specific strategies for influencing policy. Strategies should relate to three broad categories of activities:

(1) educating policymakers; (2) affecting policy decisions; and, (3) influencing underlying values (Denny et al. 1989). One study found that legislators in New England, for example, were either unaware of or underestimated the poverty levels in their states (Denny et al. 1989; note that these findings must be considered tentative because the sample was not randomly drawn). If legislators are unaware of a problem, they are unlikely to support legislation on its behalf (Denny et al. 1989). At a time when "reinventing government," "scarcity," and "change" are all political slogans of public policy, knowledge of specific advocacy strategies on behalf of children and families in poverty, as well as ways to implement those strategies, is crucial. Taken together, the two can increase the likelihood of effecting change.

Advocacy efforts may take the form of a classic social marketing strategy from the top down (e.g., as a "push") or from the bottom up (e.g., as a "pull") (Kotler and Armstrong 1989). Programs can be "pushed" down to the American people by the president and/or congressional leadership and or "pulled" up from below by the people at the grass-roots level. This section of the chapter provides an overview of key concepts and governmental mechanisms involved in influencing the legislative agenda at local community, state, and federal levels. The process comprises the following steps: (1) defining an issue and identifying a target; (2) building a coalition; (3) creating an issue network; (4) coordinating lobbying efforts; and (5) exerting pressure on the legislature. The steps represent a heuristic for understanding the legislative process. Influencing the legislative agenda in the "real world" may be more problematic than is implied by the "symbolic" framework described here.

Defining an Issue and Identifying a Target

Because conceptualization of a problem determines the objectives to be achieved and the targets to be focused upon, defining an issue is a primary step in the advocacy process (McGowan 1978). In the absence of a well-articulated and convincing issue, agreement for coalition building (discussed in the next section) is impossible (Dluhy 1990). As mentioned earlier, advocacy efforts that focus on *specific* objectives are more likely to be successful than those that target more general aims (Kahn et al. 1973: 104). Workable solutions must be offered for problems, and the issues must be well defined (Edelman 1987; Westman 1979).

McGowan (1978) has suggested that a number of questions be considered at this stage in the advocacy process relating to: the nature of the problem; the relevant target system; the objective (i.e., the desired change); and the receptivity to change of the target system. Answers to questions such as these should guide strategies and decide activities.

During the course of problem definition, data are necessary to validate the problem's existence and significance, to underscore the consequences of failure to take action, and to document the costs of a solution (Morgan 1983). In Morgan's words (1983: 99): "Facts are the fuel that drive the policy process." Information must be organized effectively and communicated to policymakers succinctly (Morgan 1983). The Children's Defense Fund offers similar advice (Morgan 1983).

Once a problem is defined, an advocate can direct his or her activities in the federal government to three levels of decision making. Hayes (1982) has presented a conceptual framework of decision making characterized by (1) the nature of the issue to be addressed, (2) resulting types of governmental action, and (3) actors participating in the debate. At the high level, policy decisions entail whether governmental activity is proper; at the middle level, decisions pertain more specifically to governmental role definition; and, at the low level, decisions relate to the actual design of such a role and its implementation (Hayes 1982).

Hayes (1982) has provided illustrations of each level of decision making. At the high level, policymaking addresses such fundamental questions as: Is there a societal problem necessitating governmental action; what is its character; and, is more or less intervention by government justified? For example, should government fund preschool education for every child? At the middle level, policymaking confronts such questions as: What type of action is needed now that it has been decided that government must act; how much money should be expended; and, what form should services and benefits take? For example, what is the best way of funding preschool education? At the low level, policymaking is concerned with such questions as: How should action be executed now that it has been decided to act and the form of that action has been ascertained? For example, how should eligibility levels and standards be conceived for preschool education? As Hayes has emphasized, knowledge of the nature of an issue is required to ascertain the level of decision making, but inasmuch as policy formation is "a fluid and dynamic process," decision making may be involved at multiple levels simultaneously (1982: 65).

At each level of activity, gaining entry to the key players is mandatory for those wishing to participate in policy formation. Namely, players at the *high* level would be the president, congressional leadership, members of the U.S. Supreme Court, and powerful private interests; players at the *middle* level would be presidential appointees, members of Congress, and the advocates' specific representatives; and players at the *low* level would be congressional staffs and officials of agencies in the executive branch. Because the middle and low spheres of activity incorporate more participants, they are more readily penetrated by "outsiders." Advocates should ascertain where they can have the most impact and direct their efforts there (Hayes 1982).

It is important to emphasize, too, that proponents wishing to influence the legislative agenda should identify as targets of their advocacy efforts the congressional committee(s) having jurisdiction over a given issue and the committee members possessing a particular interest in it. Gaining the support of key congressional representatives is essential to successful passage of legislation. Children's legislation may cut across multiple committees (e.g., Education and Labor in the U.S. House of Representatives, Labor and Human Resources in the U.S. Senate), so advocates may need to cultivate support among varied targets (Melton 1983).

Building a Coalition

Through coalition building, advocates on behalf of children in poverty can achieve more power and influence over an issue than would otherwise be possible acting alone (Dluhy 1990; Edelman 1987). A coalition has been defined as "two or more participants in a group of three or more actors who coordinate the use of their resources in controlling or attempting to control a decision" (Hill 1973: 7). Full-blown, a coalition may represent a conglomerate encompassing organizations, professions, and other groups (Dluhy 1990). Whether initiated "from scratch" or as a "spin-off" from an existing coalition, the coalition's ultimate objective is to obtain benefits by pressuring others. As a strategy for advocacy on behalf of children in poverty, coalitions possess both advantages and disadvantages (Dluhy 1990; Rickart and Bing 1989). By studying how coalitions are built to influence public policy, advocates can draw upon the information to press proposals for social change.

Coalition building may be advisable at the grass-roots level to exert pressure on decision makers, when an issue is community-wide and its resolution lies beyond the boundaries of a single agency or organization (Dluhy 1990). For example, an issue like homelessness requires broad-based coalition building so that a variety of needs and services (e.g., economic, health, housing, social, psychological, and others) can be addressed (Dluhy 1990). Over the past decade, it has become increasingly important for child advocates to direct attention to the grass roots. Weiner has advised that "where national groups . . . have been relied upon to present the views of various service components in the past . . . the new direction of government power mandates . . . activity at the state and local levels" (Weiner 1984, cited in Roberts-DeGennaro 1986: 310).

Coalitions evolve through a series of phases that imitate strategy development (Dluhy 1990), including publicizing issues in a community, advancing them on the formal agenda, activating for the adoption of specific changes, and attempting to apprehend the policy formation process.

According to Dluhy (1990), coalition building requires attention to diverse problems: namely, ways of responding to an issue, engaging in goal-seeking, realizing mutually agreed-upon objectives, and protecting the diverse bases of a coalition's membership. Other questions related to mission, time span, and membership group base have been addressed by Dluhy (1990) in the form of a coalition typology.

Creating an Issue Network

Through coalition building, groups of advocates coordinate their interests, thus forming an issue network. As defined by Heclo (1978: 103), an issue network is "a shared-knowledge group having to do with some aspect . . . of public policy." Frequently comprising a large number of participants possessing diverse degrees of mutual commitment (members may not agree on the substance of a given policy), a network is characterized by unpredictability, complexity, and fluidity (Cigler 1991). When an issue network is formed, consensus solidifies; larger numbers of advocates are brought into association; and the advocacy system expands (Dluhy 1990; Walker, Jr. 1991; Zorack 1990). The development of skillfully targeted mass communication techniques (e.g., computerized mailings, toll-free telephone lines, the media) has made it possible to rally sizable groups of widely dispersed people (Walker, Jr. 1991; Zorack 1990). To mobilize sufficient power to attain success on a major policy issue, the coordinated efforts of several organizations are frequently necessary. Only a coalition or network of coalitions is capable of mustering support broadly based enough to accomplish this aim (Smucker 1991).

Coordinating Lobbying Efforts

Lobbying has been described as the "straightforward implementation of political strategy" (Wolpe 1990: 6) and as the "discernment and exploitation of political opportunity" (Wolpe 1990: 32). Lobbying by advocacy groups is appropriate when there is a reasonable probability of its success (i.e., the opening of a "policy window"); adequate resources are available; and, a threat does not exist of its being counterproductive (Dexter 1987). As a political stratagem, lobbying can be pursued to acquire the support of a legislator or to compensate for his or her opposition. The technique comprises several fundamentals: defining the issues; being aware of contenders in the policy formation process; knowing the legislative committee system; comprehending the rationale for a policy issue; anticipating the opposition; cultivating sources of support; mastering the legislative process; engaging the support of other coalitions; gaining a bipartisan overview of the political terrain; and, finally, being polite (Wolpe 1990). Examples of lobbying efforts include blocking legislation that runs counter to one's cause; supporting legislation consistent with it; and arranging for the introduction of bills (Smucker 1991), to mention a few.

Coalition building, as noted earlier, is a critical step in the lobbying process. To achieve a broad base of support for an issue, lobbyists must identify parties sharing common interests, formulate an issue in mutually understandable terms, and inspire mutual action (Wolpe 1990). The strength of a network is related to the likelihood of its success in achieving a policy goal (Zorack 1990). According to Marian Wright Edelman, advocates for children must search constantly for common ground with others. In her words, "The key to winning big for children is for us to broaden our appeal and to push into mainstream issues that have been viewed by many as just poor or black or liberal" (Edelman 1987: 109). An example of such a broad-based issue is funding for Head Start, a program that has enjoyed strong bipartisan support in Congress (Chafel 1992).

How to frame one's message has become an issue of some dispute (DeParle 1993). Should child advocates argue on behalf of *all* children or only those living in poverty? Some say that *all* American children are vulnerable and require government assistance, not just those in poverty. Proponents of this view cite societal conditions (e.g., a culture of violence, family breakup) that render all children at risk. Furthermore, they claim that if an argument were made on behalf of poor children, it would encounter resistance from the conservatives against higher taxes in support of social programs. Other advocates claim that making a case for all children fails to address the economic forces that affect poor children and the adults who care for them. As a result, it eclipses the real issues that affect children and families in poverty. Advocates for children in poverty need to be aware of these differences of opinion. Whether a message should be framed on behalf of *all* or *some* children is a problem not easily resolved. The answer may vary depending upon the specific circumstances surrounding a policy issue.

Exerting Pressure on the Legislature

Advocates on behalf of children in poverty can direct their lobbying activities toward the local community as well as state and federal levels of government: namely, a city council, county government, state legislature, and the U.S. Congress. At this point in the process, it is important to understand how a particular legislative body of government operates, so efforts can be targeted and a decisive moment can be seized (Smucker 1991). For example, advocates must be ready to oppose or support an amendment to a bill that suddenly comes up for a vote. Because influencing policymakers depends on how many members of a coalition can be mobilized to exert pressure on government, communication with the grass roots is crucial at such a time. As defined by Smucker (1991: 105), a grass-roots network is "an organized, systematic means of communicating on short notice with volunteers at the local level who have agreed to contact their legislators on behalf of your issue." Skill in steering a bill through the legislature, securing grass-roots commitment in favor of it, and making legislators aware of that support are key to the successful passage of legislation (Smucker 1991). A number of organizations (including the League of Women Voters, the Advocacy Institute, and Independent Sector) as well as legislators currently in office all disseminate information on the legislative process and lobbying activity.

To sum up, Pertschuk (1986) has described five factors that must be present to effect change through the legislative process:

(1) a broad "outside" grass-roots movement or its proxy, an organized constituency, (2) "inside" leadership [meaning committed legislators and legislative staff], (3) a network of supportive policy professionals/ experts, (4) alert and sympathetic media, and (5) professionally sophisticated lobbyists. (Pertschuk 1986, cited by Rickart and Bing 1989: 97)

As readers will note, the elements cited by Pertschuk are relevant to both federal as well as state levels of government.

Numerous "methodologies for action" are available to assist advocates for children in poverty (Portnoy et al. 1983: 1224). A few are listed here as introductory material for readers interested in becoming advocates. These resources describe information on forming and maintaining a coalition (Dluhy 1990; Wittenberg and Wittenberg 1989); selecting tactics, strategies, and style (Dluhy 1990; Rickart and Bing 1989; Walker 1991); influencing target persons (Zander 1990); building consensus (Morgan 1983; Wittenberg and Wittenberg 1989); lobbying (Berger 1977; Children's Defense Fund 1991; Smucker 1991; Wolpe 1990; Zorack 1990); preparing for a hearing and using data (Children's Defense Fund 1990c; Wittenberg and Wittenberg 1989); working with the media (Children's Defense Fund 1990b; Smucker 1991; Wittenberg and Wittenberg 1989); analyzing social welfare legislation (Kleinkauf 1989); adopting legislative strategies that have been shown empirically to be effective (Dear and Patti 1981); and fundraising (Children's Defense Fund 1990a). In addition, Rickart and Bing (1989) described the characteristics of effective advocates and "pitfalls" to avoid. The Children's Defense Fund also publishes a monthly newsletter (*CDF Reports*) that furnishes readers with up-to-date information on the status of children nationwide, contacts with other advocates, and various strategies.

Although only a relatively small amount of data exist on the various topics just listed, research on interest groups is one area that has increased noticeably in recent years. The literature has focused on questions of scope and representativeness; how groups organize as well as attract and retain their members; and their internal workings. In addition, group impact has been studied with respect to role and tactics (see Cigler 1991 for a recent literature review). As Cigler (1991) has pointed out, some research does exist on the effectiveness of specific lobbying techniques, but the topic remains unexamined for the most part.

Schematic Example: Head Start Teacher Training

Figure 9.1 provides a schematic outline of the five-step process involved in influencing the legislative agenda as just described, applying it to a specific sample goal: funding for Head Start teacher training. As shown in the figure, advocates would first define their objective (increase funding) by performing a cost/benefit study and would then analyze and organize the information obtained about the problem. Once the objective has been defined and information gathered, targets for advocacy are identified from the top-down (e.g., the President; the U.S. House Education and Labor Subcommittee on Human Resources; U.S. Senate Labor and Human Resources Subcommittee on Children, Family, Drugs, and Alcoholism; the Administration for Children, Youth, and Families; and the Assistant Secretary for Planning and Evaluation in the U.S. Department of Health and Human Services) or the bottom up (e.g., local Head Start programs, Community Action Programs [CAPs], Head Start parents, local and state welfare agencies, and local school districts). Once targets are identified and selected, they can then receive information gathered by the advocacy group concerned with the problem.

Building agreement among these targets may not be easy, as Donald Bolce (personal communication, August 25, 1993) has pointed out. Points of dissension might be: What does Head Start teacher training mean? Is this an important issue at the local and/or national level? Responses to these questions may vary depending upon the perspective held.

In the second and third steps (see figure 9.1), those advocating for funding for Head Start teacher training should explore the merits of forming a coalition. The questions to be asked are: Is a coalition necessary to achieve the objective; and, if so, what benefits and/or costs will accrue from its formation? From the top-down, advocates may want to bring into the coalition the Children's Defense Fund, the National Council for Early Childhood Professional Recognition, the National Head Start Association, and the National Association for the Education of Young Children, in addition to the targets already mentioned, to affect the desired policy changes. From the bottom-up, the advocates would bring into the coalition the groups cited earlier as targets. If a coalition is formed around this issue, the new

Figure 9.1   INFLUENCING THE LEGISLATIVE AGENDA TO FUND HEAD START TEACHER TRAINING

Step 1: Define an Issue and Identify a Target

1. Define a specific objective: funds for Head Start teacher training
 	
   a. Perform cost/benefit analysis
   b. Analyze and organize information
 	
2. Identify a target
   A. Top down
      a. What level of government decision making: high, middle, or low?
      b. Is there a problem, and is government intervention justified?
      c. Now that we've decided to act, how much money should we spend?
      d. How should it be done?
   B. Bottom up (repeat a.–d. above)
 	
3. Disseminate information
   A. Top down
      a. High—president, congressional committees (i.e., U.S. House Education and Labor Subcommittee on Human Resources; U.S. Senate Labor and Human Resources Subcommittee on Children, Family, Drugs, and Alcoholism; the Administration for Children, Youth and Families;) and executive departments (i.e., the Assistant Secretary for Planning and Evaluation in the U.S. Department of Health and Human Services)

Steps 2 and 3: Build a Coalition and Create an Issue Network

1. Do a self-study
   a. How can a coalition respond?
   b. How can a coalition be proactive, goal-seeking, and foster mutually agreed-upon objectives?
   c. How can the coalition safeguard its membership base?
 	
Repeat Parts 2 and 3 of Step 1

Step 4: Coordinate Lobbying Efforts
1. Who are contenders for resources you want? 2. What information or knowledge about the legislative process do you need? 3. Who is your opposition? 4. Who are your sources of support? 5. Are there other coalitions that can help you? 6. Who are common stakeholders?

Step 5: Exert Pressure on the Legislature
Implement the plan developed in Steps 2 and 3

organization identifies its targets and disseminates information to them, as described earlier here in Step 1.

The fourth step in the process consists of coordinating lobbying efforts among advocates for funding Head Start teacher training. At this point, it is important to determine who may be for and who may be against the proposal and to inventory the resources at the coalition or organization's disposal to mount an effective lobbying effort at the appropriate level of government. Groups will compete for the same resources at any level of government. The question then becomes: How will this particular group distinguish itself from the rest and succeed in obtaining what it wants?

The answer to this question emanates from the final step, development and implementation of a lobbying plan. Activities are aimed at influencing federal and/or local officials who can channel resources to fund Head Start teacher training. As the lobbying effort proceeds, the lobbying plan itself evolves, as the dynamics of influencing a particular level of government and its institutions become more apparent. The success or failure of the coalition or of a single group advocating for policy changes like Head Start teaching training is dependent on a number of factors outside the group's control (e.g., changes in economic and political conditions) and it may take years before such a policy shift is realized. Therefore, regardless of the outcome, learning about the political process occurs and can then be applied to new strategies and tactics. Although the specific issue targeted for advocacy may vary (e.g., Head Start teacher training; child immunization; prenatal health care; high quality, low-cost child care), the steps involved in the process do not.

This section of the chapter has focused on government as one sector through which the needs of the disenfranchised may be served. The next section examines philanthropy as another sector through which advocates can press for change.

PHILANTHROPY

The concept of philanthropy has been associated with the history of Western civilization, evolving from its pre-Greek foundations to its entry into the English language during the 17th century (Curti 1973). A derivative of the Greek words *philein* ("to love") and *anthropos* ("man"), the term *philanthropy* denotes "actions taken for the love of humanity" (Corn 1992: 3). Broadly defined today as "voluntary

action for the public good" (Payton 1990: 179), the concept of philanthropy has come to be connected with a tradition of private voluntary
association undertaken for the betterment of society (Corn 1992). By
becoming knowledgeable about the dynamics, dimensions, and role
in American society of the philanthropic tradition, advocates on
behalf of children in poverty can use this information to broaden
and intensify their endeavors to effect social change.

Voluntary actions undertaken by private citizens to foster "the
public good" fall within a sector of American life that belongs neither
to government nor to business (O'Neill 1989). Variously referred to
as "the invisible sector," "the voluntary sector," "the independent
sector," "the third sector," "the philanthropic sector," and "the private nonprofit sector" (Commission on Private Philanthropy and Public Needs 1975, reprinted in O'Connell 1983; Corn 1992; Cornuelle
1965, reprinted in O'Connell 1983; O'Neill 1989), the third sector,
as it is referred to here, represents a veritable "kaleidoscope of human
action" (Cornuelle 1965: 280, reprinted in O'Connell 1983). Comprising it are research institutes, foundations, social action movements,
community development groups, welfare agencies, and many other
groups. Typically, organizations such as these exist to provide service
or to advance a cause. Although the service or cause may vary considerably from group to group, the commonality they all share is "some
relationship to the good of society" (O'Neill 1989: 2).

More than 150 years ago, Alexis de Tocqueville noted the American
predisposition to form independent societies:

> As soon as several of the inhabitants of the United States have taken up
> an opinion or a feeling which they wish to promote in the world, they
> look out for mutual assistance; and as soon as they have found one
> another out, they combine. From that moment they are no longer
> isolated men, but a power seen from afar, whose actions serve for an
> example and whose language is listened to. (Tocqueville 1835,
> reprinted in O'Connell 1983: 57)

Tocqueville was struck by the adeptness of Americans in proposing
a common cause to unite the efforts of many and their success in
persuading others to pursue it. More than 150 years later, the third
sector continues to deserve the keen analysis that Tocqueville gave
it.

Although the third sector has been a dynamic historic force in
American culture and responsible for pioneering a number of successful social movements (e.g., child labor legislation, mental health
care) (O'Neill 1989), it has only recently become the subject of serious

scholarly inquiry. A few references have stated that relatively little is known about it as a discipline deserving of study: its size, impact, dynamics, dimensions, or relationships to other aspects of American life (Commission on Private Philanthropy and Public Needs 1975, reprinted in O'Connell 1983; O'Neill 1989; Smith 1973, reprinted in O'Connell 1983). Payton (1990: 181) has noted that probing into the substance of philanthropy involves a "continuing exploration of open-ended social issues."

Over the course of its evolution in American society, certain distinguishing functions of third-sector activity have emerged. The Commission on Private Philanthropy and Public Needs (1975, reprinted in O'Connell 1983) has delineated several: pioneering new ideas and processes; contributing to the making of public policy; sustaining minority or local interests; dispensing services constitutionally barred from government; monitoring the activities of government and the marketplace; coordinating activities with the other sectors; distributing aid abroad; and fostering civic spirit and altruism. Smith (1973, reprinted in O'Connell 1983) has provided a comparable analysis. O'Connell (1983) singled out fostering innovation and criticism as the most significant contributions of the third sector. Such a view is consistent with an image of the third sector as an independent "advocate and critic" (O'Connell 1978: 200). In pursuit of its aims, the third sector complements government and, because it stands apart from it, is able to improve upon its capacity to benefit society (Commission on Private Philanthropy and Public Needs 1975, reprinted in O'Connell 1983).

To explain more fully (and to draw upon and to extrapolate from the above analysis provided by The Commission on Private Philanthropy and Public Needs 1975, reprinted in O'Connell 1983), the third sector can innovate in those areas of American life where knowledge is lacking or where some fear to tread (e.g., by providing experimental but controversial models of service delivery). By dissecting, refining, and focusing attention on issues for public consideration, it can foster the development of government policy (e.g., legislation on hunger and homelessness). Because the third sector need not be keyed into a broad and diverse constituency and can take risks, it can further causes that government may have to ignore due to majority prejudices (e.g., placing children afflicted with pediatric AIDS in foster care). Inasmuch as the third sector is not prohibited, like government, from entering the sphere of religious activity, it can promote religious functions (e.g., aid to Catholic schools in economically depressed areas). By engaging in oversight, it can prod the government into better protection of human rights (e.g., safeguarding low-income children from lead poisoning). Furthermore, the sector can bring together groups from both business and government to foster a common cause (e.g., restoring small businesses in Watts after the 1992 Los Angeles riots). At a time of political unrest abroad, the sector can, as an independent agent, disseminate aid in those areas where it would be unacceptable for government to do so (e.g., shipping food supplies to starving children in Iraq). Encouraging citizen involvement in a cause, it can rally them to unite in pursuit of a civic goal (e.g., forming a coalition to fight for government-sponsored clinics to provide prenatal care for low-income pregnant women). All of these areas of endeavor suggest specific ways in which advocates on behalf of children in poverty can become involved in third-sector activities.

As previously suggested, the third sector, by prompting social action (namely, influencing public opinion, lobbying government), is capable of assuming a leadership role in effecting policy change (Pifer 1987). In an article entitled "Philanthropy and Politics: New Coalitions," Bailey (1990) has reported how various segments of the third sector have, through coalition building, fashioned nonpartisan advocacy networks to win legislative support for children in need. Cooperation of this type, stated Bailey, may provide "a model for a new style of aggressive philanthropy" (p. 1). The coalitions comprise a variety of organizations embracing mainstream voters (civic, social-service, business, religious) and corporate and national foundations. Reflecting an emerging interest in attacking problems at local and state levels (Pifer 1987), they are engaging in advocacy to mobilize leaders at the grass roots. According to the Association of Child Advocates (cited by Bailey 1990), more than 85 citizen-based children's advocacy groups exist in 42 states (e.g., Florida's Vote for the Children Campaign [now called Florida Center for Children and Youth], Arizona's Children's Action Alliance). Examples of some of their activities are: producing "Religious Action Kits" to educate others on the plight of children in need, a joint project of the Children's Defense Fund and Congregations Concerned about Children; holding forums on children's issues for legislative candidates; and creating a "Children 2000 Commission" at the level of state government (Bailey 1990). Eve Brooks, of the Association of Child Advocates (personal communication, September 28, 1992), has also pointed out that other activities include monitoring of state budgets and setting state legislative agendas for children. To aid endeavors such as these,

Galaskiewicz (1989) has provided a number of research-derived suggestions for nonprofit and corporate practitioners and policymakers with respect to corporate philanthropic giving.

Recently, three large national coalitions (Coalition for America's Children, Coalition of Community Foundations for Youth, and Mobilization for America's Children) have been formed to mobilize alliances in as many as 200 cities across the country (Bailey 1992). Concerned about a variety of domestic issues affecting children (e.g., a lack of low-cost health care, poor-quality schooling), these networks are striving to persuade voters and political candidates that neglect of children's issues is detrimental to societal well-being. (By the same token, attending to these issues is "good politics" because the coalitions could swing votes and resources elsewhere.) Members of the groups include pediatricians and children's hospitals, Junior Leagues, child welfare organizations, school teachers and administrators, statewide child advocacy associations, and others. Activities consist of raising money, media campaigning, policy research and advocacy, and promoting better services for children (Bailey 1992). The partnerships illustrate how a variety of groups and individuals can become involved in third-sector activities to resolve problems and meet needs.

Although the third sector is widely perceived as fostering innovative solutions to contemporary social problems, many writers have questioned the function of the philanthropic community with respect to the impoverished in society (Gronbjerg 1990; Odendahl 1990; O'Neill 1989; Ostrander 1989; Wolch 1990). Gronbjerg (1990), for example, investigated whether nonprofit organizations focused their efforts on the poor, whether external constraints restricted their ability to do so, and whether their structure and culture directed them to this endeavor. The findings suggested that these organizations were not primarily oriented toward the poor and their problems, even when called upon by leaders in the public and private spheres to refocus their efforts. Similarly, Odendahl (1990) has argued that philanthropy does not act in the interests of the poor, but has created, instead, a constellation of institutions (social, cultural, educational) whereby the rich can maintain their own class. Wolch (1990) has asserted that government has circumscribed the ability of the third sector to advocate for reform in public policy. Dependent upon public resources, third-sector activism has in the past involved curtailment of funding by government to safeguard state prerogatives.

Today "voluntarism is in vogue" (Wolch 1990: 4). Political conservatives support it because third-sector organizations provide a structure for countering what conservatives believe to be unchecked welfare state expansion and the abrogation of private responsibility for social problems. Similarly, those with more liberal orientations have argued that voluntarism may result in a broadening of the range of welfare services, in flexibility and innovation, and in enhanced support for social causes (Wolch 1990).

In the future, the problems encountered by philanthropy are expected to increase in complexity and scope. The ability of societal institutions (e.g., government, business) to respond to these problems will be limited by a lack of resources and by restrictions resulting from the need to address other services. Demands for third-sector leadership will escalate (Van Til 1990). As the third sector assesses and redirects its commitment to the betterment of humankind, an unprecedented opportunity will arise for advocates to become involved. For all of these reasons, advocates on behalf of children in poverty need to become familiar with the third sector.

RECOMMENDATIONS

Child poverty is a problem with profound implications for our society. Unresolved, it threatens to compromise the essence of what America claims to be: a nation premised on equality of life chances, justice, and human rights. We thus have a profound ethical obligation to act on the problem of child poverty. From a more self-serving perspective, it can also be said that child poverty threatens the economic well-being of us all, as a substantial proportion of our future citizens emerge on the fringes of society unable to meaningfully contribute to it.

This final section returns to issues alluded to earlier in the chapter to suggest specific ways in which innovative modes of thinking about child poverty may be generated to further societal change. Four themes are developed: (1) pursuing research on advocacy; (2) reforming the third sector; (3) coordinating policy on children's issues; and (4) training for advocacy. The discussion considers the problematic nature of each theme and offers a rationale for action.

Advocacy Research

Serious scholarly attention has not been directed to the study of advocacy. Its scientific underpinnings, by and large, are yet to be constructed, both empirically and conceptually. Some might argue that at a time when funding to support research is limited, scarce resources should not be diverted from inquiry on the dynamics of poverty to advocacy. The underlying assumption is that advocacy is peripheral to the debate on child poverty, not a central concern. We believe otherwise. Although research on the dynamics of poverty is extremely worthwhile and unquestionably should be vigorously pursued, it is only of limited value unless the knowledge gained is used to better the life circumstances of children and families living in poverty. Advocacy can play a critical role in bringing research knowledge about poverty to those capable of influencing public policy.

Systematic inquiry is needed on the styles, strategies, and methods of advocacy that have been shown to be effective. McCall (1978), for example, has suggested that research should investigate whether the latter two variables are linked with factors such as forums (e.g., political, judicial), parties (e.g., families, subcommittees), and processes (e.g., hearings, trials), and how these elements may combine to form "typologies." Data from research on topics such as these can provide advocates with a serious conceptual framework for action. With a substantive body of empirical literature to guide their work, advocates can progress beyond what is currently known to improve conditions for children and families in poverty. The challenge for public policy is to support research of this genre. (For the limited work that does exist, see American Institutes for Research in the Behavioral Sciences 1983; Designs for Change 1983; and Kahn et al. 1973.)

Reforming Philanthropy

By virtue of its history, organizational structure, resources, and ability to unite, the third sector has the potential for leading a reform effort on behalf of children and families in poverty. Yet, as pointed out earlier, many writers have questioned whether the philanthropic community is committed to the impoverished and their problems. Data confirm that the greatest proportion of philanthropic activity "does not directly serve, advocate for, or organize the poor" (Ostrander 1989: 219). Simply doing "more" would not be enough to effect change. On the contrary, as Ostrander (1989) has pointed out, philanthropy requires a reconceptualization. Specifically: (1) the relations between the third sector and government demand reappraisal; (2) political action must be incorporated into the activities of philanthropy; and (3) the poor should become directly involved in decision making about efforts on their behalf. O'Neill (1989) has similarly argued that greater diversity of gender and ethnicity are needed in the membership profile (namely, grant recipients, staff, trustees) of institutional funders.

Empirical research can further contribute to the reform of philanthropy. The knowledge derived from such inquiry can guide professional practice related to the third sector more effectively toward serving the poor. Among topics that should be examined are the effectiveness and ineffectiveness of various types of voluntary action (Smith 1973, reprinted in O'Connell 1983); the freedom enjoyed by the third sector in launching new ventures and framing policy; and the extent to which constraints are placed on such activities by the state (Wolch 1990). Data pertaining to political activism, "innovation and risk taking," and the planning of programs with the potential for achieving serious results are also needed (Eisenberg 1991: 37). Furthermore, research should explore whether making the membership profile of institutional funders more inclusive, as just suggested, has any effect on the reform of philanthropy. Again, the challenge for public policy is to support the endeavors described here.

Policy Coordination

The target of lobbying for children's issues is diffuse and scattered across a variety of legislative and administrative structures in government (e.g., the Senate Committee on Labor and Human Resources; the U.S. Department of Education) (Melton 1983; Steiner 1976). Thus, no central place exists to which advocates for children in poverty can bring their concerns. As Steiner (1976: 251) has written, "Children are part of every member's constituency, and fit into no single committee's jurisdiction." As a result, the task of child advocacy is made more difficult because proponents must pursue multiple and varied targets.

A central coordinating structure is needed for policy development on children's issues (Steiner 1976). Such a structure may be in the making. In a recent speech at the National Summit on Children and Families, in Washington, D.C., Carol Rasco, Assistant to the President for Domestic Policy, noted:

> The details remain to be worked out. But for sure, there will be an
> ongoing, high-level focus on children and families, cutting across agency,
> departmental, and programmatic lines, coordinated by the White House,

responsible not to any single constituency but to the national interest and
directly to the President of the United States. (p. 17)

Such a framework would have a number of benefits: It would enable
advocates to target their efforts more effectively; it would give greater
public visibility to children's issues; and it would elevate these issues
to a more prestigious status. Poverty among children might assume
a place in national discourse and debate that is similar to that given
other national issues (e.g., taxes, health care). The challenge for public
policy is to create such a structure.

Advocacy Training

Numerous writers have pointed out that professionals concerned
with children's issues lack adequate knowledge of the advocacy process (e.g., Melton 1987; Portnoy et al. 1983). Child advocacy has
relevance for a variety of disciplines, but is not an integral part of
the curricula of any academic specialty. Where do advocates receive
training? By and large, they perform their role without formal education and without a clear conceptual framework to guide them.
Research suggests that the informal approach to training that now
exists is less than effective; that child advocates lack a solid theoretical framework with which to confront timely issues; and that more
adequate mechanisms are necessary if advocates are to learn from
past failures and successes (Designs for Change 1983).

If advocates are to achieve a voice through the political process,
"They must know what they can do, what they can say, and to whom
they can say it" (Portnoy et al. 1983: 1226). Graduate programs in
disciplines concerned with children's issues (e.g., education, health
care, pediatrics, psychology, social work, sociology) should incorporate into their curricula content about the advocacy process. Attention should be directed to the styles, strategies, and methods of advocacy; leadership training; identifying policy issues; forming and
maintaining coalitions; lobbying; policy formation; the policy process itself; the workings of the legislative process; and using the
media, to suggest but a few of many topics (Dluhy 1990; Portnoy et
al. 1983; Reisch 1986). Internships should be integrated into such
study. Through internships, students could apply knowledge learned
to real-life settings. The challenge for public policy is to support
advocacy training.

CONCLUSION

Children exemplify a powerless constituency whose "lives are profoundly affected by social conditions that they did not create and political decisions that are beyond their control" (Miller 1983: 72). Vulnerable and without voice, they are dependent on others to speak for them. Among the most vulnerable are children in poverty. Poverty need not be a "given" for millions of children growing up in the United States today. Blending public and private resources with political tools, advocates can prompt social action. With knowledge and commitment, they can press for change.

Notes

We express our appreciation to Paula Jorde Bloom, Eve Brooks, Michael McGuire, Marion McNairy, Maureen Pirog-Good, Leroy Rieselbach, Felicity Skidmore, and two anonymous reviewers for their helpful comments on an earlier draft of this paper.

The assistance of Donald Bolce, Linda Likins, and Shana Ritter is gratefully acknowledged.

Preparation of the appendix to this chapter was made possible by a Multidisciplinary Seminars Grant from Indiana University, Bloomington.

References

American Institutes for Research in the Behavioral Sciences. 1983. *Evaluation of the Youth Advocacy Program: Final Report*. Washington, D.C.: Author.

Bailey, A. 1990. "Philanthropy and Politics: New Coalitions." *Chronicle of Philanthropy* 3 (2, Oct. 30): 1, 10–11.

————. 1992. "Three Coalitions Join a 'Red-Alert Mobilization' to Seek Improved Conditions for Children." *Chronicle of Philanthropy* 4 (6, Jan. 14): 7.

Barnes, J. 1993. "To Clinton's Public, Less May Be More." *National Journal* 25 (Mar. 6): 582.

Berger, E. 1977. "The Compleat Advocate." *Policy Sciences* 8: 69–78.

Bowker, R. R. 1992. *Annual Register of Grant Support: A Directory of Funding Sources, 1993*, 26th ed. New Providence, N.J.: Author.

Chafel, J. 1990a. "Children in Poverty: Policy Perspectives on a National Crisis." *Young Children* 45 (5, July): 31–37.

————. 1990b. "Needed: A Legislative Agenda for Children at Risk." *Childhood Education* 66 (4, Summer): 241–42.

————. 1992. "Funding Head Start: What Are the Issues?" *American Journal of Orthopsychiatry* 62 (1, January): 9–21.

Children's Defense Fund. 1990a. *An Advocate's Guide to Fund Raising.* Washington, D.C.: Author.

————. 1990b. *An Advocate's Guide to the Media.* Washington, D.C.: Author.

————. 1990c. *An Advocate's Guide to Using Data.* Washington, D.C.: Author.

————. 1991. *An Advocate's Guide to Lobbying and Political Activity for Nonprofit Employees.* Washington, D.C.: Author.

Cigler, A. 1991. "Interest Groups: A Subfield in Search of an Identity." In *Political Science: Looking to the Future.* Vol. 4 of American Institutions, edited by W. Crotty. Evanston, Ill.: Northwestern University Press.

"Clinton Outlines His Plan to Spur the Economy." 1993. *Congressional Quarterly* 51 (Feb. 20): 399–404.

Cohen, M., J. March, and J. Olsen. 1972. "A Garbage Can Model of Organizational Choice." *Administrative Science Quarterly* 17 (March): 1–25.

Commission on Private Philanthropy and Public Needs. 1983 [1975]. "The Third Sector." In *America's Voluntary Spirit: A Book of Readings,* edited by Brian O'Connell. New York: Foundation Center.

Committee for Economic Development. 1987. *Children in Need: Investment Strategies for the Educationally Disadvantaged.* New York: Author.

Congress of the United States and the Congressional Budget Office. 1985. *Reducing Poverty among Children.* Washington, D.C.: U.S. Government Printing Office.

Congressional Research Service. 1990. *CRS Report for Congress: Federal Programs for Children and Their Families.* Washington, D.C.: Library of Congress.

Corn, K. 1992. *Philanthropy: Voluntary Action for the Public Good. A Study Guide to Accompany the Videotape.* Indianapolis: Indiana University Center on Philanthropy.

Cornuelle, R. 1983 [1965]. "Reclaiming the American Dream." In *America's Voluntary Spirit: A Book of Readings,* edited by Brian O'Connell. New York: Foundation Center.

Curti, M. 1973. "Philanthropy." In *Dictionary of the History of Ideas,* vol. 3, edited by P. Wiener (486–93). New York: Charles Scribner's Sons.

Danziger, S., and J. Stern. 1990. "The Causes and Consequences of Child Poverty in the United States." Paper prepared for UNICEF. UNICEF International Child Development Center, Project on Child Poverty and Deprivation in Industrialized Countries, Sept. 19.

Dear, R., and R. Patti. 1981. "Legislative Advocacy: Seven Effective Tactics." *Social Work* 26 (4, July): 289–96.

Denny, E., J. Pokela, J. Jackson, and M. Matava. 1989. "Influencing Child Welfare Policy: Assessing the Opinion of Legislators." *Child Welfare* 68 (3, May–June): 275–87.

DeParle, J. 1993. "Advocates Sell Antipoverty Policies Beneath Faces of America's Children." *New York Times* (Mar. 29): A8.

Designs for Change. 1983. *Child Advocacy and the Schools: Past Impact and Potential for the 1980s.* Chicago: Designs for Change.

Dexter, L. 1987. *How Organizations are Represented in Washington.* Lanham, Md.: University Press of America.

Dluhy, M. 1990. *Building Coalitions in the Human Services.* London: Sage Publications.

Edelman, M. 1987. *Families in Peril: An Agenda for Social Change.* Cambridge, Mass.: Harvard University Press.

Eisenberg, P. 1991. "Why We Know So Little about Philanthropy." *Chronicle of Philanthropy* 4 (5, Dec. 17): 37–38.

Epstein, I. 1981. "Advocates on Advocacy: An Exploratory Study." *Social Work Research and Abstracts* 17 (2, Summer): 5–12.

Fuchs, V., and D. Reklis. 1992. "America's Children: Economic Perspectives and Policy Options." *Science* 255 (5040, Jan. 3): 41–46.

Galaskiewicz, J. 1989. "Corporate Contributions to Charity: Nothing More than a Marketing Strategy?" In *Philanthropic Giving: Studies in Varieties and Goals,* edited by Richard Magat. New York: Oxford University Press.

Gale Associations. 1991. *National Organizations of the United States.* New York: Silver Platter.

Gamson, W. 1968. *Power and Discontent.* Homewood, Ill.: Dorsey Press.

Gronbjerg, K. 1990. "Poverty and Nonprofit Organizational Behavior." *Social Service Review* 64 (June): 208–43.

Hayes, C., ed. 1982. *Making Policies for Children: A Study of the Federal Process.* Washington, D.C.: National Academy Press.

Heclo, H. 1978. "Issue Networks and the Executive Establishment." In *The New American Political System,* edited by Anthony King. Washington, D.C.: American Enterprise Institute.

Hill, P. 1973. *A Theory of Political Coalitions in Simple and Policymaking Situations.* Beverly Hills, Calif.: Sage Publications.

Kahn, A., S. Kamerman, and B. McGowan. 1973. *Child Advocacy: Report of a National Baseline Study.* DHEW publ. no. (OCD) 73-18. Washington, D.C.: U.S. Department of Health, Education & Welfare.

Kamerman, S. 1989. "Toward a Child Policy Decade." *Child Welfare* 68 (July/August): 371–90.

Kingdon, J. 1984. *Agendas, Alternatives, and Public Policies.* Glenview, Ill.: Scott, Foresman & Co.

Kleinkauf, C. 1989. "Analyzing Social Welfare Legislation." *Social Work* 34 (March): 179–81.

Kotler, P., and G. Armstrong. 1989. *Principles of Marketing*. Englewood Cliffs, N.J.: Prentice Hall.

McCall, G. 1978. "The Advocate Social Scientist: A Cross-Disciplinary Perspective." In *Social Scientists as Advocates: Views from the Applied Disciplines*, edited by George Weber and George McCall. Beverly Hills, Calif.: Sage Publications.

McGowan, B. 1978. "The Case Advocacy Function in Child Welfare Practice." *Child Welfare* 57 (5, May): 275–84.

Melton, G. 1983. *Child Advocacy: Psychological Issues and Interventions*. New York: Plenum Press.

―――――. 1987. "Children, Politics, and Morality: The Ethics of Child Advocacy." *Journal of Clinical Child Psychology* 16(4):357–67.

Michael, W. H. 1991. *Official Congressional Directory*. Washington, D.C.: U.S. Government Printing Office.

Miller, G. 1983. "Children and the Congress: A Time to Speak Out." *American Psychologist* 38 (1, January): 70–76.

Morgan, G. 1983. "Practical Techniques for Change." *Journal of Children in Contemporary Society* 15 (4, Summer): 91–104.

[National Association of Social Workers] Ad Hoc Committee on Advocacy. 1969. "The Social Worker as Advocate: Champion of Social Victims." *Social Work* 14 (April): 16–22.

National Center for Children in Poverty. 1990. *Five Million Children*. New York: Author.

National Commission on Children. 1991. *Beyond Rhetoric: A New American Agenda for Children and Families*. Washington, D.C.: U.S. Government Printing Office.

O'Connell, B. 1978. "From Service to Advocacy to Empowerment." *Social Casework* 59 (4, April): 195–202.

―――――. 1983. "Introduction." In *America's Voluntary Spirit: A Book of Readings*, edited by Brian O'Connell. New York: Foundation Center.

Odendahl, T. 1990. *Charity Begins at Home: Generosity and Self-Interest among the Philanthropic Elite*. New York: Basic Books.

Office of the Federal Register, National Archives and Records Service. 1990. *U.S. Government Manual*. Washington, D.C.: U.S. Government Printing Office.

Olson, S., R. Kovacs, and S. Haile, eds. 1990. *National Guide to Funding Children, Youth, and Families*. New York: Foundation Center.

O'Neill, M. 1989. *The Third America*. San Francisco: Jossey-Bass, Publishers.

Ostrander, S. 1989. "The Problem of Poverty and Why Philanthropy Neglects It." In *The Future of the Non Profit Sector*, edited by Virginia Hodgkinson and Richard Lyman. San Francisco: Jossey-Bass, Publishers.

Payton, R. 1990. "Teaching Philanthropy, Teaching about Philanthropy." In *Critical Issues in American Philanthropy*, edited by Jon Van Til and Associates. San Francisco: Jossey-Bass, Publishers.

Pertschuk, M. 1986. *Giant Killers*. New York: W. W. Norton and Co.

Pifer, A. 1987. "Philanthropy, Voluntarism, and Changing Times." *Daedalus* 116 (1, Winter): 119–31.

Portnoy, S., M. Norman, E. Eisman, and P. DeLeon. 1983. "Effective State-Level Advocacy: A Model for Action." *American Psychologist* 38 (11, November): 1220–26.

Rasco, C. 1993. Speech to the National Summit on Children and Families, Washington, D.C., Apr. 2.

Reisch, M. 1986. "From Cause to Case and Back Again: The Reemergence of Advocacy in Social Work." *Urban and Social Change Review* 19: 20–24.

"Report Says Poor Children Grew Poorer in 1980s." 1992. *New York Times* (Mar. 24): A22.

Rickart, D., and S. Bing. 1989. *Fairness Is a Kid's Game.* Louisville: Kentucky Youth Advocates.

Roberts, M., K. Alexander, and N. Davis. 1991. "Children's Rights to Physical and Mental Health Care. A Case for Advocacy." *Journal of Clinical Child Psychology* 20(1): 18–27.

Roberts-DeGennaro, M. 1986. "Building Coalitions for Political Advocacy." *Social Work* 31 (July/August): 308–11.

Segal, E., and N. Gustavsson. 1990. "The High Cost of Neglecting Children: The Need for a Preventive Policy Agenda." *Child and Adolescent Social Work* 7 (6, December): 475–85.

Smith, D. 1983 [1973]. "The Impact of the Volunteer Sector on Society." In *America's Voluntary Spirit: A Book of Readings*, edited by Brian O'Connell. New York: Foundation Center.

Smucker, B. 1991. *The Nonprofit Lobbying Guide.* San Francisco: Jossey-Bass, Publishers.

Sosin, M., and S. Caulum. 1983. "Advocacy: A Conceptualization for Social Work Practice." *Social Work* 28(1): 12–17.

Steiner, G. 1976. *The Children's Cause.* Washington, D.C.: Brookings Institution.

Tocqueville, Alexis de. 1983 [1835]. "Of the Use Which the Americans Make of Public Associations in Civil Life." In *America's Voluntary Spirit: A Book of Readings*, edited by Brian O'Connell. New York: Foundation Center.

U.S. Congress, House of Representatives, Committee on Ways and Means. 1985. *Children in Poverty.* Washington, D.C.: U.S. Government Printing Office.

Van Til, J. 1990. "Preparing for Philanthropy's Future." In *Critical Issues in American Philanthropy*, edited by Jan Van Til and Associates. San Francisco: Jossey-Bass, Publishers.

Walker, J., Jr. 1991. *Mobilizing Interest Groups in America: Patrons, Professions, and Social Movements.* Ann Arbor: University of Michigan Press.

Washington Monitor. 1992. *Congressional Yellow Book*, vol. 18, no. 1–2. Washington, D.C.: Author.

Washington Representatives. 1992. *Washington Representatives*. Washington, D.C.: Columbia Books.

Weiner, H. 1984. "Survival through Coalition: The Case of Addiction Programs." In *Human Services at Risk: Administrative Strategies for Survival*, edited by F. Perlmutter. Lexington, Mass.: Lexington Books.

Westman, J. 1979. *Child Advocacy: New Professional Roles for Helping Families*. New York: Free Press.

Wittenberg, E., and E. Wittenberg. 1989. *How to Win in Washington*. New York: Basil Blackwell.

Wolch, J. 1990. *The Shadow State: Government and Voluntary Sector in Transition*. New York: Foundation Center.

Wolpe, B. 1990. *Lobbying Congress: How the System Works*. Washington, D.C.: Congressional Quarterly.

World Almanac. 1989. *World Almanac of U.S. Politics*. New York: Author.

Zander, A. 1990. *Effective Social Action by Community Groups*. San Francisco: Jossey-Bass, Publishers.

Zorack, J. 1990. *The Lobbying Handbook*. Washington, D.C.: Professional Lobbying and Consulting Center.

APPENDIX 9.A
NATIONAL ORGANIZATIONS PERFORMING
CHILD POVERTY AND CHILD POLICY
RESEARCH AND ADVOCACY

This appendix describes national and state organizations performing child poverty and child policy research and advocacy. It has been compiled to assist advocates who may be unaware of the large number of private and public organizations dedicated to helping children and families in poverty. Included are advocacy organizations, foundations, government agencies, and institutes that generate and disseminate information.

For readers who may wish to broaden the range of entries listed or update them in future years, the following strategy was adopted: Entries were researched from a number of data sources, including: *Annual Register of Grant Support: A Directory of Funding Sources 1993*, 26th edition; *Congressional Yellow Book; CRS Report for Congress: Federal Programs for Children and Their Families; National Guide to Funding Children, Youth, and Families; National Organizations of the United States; Official Congressional Directory; Research Centers Directory; U.S. Government Manual; Washington Representatives; World Almanac of U.S. Politics*, as well as pamphlets describing the activities of specific groups. In addition, a computer search was conducted using SPIN (Sponsored Programs Information Network, of the Research Foundation of the State University of New York). When consulting the preceding reference sources, the key terms used to guide the search were: *child abuse and neglect, children/youth, child development, sociology of the family, poverty, policy studies*, and *child welfare*.

Because the chapter focuses on a national response to the problem of poverty, organizations with a national constituency have been highlighted. To assist readers interested in state-level activity, a list of state advocacy groups is included at the end of the appendix. Finally, to limit what would be an impractically large list, groups having only a tangential emphasis on child poverty and/or policy were excluded, with the exception of certain key organizations (i.e., The Brookings Institution) whose influence suggested otherwise.

I. ADVOCACY ORGANIZATIONS

ABA Center on Children and the Law
1800 M St., NW
Washington, DC 20036
(202) 331-2250

Significant Activities: Conducts legal research and disseminates information about children's rights, lobbies for legislation affecting those rights, and trains state child welfare agency personnel on child support, foster care, termination of parental rights, child abuse, and other legal issues affecting children.

Publications: *ABA Juvenile and Child Welfare Law Reporter* (monthly), *Children's Legal Rights Journal* (quarterly), publications catalog.

Association of Child Advocates
1625 K St., NW, Suite 510
Washington, DC 20006
(202) 828-6950

Significant Activities: Acts as a clearinghouse for state and local child advocacy groups by exchanging information through newsletters, seminars, and workshops designed to build the expertise and knowledge of member organization staff.

Publication: Newsletter.

Child Care Action Campaign
330 7th Ave., 17th Fl.
New York, NY 10001
(212) 239-0138

Significant Activities: Promotes the proliferation of child care services in the United States by providing information about existing services and the programmatic gaps in them, as well as helping communities develop plans for improving and coordinating these services.

Publication: *Child Care ActioNews* (bimonthly newsletter).

Child Welfare League of America
440 1st St., NW, Suite 310
Washington, DC 20001
(202) 638-2952

Significant Activities: Provides consultation, research, library resources; develops standards for social services directed at children; and maintains an advocacy network of individuals committed to speaking out on children's behalf.

Publications: *Child Welfare—Journal of Policy, Practice, and Programs* (bimonthly), *Child Welfare League of America—From the Desk of the Executive Director* (quarterly newsletter); *Child Welfare League of America—Legislative Alert* (periodic), *Children's Voice* (newsletter, nine times yearly), *CWLA Directory of Member Agencies* (biennial), *Washington Social Legislation Bulletin* (newsletter, semimonthly), and books and monographs.

Children's Defense Fund
122 C St., NW
Washington, DC 20001
(202) 628-8787

Significant Activities: Advocates for children and teenagers through research, public education, litigation, drafting of legislation, congressional testimony, lobbying, and community organizing relating to child welfare, health, adolescent pregnancy prevention, child care, and mental health.

Publications: *Adolescent Pregnancy Prevention Clearinghouse Reports* (bimonthly), *CDF Reports* (newsletter, monthly), *A Vision for America's Future* (annual), *The State of America's Children* (annual), and several books, handbooks, and posters.

Coalition of Community Foundations for Youth
44 Bromfield St., 7th Fl.
Boston, MA 02108
(617) 338-0954

Significant Activities: Strengthens capability of community foundations to raise local awareness and advocate for children through a range of technical assistance resources.

Emergency Council of Jewish Families
2 Penn Plaza, Suite 1500
New York, NY 10121
(212) 244-3100

Significant Activities: Serves as an advocate for Jewish families before social services agencies. Recruits and advises Jewish foster and adoptive families and provides chaplaincy and legal advocacy for Jewish children in the child welfare system. Maintains a library and a speaker's bureau; offers seminars.

Mexican American Women's National Association
1030 15th St., NW, Suite 468
Washington, DC 20005
(202) 898-2036

Significant Activities: Promotes leadership, economic, and educational development training for Hispanic women in areas of pay equity, adolescent pregnancy, and children in poverty. Affiliated with League of United Latin American Citizens.

Publications: Newsletter (quarterly), "Issue Updates" (periodic).

Mobilization for America's Children
United Way of America
701 North Fairfax St.
Alexandria, VA 22314-2045
(703) 836-7100

Significant Activities: Promotes coalition building on children's behalf, develops public education campaigns, and performs advocacy for children's concerns. In partnership with the Coalition for America's Children, the Coalition of Community Foundations for Youth, and the Children's Defense Fund.

Publications: Newsletter, brochures.

National Black Child Development Institute
1463 Rhode Island Ave., NW
Washington, DC 20005
(202) 387-1281

Significant Activities: Conducts research and grassroots advocacy campaigns aimed at public policies focusing on issues of health, child welfare, education, and child care for black children.

Publications: Research reports, monographs.

Poverty and Race Research Action Council
1875 Connecticut Ave., NW, Suite 714
Washington, DC 20009
(202) 387-9887

Significant Activities: Advocates for the disenfranchised and promotes research associated with local, state, and national advocacy efforts.

Publication: *Poverty and Race* (quarterly newsletter).

II. FOUNDATIONS*

Alcoa Foundation
1501 Alcoa Bldg.
Pittsburgh, PA 15219
(412) 553-2348

Average Awards Range: $90,000

Relevant Program Areas: Health and welfare of abused children or children needing care.

---

*Foundations occasionally change their funding priorities. Therefore, the reader is encouraged to contact them directly to determine their current priorities before seeking application information.

Helen V. Brach Foundation
55 West Wacker Dr., Suite 701
Chicago, IL 60601
(312) 372-4417

Average Awards Range: $3,500–$100,000; average, $20,000
Relevant Program Areas: Teenage pregnancy, child development.

Carnegie Corporation of New York
437 Madison Ave.
New York, NY 10022
(212) 371-3200

Average Awards Range: $975–$1,000,000; average, $75,000–$150,000
Relevant Program Areas: Education and health of disadvantaged children
from birth to 15 years of age.

Carthage Foundation
Treasurer
3900 Three Mellon Bank Center
P.O. Box 268
Pittsburgh, PA 15230
(412) 392-2900

Average Awards Range: $1,000–$350,000; average, $25,000–$40,000
Relevant Program Areas: National public policy issues.

Edna McConnell Clark Foundation
250 Park Ave.
New York, NY 10017
(212) 986-7050

Average Awards Range: Open
Relevant Program Areas: Homeless and disadvantaged children and youth.

Nathan Cummings Foundation, Inc.
President
885 Third Ave., Suite 3160
New York, NY 10022
(212) 230-3377

Average Awards Range: Open
Relevant Program Area: Health programs for children living in poverty.

Danforth Foundation
231 South Bemiston Ave., Suite 1080
St. Louis, MO 63105-1996
(314) 862-6200

Average Awards Range: Open
Relevant Program Area: Educational programs that assist teenage parents and their children.

William H. Donner Foundation, Inc.
Senior Program Officer
500 Fifth Ave., Suite 1230
New York, NY 10110
(212) 719-9290

Average Awards Range: average, $20,000–$200,000
Relevant Program Area: Assistance to organizations that help disadvantaged families enter the societal mainstream.

Herman A. and Amelia S. Ehrmann Foundation
% Bear, Marks, and Upham, 21st Floor
805 Third Ave.
New York, NY 10022
(212) 702-5700

Average Awards Range: $1,000–$50,000; average, $15,000
Relevant Program Areas: Indigent, abandoned, neglected, or handicapped children.

Ford Foundation
Secretary
320 East 43rd St.
New York, NY 10017
(212) 573-5000

Average Awards Range: Programs—$3,000–$4,600,000; average for programs, $25,000–$1,500,000
Individuals—$500–$70,000; average for individuals, $2,000–$20,000
Relevant Program Areas: Urban poverty and the disadvantaged, and rural poverty and community resources.

Foundation for Child Development
343 East 46th St.
New York, NY 10017
(212) 697-3150

Average Awards Range: $3,000–$150,000
Relevant Program Areas: Promotes child advocacy activities and public policy research in child poverty.

Frost Foundation
Cherry Creek Plaza II, Suite 205
650 South Cherry St.
Denver, CO 80222
(303) 388-1687

Average Awards Range: $1,500–$170,000; average, $20,000
Relevant Program Areas: Children's health, assistance to the poor.

General Mills Foundation
P.O. Box 1113
Minneapolis, MN 55440
(612) 540-7891

Average Awards Range: Open
Relevant Program Areas: Advocacy, education, and social programs aimed at supporting child development.

Edward D. Hazen Foundation
505 8th Ave., 23rd Floor
New York, NY 10018-6505
(212) 967-5920

Average Awards Range: Open
Relevant Program Area: Development of youth living in poor communities.

W. K. Kellogg Foundation
Executive Assistant for Programming
One Michigan Ave. East
Battle Creek, MI 49017-4058
(616) 968-1611

Average Awards Range: Programs—$494–$20,000,000; Individuals—Grants to individuals totalled $4,660,000. (No range published.)
Relevant Program Areas: Organizations assisting families, neighborhoods, and community health services.

A. L. Mailman Family Foundation, Inc.
707 Westchester Ave.
White Plains, NY 10604
(914) 681-4448

Average Awards Range: Open
Relevant Program Areas: Early childhood education, support for families in crisis.

Andrew W. Mellon Foundation
140 East 62nd St.
New York, NY 10021
(212) 838-8400

Average Awards Range: $5,000–$2,000,000
Relevant Program Area: Prevention of adolescent pregnancy.

Charles Steward Mott Foundation
1200 Mott Foundation Bldg.
Flint, MI 48502
(313) 238-5651

Average Awards Range: $10,000–$150,000
Relevant Program Areas: Prevention of teenage pregnancy, expanding life options for teen parents and their children, and early childhood and parenting education.

Nike, Inc.
One Bowerman Dr.
Beaverton, OR 97005-6453
(503) 671-6453

Average Awards Range: $500–$5,000
Relevant Program Area: Support for education of low-income youth.

The Pew Charitable Trusts
Executive Director
One Commerce Square
2005 Market St., Suite 1700
Philadelphia, PA 19103-7017
(215) 575-4939

Average Awards Range: $50,000–$500,000
Relevant Program Areas: Public policy, health and social services, and education services that promote interdisciplinary approaches to solve community problems.

Public Welfare Foundation, Inc.
Executive Director
2600 Virginia Ave., NW, Suite 505
Washington, DC 20037-1977
(202) 965-1800

Average Awards Range: $5,000–$240,000; average, $36,162
Relevant Program Area: Low-income populations.

Reebok Foundation
100 Technology Center Dr.
Stoughton, MA 02072
(617) 341-5000

Average Awards Range: Open
Relevant Program Area: Programs that could significantly assist disadvantaged youth.

Rockefeller Foundation
1133 Avenue of the Americas
New York, NY 10036
(212) 869-6500

Average Awards Range: Open
Relevant Program Area: Organizations that assist the disadvantaged, especially those living in urban areas.

Dorothea Haus Ross Foundation
1036 Monroe Ave.
Rochester, NY 14620
(716) 473-6006

Average Awards Range: average, $4,600
Relevant Program Area: Disadvantaged children.

Russell Sage Foundation
Program Officer
112 East 64th St.
New York, NY 10021
(212) 750-6000

Average Awards Range: Open
Relevant Program Area: Poverty research.

Smith Richardson Foundation
266 Post Road East
Westport, CT 06880
(203) 454-1068

Average Awards Range: Open
Relevant Program Areas: Programs, research, and public policies that assist those who live in chronic poverty.

Xerox Foundation
800 Long Ridge Rd.
Stamford, CT 06904
(203) 968-3306

Average Awards Range: $5,000–$30,000
Relevant Program Areas: Community social service programs, educational opportunities for the disadvantaged, organizations that conduct public policy research and advocacy.

III. U.S. CONGRESSIONAL COMMITTEES AND EXECUTIVE DEPARTMENT AGENCIES WITH OVERSIGHT OF CHILD PROGRAMS AND POLICIES

U.S. Congressional Committees—U.S. Senate

Agriculture Committee
SR-328A Russell Senate Office Bldg.
Washington, DC 20510-6000
(202) 224-2035

Nutrition and Investigations Subcommittee—Jurisdiction over Food Stamp and school nutrition programs.

Appropriations Committee
S-128 Capitol Bldg.
Washington, DC 20510-6025
(202) 224-3471

Labor, Health and Human Services, Education and Related Agencies Subcommittee—Jurisdiction over budgets of these agencies.

Banking, Housing, and Urban Affairs Committee
SD-534 Dirksen Senate Office Bldg.
Washington, DC 20510-6075
(202) 224-7391

Housing and Urban Affairs Subcommittee—Jurisdiction over public and private housing constructed through government contracts.

Finance Committee
SD-205 Dirksen Senate Office Bldg.
Washington, DC 20510-6200
(202) 224-4515

Social Security and Family Policy Subcommittee—Jurisdiction over health programs under the Social Security Act and health programs financed by a specific tax or trust funds (e.g., Medicaid and Medicare, Supplemental Security Income [SSI]).

Labor and Human Resources Committee
SD-428 Dirksen Senate Office Bldg.
Washington, DC 20510-6300
(202) 224-5375

Children, Family, Drugs, and Alcoholism Subcommittee; and Education, Arts, and Humanities Subcommittee—Jurisdiction over education, labor and employment, health and public welfare.

U.S. Congressional Committees—U.S. House of Representatives

Agriculture Committee
1301 Longworth House Office Bldg.
Washington, DC 20515-6001
(202) 225-2171

Domestic Marketing, Consumer Relations, and Nutrition Subcommittee—Jurisdiction over agricultural legislation, human nutrition and home economics, Food Stamp, and other related programs.

Appropriations Committee
H-218 Capitol Bldg.
Washington, DC 20515-6015
(202) 225-2771

Labor, Health and Human Services, Education, and Related Agencies Subcommittee—Jurisdiction for appropriating money to support these agencies' activities.

Education and Labor Committee
2181 Rayburn House Office Bldg.
Washington, DC 20515-6100
(202) 225-4527

Elementary, Secondary, and Vocational Education Subcommittee and Human Resources Subcommittee—Jurisdiction over education, labor, and employment legislation; includes programs and services for the elderly, elimination of poverty, and care and treatment of children, including Head Start and early childhood services.

Energy and Commerce Committee
2125 Rayburn House Office Bldg.
Washington, DC 20515-6115
(202) 225-2927

Health and the Environment Subcommittee—Jurisdiction over communication, energy, and consumer matters related to health, including Medicaid and Medicare insurance.

Ways and Means Committee
1102 Longworth House Office Bldg.
Washington, DC 20515-6348
(202) 225-3625

Human Resources Subcommittee—Jurisdiction over legislation dealing with public assistance: welfare reform, supplemental security income, AFDC, social services, child support, Food Stamp eligibility, and low-income energy assistance.

Executive Department Agencies and Offices

Office of Management and Budget
Old Executive Office Bldg.
Washington, DC 20503
(202) 395-3000

Prepares federal budget the president sends to Congress each year. The office is divided into several subunits, each responsible for helping executive departments create their budgets in line with the president's objectives.

Department of Agriculture
Independence Avenue, between 12th and 14th Sts., SW
Washington, DC 20250
(202) 655-4000

Food Stamp Program. Provides food coupons through state and local welfare agencies to help people who need assistance meeting their food budgets.

Special Nutrition Programs. Includes National School Lunch program; School Breakfast program; Summer Food Service Program for Children, Child Care Food Program; Summer Food Assistance Program; and Special Milk Program.

Division for Child Nutrition. Provides grants to promote nutrition education and in-service training of food service and teaching personnel.

Division of Food Distribution. Makes food available through children's nutrition programs, food banks, charitable institutions, local government agencies, and Indian reservations.

Division of Supplemental Food Programs. The Special Supplemental Food Program for Women, Infants, and Children (WIC) provides food and nutrition education for pregnant women, nursing women up to 12 months postpartum, non-nursing women up to 6 months postpartum, and children up to five years of age. An additional program, the Commodity Supplemental Food Program, gives supplemental food and nutrition education to infants and children and to pregnant, postpartum, and breastfeeding women.

Department of Education
400 Maryland Ave., SW
Washington, DC 20202
(202) 401-3000

Administers several grants meant for state education agencies and local school districts, which include homeless children and youth, school dropouts, and other special needs.

Office of Elementary and Secondary Education. Oversees disadvantaged and neglected and delinquent children programs. Manages the Even Start and Follow Through programs, which are supplements to the Head Start Program.

Office of Special Education and Rehabilitative Services. Manages programs for emotionally, mentally, and physically disabled children.

Department of Health and Human Services
Hubert H. Humphrey Building
200 Independence Ave., SW
Washington, DC 20201
(202) 245-7000

Assistant Secretary for Planning and Evaluation, Children and Youth Policy Division. Formulates policy and legislation, reviews regulations, performs research, and conducts budget analysis of programs and policies related to matters affecting children, youth, and families. Also administers grants to integrate services directed at low-income families.

The Administration for Children, Youth, and Families. Manages adoption and foster care opportunities, temporary child care and crisis nurseries, discretionary grants providing Head Start services and runaway youth facilities programs. Also promotes demonstrations of comprehensive family support services, and enforces the Child Abuse Prevention and Treatment Act.

Public Health Service:
Office of Adolescent Pregnancy Programs
Office of Family Planning
Office of Minority Health
Bureau of Maternal and Child Health and Resources Development
Manage policies and programs pertaining to health care facilities, education, and family planning.

National Institute of Child Health and Development
National Institutes of Health
9000 Rockville Pike
Rockville, MD 20205
(301) 496-2433

Administers research programs relating to health of mothers and their children, incidence and treatment of mental retardation, treatment of people with physical and learning disabilities, and research into dynamics of the family.

Family Support Administration and Office of Child Support Enforcement
Aerospace Bldg., Sixth Fl. East
370 L'Enfant Promenade, SW
Washington, DC 20447
(202) 252-4500

Enforces obligations owed by absent parents to their children through state governments by locating parents, establishing paternity, and obtaining child support payments.

Office of Family Assistance. Carries out Aid to Families with Dependent Children (AFDC) program, which subsidizes children who do not have adequate parental financial support. Also administers the Jobs Opportunities and Basic Skills (JOBS) program, a mandatory work program for custodial parents whose children are at least three years old.

Social Security Administration. Extends Supplemental Security Income (SSI) and dependents benefits to children.

Department of Housing and Urban Development
Housing and Urban Development Bldg.
451 7th St., SW
Washington, DC 20410
(202) 708-6417

Assistant Secretary for Public Housing. Administers public housing programs and provides technical assistance to low-income housing projects.

Federal Housing Administration. Provides eligible persons the possibility of owning their own homes through guaranteed mortgages. Programs include home ownership and rental housing assistance to those with low and moderate incomes.

Department of Labor
Frances Perkins Bldg.
Third St. and Constitution Ave., NW
Washington, DC 20210
(202) 523-6666

Employment and Training Administration. Administers the Job Training Partnership Act, which includes the Job Corps and the Summer Youth Employment and Training Program, which help low-income youth obtain job training and experience.

Department of the Treasury
15th St. and Pennsylvania Ave., NW
Washington, DC 20220
(202) 566-5300

Internal Revenue Service
Internal Revenue Bldg.
1111 Constitution Ave., NW
Washington, DC 20224
(202) 566-5000

Administers U.S. Tax Code, whose primarily policy instruments to aid children living in poverty are the Dependent Tax Exemption and the Earned Income Tax Credit.

IV. KNOWLEDGE GENERATION AND DISSEMINATION ORGANIZATIONS

American Enterprise Institute for Public Policy Research
1150 17th St., NW
Washington, DC 20036
(202) 862-5800

Significant Activities: Conducts research on domestic and international economic policy, foreign and defense policy, and social and political studies that seek to preserve free enterprise, limit government, promote strong defense and foreign policy postures, and protect existing mainstream cultural and political values. Sponsors an annual meeting and a monthly seminar, Election Watch, during national election years.

Publications: *The American Enterprise* (bimonthly), books.

The Brookings Institution
1775 Massachusetts Ave., NW
Washington, DC 20036
(202) 797-6000

Significant Activities: Produces nonpartisan research and publications in economics, government, and foreign policy; maintains a library of 85,000 volumes; and conducts numerous conferences, forums, and seminars.

Publications: Annual report, directory (annual), Papers on Economic Activity (semiannual), *Brookings Review* (quarterly), program brochure (annual), books, staff papers, and reprints.

The Bush Center in Child Development and Social Policy
310 Prospect St.
New Haven, CT 06511
(203) 432-4581

Significant Activities: Provides information, research, and policy analysis to government and others about the developmental needs of children.

Publications: Studies and research projects related to child development.

Carnegie Council on Adolescent Development
2400 N St., NW, 6th Floor
Washington, DC 20037
(202) 429-7979

Significant Activities: Conducts research on adolescent development focusing on the problems associated with school dropout, youth crimes, teenage pregnancy, drug and alcohol abuse, and teenage suicide.

Publications: Carnegie Council of Adolescent Development Working Papers (periodic), *Turning Points: Preparing American Youth for the 21st Century* (book).

Center on Budget and Policy Priorities (CBPP)
777 N. Capitol St., NW, Suite 705
Washington, DC 20002
(202) 408-1080

Significant Activities: Acts as an information clearinghouse concerning the impact that government spending has upon low- and moderate-income families and individuals. Maintains a library and compiles statistics about national poverty trends, income tax policy, housing affordability, effectiveness of and funding for social programs including hunger and nutrition issues, unemployment, and the minimum wage.

Publications: *Women, Infants, and Children Newsletter* (monthly), fact sheets, articles, and reports.

Chapin Hall Center for Children
University of Chicago
1155 East 60th St.
Chicago, IL 60637
(312) 753-5900

Significant Activities: Child poverty, welfare, and children's policy research.

Publications: Discussion papers.

Child Trends, Inc.
2100 M St., NW, Suite 610
Washington, DC 20037
(202) 223-6288

Significant Activities: Compiles statistics and maintains a speaker's bureau and a library to educate the American public about how social trends affect children. Also provides funding for research scholars to interact with federal policymakers.

Publications: *Facts at a Glance* (annual), monographs, pamphlets, and reports, including *U.S. Children and Their Families: Current Conditions and Recent Trends.*

Child Welfare Research Center
1250 I St., NW, Suite 503
Washington, DC 20005-3922
(212) 371-1565

Significant Activities: Child policy research as it relates to child welfare and children's services.

Publications: Working papers.

Committee for Economic Development
2000 L St., NW, Suite 700
Washington, DC 20036
(202) 296-5860

Significant Activities: Research and reports about public policy issues relating to interests of the American business community. The committee has taken a greater interest in social issues and contributes to the public policy debate about child care and development.

Publications: Books, monographs, policy statements, research reports.

Families and Work Institute
330 Seventh Ave.
New York, NY 10001
(212) 465-2044

Significant Activities: Conducts policy research, acts as an information clearinghouse, and performs consulting and training services for organizations and individuals wanting to know more about work/family needs and issues.

Publications: Research studies, books, reference sources.

Family Impact Seminar
1717 K St., NW, Suite 407
Washington, DC 20006
(202) 429-1825

Significant Activities: Produces policy research and conducts monthly seminars about family policy issues for government policymakers. This nonpartisan unit of the American Association for Marriage and Family Therapy also awards research grants, awards, fellowships, and scholarships to promote family policy research.

Publications: Research reports.

Family Research Council
601 Pennsylvania Ave., Suite 901
Washington, DC 20004
(202) 393-2100

Significant Activities: Provides research information on family-related issues: including income tax policy, adolescent pregnancy, teen suicide, alternative education, and support for single parents.

Publications: *Family Policy* (bimonthly), *Washington Watch* (monthly newsletter), reports on topics of interest.

The Heritage Foundation
214 Massachusetts Ave., NE
Washington, DC 20002
(202) 546-4400

Significant Activities: Analyzes public policy issues to preserve free enterprise, limit government influence, and maintain a strong military defense. Conducts seminars and conferences, sponsors research, maintains a library and a speaker's bureau, and acts as an information clearinghouse for academics and policy research groups.

Publications: *Backgrounder/Issue Bulletin* (weekly), *Educational Update* (quarterly), *Heritage Members' News* (quarterly), *Heritage Today* (bimonthly), *Policy Review* (quarterly), publications catalog, research papers, monographs, studies, and books.

Institute for American Values
250 West 57th St., Suite 2415
New York, NY 10107
(212) 246-3942

Significant Activities: Researches American family values and issues such as child care, education, the workplace, and income tax policy. Provides a database on such issues.

Publication: *Family Affairs* (quarterly).

Mathematica Policy Research
P.O. Box 2393
Princeton, NJ 08543-2393
(609) 799-3535

Significant Activities: Provides research and data collection services for clients in areas of welfare, food assistance, employment and training, unemployment insurance, disability, health care, long-term care for the elderly, and retirement security.

Publications: *Innovations/Contributions* (brochure), research reports.

National Association of Child Care Resource and Referral Agencies
2116 Campus Drive, SE
Rochester, MN 55904
(507) 287-2220

Significant Activities: Promotes accessible, quality child care for all families by providing the public with a range of educational materials about the availability, affordability, and quality of child care services.

Publications: *The Complete Guide to Choosing Child Care*, policy and technical assistance papers.

National Center for Children in Poverty
Columbia University
154 Haven Ave.
New York, NY 10032
(212) 927-8793

Significant Activities: Performs research and analysis on subjects related to poor children under age six and their families. Specific research in areas of maternal and child health, early childhood care and education, and child and family poverty.

Publications: Monographs, newsletters, and *Five Million Children: A Statistical Profile of Our Poorest Young Citizens* (updated annually).

National Council of Jewish Women
53 W. 23rd St.
New York, NY 10010
(212) 645-4048

Significant Activities: Sponsors education, social action, and community services to improve the quality of life for all people. The Center for the Child conducts research on issues and actions necessary to shape policies affecting children.

Publication: *NCJW Journal* (quarterly).

University of Wisconsin
Institute for Research on Poverty
1180 Observatory Dr.
3412 Social Science Bldg.
Madison, WI 53706
(608) 262-6358

Significant Activities: Conducts research on poverty-related topics in a wide variety of disciplines. Promotes support for scholarly research through small grant programs at the institute.

Publications: Newsletter, monographs.

The Urban Institute
2100 M St., NW
Washington, DC 20037
(202) 833-7200

Significant Activities: Conducts research about national social and economic problems, and issues reports and policy recommendations on the basis of research results.

Publications: *Policy and Research Report* (3 times per year), books, reports.

V. STATE ORGANIZATIONS PERFORMING
CHILD ADVOCACY ROLES†

WEST

Alaska
Action for Alaska's Children
2363 Captain Cook Dr.
Anchorage, AK 99517
(907) 248-0834

Arizona
Children's Action Alliance
4001 N. 3rd St., #160
Phoenix, AZ 85012
(602) 266-0707

California
Children Now
1212 Broadway, #530
Oakland, CA 94612
(510) 763-2444

Children's Advocacy Institute
University of San Diego Law School
Alcala Park
San Diego, CA 92110
(619) 260-4806

Coleman Advocates for Children and Youth
2601 Mission St., #708
San Francisco, CA 94110
(415) 641-4363

Hawaii
Hawaii Advocates for Children and Youth
1154 Fort St. Mall, #305
Honolulu, HI 96813
(808) 521-5986

Utah
Utah Children
401 12th Ave., #112
Salt Lake City, UT 84103

---

†We gratefully acknowledge the National Association of Child Advocates for its permission to reproduce its membership list in this appendix.

Washington
The Children's Alliance
172 20th Ave.
Seattle, WA 98122
(206) 324-0340

SOUTH

Florida
Florida Center for Children and Youth
P.O. Box 6646
Tallahassee, FL 32314
(904) 222-7140

Georgia
Georgians for Children
3109 Maple Dr., NE #200
Atlanta, GA 30305
(404) 365-8948

Kentucky
Kentucky Youth Advocates
2034 Frankfort Ave.
Louisville, KY 40206
(502) 895-8167

Mississippi
Human Development Center of Mississippi
P.O. Box 68051
Jackson, MS 39286
(601) 355-7784

North Carolina
North Carolina Child Advocacy Institute
1318 Dale St., #110
Raleigh, NC 27605
(919) 834-6623

Oklahoma
Oklahoma Institute for Child Advocacy
4030 North Lincoln, #208
Oklahoma City, OK 73105
(405) 424-8014

South Carolina
Alliance for South Carolina's Children
P.O. Box 11644

Columbia, SC 29211
(803) 343-5510

Tennessee
Black Children Institute of Tennessee
1031 15th St., South
Nashville, TN 37212
(615) 242-7209

MIDWEST

Illinois
Voices for Illinois Children
208 S. LaSalle St., #1580
Chicago, IL 60604
(312) 456-0600

Kansas
Kansas Action for Children
P.O. Box 463
Topeka, KS 66601
(913) 232-0550

Nebraska
Voices for Children in Nebraska
14643 Grover St.
Omaha, NE 68144
(402) 334-1194

Wisconsin
Wisconsin Council on Children and Families
16 North Carroll St., #420
Madison, WI 53703
(608) 258-4380

EAST

Maryland
Advocates for Children and Youth
300 Cathedral St., Suite 500
Baltimore, MD 21201
(410) 547-9200

New Hampshire
New Hampshire Alliance for Children and Youth
125 Airport Rd.
Concord, NH 03301
(603) 225-0900

New Jersey
Association for Children of New Jersey
35 Halsey St.
Newark, NJ 07102
(201) 643-3876

New York
Citizens Committee for Children
105 East 22nd St.
New York, NY 10010
(212) 673-1800

Statewide Youth Advocacy, Inc.
40 Sheridan Ave.
Albany, NY 12210
(518) 436-8525

Westchester Children's Association
470 Mamaroneck Ave.
White Plains, NY 10605
(914) 946-7676

Pennsylvania
Juvenile Law Center
801 Arch St., 6th Fl.
Philadelphia, PA 19107
(215) 625-0551

Pennsylvania Partnership for Children
931 North Front St., Suite 101
Harrisburg, PA 17102
(717) 236-5680

Philadelphia Citizens for Children and Youth
7 Benjamin Franklin Pkwy.
Philadelphia, PA 19103
(215) 563-5848

Rhode Island
DAWN for Children
P.O. Box 3267-09
Providence, RI 02909
(401) 351-2241

West Virginia
Children's Policy Institute of West Virginia
1205 Quarrier St., LL
Charleston, WV 25301
(304) 344-3970

CONCLUSION: INTEGRATING THEMES ABOUT CHILD POVERTY IN SEARCH OF A SOLUTION

Judith A. Chafel

The authors contributing to this volume have surveyed child poverty from a variety of perspectives: case study methodology, demographics, social policy, child advocacy, and more. Each author has analyzed the problem from his or her chosen angle of inquiry and has shed light on possible solutions.

Judith Musick, in chapter 2, has drawn upon the words of those living in poverty to illuminate what it means to be impoverished. The "stream of experience" that she provides underscores the destructive nature of poverty, as well as the remarkable challenges faced by the poor and, by implication, society in resolving the problem. Whereas Musick employs qualitative evidence, William Scarbrough, in chapter 3, quantifies and analyzes demographic data on the poor population. The picture he provides of the incidence of child poverty enables readers to apprehend the "heterogeneity" of the poor population and to appreciate how misleading stereotypical thinking can be about who comprise "the poor." Confronted with such diversity, the reader must inevitably note the complexity of the dilemma faced by our society. Suzanne Bianchi, in chapter 4, examines the interplay of factors giving rise to poverty, emphasizing the complex, multivariate nature of the problem and advising that translating what is known about causes into action represents "a very large additional step." Joan Vondra, in chapter 5, cogently illustrates the efficacy of empirical research in enlightening our understanding of poverty as a "risk factor" for human development, the limitations of that research in pointing out solutions, and ways in which the existing body of empirical knowledge can be transformed into public policy. In the following chapter 6, Elsie Moore demonstrates that research has both informed and misinformed us about ways in which the child of poverty has been conceived and how intervention should be envisioned. Once again, the reader is left with clear messages about the complexity of the problem and the danger of oversimplifying solutions. Sandra Hofferth, in chapter 7, analyzes the dynamics of the successful passage of legislation affecting children and families in poverty in the 101st Congress. The discussion provides a narrative account of domestic agenda-setting and the ways it can be influenced. Harold Watts, in chapter 8, uses the concept of "human capital" to explain the connection between child development and the nation's economic well-being. He establishes the need for a social policy to alleviate the deficits of poverty and suggests how it might be funded. In chapter 9, Kevin Condit and I consider the role of government and philanthropy in assisting the impoverished, offering readers a further vision of what can be done to effect change.

In this final chapter of the volume, I invite the reader's further reflection about the problem of child poverty and possible ways to alleviate it. My aims are to identify themes that echo through the volume, to synthesize these themes, and to provide the reader with a concluding statement. The analyses and conclusions contained here are mine, and the authors cited should not be held accountable for my interpretations of their work.

Four broad themes emerge from the essays and blend the volume into a cohesive whole. They are the following:

1. The poor face remarkable challenges;
2. Poverty is a diverse, complex phenomenon;
3. Empirical inquiry is needed to illuminate the problem and to suggest viable solutions; and
4. Challenges exist for public policy.

The following discussion is organized around these broad constructs. Within each construct, more specific themes, issues, and questions emerge. While no attempt is made to summarize the essays, I do draw upon them liberally. Overall, the question is raised: "Where do we go from here?"

THE POOR FACE REMARKABLE CHALLENGES

The conception that the poor face remarkable challenges may seem "axiomatic" to some, whereas others may regard it as merely an "illusion." In other words, it is not without controversy. For that very reason, it is an extremely important conception to contemplate.

In the absence of broad societal consensus about its veracity, meaningful change for children and families in poverty is unlikely.

Three of the essays in the volume emphasize the theme. The "stream of experience" offered by Judith Musick (chapter 2) demonstrates unequivocally the devastating psychological consequences of poverty, as evidenced by the words of those who either live or are affected by it. The chapter forcefully conveys the destructive character of economically deprived environments from the perspective of the poor themselves.

Poverty, as Joan Vondra (chapter 5) points out, increases the likelihood of an array of chronic and acute stressors with negative impacts on family well-being: economic hardship and deprivation, inadequate housing and residence in an unsafe environment, the absence of a social network of supports, a culture of violence, and more. Dynamics such as these render the child of poverty susceptible to injury and harm.

Acute or chronic poverty, as Elsie Moore (chapter 6) notes, serves as a predictable risk factor for child development. Myriad negative outcomes emanate from it: lowered school achievement, adolescent childbearing, poor nutrition, alcohol and drug abuse, and HIV infection. As Moore explains, certain societal conceptions have served as negative filters through which the child of poverty historically has been viewed. The impoverished child has been variously perceived as "culturally deprived," "socially disadvantaged," "vulnerable," and "at risk." The terms exemplify labels that denote "deficient" development. While representing an effect of impoverishment, they may act as another cause of it. If school achievement is affected by a teacher's expectations of failure for a child, negative labels such as these may promote a "self-fulfilling prophecy."

Musick, Vondra, and Moore have each provided evidence in support of the assertion that poverty is a pernicious phenomenon affecting millions of children in the United States today. Confronted by the ravages of poverty, the impoverished indeed face remarkable challenges. Judith Musick has suggested that the poor "are called on to do and be far more than their middle-class counterparts, with fewer resources to support them in this role, and many more burdens to contend with." As she explains, parents who reside in high-risk environments "must be better than good." Merely being good is not "good enough." While performing their childrearing role, the parent of poverty must continuously "mediate," "counteract," "shield," and "shelter" the child. This conception represents a novel way of viewing the impoverished, one that runs counter to prevailing societal images in which the poor are viewed as being "undeserving" or "not good enough."

Musick is not the only author in this volume to reflect the idea that parents in poverty must be "better than good." Citing Pelton (1978), Vondra (chapter 5) notes that a middle-class parent may be able to do what a parent in poverty cannot do without jeopardizing a child's well-being. For example, carelessness with money on the part of the former may bear no serious consequence for the child, whereas such behavior on the part of the latter may deprive the child of poverty of basic necessities. Similarly, if child maltreatment arises from severe need due to a complicated combination of factors (whether economic, situational, social, or personal in nature), then, by implication, parents in poverty need to be "better than good" to overcome their destitution. In addition, whereas the middle-class parent benefits from numerous buffers that promote healthy child development (e.g., high-quality health and child care), the parent living in poverty, as both Vondra and Musick suggest, is undermined by the nonexistence or inferior value of these very services, when they are more urgently needed. A middle-class environment with numerous social and economic supports can minimize the occurrence of impaired child development; an economically deprived setting, on the other hand, can intensify it. Bereft of valuable resources for parenting and sabotaged continuously by a hostile environment, parents in poverty must be exceptionally competent if they are to achieve "success" in their childrearing role.

Few would dispute that large segments of American society judge the impoverished negatively. Capitalizing on the "stigma of poverty," the Reagan administration mobilized a broad coalition of Americans with negative perceptions about the impoverished and substantially reduced governmental support for the poor (Waxman 1983). Reagan's message to the American people was not difficult to grasp. Lekachman deduced, "To the poor, the injunction [was] to get off your butts and start working like the rest of us" (Lekachman 1982: 102, cited in Waxman 1983: 130; also cited by Chafel 1990: 32). An underlying assumption behind such a statement is that the impoverished are to blame for the circumstances in which they find themselves and, as a result, are in need of reform. According to this view, unless the poor were seriously inadequate, why would they situate themselves outside mainstream American society (Keniston 1977, cited in Chafel 1990)? This position contrasts sharply with the one advanced here of having to be "better than good" to survive. The Clinton administration has created a more promising outlook for the poor in our society by emphasizing the economic empowerment of all. Yet, negative stereotypes about the poor still widely persist.

The image of the "undeserving poor" is an enduring theme in American culture. That the impoverished must assume personal responsibility for their condition has its origins in the Protestant ethic and the spirit of capitalism. Concerning these origins, Max Weber noted that:

> In conformity with the Old Testament and in analogy to the ethical valuation of good works, asceticism looked upon the pursuit of wealth as an end in itself as highly reprehensible; but the attainment of it as a fruit of labor in a calling was a sign of God's blessing. And even more important: the religious valuation of restless, continuous, systematic work in a worldly calling, as the highest means to asceticism, and at the same time the surest and most evident proof of rebirth and genuine faith. (Weber 1958, cited by Blank 1989: 158–59)

As Blank (1989) has pointed out, few churches in American society today explicitly speak such a message. Yet, the image of the undeserving poor and the belief that the impoverished are "just not trying hard enough" lingers on (Blank 1989: 159).

Society's response to the dilemma of poverty is influenced by the images its members hold of the impoverished and their condition. These images act as constraints on the political process and shape policy formation (Blank 1989; Chafel 1990). Societal images provide not only a justification for targeting programs to certain groups but also a rationale for designing programs in certain ways. If the impoverished are viewed generally as being "undeserving," then the assumption is that they have a responsibility to work, which is not being met. Therefore, programs are designed for the "deserving" poor, those members of society who either are physically unable to work (e.g., the disabled) or are morally exempted from it (e.g., mothers of very young children) (Blank 1989). Others are excluded from assistance because they are judged to be unworthy of it.

As mentioned earlier, the conception of having to be "better than good" to survive represents an alternative way of viewing the impoverished in our society. Public policy constructed around this reality would provide basic economic support and a broad array of social services to assist the impoverished in overcoming the virulent, destructive consequences of their life circumstances. An underlying assumption of this view is that *every* individual possesses certain basic rights to the necessities of life, and that society has an obligation to render these needs attainable when they are being threatened.

Society's obligation to the impoverished would end, if and when members of this group were able to provide for themselves. To be sure, an important part of society's responsibility to the impoverished would be fostering self-reliance. The individual's obligation, in turn, would be to accept responsibility for meeting that challenge. This is similar to the social-contract approach described by Blank (1989).

POVERTY IS A DIVERSE, COMPLEX PHENOMENON

Reference is frequently made to *the poor* in our society. Although the term *the poor* is commonly used to denote a single population, no such cohesiveness exists among those living in poverty in the United States today (Blank 1989). In reality, a broad spectrum of society is represented among the poverty population; and a complex interplay of factors is responsible for their impoverishment. Judith Musick (chapter 2), William Scarbrough (chapter 3), Suzanne Bianchi (chapter 4), and Elsie Moore (chapter 6) all address the theme that poverty is a diverse, complex phenomenon. Moreover, they provide support for the notion that *many of the distinct groups comprising the impoverished are poor through no fault of their own.*

The term *the poor* should not be considered anything more than an aggregate term for a disparate collection of groups comprising the poverty population (Blank 1989). Scarbrough's essay lends credence to this point. Poverty is distributed across all racial and ethnic groups. According to his analyses, 14.3 million children under 18 years of age were poor in 1991. Of the number living in poverty, 39 percent were white, 34 percent were African-American, 23 percent were Latino, and 4 percent belonged to other racial and ethnic groups. Poverty rates (the proportion of poor children) are disproportionately higher for minorities: 46 percent for African-Americans; 40 percent for Latinos; and 32 percent among Native American, Asian-American and other cultural groups, as compared with 12 percent for whites. Demographic diversity among *the poor* is not limited to racial and ethnic composition. Geographically, poverty among children is found in virtually every region of the country: in the central cities, rural areas, and suburbs. In addition, poverty occurs among both one- and two-parent families, and among working parents. Scarbrough's analysis disputes the accuracy of commonly held stereotypes: e.g., that all of the impoverished are members of minority groups, that all of them do not work, and that they all reside in urban areas.

Similarly, Musick's psychological ethnography draws on data from a broad representation of poor families. These families are characterized by their diversity with respect to geographic locale, race and ethnicity, and family structure. They reside in small towns, isolated rural communities, and large cities; they are African-American, white, and Hispanic; and they reside in single and two-parent families, and extended family households. In Musick's words, "Poverty takes many forms, affecting different groups in different ways."

Consistent with Scarbrough's depiction of the demographic diversity of the child poverty population is Bianchi's analysis of the complex, multivariate nature of the causes of child poverty. As she notes, "Poor macroeconomic performance continues to move more children into poverty, but good macroeconomic performance seems less able to do the opposite." Growing inequality of earnings, government income transfers and taxation, and family formation and dissolution are all key factors giving rise to poverty.

Why are children poor? Are their parents "deficient" or "lacking in self-discipline"? Are they responsible for their children's poverty? Bianchi's analysis suggests otherwise for some segments of the poverty population. An important trend in our society is the declining ability of fathers in two-parent households to earn sufficient income to keep their families out of poverty. They are not responsible for their impoverished condition; rather, the declining value of their wages is to blame. For other segments of society, the answer to the question posed at the beginning of this paragraph is not so clear. As Bianchi points out, another significant poverty-enhancing variable has been the disappearance of paternal income from a growing proportion of families with children. The result has been that children are left in female-headed families without adequate support. Complicating the picture, as she explains it, is that female-headed families in poverty increasingly comprise young, never-married women with children, who are less likely to receive support from absent fathers. In addition, they are not competitive in a job market that has increasingly become less likely to employ "the unskilled."

The issue then arises as to whether the growth in mother-only families is a cause or effect of poverty. The answer has been unavoidably "politicized." The politically conservative view would see the individual as "lacking," while the politically liberal view would view the system as being "deficient." As Bianchi explains, the former would lay the blame for poverty on marital breakup and out-of-wedlock childbearing resulting from a welfare system that spawns individual dependency and a lack of paternal responsibility for children. The latter would argue that poor macroeconomic conditions have thwarted the ability of fathers to provide for a family and, as a result, have encouraged either marital disruption or out-of-wedlock childbearing. Overall, Bianchi concludes that "although there may be a causal relationship between welfare and dependency, no research to date convincingly shows that effect to be large."

The issue of race and ethnicity further complicates and politicizes the consideration of causes. Scarbrough has pointed out that children of color are more likely to experience poverty and to remain in poverty longer than white children. Furthermore, children of color constitute a larger proportion of the child poverty population than previously. In 1960, 26 percent of the poor child population were children of color; in 1991, they comprised more than 61 percent of poor children. Moore has similarly emphasized the association of race and ethnicity with poverty.

What is responsible for the disproportionate representation of African-Americans, American Indians, and Mexican-Americans among the ranks of the poor in our society? One explanation, cited by Moore, has been offered by Ogbu (1982). Involuntarily and immutably incorporated into a "castelike minority group," ethnic minorities like those just mentioned experience a "job ceiling" that selectively relegates them to an inferior position in society, while members of the dominant group are allowed to compete more easily for status and power. Following Ogbu's conceptualization, the responsibility for poverty would rest with "the system," not with the individual; and the rise of female-headed families would be assumed to be an effect, not a cause, of poverty. Existing structural barriers in society have undermined the ability of some ethnic minorities to obtain employment and to provide for a family.

Whether one believes that the individual or the system (namely, society) is responsible for poverty has profound implications for how solutions to the problem are conceived. If the cause of poverty rests with the individual, then the solution lies with the individual. On the other hand, if society is the cause, then society bears responsibility for doing something about the problem. According to Bianchi, public opinion increasingly has been shifting toward a solution that rests with the individual. She notes that escalating welfare caseloads, current economic trends, and the prevailing political climate have all increased public skepticism of the "deserving poor." On the other hand, as Sandra Hofferth suggests in chapter 7, society increasingly has come to accept responsibility for alleviating the problem of poverty, as state governments and the business community alike, concerned about economic productivity and educational achievement, support public and private investment in programs for the disadvantaged.

Statistical evidence corroborates the view that the majority of families with children in poverty are impoverished through no fault of their own. Most are not recipients of welfare; and, many are two-parent families who comprise the "working poor" (Bane and Ellwood 1989). Based on calculations derived from the 1988 Current Population Survey, Bane and Ellwood (1989) pointed out that nearly 45 percent of two-parent families in poverty have a full-time worker year-round; and, more than 50 percent with two healthy parents have at least one worker. These figures verify that work does not always ensure that families with children will not be poor; they belie the commonly held stereotype that poverty emanates from individual inadequacy.

Other findings support this conclusion. According to data compiled from the 1991 Current Population Survey and reported by Lamison-White (1992), approximately 45.4 percent of female-headed families in poverty with children worked in 1990. Of these, 8.2 percent worked full-time, year-round. The proportion of working non-poor female-headed families with children was 69.4 percent. Of these, 39.8 percent worked full-time, year-round. Among the two groups (poor and nonpoor), the primary reason given for not working was family responsibility, 64.1 percent and 69.5 percent, respectively. These data corroborate the view that multiple reasons exist as to why some families with children live in poverty; they support the notion that individual inadequacy cannot always be assumed to be the only cause.

If the causes of child poverty are multivariate and complex, then accompanying solutions must reflect this fact (Blank 1989). Neither individual inadequacy nor societal inequity completely explains why child poverty exists. Therefore, polar extremes should be avoided in conceptualizing a solution to the problem of poverty. Ongoing policy debate should address two interrelated questions: What is the individual's responsibility to society? And, conversely, what is society's responsibility to the individual? Answers may differ, depending upon why a particular group in poverty is poor. By considering both individual as well as societal responsibility for the problem, it should be possible to achieve a consensus on solutions among both the politically conservative and the politically liberal sectors of our soci-

of our society.[1] The dichotomous nature of much current thinking and discourse has resulted in a lack of agreement among these groups about how to alleviate poverty. Unanimity and compromise are needed to effect change.

EMPIRICAL INQUIRY IS NEEDED TO ILLUMINATE THE PROBLEM OF CHILD POVERTY

Although this volume's authors have drawn upon the best available research knowledge, that knowledge both illuminates and constrains the reader's understanding. Inasmuch as the knowledge represents the "cutting edge" of what is known about child poverty, it enlightens; yet, at the same time, various chapter authors have noted the limitations of the research cited for informing and/or influencing public policy.

The large proportion of children living in poverty underscores the urgency of the need to remediate their dilemma. If research is to contribute optimally to this endeavor, then more policy-relevant empirical inquiry is indicated. Questions must be framed, methodological paradigms utilized, and research audiences addressed in ways that both bridge the gap between the generation and application of knowledge and that have direct implications for improving the lives of children and families in poverty. Joan Vondra (chapter 5), Elsie Moore (chapter 6), and Kevin Condit and I (chapter 9) all specify directions for such research.

Vondra notes with respect to child maltreatment that the most important unresolved questions relate to definitions, extensiveness of services, and cost-effectiveness. Because a conception of what comprises child maltreatment varies across disciplines, researchers need to pursue inquiry that bridges these domains. One way of doing so is methodological in nature, that is, through the careful selection and description of subject samples. Systematic sampling of subjects representing specific configurations of background, context, or functioning may result in data with direct implications for modifying the system of service delivery. Further empirical inquiry is also needed, as Vondra notes, to establish the scope of intervention, that is, through careful sampling of "types" of troubled families and "types" of services to ascertain the most effective combination of resources. Finally, society has increasingly come to demand evidence of savings accrued (i.e., cost-effectiveness) as a result of expenditures made for human services. Accordingly, Vondra indicates that research must document longitudinal differences in quality of functioning and/or differential use of services among comparison groups. Future funding by government is dependent upon empirical confirmation of program effectiveness.

Condit and I point out that there is a dearth of existing empirical research on two areas of profound importance to the alleviation of child poverty: the pursuit of advocacy and the conduct of philanthropy. We contend that research questions should be framed to address a variety of topics, ranging from the styles, strategies, and methods of advocacy shown to be effective in influencing social policy to the resulting benefits for society of involving ordinary citizens in voluntary action for the "public good." Research should investigate political activism by the third sector, "innovation and risk-taking," and the extent to which the state constrains philanthropic efforts to shape policy (Eisenberg 1991: 37; Wolch 1990). With knowledge emanating from such inquiry, as Condit and I note, advocates would be better prepared to focus their efforts on the existing system to improve conditions for children in poverty.

Moore also suggests directions for future research. She points out that the way the child of poverty has been conceived historically has influenced the construction of social policy. A conception of *innate* deficiency lessens, if not negates, the significance of environmental intervention. Conversely, if deficits are assumed to be environmentally induced, then environmental intervention is seen to ameliorate them. Moore's historical examination leads to the inference that further process-oriented research is needed to delineate the complex cause-and-effect relations that exist between variables associated with poverty and aspects of developmental functioning. Such knowledge is required to progress beyond what we currently "know" in order to design better intervention strategies for children in poverty.

Citing Baratz and Baratz (1970), Moore notes that research is also needed to illuminate ethnic group behavior. Empirical evidence of this sort would enable policymakers and others to allow for cultural differences in designing programs to help minority children in poverty preserve their individual identity and heritage, while assimilating into the mainstream. Similarly, Ogbu's (1982) conceptualization of a "castelike minority status" among blacks that operates to effect a "job ceiling" needs to be clarified by empirical research. Based on Moore's analysis, one could pose the question: How do existing social structural barriers in society affect developmental outcomes for minority children in poverty and what are the social policy implications emanating from such research?

Another promising area of further research pertains to the concept of resiliency and child poverty. As Moore points out and as Garmezy (1991) has suggested, research should search for those protective factors that support healthy development in children who are at risk of negative outcomes. Intervention strategies might subsequently be designed to take account of these protective factors. Through intervention, these factors might be provided to children in poverty lacking such resiliency.

Ethnography is ideally suited to the investigation of many research questions pertaining to child poverty. As a methodological paradigm, it seeks to comprehend "multiple constructions of reality" from the perspectives of those studied in their natural surroundings (McMillan and Schumacher 1989). As a result, ethnography is capable of illuminating the inner dynamics of life experience in ways often imperceptible to an "outsider" (Bogdan and Biklen 1992; McMillan and Schumacher 1989). What do children and families in poverty experience, and how do they interpret their experiences? How do they interpret events in their daily lives? Ethnography can address questions such as these and convey "the reality" of what it is like to be impoverished. The rich description emanating from ethnographic inquiry into childhood poverty can profoundly influence societal images, and thus public policy, regarding the poor.

In addition, as Musick has asserted, qualitative data can clarify underlying processes that mediate and thereby explain developmental outcomes. Such data, I submit, would increase understanding of the lived experiences of those in poverty and of how poverty affects the many dimensions of human functioning. With the knowledge resulting from such study, better interventions could be designed for children and families in poverty.

Policy-relevant "applied" research has traditionally been assigned a low status by academicians, a point noted by Vondra. By contrast, Bronfenbrenner (1974: 4) has asserted that issues of social policy may serve as "points of departure for the identification of significant theoretical and scientific questions." In other words, policy-relevant research is as valuable and important to the development of the disciplines as other more "basic" research and should be pursued. In the past, the low status given applied research has discouraged some researchers from engaging in it. Inducement by government (e.g., funding in the form of traineeships; "seed money" to pursue specific research questions, and so on) is needed to encourage policy-relevant research on child poverty. Incentives should be constructed to promote the development of a community of scholars distinguished by its diversity, both with respect to disciplines and the ethnicity of its members. During the 1960s when antipoverty policy was in vogue, research on child poverty was fashionable; but not today. Incentives are thus needed to stimulate research on a broad range of topics related to child poverty, to reflect minority perspectives, to foster cross-disciplinary efforts, and to generate policy-relevant empirical inquiry on child poverty in disciplines where recent studies are scarce.

The pursuit of policy-relevant research requires collaboration between researchers, policymakers, and practitioners. I agree with Vondra that cooperation is needed to conceptualize problems; to select and utilize methodological paradigms; to disseminate applied research findings; to establish their relevance for public policy; and to formulate policies that complement theoretical and empirical strides. Vondra envisions the need for a central coordinating structure, an "umbrella agency," to promote collaboration on child maltreatment. If such a structure is to evolve, governmental support will be required.

Empirical investigations of child poverty should be carefully constructed to increase the likelihood that resultant findings will provide information useful to policymakers. Research has identified several characteristics that promote the use of scientific findings in the policy formation process: (1) quality; (2) conformity to the user's ideas, position, and values; (3) explicit recommendations or direct implications pertaining to a course of action; and (4) the presentation of a challenge to existing arrangements or assumptions, or an implied need for substantial revision of organization, philosophy, or services (Weiss and Bucuvalas 1980). The usefulness of a study depends on the extent to which its recommendations mirror those economic, political, and social realities that influence decision making by government (Bergen 1987, cited by Gaskell 1988). Policymakers reportedly experience difficulty in translating the implications of research "for the needs at hand" (Brim and Dustan 1983: 85). Thus, brevity and clarity of presentation of findings are also essential (Brim and Dustan 1983; Coleman 1975; Weiss 1977).

Researchers can increase the likelihood of having their findings utilized by ascertaining when a "policy window" opens. Chapter 9's appendix describes a variety of congressional committees and agencies of the executive branch of the federal government where researchers interested in child poverty might direct their findings.

Gaskell (1988: 415) has stated that "policy researchers should see themselves as political actors and work to have their research reflected in political debates."

CHALLENGES EXIST FOR PUBLIC POLICY

Each chapter author has been asked to consider challenges for public policy from the unique perspective of his or her special topic. This final section synthesizes these inferences. A brief outline of challenges highlighted by the authors is provided first, to emphasize the breadth and complexity of potential solutions to the problem of poverty.

Among the challenges identified by the authors are the following: creating better opportunities (both social and economic) for helping the impoverished to participate in the mainstream of American life; establishing a national network of comprehensive and intensive community-based family support programs; designing and implementing a variety of interventions (e.g., Head Start, adolescent pregnancy prevention and parenting programs, job training); and constructing institutionalized structures for promoting the collaboration of practitioners, researchers, and policymakers in conceptualizing solutions to the problem of poverty. Other challenges for public policy involve reexamining the official (federal) definition of poverty; implementing welfare reform; converting appropriations-limited programs to entitlement programs; enacting a system of universal health care; using the tax system to provide assistance to the poor (e.g., the Child and Dependent Care Tax Credit, the Dependent Care Credit, the Social Security Trust Fund); assuring better child support enforcement; creating a minimum child support guarantee; initiating school reform; and designing a focal point in government to coordinate federal policy for children. Still others pertain to the provision of easily accessible and affordable high-quality child care, a prerequisite if families in poverty are to become economically self-reliant.

Harold Watts' proposal (in chapter 8) to set aside a portion of the Social Security Trust Fund to finance social policy for children and families in poverty deserves special emphasis. Perceiving human capital as "the biggest deficit" of child poverty, he advances the idea that a Human Capital Account be created from the surplus as a source of money to fund initiatives to support child and family development among the impoverished. Inasmuch as the Social Security Trust Fund is endangered by a neglect of human capital investment, as Watts explains, the former is a logical source of money for sustaining the latter.

Overall, as Watts suggests, social policy designed to alleviate child poverty should combine income support with direct services to the poor. He asserts that both of these vehicles are necessary, while neither alone may be sufficient to support family development. What particular combination of financial assistance by government should be offered to provide an optimal "balance" between the two remains unclear.

Throughout the volume, numerous other issues are raised that warrant further study. For example, Scarbrough (chapter 3) points out the failure of the official (federal) definition of poverty to identify all people who are "poor" and to link those in need with government programs. Bianchi (chapter 4) refers to the gender inequality in our society that affects wage-earning capacity and responsibility for rearing of children. Vondra (chapter 5) mentions a custom of ethnic bias in the child welfare system that "victimizes" disadvantaged minority children and their families. In addition, she speaks of the dilemma that exists (given scarce resources) between adopting a policy strategy of prevention versus intervention with respect to child maltreatment. Still another issue relates to the inadequate coordination of research, policy, and practice, which hinders the pursuit of systematic inquiry on topics of significance to child maltreatment. The absence of structures for promoting collaboration impedes policy-relevant advances.

As noted earlier, Moore (chapter 6) alludes to the "castelike minority status" of ethnic minorities (blacks, Native Americans, Mexican-Americans) that relegates them to a position of inferiority. Racism and ethnocentrism are institutionalized in the very structures of society. The interpretation is supported by Scarbrough's demographic analysis indicating that poverty rates for minority children are three to four times higher than those for white children.

Furthermore, as Moore's analysis suggests, and as pointed out here earlier, the way in which the child of poverty has been envisioned (i.e., an underlying assumption of deficiency) may represent both a cause and an effect of poverty. The "at-risk" perspective, widely employed in current discourse, may not serve the impoverished well; that is, it conceals poor children's unique developmental status and attenuates, if not negates, a policy designed specifically for them. Moore leaves the reader with a haunting question about whether "the deficient child perspective on poor children is a social construction designed to perpetuate the existing economic stratification and social inequalities."

Scarbrough (chapter 3) asserts that "commonly held stereotypes" persist about children and families living in poverty in the United States today. As noted earlier here, most poor people are not recipients of welfare; and many are two-parent families who comprise the "working poor" (Bane and Ellwood 1989). Yet, facts such as these, as Scarbrough points out, rarely are publicized, thereby perpetuating negative societal images about the poor.

Hofferth's (chapter 7) analysis of legislation in the 101st Congress highlights unresolved issues pertaining to implementation of legislation: elevating the quality of early childhood services; establishing funding priorities for Head Start (that is, broadening enrollment versus improvements in program quality); advancing coordination of an intricate array of federal programs for the care and education of children; and, finally, more fully supporting family leave.

Numerous other societal barriers exist to obstruct the achievement of a viable social policy for children and families in poverty. First, a pervasive public attitude endures that the task is too "formidable"; that "throwing money at problems" (e.g., the War on Poverty implemented during the sixties) has not worked in the past; and that government has become too big and unwieldy to deal effectively with human problems. Coupled with this perspective is the commonly held conception that the impoverished are "undeserving" of support. As Bianchi noted in chapter 4, this belief has been fueled by a number of factors (e.g., growing income inequality, diminishing wage-earning capacity, increasing taxation on wages), which have negatively influenced public generosity to the impoverished. Second, as Musick (chapter 2), Moore (chapter 6), and Condit and I (chapter 9) all have indicated, change is limited by existing societal institutions (e.g., the schools, the philanthropic community) that reflect prevailing values. Profoundly conservative in nature, these institutions are committed to sustaining the status quo. Third, the current economic outlook (as reflected by the limited growth rate of the economy and the budget deficit) constrains the amount of public funding available to ameliorate the problem. Watts has persuasively argued in chapter 8 that the human capital deficit has far more serious implications for societal well-being than the federal budget shortfall and therefore merits first priority.

Perhaps, the most significant unresolved issue with respect to child poverty concerns how a broad national consensus might be constructed on behalf of the poor. As Hofferth (chapter 7) notes, the impoverished in our society have captured public interest, owing to the present outlay of public assistance they require, as well as the future cost to society that will be incurred if their offspring are not incorporated into the mainstream. This statement suggests that concern about national self-interest has taken precedence over altruism. How likely is it that, in the words of Kingdon (1984), a "window of opportunity" will soon open for the poor population? The probability of this occurring depends to a large extent on whether coalitions can be made to coalesce on their behalf. Issue networks can be formed and national alliances created, if altruistic motives for advocacy (that is, the ideal of social justice) are joined with those inspired by national self-interest (that is, the escalating apprehension that neglecting children's issues may be detrimental to societal well-being). Concerned about child and family development, professionals devoted to children's issues can align with representatives of state government and the business community, who are becoming increasingly worried about educational achievement and economic productivity. As Hofferth's analysis of legislation in the 101st Congress has illustrated, state government concern about poverty laid a foundation both for welfare reform legislation and, then, child care.

Ways can be found to challenge the prevailing societal image of the poor as being "undeserving" of assistance. As private citizens, each of us has the power to vote; to write to our elected representatives; to publish editorials. As practitioners, educators, health care workers, pediatricians, psychologists, public policy analysts, and social workers, we can generate change through our professional associations: by speaking out about the problem of poverty, developing position statements, and establishing connections with other groups. As Hofferth demonstrates, smaller groups can join with larger ones to create local, state, and national alliances; legislative developments can be monitored; and education campaigns can be mounted, to enumerate but a few of many strategies. Influencing the legislative agenda at all levels of government, as Condit and I (chapter 9) explain, requires knowledge of advocacy strategies and how to implement them. In the past, professionals concerned with children's issues have not, on the whole, envisioned their role as encompassing advocacy, although they have increasingly come to do so. A rationale for advocacy, as Condit and I assert, emanates from a number of considerations, including: the sizable proportion of children living in poverty; the risk factors for such children; the absence of a comprehensive social policy to address the problem; and the political vulnerability of the poor.

This book has analyzed the complex nature of child poverty in the United States today. A central focus has been the interface of that problem with public policy. Legislation, as Kingdon (1984) has argued, ensues when problems, policies, and politics converge. If a "window of opportunity" is to open for the impoverished in our society, then each citizen must work within the political process to bring it about. Political streams must be created to merge the problems of the poor with viable solutions to alleviate their plight. As Hofferth put it, "The 101st Congress helped to illuminate an agenda for children in poverty," but as she also pointed out, it "remains unexecuted."

Notes

I would like to express my appreciation to Jesse Goodman and Marion McNairy for their helpful comments during preparation of this chapter.

1. Marion McNairy helped me clarify this idea.

References

Bane, M. J., and D. Ellwood. 1989. "One Fifth of the Nation's Children: Why Are They Poor?" Science 245 (Sept. 8): 1047–53.

Baratz, S., and J. Baratz. 1970. "Early Childhood Intervention: The Social Science Base of Institutional Racism." Harvard Educational Review 40: 29–50.

Bergen, J. 1987. "Government Sponsored Private School Studies in Alberta and Ontario." Alberta Journal of Educational Research 33(4): 292–306.

Blank, R. 1989. "Poverty and Policy: The Many Faces of the Poor." In Prophetic Visions and Economic Realities, edited by C. R. Strain. Grand Rapids, Mich.: Eerdman's Publishing Co.

Bogdan, R., and S. Biklen. 1992. Qualitative Research for Education. Boston: Allyn & Bacon.

Brim, O., and J. Dustan. 1983. "Translating Research into Policy for Children." American Psychologist 38(1): 85–90.

Bronfenbrenner, U. 1974. "Developmental Research, Public Policy, and the Ecology of Childhood." Child Development 45: 1–5.

Chafel, J. 1990. "Children in Poverty: Policy Perspectives on a National Crisis." Young Children 45(5): 31–37.

Coleman, J. 1975. "Problems of Conceptualization and Measurement in Studying Policy Impacts." In Public Policy Evaluation, edited by K. Dolbeare. Vol. 11 of Sage Yearbooks in Politics and Public Policy. Beverly Hills, Calif.: Sage Publications.

Eisenberg, P. 1991. "Why We Know So Little about Philanthropy." Chronicle of Philanthropy 4(5, Dec. 17): 37–38.

Garmezy, N. 1991. "Resiliency and Vulnerability to Adverse Developmental Outcomes Associated with Poverty." American Behavioral Scientist 34(4): 416–30.

Gaskell, J. 1988. "Policy Research and Politics." Alberta Journal of Educational Research 34(4): 403–17.

Keniston, K. 1977. All Our Children: The American Family under Pressure. New York: Harcourt Brace Jovanovich.

Kingdon, J. 1984. Agendas, Alternatives, and Public Policies. Glenview, Ill.: Scott, Foresman & Co.

Lamison-White, L. 1992. Income, Poverty, and Wealth in the United States: A Chart Book. U.S. Bureau of the Census, Current Population Reports, ser. P-60, no. 179. Washington, D.C.: U.S. Government Printing Office.

Lekachman, R. 1982. Greed is Not Enough: Reaganomics. New York: Pantheon Books.

McMillan, J., and S. Schumacher. 1989. Research in Education. Glenview, Ill.: Scott, Foresman & Co.

O'Connell, B. 1978. "From Service to Advocacy to Empowerment." Social Casework 59(4): 195–202.

Ogbu, J. 1982. "Societal Forces as a Context of Ghetto Children's School Failure." In The Language of Children Reared in Poverty, edited by L. Feagans and D. Farran. New York: Academic Press.

Pelton, L. 1978. "Child Abuse and Neglect: The Myth of Classlessness." American Journal of Orthopsychiatry 48: 608–17.

Waxman, C. 1983. The Stigma of Poverty: A Critique of Poverty Theories and Policies. New York: Pergamon Press.

Weber, M. 1958. The Protestant Ethic and the Spirit of Capitalism. New York: Charles Scribner's Sons.

Weiss, C. 1977. Using Social Research in Public Policy-Making. Lexington, Mass.: D. C. Heath.

Weiss, C., and M. Bucuvalas. 1980. "Truth Tests and Utility Tests: Decision-Maker's Frames of Reference for Social Science Research." American Sociological Review 45: 302–13.

Wolch, J. 1990. The Shadow State: Government and Voluntary Sector in Transition. New York: Foundation Center.

ABOUT THE EDITOR

Judith A. Chafel is associate professor in the School of Education at Indiana University, Bloomington, and adjunct associate professor at the Center on Philanthropy. Her publications focus on young children's play and social cognition, child and family policy, and child poverty. In 1989, she was awarded a Congressional Science Fellowship by the Society for Research in Child Development. As a Congressional Fellow, she spent a year working in the U.S. House of Representatives. In that capacity, she studied and wrote about child poverty and acquired a firsthand acquaintance with the policymaking process. In 1990, she received two grants from Indiana University to support her work on child poverty: one, to establish a Multidisciplinary Forum for the Study of Poverty and Adolescent Parenting, and another from the Center on Philanthropy to develop a doctoral seminar on child poverty.

ABOUT THE CONTRIBUTORS

Suzanne M. Bianchi is a demographer in the Housing and Household Economic Division of the U.S. Bureau of the Census. Her current research focuses on the relative economic well-being of children and their absent fathers in the year following divorce. Her publications on children's well-being include a Census Bureau report, "Family Disruption and Economic Hardship: The Short-Run Picture for Children" (with Edith McArthur); "America's Children: Mixed Prospects," *Population Bulletin*, vol. 45, no. 1; and "Children's Contact with Absent Parents," *Journal of Marriage and the Family*, vol. 50, no. 3 (with Judith Seltzer). She is also author of two books: *Household Composition and Racial Inequality* and *American Women in Transition* (with Daphne Spain).

Kevin Condit is a doctoral student at Indiana University, Bloomington, in the School of Public and Environmental Affairs. He has previously served as a professor of business, a departmental administrator, a health systems analyst, and an intern for state and local governments. At Indiana University, he has worked with the Multidisciplinary Forum for the Study of Poverty and Adolescent Parenting, a group devoted to analyzing problems of the poor. His interests include American social welfare issues, especially those pertaining to family policy.

Sandra L. Hofferth is senior research associate in the Population Studies Center at the Urban Institute in Washington, D.C. Dr. Hofferth has been engaged in research on children, youth, and family issues for 16 years. She has testified on the Hill six times. In 1987 and 1988 she testified on the 1990 child care legislation which is the focus of her chapter. Recent publications include the *National Child Care Survey, 1990; A Profile of Child Care Settings: Early Education and Care in 1990;* and *Learning Readiness: Promising Strategies.*

Elsie G. J. Moore is associate professor in the Division of Psychology in Education, College of Education, at Arizona State University.

Her research interests include ethnic group and socioeconomic status effects on children's cognitive test performance and specific skill development; psychological tests and test policy; and school factors related to children's achievement and educational attainment. In 1986, she co-authored with R. Darrell Bock a book titled *Advantage and Disadvantage: A Profile of American Youth.*

Judith S. Musick was the first director of the Ounce of Prevention Fund, and currently serves as the vice chair of its board. She is a visiting faculty member at the Erikson Institute for Advanced Study in Child Development. She has spent the last fifteen years developing and studying prevention and intervention programs for at-risk children, youth, and parents. She was the recipient of a multi-year grant from the Rockefeller Foundation to synthesize and write about her work with adolescent mothers. Dr. Musick is the author of *Young, Poor and Pregnant: The Psychology of Adolescent Motherhood* (1993); and the forthcoming *Infant Development: From Theory to Practice, Second Edition.*

William H. Scarbrough is senior associate at CSR, Incorporated, a private social science research firm located in Washington, D.C. He is responsible for designing, conducting, and supervising large-scale evaluations of federal programs dealing with the growth and development of low-income children and their families living in the United States. He has studied and published in the areas of income transfer policy, poverty measurement, and early childhood development. Prior to joining CSR, he served in a variety of capacities, including associate director for research at the National Center for Children in Poverty at Columbia University. He has testified as an expert witness at Congressional hearings.

Joan I. Vondra is assistant professor of human development and family studies in the Department of Psychology in Education at the University of Pittsburgh. She has an extensive background in child development and family studies through graduate and post-doctoral training and research on the determinants of parenting, parental influences on child development, and child maltreatment. Her work on parenting and child development appears in major journals and books devoted to child maltreatment, family relations, and developmental psychopathology. She is currently principal investigator of a large, federally funded longitudinal study of developmental vulnerability among children from urban, low-income families.

Harold Watts is professor of economics and public affairs at Columbia University in New York. In 1975, he was awarded a Guggenheim Fellowship and spent several months in Paris and London collecting data on the cost of childbearing in European countries. He is the founding director of the Institute for Research on Poverty at the University of Wisconsin at Madison. His publications include articles in the *American Economic Review,* the *American Sociological Review,* and the *Population Research and Policy Review.* His research interests have focused on the study of poverty, income and wealth inequality, and public policies related to these variables.